INCLUSION

INCLUSION

How Hawai'i Protected
Japanese Americans from Mass
Internment, Transformed Itself,
and Changed America

Tom Coffman

University of Hawai'i Press
Honolulu

Library of Congress Cataloging-in-Publication Data

Names: Coffman, Tom, author.

Title: Inclusion : how Hawaiʻi protected Japanese Americans from mass internment, transformed itself, and changed America / Tom Coffman.

Description: Honolulu : University of Hawaiʻi Press, 2021. | Includes bibliographical references and index.

Identifiers: LCCN 2021009481 | ISBN 9780824888541 (hardcover) | ISBN 9780824888558 (paperback) | ISBN 9780824890209 (kindle edition) | ISBN 9780824890193 (epub) | ISBN 9780824890186 (adobe pdf)

Subjects: LCSH: Japanese Americans—Evacuation and relocation, 1942–1945. | World War, 1939–1945—Japanese Americans. | Japanese Americans—Hawaii—History—20th century. | World War, 1939–1945—Participation, Japanese American. | Hawaii—Ethnic relations—History—20th century. | Hawaii—Politics and government—20th century.

Classification: LCC D769.8.A6 C54 2021 | DDC 940.53/969089956—dc23

LC record available at https://lccn.loc.gov/2021009481

University of Hawaiʻi Press books are printed on acid-free paper and meet the guidelines for permanence and durability of the Council on Library Resources.

Cover art: *Foreground (left to right)*, Charles Hemenway (Nippu Jiji/Densho Digital); Hung Wai Ching (Ching family collection); and Shigeo Yoshida (Yoshida family collection). *Background*, 442nd Regimental Combat Team standing in formation at ʻIolani Palace, Hawaiʻi, prior to a departure for training, March 1943 (Hawaiʻi State Archives).

Cover design: Aaron Lee

For Lois again and forever,
and for Harry, Nate, and Makena,
Justin, Jackie, and Alina;
Eli and Micah;
Anya, Rose, and Reyn;
and Mosiah

CONTENTS

Part V   Home Front and Battlefront

Acknowledgments

Of the many dozens of people who helped with this book, the late Ted T. Tsukiyama is foremost. Ted was my friend, research companion, mentor, interpreter of obscure events and names, and link to then-living historical sources.

Most importantly among Ted's relationships was Hung Wai Ching, whose vast energy and persistence made this book imperative. Shigeo Yoshida had passed away before I realized what he had done, but I became acquainted with him through Hung Wai and then through his writing and archiving. Without the two of them, there would be no story.

Sons King Lit Ching and Sai Lit Ching shared their family archives, as did Gerald and Bonnie Yoshida. The late Sue Isonaga shared the personal file of Robert Shivers.

Two scholars of national stature encouraged my inquiry: Dr. Tetsuden Kashima, emeritus, University of Washington; and Dr. Greg Robinson, University of Quebec at Montreal. As many scholars have not, they see that the history of Hawai'i matters. Close to home, the writer Mark Matsunaga and the researcher/analyst W. R. Wright helped me deal with battlefield history.

Robbie Alm organized crucial support for the earlier years of the work. Attorney Vernon Char, founder of the Manoa Forum, and Dr. Richard Dubanoski, emeritus, dean of Liberal Arts and Sciences, University of Hawai'i, gave the book a vigorous boost midway. Various Sons and Daughters of the 442nd Regimental Combat Team helped power the finish.

I am also indebted to the far-flung archivists, particularly James Cartwright, Sherman Seki, and Lynn Davis of the University of Hawai'i Archives and Manuscripts Room. Michi and Warren Nishimoto and their faithful development of the UH Center for Oral History provided support and encouragement. Masako Ikeda, acquisitions editor of UH Press, kindly welcomed me back through the publishing door.

Elinor Langer, a valued at-distance writing partner, read parts of the manuscript. Lois U. H. Lee, Dr. Kashima, and Michi Kodama-Nishimoto read parts and provided valuable perspectives. Mark Matsunaga shared resources from his deep research, read the manuscript in whole or part repeatedly, and also applied his sharp pencil.

A combination of personal and institutional donations and grants helped support what turned out to be an off-and-on ten-year journey. Donors included ABC Stores, Kenneth Akinaka, Allan Akita, Juanita Allen, Robbie Alm, Dr. Mary Bitterman, Michael Broderick, Vernon Char, Stephen Chinen, King Lit Ching, Rowena Chow, Dr. Richard Dubanoski, Jonathan Ego, Grace Fujii, Glenn Goya, Hawaiian Electric Company Educational Foundation, Lynn Heirakuji, Suzie Henyan, Phyllis Hironaka, Jon Ishihara, Island Insurance Foundation, Mae Isonaga, Dr. Satoru Izutsu, Japanese American Citizens League (Honolulu Chapter), Ann Kabasawa, Beverly Kaneshiro, Mark Matsunaga, Military Intelligence Service Veterans Club of Hawai'i, Anita Nihei, Mark Oshiro, Tracy Sakai, Thomas Sakata, Carol Sullivan, David Takagi, Barry Taniguchi, K. Taniguchi Ltd., the Hawai'i Council for the Humanities, Jason Wright, Wendy Wright, William R. Wright, Barry Yamashita, Bryan Yamashita, Byrnes Yamashita, and Gerald and Bonnie Yoshida. Probably more people helped support this book than I can accurately recall. My apologies for oversights.

PROLOGUE

The American period of Hawai'i's long history flows from two events. The first is the American takeover of 1898, which I described in my book *Nation Within*. The second is the crisis brought down by World War II, which I explore here. In the aftermath of Japan's attack on Pearl Harbor, the dark question for Hawai'i was the fate of its large Japanese-ancestry population. This was a question that went to Hawai'i's character no less than to the character of the United States.

As the U.S. government began indiscriminately rounding up people of Japanese ancestry on the West Coast, a combination of public officials and private citizens in Hawai'i resisted. Audaciously for an overseas territory in a war zone, they attempted to create an alternative course. How and why is the arc of this book.

In the course of the work, I saw instances in which the relationship between Hawai'i and Washington, D.C., was interactive. Through this two-way process, Hawai'i contributed to changing the policies, behavior, and standards of the federal government.

I first glimpsed the possibility of such a pivot point as a young political reporter for the *Honolulu Star-Bulletin*. The moment was 7 a.m. on a particular day in January 1971 when, by appointment, I rang the doorbell of Washington Place. Washington Place was originally the home of Hawai'i's last monarch, Lili'uokalani, and was by then the residence of the elected governor of Hawai'i, John Anthony Burns. Mr. Burns answered the door himself, just as he sometimes answered the house telephone. We passed through the queen's household area to a family-like breakfast table of relative informality, and there we started on the first pot of coffee.

When I told him I hoped to write a book about the politics of Hawai'i, he well might have thought my youthful interest exceeded my understanding. He was sixty-two years old and was widely thought of as a living legend. He had led the Hawai'i democratization movement in the 1950s, guided the statehood bill through Congress in 1959, and most recently had been reelected to a third four-year term as governor. I began by asking that most routine of twentieth-century questions, "Could you talk to me about where you were and what you were doing on December seventh?" He grimaced. Possibly he thought I knew the answer, although I did not. He paused, as if traversing a distance, then spoke with a growing intensity.

On December 7, 1941, he was an acting captain in the Honolulu Police Department. He had met with the agent in charge of the Honolulu FBI office, a man named Robert L. Shivers. Together they reviewed the internal-security arrest list. Burns described himself as saying, in response to certain names, "I know so-and-so, and he is a damn fine American." Sometimes, he said, a name would be removed from the list at this last moment. He and Shivers then supervised the arrests of several hundred people. (I was, for my part, astonished that he was involved in anything of the sort, in that his political base was particularly strong among Japanese American voters—a reaction I kept to myself.)

Reviewing my interview notes, unearthed from a closet, I see the names of people then new to me. Burns often mentioned Hung Wai Ching and Shigeo Yoshida, as well as other names I would ask him to spell, such as Katagiri: K-a-t-a-g-i-r-i. He talked about the crucial importance of the prewar months to minimizing the arrests. He talked for more than five hours, and it was neither statehood nor the rise of the Democratic Party that rocked the cradle of his narrative, but what had occurred in the crisis of war.

In my subsequent book, *Catch a Wave*, I nonetheless wrote only briefly about the war period. While this may now seem extremely naïve, it reflected the times. We were in the trough of a great wave. World War II was deep history, and Hawai'i was moving on. What Burns thought of as monumental had been obscured.

Fifteen years later, in 1986, a group of Japanese Americans in Honolulu organized themselves around the idea of actively appreciating individuals who had befriended them during the war. This was a significant moment in the community's reworking of the past. The Japanese word retrieved for the occasion was *kansha*, which has to do with gratitude. The *kansha* observance filled the Honolulu Civic Center. Prominent

X FOR THE PRO

HONOLULU, HAWAII

How It Started

al scene grew steadily worse and part'
lted States and Japan became more and
ng the people of certain races in Haw
as evidence of a growing feeling of d
mistakable although there appeared r
g or wholesale dismissal from employm
ver, there were wild rumors coursing
ibtless in other sections of the Terr
s were dismissing their Japanese emp
of constructing concentration camps
as soon as the "inevitable" war be
not a single American citizen of J
vice, that every sampan in Hawaii w
ist the Japanese fleet, etc.
basis for much of these r
passed them on
med ev

How It Started. In a moment when the future of Hawai'i hung in the balance, Shigeo Yoshida described the background and contacts of the Council for Interracial Unity.

among the several honorees still living, the Chinese American Hung Wai Ching was thanked with a special enthusiasm.

I was subsequently introduced to Mr. Ching. He was past eighty years old, but his energy level was astonishing. He quickly got into his story. "Do you understand?" He waved the air. "You get that?" He loved irony. "You know who wrote the general's speech? Calmed the people down? Japanese guy! Shigeo Yoshida! A Buddhahead wrote that speech!" His laughter was uproarious.

He said the real story was in the files, but where were the files? Without validation, he feared being taken for a self-aggrandizing old man. "What about my meeting with Roosevelt?" he asked. "Who's going to believe that?" He often referred to Shigeo Yoshida as if Yoshida could vouch for him, but Yoshida was by then deceased. "Shigeo did all the writing," he said, "Shigeo was the idea man." Because Yoshida was of Japanese ancestry, he did not have a security clearance. As a result, he took care of the work in Honolulu while Ching, with his high-level clearance, was on the move, traveling often and talking to people in positions of power. Ching framed a stage whisper with his inordinately long fingers. "Shigeo was the brains. I was the mouth." He winked.[1]

In 2004, I was researching a documentary film on the crisis of the home front in wartime Hawai'i. The director of the University of Hawai'i's Archives and Manuscript Collections (UHAM) called my attention to three vintage cardboard boxes of possibly interesting matter. They had come to light in a recent move into the library's new wing, but the contents had never been accessed. They were filled with aging brown folders, bulging with notes and memos, with labels written mostly in pencil, such as Internment, Emergency Service Committee, 100th, 442nd, VVV, Haole, Chinese, Filipino, Maui, Kona, and, yes, Burns and Ching.

These were the files.[2]

Inclusion

PART I

From the Ground Up

CHAPTER 1

On the Ground

WITHIN THE REALITIES OF HAWAIʻI, the time horizon for the onset of World War II was not a day but more than four decades. From the 1898 American takeover forward, the U.S. naval base at Pearl Harbor connected a previously independent small nation to the downward drift of world events. As the United States military developed the harbor, it was often described as America's Pacific Gibraltar. When its guardians so famously slumbered, Americans were inveighed to focus on one thing: *Remember Pearl Harbor.*

The U.S. Navy was crippled, and more than twenty-four hundred Americans were dead. Terrified people across the country demanded to know how Japan could have attacked with such success. Roughly, the national answer became this: a faceless enemy had laid the groundwork from within. Surely Japan's triumph was a matter of subversion, espionage, and sabotage.

In an attempt to counter the growing hysteria, Shigeo Yoshida, then a young teacher, wrote an account of a small interracial group in Honolulu that had met for more than a year in anticipation of a war. The Council for Interracial Unity, as Yoshida called it, had determined that if war broke out, it would attempt two things. One was to prevent a mass internment of Hawaiʻi's large Japanese-ancestry population. The second was to maximize participation of Hawaiʻi's people in the war effort.

Yoshida's account likely was written hurriedly in mid-December of 1941, nine or ten days after the bombing. Adapted to the demands of the moment, it was akin to jamming a foot in a closing door. Flawlessly typed, it ran to five single-spaced pages. The original passed among several of the most important figures in the territory of Hawaiʻi, and an onionskin copy came to rest in the first of Yoshida's cardboard boxes.[1] Yoshida recounted how fewer than a dozen people of varied racial ancestries had gathered the previous year at a residence in Honolulu to address what might occur if Japan and the United States went to war. The group, he wrote, was brought together by "a rising tenseness." He wrote of rumors that the Caucasian firms were dismissing their Japanese employees, and that the U.S. Army was building concentration camps for use when "the inevitable war" began. He wrote of fears that "not a single American citizen of Japanese ancestry would be inducted into service. . . . Misinformation could," he said, "destroy the unique, though not perfect, interracial good will which has been built up in Hawaii." Optimistically, he had in mind a time frame that looked through the war and past it: "How we get along during the war will determine how we get along when the war is over."

Those present at the meeting were of Japanese, Chinese, and Caucasian ancestries. The connecting person was a patrician figure named Charles H. Hemenway. Yoshida eventually was to name his two sons after Hemenway, but as of 1941 Yoshida simply described him as older and more established, while others were younger and "just coming into positions of leadership." Yoshida himself was thirty-two, and his closest associate, Hung Wai Ching, was thirty-five. Additional people were invited to discussion meetings. Some came and went, but a handful stuck together, attending repeatedly.

The meetings revealed three points of view. One, war was not sufficiently imminent to do anything. Two, the situation was quickly worsening, "but nothing could be done about it by way of an organized movement." This second group nonetheless wanted to continue meeting with the idea of reinforcing interracial friendships. The third group held that the onset of war was only a matter of time, and they must redouble their efforts to maintain a stable community.

The latter was a grand notion. Being an overseas possession of the United States, the territory of Hawai'i lacked the governmental mechanisms to achieve such a goal. This relegated the means to community relationships so elemental as to not usually be associated with the hard stuff of policy and history. These included personal acquaintances, work relationships, social practices, and social standards, or what members of the Council for Interracial Relations referred to as the spirit of *aloha*.

The group became a committee. In addition to Hemenway, Yoshida, and Ching, it consisted of Dr. Miles H. Cary, a renowned high school principal, and several other individuals who had worked with one another through the YMCA. From the federal intelligence agencies, there were

Charles Hemenway *(center)*, the father figure of the University of Hawai'i, mentored both Hung Wai Ching *(left)* and Shigeo Yoshida *(right)*.

two people: the agent in charge of the Honolulu FBI office, Robert Shivers, and the chief intelligence officer of the U.S. Army's Hawaiian Department, Colonel M. W. Marston. Taken together, their life experiences illuminated a territorial Hawai'i that often was described as languid and unchanging but was not quite what it appeared.

By accident of family decisions, Shigeo Yoshida was neither a city boy nor a country jack. He was from a semirural part of Hilo, the most populous town on the Big Island of Hawai'i. As a result, he grew up with insight into the two disparate lifestyles that dominated the territory. One was the inherently backward and hierarchical world of the plantations. The other was an emerging and more open urban society.

Shigeo was the fourth of eight children of Naohiko and Ichi Yoshida, who had immigrated as a couple in 1898, the year of Hawai'i's forced annexation to the United States. With duty-free access to the American sugar market, plantation agriculture was expanding rapidly, and the planters were luring Japanese workers by the tens of thousands, giving the lie to their often-rumored fear that Japan would take over Hawai'i.

Naohiko Yoshida was twenty-six years old, the son of a samurai. As such, he was the inheritor of the two swords of the warrior class, but he himself was without status in Japan, the entire class having been displaced by mechanization and firepower. It may reasonably be inferred that Naohiko had looked to Hawai'i to recoup the status that his family had lost to modernization. There is no record of him laboring for the plantations. What did survive was an account in which he attempted to function—without apparent success—as a headman within a plantation camp made up of Japanese families, who tended to be isolated as a matter of calculation by the plantations and also as a result of their large numbers and their inclination to stick together.[2]

By 1910, the U.S. Census listed Naohiko as a sugarcane farmer and his wife Ichi, six years younger than he, as a laborer on a "home farm." Two Japanese boarders were listed at their address as cane cutters. Together the notes suggest that Naohiko might have become an early day sharecropper, or "contract farmer," as it was called. This was noteworthy because it provided him a margin of autonomy that wage labor did not. Naohiko acquired a horse, then a car. He bought a flat-crowned straw boater hat, a white shirt, a necktie, and knee-high boots of the sort worn by plantation overseers. The 1920 census reported that he was able to read and write, meaning he had become literate in English. In contrast, Ichi was marked "No" and "No," meaning she neither spoke nor read English. Initially their neighborhood in Hilo was entirely Japanese, but with time they were joined by Portuguese, Puerto Ricans, and Koreans.

That Naohiko and Ichi had emigrated as a couple was an exception to the usual pattern, in which the Japanese male came as a bachelor and, some years later, either returned to Japan or sent to Japan for a bride. Their arrival as a previously married couple accounted for creating American-born children who were nearly a full generation older than most Nisei. Yoshio, a son, was born shortly after their arrival, followed by two girls. Shigeo was born in 1907, followed by four more children. Yoshio went to sea on Japanese merchant ships, returned to Hilo, lived next door with his young wife, and took up carpentry. The two older sisters likewise went to work at a young age. As the fourth child, Shigeo Yoshida benefited from his place in the birth order. Where his older siblings went out to earn wages, Shigeo would have the luxury of pursuing an advanced education.

Through the American public school system, Yoshida began to realize his intellectual potential. He was an A student, a member of the student council and the literary society, and the president of his class. He also was a writer and a debater, skills that sharpened the use of logic and the vigorous presentation of ideas. His high school's faculty was made up entirely of Caucasians from the U.S. Mainland, some of whom were highly educated. His English teacher had a doctorate degree from the

University of Chicago. His history teacher was a graduate of Occidental College, and the other twenty-one faculty members had degrees from state universities and small colleges.

Yoshida's slogan in the Hilo High School annual was, "Working Constantly for a Purpose." Foreshadowing key events in his adult life, he won a territory-wide speaking contest as a high school sophomore. As a junior he won first prize in a peace essay contest, and as a senior he was captain of the Hilo High School debate team. He edited the school yearbook, to which he contributed two poems. One was an ode to the mountain above Hilo, Mauna Kea, the second an ode to the future. He tracked the key events of the year. The Punahou School football team came from Oʻahu for a game, then stayed on for the school dance and a field trip to Kīlauea Volcano. A group from McKinley High School came to explore the volcano, and so on.

The school's effort to enrich extracurricular life was evident. During Yoshida's attendance, Hilo High started a student government, a student newspaper, and a Hi-Y (YMCA) Club. A Japanese Student Association was organized with a disclaimer that although it was "distinctly racial in membership, [it] is not such in character." The purported goal was to help Japanese Americans "better meet their problems and prove themselves useful and better citizens." Yoshida joined the club, possibly with some ambivalence, given his later misgivings about ethnic organization.

More than half of Hilo's student body was of Japanese ancestry, followed by a substantial group of Chinese and a scattering of Hawaiians, Caucasians (haole), and Koreans, but no Filipinos.

Despite the faculty being entirely haole and the student body being heavily Japanese, the main editorial theme of the student annual was diversity. The lead piece described Hilo High as an international showcase. "Lying at the Crossroads of the Pacific, it is but natural that the different races should come together so well," it said. "We know no racial prejudice, no discrimination of creed or color." The yearbook praised the aloha spirit and the importance of student self-government as a path to responsible citizenship.

In such an atmosphere, Yoshida—like many Nisei—resisted the teachings of Japanese-language school. "We could see, young as we were, what influence Japan could have on us through the language school," he was to tell an interviewer.[3] "We celebrated the Emperor's birthday, for instance, and I felt that there was no such place for that in a school in America." His parents, his mother in particular, persisted in arguing that knowledge of the Japanese language might help him find a job, such as clerking, when he grew up. His response was, "I'm American," and he prided himself on slacking and playing hooky from the language school.

His issue of identity must have been heightened at age eleven with the arrival of his samurai grandfather from Japan. Juhei Yoshida was a small, wrinkled figure who dressed in peasant clothes. His life as a samurai had come to rest on a shoal of history, much as his two swords eventually would come to rest in Shigeo Yoshida's closet.

Lifelong, Hung Wai Ching remembered the animosity of his Chinese-language schoolteacher for Japanese Americans. "Oooh, he was such a Chinese nationalist," Ching said. "Taught us to hate the Japanese. I used to beat up on these little Japanese kids. A big Japanese kid [would] come along, I'd run like hell."

The traceable history of Hung Wai Ching's family commenced around AD 1700. In response to invasions, the Chings settled in the Pearl River delta of southern China, near the trading center of Canton (now Guangzhou). The family household, as well as the Ching clan's temple, was located in a rice-growing village named On Ding, one of six villages in the municipality of Nanlang, which in turn was part of the city of Chung-shan (now Zhongshan).

Most villagers were tenant farmers, but Ching's grandfather owned his own land and also a textile business. As a result, his children were born to a certain level of privilege. Family names then being stated first, Hung Wai Ching's father was known as Ching Yei. Although Ching Yei eventually would be described in newspaper accounts as an itinerant cook in the New World, an oil portrait survived of what was taken to be him as a young man, dressed in fine silk. He sat beside a lacquered table, next to a stack of books and a vase of roses.[4]

Ching Yei was betrothed to a young woman of Chung-shan through a matchmaker, who was said to have consulted the zodiac calendar and the position of the stars. Ching Yei's bride, originally a Fong, became Ching Fong Shee. She was a second child, separated from her older brother by eighteen years. In that long interim, her father had gone to California during the gold rush and returned to Chung-shan with Bull Durham tobacco sacks of gold nuggets. When Ching Fong Shee was born, her parents bound her feet, which suggested that she would

Courtesy of Yoshida album.

Courtesy of Ching album.

While Yoshida *(left)* lit up the art of debate at the university, Hung Wai Ching *(right, back row center)* was making a name for himself as a youth worker.

become a person of privilege, waited on by others. The development of her feet was stunted in a way thought to be delicate and visually pleasing, but the pain of it was horrendous. To protect his ears from the sound of her weeping, her father was said to have left the house for several years.

While the specific reasons for Ching Yei and Ching Fong Shee emigrating to Hawai'i are obscure, the two were part of a trend of their time. Coastal China was wracked by foreign incursions, of which nearby British-controlled Hong Kong and nearby Portuguese-controlled Macau were the best known. The Pearl River area, Chung-shan in particular, was famous among Chinese for producing large numbers of out-migrants and creating wide interaction with Hawai'i and North America.

In or around 1894, Ching Yei set out for the New World. He first went to South America but soon doubled back to Hawai'i, which was regarded by the Chinese as a place of opportunity. He briefly worked in the sugarcane fields, then washed dishes in Chinatown. Several years into this, Ching Fong Shee boarded a schooner bound for Hawai'i to join him. The passengers were crowded into large open holds, plagued by seasickness and a lack of decent sanitation. For a month in transit, Ching Fong Shee lurched about on her damaged feet, unaided, before arriving at her new island home.

In subsequent photographs, she was consistently seated, while others around her stood. Her face was a pleasant oval, open and wide eyed, suggesting approachability, in contrast to the craggy features of Ching

Yei. They first lived in a small apartment above Honolulu Harbor in Chinatown, a catacomb of fish and vegetable markets, herbalists, bars, restaurants, gambling houses, and opium dens. The residential dwellings were tenements with tiny rooms and shared kitchens and baths. Overwhelmingly, Chinatown was made up of men less fortunate than Ching Yei, in that they were single and alone.

With the birth of children, Ching Yei and Ching Fong Shee moved up the hill to a house on Christley Lane near Fort Street, which was literally a stone's throw from Royal Elementary School. Hung Wai was the middle of five children, born in 1904. As a boy, he learned how to shoot craps from the Chinatown gamblers, and he also boasted of knowing which doors opened to the opium smokers. But if in age he enjoyed portraying himself as a free spirit who flirted with the low life, in reality he was deeply influenced by Christian youth workers.

The Christian movement in Chinatown was imported both by American missionaries and by Chinese missionaries who had converted in China. By the time the Ching family arrived, the Fort Street Chinese church was well established. Christianity was associated with modernity, equality, and an affirmation of each individual's worth. This was particularly so with the Chinese church on Fort Street, because it was a Congregational church, in which members discussed and voted on questions of how to conduct their affairs.

Mother Ching had studied the Bible in China as a girl. Her interest in Christianity was reinforced by a missionary named Jessie Mackenzie, who lived among the people she served. Mackenzie comforted the Chinese women who were isolated in their dwellings, who spoke little or no English, and who might even be struggling to converse with their American-born and mainly English-speaking children. She also worked with the youth of the neighborhood. One was Hung Wai, who remembered her as an imposing woman who snared children into Sunday school.

A progressive minister from the U.S. Mainland organized the young people into clubs, each of which had colors, a motto, a constitution, and a governing council. The clubs offered socializing and sports activity and as much or little religion as an individual wanted. It was more than anything a project of Americanization. For example, a group discussion addressed the following: "Should young people remain with the old ways, be always accepting without questioning, [and] be bound by their parents' philosophies without learning the American Way?"

As the Ching family grew, Ching Yei began working as a cook on an interisland steamship. He left home frequently, and one day he did not return. This conceivably might have resulted from his ship being forced into national service during the First World War, but the war alone does not explain his long absence. Ship logs show that Ching Yei sailed in and out of the ports of North and South America many times. Conflicting stories about the family's well-being made the rounds. One was told by a YMCA worker, John Young, who found the Ching children living in what he took to be poverty. He embraced a tale told repeatedly to the effect that Ching Yei had been washed overboard, never to return. This was a fable that not only traveled conversationally but was to be published years later, when the Ching brothers had gained a measure of fame. The second story was recorded by Ching Yei's youngest daughter, who believed that he sailed the seas to earn money and function as a dutiful provider, sending most of his earnings home.[5]

In Ching Yei's absence, Ching Fong Shee's brother—the brother eighteen years her senior—immigrated with his family from Chungshan to Honolulu. He, too, worked as a dishwasher. His wife was stricken by tuberculosis. As she lay dying, she implored Ching Fong to take care of her five children. Thereafter, Ching Fong mothered the Fongs, in addition to her own six children. Her limited mobility kept her from working outside the house, but she made money as a piecework seamstress, sought out by tailors and dressmakers for her skills with buttonholes and embroidery.

When the house was wired for electricity in 1913, the family members gathered to stare in amazement at their one dangling lightbulb.

In photographs, Ching Fong Shee's expression remained serene. She maintained a taste for high culture. When a new exhibit opened at the Honolulu Academy of Arts or the Bishop Museum, she and her daughter Bessie would catch a bus to take it in.

The nearby Royal School was one of the few public schools on Oʻahu. The children were expected to earn As, and they did so. The principal was a disciplinarian named Cyril O. Smith. At his command, students fell into a military formation to raise the American flag and recite the Pledge of Allegiance. They stood when Smith visited a classroom and responded to his questions with, "Yes, sir," and "No, sir." The YMCA's John Young called him "Billygoat Smith." Hung Wai Ching said that one either liked him or was scared stiff of him. Out of his own pocket, Smith hosted dances on Friday afternoons to teach the children social skills.

The Chings were among his passions. The youngest brother, Hung Wo, greeted visitors to the school by announcing that he was Smith's assistant, and he eventually became the executor of Smith's estate.

With Ching Yei at sea, the firstborn Hung Chin Ching became the man of the house. People called him "Joe Gans," meaning he fought like a famous black boxer of that time. He fought both the Asian kids and the much bigger Hawaiians, who were often the "bulls" of their turf. He dropped out of school in the fifth grade and started a janitorial business, securing the cleaning jobs and directing his siblings in the work. In adult life, Hung Chin Ching became a policeman and the least known of the Ching brothers, but his contribution to the future of the family was immense. Similarly, sister Annie, the oldest girl, planted a garden and was heavily tasked with household work, sacrificing her labors to the family's future.

Although Hung Wai Ching shined shoes and sold newspapers, he realized it was primarily Hung Chin and Annie who provided him the space in which to grow. When he asked Hung Chin's permission to enroll in high school, Hung Chin easily could have told him no, that the family needed him to work full time. Hung Chin said yes, for which Hung Wai was always grateful.[6]

To what extent the Chings were awakened by the democracy movement of the time is a question. Hawai'i was important to China. In particular it was important to the groundwork of the revolutionary Sun Yat-sen. Like Ching Yei, Sun Yat-sen was from one of the villages around Chung-shan, a village called Cui Yeng.[7] As a young student intent on defying tradition, Sun Yat-sen had defaced figures in the village temple, causing him to be banished to the care of his adventurous older brother in Hawai'i. There he attended the private Episcopal school, 'Iolani. He cut off his braided queue and converted to Christianity. He organized his first revolutionary group in the home of a friend in the year of Ching Yei's arrival in the Honolulu Chinatown. Only twenty-four people attended, but it proved to be a tremor in a revolutionary earthquake. Like hundreds of fellow Chinese in Hawai'i, Ching Yei supported Sun Yat-sen's campaign. Just down Christley Lane from the Chings, for example, was a man named Chang Kim, who first put Sun Yat-sen up on weekends, and who later risked his life fighting in China.[8]

During the years in which Hung Wai Ching was growing from infancy to awareness, Sun Yat-sen launched insurrection after insurrection.

Ching was eight years old when Sun Yat-sen, on his eleventh try, top-pled the imperial throne that had defined China for more than two thousand years. He credited overseas Chinese with his success, and he credited the Chinese of Hawai'i most of all. The newspapers that Hung Wai sold in the streets of Honolulu announced his earthshaking victory. Inherent in the story was the ideal of democracy and the feeling that anything was possible.

For most nonwhite people of the time, education beyond the eighth grade was not a birthright but a privilege. There being no junior high schools, Hung Wai Ching completed elementary school, then passed an entrance examination to enter high school. He counted himself a beneficiary of the territory of Hawai'i's expansion of the public school system during the 1920s. He was acutely aware that in the early years of the territory, many of the influential corporate executives were still direct descendants of missionaries. Christian doctrine was their original basis of existence in Hawai'i and, in Ching's view, created a paradox. He paraphrased the oligarchy's dilemma as "Should we or should we not educate the children of our plantation immigrants? If we educate them, they're not going to stay on the plantations and become labor-ers." He came to believe that while the white elite seemed all powerful, public education was the crack in the wall. The most elemental issue was whether people were inherent equals before the Deity. What of the standard that Charles Hemenway promoted, which was that everyone should be provided the opportunity of education? It was within this framework that public education evolved as—the educators' word of choice—a "progressive" force.

To be taught by white people was assumed. Innumerable anecdotes would be told about strong-willed white Americans in the roles of prin-cipal and schoolmarm who followed the U.S. flag into the Pacific. They tended to give Western names to their nonwhite students and to pound away on the use of proper English. In memory, many students honored them for their dedication and determination. In a contrary vein, the educational scholar Eileen Tamura was to write that while some were kind and inspirational, an element of this teacher force was "mean-spirited and bigoted."[9]

Ching remembered virtually all of his teachers as white. At McKin-ley High School, thirty-one were women and seven were men. All had undergraduate degrees, and six had master's degrees. Five had graduated from Stanford University, four from Oberlin College, and two each from Columbia University and Wellesley College.

Although the McKinley faculty did not reflect the student population, *aloha* was held up as the guiding ideal. The lead essay of the 1921 McKinley High School annual compared McKinley favorably in terms of racial integration to the private high schools such as Punahou (which it dismissed as predominantly haole), Kamehameha (Hawaiian), and Mills Institute (which served many Japanese student boarders). The essayist wrote that racial prejudice could only be cured by "mutual friendship and constant mingling" of different groups. "To this end McKinley High School is working."[10]

In the 1921 graduating class of ninety students, Chinese and Japanese were represented disproportionately. Only five were haole. Three or possibly four were Hawaiian or part Hawaiian. Isolated in the plantations, Filipinos were, again, absent. Undaunted by the actual ethnic distribution, the essayist proclaimed McKinley to be the real melting pot of the Pacific: "[It] aims to solve the problem of race prejudice through thorough understanding and mutual friendship. . . . May each and every student go out into the world, trying to solve this great world problem!"

Ching thrived at McKinley. He was bigger, quicker, and more verbal than most of his classmates. He was a first lieutenant in the school's Reserve Officer Training Corps (ROTC). He was a leading character in school plays. In his senior year, after again consulting Hung Chin, he went out for the track team and immediately became its star performer.

Statistics fail to convey the excitement of McKinley High School during this period. The reason, given over and over by the students, was the progressive educator Miles Cary, who would eventually serve on the Council for Interracial Unity along with Ching and Yoshida. Cary was extraordinary both for his educational philosophy and his demonstrable moral courage. He arrived at McKinley in 1923 as a teacher after graduating from the University of Washington. He had wavy hair, a cleft chin, and a ready smile. He seemed to make person-to-person contact no matter how casual the circumstance. His driving vision was to engage students in a genuinely democratic school life. Student government took on substance where so often there is only form.[11] Classrooms held elections, and classroom representatives served on the student council, which in turn elected class officers. Each student undertook a community service project. The size and frequency of the school newspaper doubled. Where other voices were advising young people to stay on the plantations, Cary proclaimed McKinley to be a school that "teaches all who come within its walls to dream dreams and tackle big enterprises." The school's many clubs included a Citizenship Club and a YMCA club. Both focused on leadership development.

When the 1923 track season started with no coach and no track, Cary filled in, arousing the athlete in Hung Wai Ching. The 1923 *Black and Gold* student annual was dedicated to Cary, the first-year teacher, as "One Who Is Unquestionably the Greatest Friend of McKinley High School." Within the year, he was named principal.

Students were told that McKinley High was a force of destiny: "It represents what Hawai'i stands for, the Melting Pot of the Pacific, the Key to the East and West." For some people, such a line must have seemed ridiculously disconnected from the realities of the plantation system, the conditions of work, the low wages, and the job discrimination based on ethnicity. But in McKinley's telling, the plantations seemed a world away. Likewise, McKinley gave no hint of the deteriorating relationship between Japan and the United States or of the fact that in 1924 the U.S. government adopted a purely race-based system of immigration. The themes of Aloha, Democracy, and the Melting Pot were repeated over and over, as if taking on a life of their own. What people in Hawai'i remembered most about 1924 was McKinley High School's high-achieving graduating class, including Hung Wai Ching, Masaji Marumoto (Harvard Law), the eventual U.S. senator Hiram L. Fong, and the colorful entrepreneur Chinn Ho, who like Ching was from Christley Lane.

When Ching continued his education at the University of Hawai'i (UH), his eldest brother again approved, but on the condition that Hung Wai major in a field that would yield solid employment. Ching reluctantly chose engineering, but he stood out on campus for his social skills. He made innumerable friends and attracted the acclaim of his peers. He was class president in his sophomore, junior, and senior years. He was president of the Chinese Student Alliance, president of the Cosmopolitan Club, and editor of the school annual, *Ka Palapala*. He supported himself by running a used bookstore.

Willowy and tall for an Asian, he was a three-year letterman in basketball, a four-year letterman in track, and the captain of the track team. For lack of air travel, most athletic competition was limited to club sports around Honolulu, but Ching's level of performance would have made him competitive in any setting. The Amateur Athletic Union had begun to keep records in Hawai'i, and Ching became the Hawai'i record holder in the 220-yard hurdles, the 100-yard dash, and the broad jump. His broad jump of 20 feet 2 inches would have placed him among the qualifiers in the 1924 Olympics.

He was again a standout in ROTC, attaining the student rank of major, and he was a member of the ROTC rifle team. That both McKinley High and UH had ROTC units was in itself remarkable. The rifle team reflected a desire on the part of the U.S. Army to develop and train local defenders of Hawai'i, as well as an openness—if seemingly unconscious and uncharted—to developing nonwhite officers, this being many years before the United States considered the racial desegregation of its military.

After Ching's sophomore year at UH, he made his first trip to the U.S. continent. His purpose was ROTC training. He spent two weeks at Fort Lewis, where he was commissioned a second lieutenant in the territory's national guard. He traveled with a fellow ROTC member, Dan Ainoa, a pure Native Hawaiian with dark-brown skin.[12] En route they stopped in San Francisco. For the first time, Ching saw the Presidio of San Francisco, the army fort to which he would return in a crucial moment of the war. He and Ainoa swam at an army pool without incident. They next went to a municipal pool for a swim but were turned away based on their racial backgrounds. When Ching attempted to get his hair cut in a five-dollar shop on Market Street, he likewise was turned away, then got a fifty-cent haircut in Chinatown. At training camp, they were given to understand they were not to attend a dance that was attended by white girls.

Ching did not suffer discrimination lightly. On the contrary, he was inclined to actively protest racial slights. In this regard, his level of awareness and determination likely was heightened by his deep involvement with the YMCA, which during this period was beginning to discuss the issue of racism in America in critical terms.

Although the YMCA had existed for more than half a century in Hawai'i, the 1920s were a period of rapid expansion. By the time Ching arrived at UH, the University "Y" was the biggest club on campus. Ching became its president. Likely at the YMCA's expense, he sailed to the West Coast a second time—in this instance for a student conference at the YMCA's Camp Asilomar, an idyllic retreat by the sea on the Monterrey peninsula of California. According to one account, several hundred students attended this conference from colleges in the Western states to discuss prejudice and racial segregation. Ching led ten delegates from Hawai'i.

While in California, Ching received a call saying that his father had been arrested by immigration authorities under the terms of the Chinese Exclusion Act for illegal entry into the continental United States. Ching Yei was being held for potential deportation in the San Francisco jail. With Hung Wai's help, Ching Yei was set free, at which point he returned to Honolulu and rejoined his family.[13]

Between the YMCA and ROTC, Ching gained a comfort with the world outside of Hawai'i. One of his most distinguished contemporaries, Shunzo Sakamaki, had won an oratorical contest by proclaiming that island youth of Asian ancestry struggled with "a subtle sense of inferiority," a phrase that John Burns eventually embedded into the political vocabulary of Hawai'i. Ching seems to have had no such sense, subtle or otherwise. He sought to engage with practically everyone he encountered. If anything, he imagined himself as he appeared in his scrapbook—as the extraordinary person who led the way, who won races and set records.

In addition to his many other activities, Ching was a member of the debate team, the Hawai'i Union, playing a role that he described with an uncharacteristic humility. His personal taste was to speak pidgin, delighting in its word play and humor. As a debate team member, he took care of the treasury and once or twice a month, at Hemenway's house, he served as a foil in practices. And it was there that he made the acquaintance of Shigeo Yoshida.

Debating was then a major pastime, and Yoshida stood out from the first moment. As a freshman, he led his class team to victory over the sophomores and then over the mighty seniors. In the process, he came to the attention of Hemenway, a godfather of the debaters and a moving force in an intercollegiate series called 'Round the World. Reflecting the extant interest in international life, the series tackled progressive political topics such as, "Be it resolved: That Foreign Powers Immediately Abandon All Extraterritorial Privileges in China," and, "Resolved, That the United States Grant the Philippines Complete, Immediate Independence." When a debate team came from Australia, the topic became a critical examination of Australia's then whites-only immigration policy.

Yoshida made the traveling team, which meant that in 1929 he toured Japan. The finale was a grand tour in 1930 of the U.S. West Coast. The

United States was sinking into its great economic depression, but Hemenway was undaunted. He chaired a panel of judges who picked Yoshida to lead a three-member team along with two of his friends, Chinese American Dai Ho Chun and a haole, Donald Layman. The face that Hawai'i showed to the West Coast was a sensitive matter in 1930, since Japanese Americans were not allowed into the U.S. Mainland without a permit. Only six years previously, Congress had passed the Japanese Exclusion Act, by which the United States for the first time had adopted a completely racist system of immigration, and Jim Crow segregation was the law in much of the country.

The itinerary of potential destinations was four pages long, filled with notes on who to see and what to debate. Most were marked with a "Yes." A few were labeled "Maybe. Call on arrival." Yoshida, Chun, and Layman departed on a ship bound not for the United States but Vancouver, Canada. When Canadian customs agents studied Yoshida, one marveled aloud that someone of his physiology could be an American. The agents at first insisted that Dai Ho Chun, being of Chinese ancestry, had to put up a bond as a guarantee he would leave the country. After a discussion of the debate tour, the bond was waived.

Their original plan was to ride a train from Canada to Seattle, but they now feared being turned back at the U.S. border. As an alternative, they took a ship to Seattle, then caught a train to Salem, Oregon, home of Willamette University. Six hundred people crowded into the hall, setting a Willamette record. Yoshida stepped forward with orange paper leis. When he presented them to the Willamette debaters, everyone cheered. The two teams debated the proposition that the nations of the Earth should disarm. Yoshida's team argued the affirmative, contending that weapons were costly and their very existence created fears that led to war. UH won.

The team next stopped at Oregon State University at Corvallis. They stayed at a fraternity house, presumably all white at a time when fraternities were racially segregated. Press reports said they visited a sorority but suffered from shyness, which Yoshida was quoted as denying. This time seven hundred people packed into the debate hall—another record—and others were turned away. UH won again. At the University of Oregon, they lost for the first time, on a single vote. They then headed south to the University of California at Berkeley. An opponent said he had not known whether the Hawai'i debaters could speak intelligible English, or even whether English was spoken in Hawai'i's schools.

The debate was a draw. The team went on to Stanford (no decision) and then to the University of Southern California, where the press described Yoshida as showing "splendid oratorical powers and an unmatched vocabulary." Nonetheless, UH lost. Debates at Redlands (a win), UCLA (a loss), Pacific University (no decision), and Southwestern University (a loss) resulted in an overall record of three wins, four losses, and three debates with no decision.

After five weeks, the team returned home on the *City of Honolulu* and was welcomed by a large crowd. The press headline read, "Debaters Back After Invading the Mainland." Wherever they had gone, the story said, they had been greeted by ovations.[14]

At a later time, an undergraduate record of Yoshida's caliber would have vaulted him into the top graduate schools in the country. Yoshida wanted to do graduate work, but ties to Mainland schools were comparatively weak, and the country's economy was sinking. His father was sixty, and his grandfather was past eighty. A younger sister had just won the territory-wide speech contest that Yoshida had won as a sophomore at Hilo, and if she was going to college she needed help.

Following graduation, Yoshida taught school. With the public system swelling, he was much in demand. He taught at Lili'uokalani Intermediate School from 1932 to 1936, then transferred to Central Intermediate School, which served students in the harbor district. One was a stevedore's son who lived in a board tenement in the heart of Chinatown, George R. Ariyoshi. Yoshida instructed him in news writing while Ariyoshi was thinking about a career in journalism. Only later did Ariyoshi set his sights on law, which would lead long afterwards to his becoming governor of Hawai'i. Ariyoshi's friend from Beretania Street, George Akita, had taken the admittance exam for one of the territory's several English Standard schools, which mainly admitted haole students and were therefore widely regarded as a manifestation of de facto segregation. Despite his keen mind, Akita was rejected. He was a seventh grader at Central Intermediate when Yoshida began coaching him in speech competition. Akita was known for talking incessantly and was sometimes disciplined for talking in class. He thought of himself as speaking two languages, pidgin and Japanese. Every day for an hour after school, Yoshida put Akita on the auditorium stage by himself. Akita found his new coach both charismatic and exacting. Yoshida would tell him when to raise his voice, when to hold steady, and when to drop his voice. This went on for several months. Yoshida taught Akita not only to pronounce and intone words but to understand their nuance. "It was magical," Akita was to recall. "At some point I spoke proper English."

Yoshida never mentioned his own competitive accomplishments to Akita. This was about the student, not the teacher. In 1939, Akita won second prize in the *Honolulu Star-Bulletin* oratorical contest, which was held at McKinley High School. The next year, he won the territory-wide speech contest. The following year he was on his way to a repeat. On December 5, 1941, he won the O'ahu contest and prepared to debate students from the other islands. The news of his achievement ran on an inside page of the newspaper on Sunday, the seventh day of December.[15]

As an early acknowledgment of Yoshida's teaching skills, the Department of Public Instruction put him in charge of training probationary teachers at Central Intermediate—a skill that was much needed because of the burgeoning school population. In 1900, the schools had eleven thousand students. By 1920, the number had nearly quadrupled. Of these, Japanese American youth were the fastest growing element. Where in 1900 the system had a mere 1,352 students of Japanese ancestry, this number was 19,354 by 1920 and 45,930 by 1940. Throughout this period, about half of the entire public school population was Nisei.[16] In response, the territorial government established sixteen junior high schools. Where there were only four public high schools in 1920, there were ten high schools by 1930.

In contrast to the often-negative portrayals of the territory during this period, Dr. Kazuo Miyamoto, in his epic *Hawaii: End of the Rainbow,* described these years enthusiastically. "Modernization programs in all fields of industrial and cultural endeavors became marked. Great strides were made," he wrote. "Public schools were opened in the remotest villages of the islands and attendance was made compulsory." The melting pot, Miyamoto announced, was a success: "Youngsters were being instilled with the ideals of democracy without letup and each was made to feel that he was just as good an American as the direct descendants of the Mayflower. . . . It was a startling achievement that the children could be so Americanized."[17] Nuances aside, the people of Hawai'i benefited significantly between 1920 and 1940 from the improving education system. The trajectory was clear. The public schools were changing Hawai'i from the bottom up.

Yoshida, with his partner from the UH debate team, Dai Ho Chun, attended the national conference of the Progressive Education Association. The light of this movement was John Dewey, a giant of ideas in

American history. To be a progressive in Dewey's name was to challenge fixed learning curricula and rote learning. It was to embrace his slogan, "Learn by Doing" and to engage "the whole child." A generation before Yoshida, Dewey had inspired missionary descendants to found the first preschools and kindergartens in Hawai'i. In Yoshida's time, Dewey was an obvious influence on the McKinley principal Miles Cary.

Yoshida became a man with a mission. He and Dai Ho Chun coauthored an article attacking the student evaluation system as sterile and inflexible. They proposed instead a dialogue between student and teacher, in which the student became engaged in self-evaluation. Yoshida then published a second article attacking the standardized testing of reading skills: "It emphasizes group achievement, grade standards, norms and total reading scores (whatever they mean) and denies, at least in practice, individual differences in interests, purposes and needs." As previously, he proposed involving the child in self-evaluation: "If we have faith in the child's ability to choose and adjust his learning experiences in terms of his own needs and interests, then we should also have faith in the child's ability to evaluate the worthwhileness to him of these experiences."[18]

His medium for sharing ideas was the monthly periodical of the Hawaii Education Association (HEA). Through the HEA, Yoshida exerted leadership in the company of much older and more credentialed men. He served as first vice president of the HEA in 1939 and as the program chair of its annual convention. The 1939 agenda was heavily colored by the threat to democracy posed by the militarism of Japan and Germany. Miles Cary discussed "Social Education and Democracy." One of Hawai'i's great painters, Madge Tennent, led a discussion of "Art Education and Democracy." Others who were distinguished in their subjects led panels on "Personality Education and Democracy" and "Science Education and Democracy." Ethnically, the 1939 HEA convention was a grafting of the UH debate team onto a gathering of mostly white liberal reformers, many of whom were immigrants from Mainland America. As a group, their attitudes were much like Hemenway's. They were excited by Hawai'i's possibilities and appalled by its feudal and colonial aspects.

All grasped—certainly Yoshida grasped—that global history was taking a frighteningly dark turn. As the military successes of fascism spread, Yoshida became an active voice for the view that democracy must save itself by a more genuine practice of democracy. Democracy needed more democracy. The *Educational Review*, which Yoshida edited, editorialized: "If democracy is not to be destroyed in our own land we, the citizens of a free country, must see the situation clearly. The unemployed, the underpaid, the sharecropper, the migrant—these are our 'Fifth Column'; these are our undermines, these represent the failure of democracy." This was an interesting twist. The "Fifth Column" was not the enemy within (such as the Japanese community), but rather poverty, injustice, and human ignorance.

The same article boasted that the Parent Teacher Association (PTA) in Hawai'i had the most active membership of any place in the country. The PTA was "devoted to the democratic ideal, an organization that exists for the sole purpose of getting results in the way of better homes, better schools, and better communities through the cooperative effort of its members."[19] The quest for building a more democratic society and the possibility of fighting an antifascist war were being woven together, but as yet there was no war.

Hung Wai Ching was one of eighty-four students to graduate from the University of Hawai'i in 1928. Thirty-four were Caucasians, twenty-five were Chinese, and seventeen were Japanese. Five were Hawaiian, two were Korean, and none were Filipino. Kekaha Plantation on Kaua'i offered Ching an engineering job for sixty dollars a month, and he had similar offers from American Factors and the territorial government. The YMCA offered him eighty-five dollars a month, which he accepted, launching his career as a youth worker. It was the first of several instances in which Ching uncannily became the right person in the right place at the right time.

The YMCA had deep roots in Hawai'i, dating to the 1870s. Two Christian immigrants from China—the Rev. Samuel P. Aheong and a YMCA worker Sit Moon—converged to serve the youth of Honolulu's Chinatown. During the week, Ching was employed by the Nu'uanu YMCA. On weekends he volunteered at the Beretania (Street) Settlement. On Sunday morning, he taught a Bible class at the Chinese Congregational Church. In this way, he served as a connecting point among the three institutions. He was among Chinese Christians of the period who were, in the writer Diane Mark's view, "independent-thinking individuals who thrived on the latitude allowed in the Congregational churches, where much of the governing was based on democratic principle and where each member was given a vote."[20] One of the important voices of the

Chinese churches was the Rev. Stephen Mark, who implored his congregation to pursue education, to be open to new ideas, and to care actively for the condition of society. He urged them to not take discrimination lying down. He said his congregants should "comfort the afflicted and afflict the comfortable." "The word of God is double-edged," Mark wrote. "It brings healing to suffering souls on the one hand, but it also judges the proud."[21]

As with the YMCA, the Beretania Settlement and the Congregational Church approached youth on the basis of service and engagement. Christian doctrine provided a framework, but proselytizing was kept to a minimum. The message was rooted in the idea that all people are inherently equal and equal in the eyes of God—a simply stated doctrine with far-reaching political, social, and economic ramifications.

The Nu'uanu YMCA of Ching's tenure was playing a pivotal role in bringing the various ethnic groups of Hawai'i to the same table. In the late nineteenth and early twentieth centuries, the Chinese YMCA, Japanese YMCA, and Korean YMCA each served their respective ethnicities, while the Central YMCA served Caucasians and Hawaiians. Thus the YMCA in this period was a mirror of oligarchic society. Caucasians—with a few Hawaiian companions mixed in—were "central," while Asian ethnics were separated not only from whites but from one another. The YMCA's institutional guideline during the 1920s was for the Nu'uanu YMCA to be 90 percent Asian and 10 percent Caucasian and Hawaiian. The Central YMCA was supposed to be the reverse.

The Nu'uanu YMCA was in the forefront of developing an interethnic model. In 1921, it formed a multiracial board of directors consisting of a Chinese American businessman, C. K. Ai, founder of the building-supply company City Mill; Dr. Iga Mori, a well-known physician and a founder of the Japanese Hospital (now Kuakini Hospital); Dr. Syngman Rhee, the Korean nationalist who in the postwar period would become president of the Republic of Korea; and two Caucasians of an internationalist bent, the Big Five's Frank Atherton and W. D. Westervelt, a university professor and writer.

The idea that youth workers such as Ching could have a substantial impact on society may stretch the contemporary imagination. Partly it was a matter of scale. A YMCA executive, visiting in 1922, announced, "There is more 'Y' work per square foot on O'ahu than any other place I know of in the world."[22] A national YMCA study in 1922 found that the YMCAs of Honolulu had the most members per thousand population of any American city of comparable size. During the 1920s and 1930s, the YMCA reached far and wide into the lives of the young people of Honolulu. It addressed their need to be physically fit, to socialize, and to make acquaintances across ethnic lines.

The YMCA attracted charismatic people to its staff, and they had few competing distractions. As a type, they seem to have been likeable and energetic. They shared progressive attitudes toward race. They were dedicated to serving others without pushing Christian doctrine. They approached young people with a view to their potential and without condescension. Further, they either had experience with Asians in Hawai'i or in Asia or both. From experience, they did not think of Asians as odd, or as "celestials," or "coolies."

Ching followed in the spiritual footsteps of a well-known youth worker named Leigh Hooley, originally of the Beretania Street Settlement. Hooley had arrived in Honolulu in 1920. A second archetype was the even more widely known John Young, who had hovered over the Chings as children. Young was from Brooklyn, New York. He was born in 1902 into a world of ethnic and racial slurs aimed not only at the suppression of black people but all minorities. He would often recall with great bitterness the hateful vocabulary of his childhood, in which Poles were called Polacks, Italians were Dagos, Jews were Kikes, Hispanics were Spics, and anyone of Asian appearance was a Chink. When Young decided to work with nonwhite people in Hawai'i, his Scots father disowned him.

John Young had a large following among YMCA youth, organizing several dozen YMCA clubs in Honolulu in the late 1920s, including the first club in the Tin Pan Alley slum. He organized Pioneer clubs and Friendly Indian clubs, which promised adventure, and Hi-Y clubs, which promised socialization and leadership development. While this was "soft" organizing by the standards of labor or politics, it nonetheless had real ramifications, because the end goal was the development of leadership skills.

While the clubs were multiethnic, Japanese Americans participated heavily, owing to the rapid urbanization and demographic bulge of Nisei. According to one account, one of the subjects for discussion groups was the threat of a Pacific war, which no doubt put them on the spot. What would they do in the event of war between Japan and the United States?

Young estimated that twelve hundred boys were actively involved in one or more of his clubs. Diane Mark quoted him as saying, "The basic purpose of the clubs was to help lead good lives, period. If you want to call a Christian moral, all right, but it wasn't stuffing religion down their throats."

Young boasted that, after years of intense work, he was acquainted with thousands of Asians and Hawaiians and only fifteen Caucasians. In 1928, he left Honolulu to work for the YMCA in Japan and then in China. A year later, Hooley departed to study philosophy and theology, leaving Ching as the most high profile youth worker on the scene.

By skills and temperament, Ching was ideally suited to the task. He was a sharp conversationalist. He loved to tell stories. He was interested in philosophy. He had played numerous leadership roles and traveled widely. He relished acquaintance with people high and low. He was always thinking things through and talking things through. He had an instinct for trusting the right people.

He was photographed with group after group of boys and also in retreats with fellow YMCA workers. He was supremely comfortable with himself. When he organized athletic competitions, he had the unforced authority of a star athlete. He led the Nuʻuanu YMCA track team to victories over the Army Club, the Outrigger Club, and the Palama Settlement Club, thereby defeating the powerful, the privileged, and the tough. In the process, he set a new AAU Hawaiʻi record in the 220-yard hurdles.

Nuʻuanu YMCA had a large outdoor swimming pool, which was a magnet. A young boy named August Yee would remember traveling from his home in upper Kalihi Valley to swim at Nuʻuanu, and Sidney Kosasa would travel all the way from Palolo Valley for a swim. Nuʻuanu YMCA also had showers, which were especially useful to boys who lived in the tenements, where baths were shared by entire floors of occupants, and many still bathed in public *furo*.

With his engineering background, Ching took on broad responsibilities for developing the Y's facilities. One of his special assignments was to develop the YMCA's campground retreat on the North Shore of Oʻahu, Camp Erdman, an idyllic place next to a sandy inlet. For years, the Nuʻuanu Y had tried to build a second major building that included a dormitory. The Great Depression caused development of the new building to be shelved, but the needs of a growing membership revived the idea. To scope out the building and raise money, the YMCA formed the Committee of 100, with Ching as its supporting staff. Initially, the building was to be two stories high and cost $100,000. Ching advocated for adding a dormitory, which would result in a three-story building at a cost of $150,000. He said that if the YMCA leadership could raise $100,000, he would raise another $50,000 "from my people." On the haole side of this divide, Frank Atherton gave a major gift. Ching raised his $50,000. The building went up one floor, and Ching's sense of ownership of the YMCA program rose with it.

The building project was in 1937, foreshadowing the relationships of wartime. In addition to Ching, a young Nisei named Masa Katagiri served on the steering committee. Frank Atherton swung the pick that broke ground for construction.[23] On the building's completion in 1938, Charles Hemenway gave the principal remarks. "There is still to come a community of good citizens," he said. "The task still ahead is to make this dream of a community of good citizens come true."[24] Ching's effectiveness underscored the fact that he was unfazed by the widely assumed dominance of the haole. On the contrary, he was curious about their influence, their money, and their foibles. He was learning whose doors were open, who contributed to philanthropic projects, who drank, who liked to tell jokes, and who was game to sit up talking late into the night.

As a youth worker, he continued to travel often. In summer 1930, he was a delegate to an international YMCA meeting in Toronto, Canada, at which people of Asian ethnicities were strongly represented. At the international border, a Canadian border agent asked Ching why he wanted to enter the country. Ching replied that he was a U.S. citizen. He produced his passport. Others of Asian descent on the train told the agent they were going to a YMCA conference, about which the agent was informed. The agent pressed Ching. Why did he want to enter Canada? Ching repeated that he was a U.S. citizen and that he was traveling into Canada as would any U.S. citizen. The agent pressed harder. Ching stood his ground, refusing to identify himself as an employee of the YMCA bound for a YMCA-related conference. He was taken from the train, separated from his travel companions, and thrown off schedule.[25] The incident made news in both Canada and the United States. On his return home, Ching protested that his ethnicity and citizenship had been confused. "My American citizenship didn't mean a thing," Ching wrote. "It was just a scrap of paper."[26] The *Honolulu Advertiser* gave him tepid support: "Something should be done about it." The *Hawaii Chinese News* wrote, "It was because he was Chinese, because his skin was yellow." Hawai'i's nonvoting delegate to Congress, Victor Houston, helped him lodge a complaint with the U.S. State Department. The complaint went up to U.S. Secretary of State Henry Stimson, who asked the Canadian government what had happened. The Canadian government's response, which took four months, continued to claim the problem was Ching's refusal to say he was going to a YMCA conference. Stimson relayed the Canadian response to delegate Houston, along with a note saying it appeared the Canadian border agent had behaved courteously, and that the problem was of Ching's making. He ignored Ching's contention that, as an American, he had a right to enter Canada with no questions asked.

Not long after the incident, Ching enrolled in the University of Chicago School of Divinity. He said his purpose was to gain a deeper understanding of theology and to communicate with highly educated Christians on their own terms.[27] He enrolled in such courses as "Development of the Social Conscience of America," "The Church and Society," and "The Psychology of Religion." He was excited by the university's environment. Robert Maynard Hutchins, a boy wonder of higher education, had just been installed as president. Hutchins set new standards for interdisciplinary collaboration, Socratic dialogue in class, and academic freedom. He attacked the snobbishness and racism of the white fraternities and actually tried to shut them down. He abolished the football team.

Before completing the course of study, Ching followed a professor of theology to Yale University. Where the University of Chicago was about social reform, Yale was about God and country. It had educated many of the original missionaries to Hawai'i, and soon it was to supply America's intelligence agencies with many of its leading figures. At Yale, Ching was awarded a master of divinity degree. Thereafter he studied social work at New York's Columbia University before returning to Hawai'i.

Through his study at three of the country's leading universities, Ching had gained an even higher level of self-confidence. He enjoyed theology. He conversationally played with its possibilities, sometimes portraying himself as a Buddhist among the Christians, as if he were the borderland joining the two, but in reality he was rooted deeply in Christian belief.

He courted and married a smart, stylish classmate, Elsie Ting, who had finished third in the McKinley Class of 1924, served as treasurer of the Chinese Student Alliance, and acted in Ching's senior class play. Hung Wai and Elsie were seemingly a foregone conclusion of long standing. After graduation, she had taught school in rural Hawai'i

Island. She had toured the Mainland United States, climbed the Great Wall of China, and explored niches of Hawai'i that Hung Wai had not—the ancient City of Refuge, Honaunau, on the island of Hawai'i, and the inside of Haleakalā Crater on Maui, among others.

Despite the economic depression, the Ching family moved from the duplex on Christley Lane to a house on Dole Street near the university. Ching Yei, Ching Fong Shee, and several of their adult children shared the cost of a new house, Hung Wai among them. In the nuance of location, their address was on the lower end of largely haole Mānoa Valley—what some of the Chinese referred to whimsically as "Haolewood."

During this period, both Ching and Yoshida, separately, made life-long commitments to the most socially progressive churches in Hawai'i. Ching's mentor Leigh Hooley had resumed his ministry through the Chinese Congregational Church of Honolulu. In 1934, Hooley led the younger members in forming their own congregation, in which Ching played a central role. "We purport to be democratically Christian," the new congregation declared, "believing that the democratic process is the most educative in the development of the personality. . . . We purport to be a community church in fact," its declaration went on, "supra-racial and supra-national, open to all, regardless of race, class or caste."[28] In one breath, their statement evoked democracy, inherent equality, the advancement of education, and "the development of the personality." Ching was vice president of the new congregation. He attracted others and soon led a group of university students who regularly participated in the new church. In its maturity, this group became Community Church, relocated from Chinatown to the upland of Nu'uanu Valley next to the Royal Mausoleum of the Kingdom of Hawai'i.

Yoshida became part of a new multiethnic Christian congregation that likewise was dedicated to practicing interracial equality. At first it was called the Young People's Church. Most members were students of either Japanese or Chinese ancestry. They variously had roots in McKinley High School, the University of Hawai'i, and Mid-Pacific Institute. The Young People's Church was located downhill from UH. In 1923, it became the Church of the Crossroads under the leadership of yet another influential migrant from Mainland America, Dr. Galen Weaver.[29] Yoshida joined Crossroads in 1937 or thereabouts. Among its members were the sociologist Dr. Andrew H. Lind; the schoolteachers John and Aiko Reinecke, who were active in the radical wing of the labor movement; and Alice Cary, the spouse of Miles Cary. Yet another remarkable member, likely their oldest, was Theodore Richards, a visionary and somewhat iconoclastic in-law of the wealthy and influential Athertons. When Richards heard of a young people's church, he announced he was tired of the old ones.

Like Ching's Community Church, Crossroads pursued intellectual inquiry and social action. Weaver preached clear thinking and "courageous acting." The church studied Christianity in dialogue with other world religions, particularly with Buddhism, and it none too subtly incorporated a wide range of cultural and religious emblems in its architecture and décor. Although Crossroads was identified strongly with the creation of an interwar multicultural movement, early financial contributors included not only Richards but members of his Cooke and Castle relatives, as well as the Wilcox family—all of whom descended from the early day missionaries. Through such contributions, the elite maintained ties to young progressive Christians.

The two experimental churches, Yoshida's Crossroads and Ching's Community Church, were enclaves of mutual support for dissenters and a safe haven for relationships that transcended ethnic lines. Their existence suggested that, here and there, ethnic ties were giving way to consciously multiethnic models.

Such interracial projects occurred in a long context of relationship building. In a rare attempt to describe this in sociological terms, Andrew Lind returned to the original encounter between Native Hawaiians and the outside world. He began with the vibrant, populous society, on whom the British explorer James Cook depended for food and fresh water. "The fact that initial contacts occurred on an inherently equalitarian level of trade played an important role in establishing a 'live and let live' type of cross-cultural association," Lind contended.[30] In 1797, Kamehameha the Great had proclaimed, "O my people, Honor thy gods; Respect alike men great and humble; see to it that our women, our aged, and our children lie down by the roadside without fear of harm." In 1839, with the development of constitutional governance, Kamehameha III had proclaimed a similarly inclusive concept: "God hath made of one blood all nations of men to dwell on the earth, in unity and blessedness."

The overthrow of the Native Hawaiian government and America's annexation of the kingdom coincided with the triumph of social Darwinism in America—that is, with the distortion of Darwin's theory of evolution into a belief that the races had evolved to different levels, and that Europeans were the most highly evolved and therefore were the most entitled to wealth, prestige, and positions of leadership.

As a result, Ching and Yoshida came of age in a contradictory social and political environment. On the one hand, equalitarian values were at work in island culture. On the other, a network of the white elite controlled the economy, dominated the territorial government, and inflicted social wounds through the maintenance of whites-only social clubs and exclusionary real estate clauses. To be white and align oneself with the interests of the oligarchy meant gaining admission of one's children into Punahou School, and it insulated oneself from developing calluses on the hands. In the first several decades of the territory, many people never saw whites perform physical labor.

In 1917, the annexationist W. R. Castle published a book that aimed at readers who might move to Hawai'i. He warned the potential new-comer that household management for white women was not easy, because the servants were Orientals, "admirable as far as they go, but with inevitable limitations." Castle advised that Chinese servants were preferable to Japanese, even though the Chinese were inclined to go missing for several days at Chinese New Year. Furthermore, Chinese servants often gave their employers "expensive and usually hideous presents, which must be prominently displayed for months after." Overall, the Japanese were less reliable than the Chinese, but they were good cooks and potentially colorful additions to a household: "Japanese maids in their bright kimonos are picturesque around the house."[31]

It was for such arrogance that the prolific Miyamoto, who generally described the U.S. territory of Hawai'i so positively, made an exception for the dominant haole group: "Among the common people, racial barriers were minimal, and one person was as good as another. Only the ruling race, the Anglo-Saxons, held themselves haughty and aloof, priding themselves on racial superiority."[32]

The annexationists Thurston and Dole dominated the early written history of the American period—incessantly replaying their criticisms of the latter days of the kingdom as a means of rationalizing the taking of Hawai'i. The nurturing grassroots social culture of the territory was largely ignored, resulting in a void of understanding that was to persist across the decades. The contradictions of 1898 to 1941 went unanswered. The period was a kind of black hole. What was the interior story of these forty-some years? How might the paradox of this time be explained?

One answer lay in the broad notion that the values of democracy and aloha partially offset the weight of colonialism and racism. Democracy and aloha bubbled upward, pressuring federally appointed governors and judges to honor the promises of America. Democracy and aloha nurtured progressive ideas and progressive individuals and movements in competition with the status quo of white privilege. The welcoming inclusivity of Hawaiian culture continued to exert itself. More subtly, an increasingly cosmopolitan urban life challenged the hierarchical system of plantation agriculture.

It was in this environment that Ching and Yoshida and their like-minded acquaintances matured and labored, anticipating America's entry into a second world war. As the organizers of what Yoshida called the Council for Interracial Unity, they emerged as optimists—eager for social and political change—in a time of a gathering peril.

CHAPTER 2

Next to the Ocean

IN A STUDY OF PREJUDICE AGAINST JAPANESE AMERICANS, the writer
Carey McWilliams severely criticized his fellow Californians for failing
to grasp the international implications of their small-mindedness and
venom. Californians, he wrote, "insisted on regarding this agitation as a
manifestation of provincial prejudice unrelated to what was happening
in the Far East and throughout the Pacific Basin. . . . We [Californians]
seemed incapable of visualizing this area as a world region of which our
West Coast was an integral part."[1] McWilliams recounted the racism of
California's white settlers, the segregation of Chinese schoolchildren,
the California-induced war crisis of 1907, and finally California's contribution to the Japanese Exclusion Act of 1924. McWilliams described
this record as a California-Japan war. In contrast, the combined lega-
cies of the Kingdom of Hawai'i and an internationalist movement in
territorial Hawai'i worked to minimize the psychological distance and
conflicts between Japan and the United States.

From the time of Kamehameha forward, nation-state responsibilities
required the Hawaiian Kingdom to interact with the leading countries
of Europe and the Pacific. In the more than one century of its existence,
the kingdom established diplomatic relations with eighty nations, most
importantly the United States, Great Britain, and Japan. David Kalākaua,
the king of Hawai'i from 1874 to 1891, was the first head of state to
circumvent the planet. It was he who pried open the door to the large-
scale emigration of workers from Japan, and he personally welcomed
the first shipload of Japanese workers to Honolulu. As an expression of
his interest, he sent a contingent of bright young Hawaiians to study in
Japan. His successor, Queen Lili'uokalani, maintained this cordial relationship, exchanging medals with Japan's royal family.

Among the Hawai'i missionaries, a Congregationalist of the nineteenth century named Samuel Chenery Damon was a particularly notable

builder of bridges to Japan. He ministered to the passing ships and the doings of the port. He befriended and helped educate the legendary Japanese traveler Manjiro Nakahama, who had been rescued from a shipwreck by whalers and who eventually led the first Japanese delegation to Washington, D.C., to commence Japan's diplomatic relations with the United States.

In the early years of the territory, Theodore Richards coupled his interest in Japan to his concern for the Japanese workforce in Hawai'i. As a young man in New York City, Richards had attended a lecture by a retired Civil War general, Samuel C. Armstrong, an offspring of the original Hawai'i missionaries. Armstrong was famous for commanding a regiment of freed slaves in the Civil War and, thereafter, for founding Hampton Institute in Virginia, a boarding school dedicated to the education of African Americans and Native Americans. The general called to the audience for volunteers to teach at the newly organized Kamehameha Schools for Native Hawaiians and Theodore Richards, in response, abandoned law school and migrated to Hawai'i. Among many other things, he wrote the lyrics for the Kamehameha School song ("Be Strong and Ally Ye, O Sons of Hawai'i"), achieving a sort of musical immortality. He served as the school's second principal. He married Mary Atherton, a granddaughter of the particularly influential missionaries Amos Starr and Juliette Montague Cooke and, as a result, became privy to the deep history of the missionaries.

In the early 1900s he took charge of the fund-raising and publishing of the Hawaii Board of Missions. He resuscitated the missionary newspaper, *The Friend*, which claimed to be the oldest newspaper west of the Mississippi River. He developed publications in Japanese, Chinese, Hawaiian, and a dialect of Filipino. He was at once egalitarian and evangelical. He believed, as his biographer wrote, that "Americanization and Christianization went hand in hand." He first began volunteering for the YMCA in 1891 and went on to serve on the board of the interracial Nu'uanu YMCA.[2]

Inevitably, Japan and the Japanese community rose to the top of Richards's concerns. In 1912, he wrote an article predicting that many Japanese would leave the plantations but nonetheless settle in Hawai'i and also that they would rise economically and marry across racial lines.[3] Referring to race prejudice, Richards celebrated Hawai'i "as the highly privileged leader in the great silent change in the thought of mankind which promises to rob the world of its most pregnant source of

strife." Picking up where Kalākaua had left off, he developed a student
exchange program with Japan that he called the Friend Peace Scholarship, mirroring Japan's Prince Fushimi scholarship that, incidentally,
would eventually support the education of Shigeo Yoshida.

Richards acted out of a deep concern for the friction between the
United States and Japan that had resulted from the San Francisco
school crisis and the Alien Land laws of the Western states. In the tradition of Damon, he traveled to Japan, where he was received in the home
of the former premier of the Japanese government, Count Shigenobu
Ōkuma, one of the several dominant figures of the Meiji Restoration.
He met with the mayor of Tokyo, who asked a variation of the recurring question of Japan: If Japan sent students to Hawai'i, would they be
received as equals? He met with Dr. Inazō Nitobe, author of *Bushido,
the Soul of Japan.* He became acquainted with the president of Doshisha
University, Dr. Tasuku Harada, who became deeply involved in student
exchanges and who moved to Hawai'i in 1920 to found the university's
Japan Studies program.

Richards voiced unpopular positions with abandon. He insisted that
the plantations pay their workers more and house them better. He promoted sharecropping and profit sharing of the sort undertaken by Shigeo Yoshida's father. He assailed Hawai'i's public education system as
inadequate, insisting that future relations depended on providing an
equal education for all. He envisioned an ever-improving relationship
with the Nisei Japanese Americans, writing, "[We] hope to bind them
to us by ties of friendship which no shock of war or industrial cataclysm
can disrupt."

The First World War illuminated the oddities and contradictions at
work in Hawai'i. On the one hand was a budding internationalism.
On the other was a jingoistic patriotism, aroused and orchestrated by
the annexationists, who were still very much in charge of things. Until
America's belated war declaration in 1917, the United States was nominally neutral. Hawai'i nonetheless became involved in the war against
Germany, which had far-flung holdings in the Marshall Islands, the Mar-
iana Islands (Saipan and Tinian, for example), the Solomon Islands
(including Guadalcanal), and the western Samoan islands, such as
Savai'i. Compared to Hawai'i, the German-held islands of the Pacific
were of modest strategic value, and they were so remote from Germany
as to be indefensible. Nonetheless, they were of considerable interest to

Japan, which for purposes of World War I was allied with Great Britain against Germany.

In 1915, nine German ships, two of them warships, sought refuge from Britain and Japan in the supposedly neutral port of Honolulu. Two Japanese ships stalked the German ships, lying outside the harbor, waiting to attack. The Japanese navy actually captured a German schooner, removed the crew, and torched the ship. Japan's navy departed only after the German ships disarmed and submitted to a long-term agreement to dock in Honolulu. Thereafter the demobilized German ships took up useful space on the Honolulu waterfront, and people worried that the German crews might sabotage their own vessels, damage the wharves, and clog the mouth of the harbor. One German crew actually attempted to do so, setting their ship on fire and burning their papers, which brought the Honolulu Fire Department to the rescue of the wharf.

When the United States declared war on Germany in the spring of 1917, a fevered patriotism arose in Honolulu. A group called the Hawaiian Vigilance Corps formed. Its jingoism was reflected in a letter to the territory's public schoolteachers telling them that their primary role was to produce loyal Americans. It demanded—yes or no?—that teachers say whether they were promoting "loyal Americanism." All said yes. Nonetheless, six public schoolteachers were accused of insufficient patriotism and removed from their jobs.[4]

In a widely noted incident, the loyalty question was directed at a German-language teacher at the University of Hawai'i named Maria Heur. Professor Heur said she was opposed to war and would not support any of the warring countries. Despite the support given to her by Charles Hemenway on the Board of Regents, she was pushed out of her job. The Department of Public Instruction mandated that all teaching be in English. The teaching of German—then the principal international language of science—was banned from public schools until 1927. Certain individuals of German descent were removed from their jobs and made destitute. Oil paintings of Prussian kings that had been given to the Hawaiian Kingdom were removed from 'Iolani Palace. German aliens were required to register with the government, restricted from the wharves, and constrained from interisland travel except by permit. A public rally at 'Iolani Palace voted approval for a resolution to intern anyone who sympathized with enemy aliens or who expressed "disloyal or unpatriotic wishes."[5] The legislature passed a resolution urging the federal government to build an internment camp in Hawai'i, but the U.S. Department of Justice declined to do so. It suggested that the territory of Hawai'i was pushing patriotic ardor to an extreme.

The Justice Department quoted President Woodrow Wilson on the proper handling of resident aliens from an enemy nation in time of war, saying that as long as aliens lived by the law, "they shall be undisturbed in the peaceful pursuit of their lives and occupations and be accorded the consideration due to all peaceful and law-abiding persons." Wilson instructed the public to treat enemy aliens "with all such friendliness as may be compatible with loyalty and allegiance to the United States."

Wilson made this statement on the day that America declared war, April 2, 1917. His clear intent was to maintain most people of German ancestry as functioning members of American society. The test for German aliens and German Americans was not what went on in the recesses of their minds but rather whether they were willing to live amicably by U.S. law in wartime.

Although Wilson leaned in the direction of keeping people in the normal functioning of their lives, he stopped short of altogether prohibiting internment. He made an exception for the safety of the country. He also broached the insidious idea of confining people for their own protection.

By following Wilson's standard, internment of resident aliens in the United States was minimized. In the course of the conflict, just over two thousand persons of German citizenship or German ancestry were interned throughout the United States.[6] A few of these were individuals shipped from Hawai'i to internment centers on the Mainland, their stories seemingly forgotten.

In Hemenway's experience as a corporate executive, the most enduring legacy of anti-German prejudice was the dismemberment of a Big Five company, the German-owned H. Hackfeld & Company, a business of long standing that previously had been securely embedded in the white oligarchy. One of its officers, Georg F. Rodiek, was president of the Hawaiian Sugar Planters Association, and a second, J. F. C. Hagens, was president of the Chamber of Commerce of Honolulu. Both were from Bremen, Germany. They had immigrated to the Kingdom of Hawai'i as young men, worked their way up, and become U.S. citizens following annexation.

The assault on the Hackfeld company was touched off by its representing the immobilized German ships for port purposes. After America declared war, the alien property custodian of the U.S. government took over H. Hackfeld, setting a precedent of ruthless disregard for alien holdings. Hackfeld's shares were redistributed. New officers and directors were drawn from the remaining four of the Big Five corporations, forming an interlocking corporate directorate to manage the new company. The Hackfeld name was obliterated from the edifice of its Honolulu headquarters in 1918 and a new name was carved in stone— American Factors, Ltd. Its chain of department stores became Liberty House.[7]

Such discrimination as occurred raised a sobering question. If this was what happened to supposedly secure white people in response to a war, what might happen to previously marginalized nonwhite people caught up in wartime?

A partial answer lay in the subjective realm of territorial Hawai'i's political development, or lack thereof. At the onset of the First World War, Hawai'i had been incorporated into the United States for only seventeen years. Lorrin Thurston, strategist of the overthrow of the Hawaiian monarchy, still owned the morning newspaper, the *Honolulu Advertiser*, which dripped with the editorial animosity that poisoned the relationship with the German community. The leading figure in the newly organized Red Cross of Hawai'i was the author W. R. Castle, a leading coconspirator of Dole and Thurston's in the 1890s. John H. Soper, commander of the Provisional Government's troops in 1893, was the original proponent of the internment camp idea. The George R. Carter who led the Hawaiian Vigilance Corps, far from being an extremist on the margin of society, had served as governor of the territory from 1903 to 1907, succeeding Sanford Dole.

The World War I territory of Hawai'i bristled with fund drives, posters, and parades. The throne room of 'Iolani Palace became a center for rolling bandages and packing clothes and blankets. Hawai'i sent ten thousand jars of guava jelly to France. The deposed queen endorsed a fund-raiser for Belgium. "Feeling as I do the deepest sympathy for the Queen of the Belgians and her stricken people," Lili'uokalani said, "I wish every success for the 'Belgian Day' in Honolulu." Schools, churches, Boy Scouts, Girl Scouts, and the Knights of Columbus all became engaged in patriotic projects.

The YMCA and YWCA became interwoven with the U.S. military during this period. The YMCA organized classes for men who sought commissions as military officers. It supplied registrars for a day devoted to signing up men for the draft. Its first aid class focused on war wounds. Construction and operation of the army and navy YMCAs of Honolulu resulted from the war effort.

What seemed to matter most was how Hawai'i was perceived by outsiders. The historian Ralph Kuykendall believed the overarching objective was to establish the citizenry's bona fides as Americans. "There was never any doubt of the patriotism of Hawaii or of her loyalty to the cause of the United States and the Allies in the Great War," he wrote. The American spirit was "frequently the subject of favorable comment by visitors who came here from other parts of the country." Kuykendall quoted the puffery of the U.S. secretary of interior, whose department supervised American territories: "I have been astonished on my trip through these islands to discover how nearly, how well, how certainly the most remote people, the children of the schools, the men and women of the plantations, and in the upper reaches of the grazing country, knew what the significance was of this great war."[8]

In addition to self-congratulation, the war activated a streak of opportunism. When the fighting began in Europe, according to Kuykendall, "the first real issue" was how tourists might reroute themselves to Hawai'i.[9] The moralist in Theodore Richards bristled, proposing an alternative identity for Hawai'i based on compassionate war relief. It was then that Sanford Dole, described in a 1917 Who's Who as "The Grand Old Man of Hawai'i," emerged as the chairman of the war relief program. Committee by committee, virtually all were Caucasians.

A wartime poster showed a dozen ethnically diverse people queuing up behind Uncle Sam, who led them through the doorway to their patriotic duties. Foremost was a Japanese woman in a kimono. A caption translated into Japanese, Korean, Hawaiian, Chinese, Portuguese, and Ilocano said, "Own Shares in the Country that Protects You." When the Japanese press finally expressed dissatisfaction over Japanese not being represented on the territory's Food Commission, a subcommittee was appointed made up of the pineapple king James Dole, John Waterhouse, and three Japanese, Dr. Iga Mori, G. Negoro, and K. Ishida.

Hawai'i's experience with combat was minimal but nonetheless shed light on the tenuous condition of the U.S. military in Hawai'i. By one count, only about one-tenth of the total were of Japanese ancestry, mainly first-generation immigrants, resulting in a (segregated) all-Japanese outfit of about five hundred troops.[10] Most of the guardsmen were Caucasian, Native Hawaiian, Chinese American, or Filipino. The latter, mostly immigrants from America's Philippine colony, were widely recruited from the plantations and deemed to be Americans for purposes of military service.

The U.S. war declaration of April 1917 came and went without the federal government mobilizing Hawai'i's National Guard. When news arrived that guard troops from the Philippines were being sent to France, the territorial governor of Hawai'i wrote, "[If] Filipino organizations get first chance, Hawaiian guardsmen will seriously feel apparent discrimination." It was an awkward fix for the federal administration of America's recently acquired possessions in the Pacific. In response, the War Department called Hawai'i's guardsmen to active duty. The soldiers camped around Honolulu in pup tents and were only incrementally shuttled to the army's training center at Schofield Barracks. When the war ended on November 11, 1918, most of the Hawai'i contingent of about four thousand men were still at Schofield Barracks.

Seventy-eight were memorialized as casualties of the war. Most were noncombatants. The last to die in Europe, Clarence J. Watson, died on November 7, 1918, four days before the armistice. Nonetheless, the territorial government ardently pursued a highly visible memorial to the fallen. This became a saltwater swimming pool next to the ocean at Waikīkī, enhanced by an elaborate arched entryway and concrete bleachers, called the Natatorium. For a while it became a showcase for the talents of the Olympian swimmer Duke Kahanamoku and others, and then it became an albatross of the City and County government of Honolulu, the subject of decades of dispute over its costly maintenance.

Obviously, the First World War stirred up the white community. Information on how it affected the Japanese community is fragmentary. Seemingly the overall idea was to keep the Japanese community on the margin, and there was little pushing back, reflecting the dominance of the white oligarchy and also suggesting a comparatively weak state of Japanese community development. In the long reach, the first of the world wars was a window into Hawai'i's early territorial period. Only two decades had elapsed between the annexation and the armistice. During this time, society in Hawai'i was based on an unequivocal system of white dominance and white privilege.

What followed in the 1920s was, if not a distinct turning point, at the least characterized by increased social interaction of the races and accelerated community development. Support for public education expanded. The University of Hawai'i brought in key people in such crucial areas as sociology and Japan studies. The U.S. Army opened itself to greater contact with young people through its Reserve Officers Training Corp (ROTC) program. Youth work became more of a social force. Immigrants established niches of expanded autonomy, and people of Asian ancestry began to assert themselves more vigorously. Finally, a labor-organizing movement made a fundamental—that is, structural and demographic—contribution to the process of social change.

Prior to the 1898 annexation, immigrant plantation workers were bound by three-year contracts, which were enforced by a law suggestively known as the Masters and Servants Act. The earliest immigrants lived in stick and thatch huts, and then in barracks. Workers might be ill but were often forced to work. Workers who ran away from their contracts were tracked down and sometimes beaten by overseers. If not slaves, neither was a contract worker quite free. Following annexation, the tyrannical ties of labor contracting were no longer legal.

Contrary to the stereotype of passivity, first-generation Asian immigrants engaged in numerous protests and wildcat strikes.[11] In the earliest conflicts, the plantations always won on the face of things. Strikes were broken, and workers returned to their tasks without visible gains. In 1909, coordination among the scattered labor actions of the Oʻahu plantations reached a critical mass through the Japanese-language press of Honolulu. The editors Yasutaro Soga of the *Nippu Jiji* and Fred Makino of the *Hawaii Hochi* mobilized the discontent of Japanese workers into an island-wide plantation strike. Soga and Makino and two of their reporters were jailed. The strike was beaten down. Freedom of speech, freedom of assembly, and due process of law were trampled to maintain the plantation labor system, but the strike nonetheless was revelatory. Immigrants might become authors of history.

The second large strike began in 1919 and continued into 1920. It challenged the white colonial system of class and race that had run amok between the annexation and World War I. Contrary to the image of a Pacific paradise, "there are thousands of laborers who are suffering under the heat of the equatorial sun, in the field and in factory, and who are weeping with ten hours of hard labor and a scanty pay of 77 cents a day. . . . Certain capitalists may regard us as ignorant creatures," the Japanese Labor Federation said, but the strikers were "endeavoring to safeguard justice and humanity as the members of the great human family."[12]

As in the 1909 strike, Japanese organizers led the 1920 strike, except now they were genuine labor leaders, not newspaper editors. Work stoppage originated on the plantations of O'ahu and spread to the Neighbor Islands and also to Filipino organizers and workers. Although this alliance had its problems, it was a step toward working people achieving solidarity across ethnic lines. The sugar companies retaliated by evicting workers and their families from their plantation-provided housing, causing them to converge on Honolulu. According to one account, about twelve thousand people were homeless.[13] Some stayed with relatives. Others stayed in camps in parks and along stream banks. Soup kitchens fed people. Jack Burns, then a ten-year-old, remembered his mother taking food to the soup kitchens in urban Kalihi. On April 3, 1920, three thousand workers marched through Honolulu. Their banners called for such basics as an eight-hour workday. Others said, "We want to live like Americans"; "We pledge to God we are not radicals—we are laborers who wallow in the brown dirt to produce sugar." The last banner in the march said, "God has created us equal."[14]

The strike leaders were the object of a fiercely anti-Japanese propaganda campaign. Its centerpiece was the allegation that Japan was trying to control Hawai'i's economy. The words "Japanese conspiracy" were employed to play on fears first contrived twenty-five years earlier to facilitate America's takeover of Hawai'i. Prominent politicians and businessmen focused on the presence of a labor organizer from Japan.[15] Although the linking of the strike to Japan's government was fallacious, the conspiracy theory persisted.

The strike ended without formal concessions from management, but workers soon were given pay raises, and conditions of work improved. Nonetheless, many refused to return to the plantations. The number has been estimated as high as half of all the strikers, with some subsequently trickling back to the plantations after realizing that opportunity in Honolulu was limited.[16] The net effect was that Honolulu swelled— the city that sheltered thoughts of democratization, the aloha spirit, and the Melting Pot.[17] The city became more Japanese in character and atmosphere. The Japanese population of Honolulu increased by two-thirds during the 1920s. With urbanization and expansion of the school system, Japanese Americans grew up with ever-increasing access to elementary schools, McKinley High School, and the University of Hawai'i. Heavily Japanese neighborhoods expanded in upper Kalihi Valley, Palama, Liliha, the McCully district, Moiliili, Palolo, and Kapahulu. Half of Chinatown was Japanese. Its western (or 'Ewa) part, along the banks of Nu'uanu Stream, was more accurately Nihonmachi (Japantown).

Japanese grocery stores, dry goods stores, restaurants, sake shops, and Japanese-style hotels encircled A'ala Park, catering both to the city dwellers and to the remaining thousands of plantation workers who disembarked from the train that carried them from the countryside to the end of the O'ahu Rail and Land Company line.

Where the original Japanese had migrated to Hawai'i with the idea of returning to Japan, only about a third did so. Many pushed on to the better wages and spacious farmlands of the West Coast states, but a larger group stayed in Hawai'i. Although well less than half of the original migration, the Japanese of Hawai'i were a fraction of a large base number. By 1920, the 61,000 of 1900 had grown to more than 100,000.

It would often be said that the first generation of immigrants pulled itself up by its bootstraps. While their achievements were remarkable, it is more accurate to say that the Asia of their youth, in the late nineteenth and early twentieth centuries, was suffering through a time of turbulent transition. The common denominators of stress on Asian countries were the aggressive impact of the West and the shocks of modernization. In the early years of the resulting migrations, most immigrants were childless single males, which meant that childbearing couples were a special subset. Among the Japanese couples, their children were the advance contingent of the second generation. A few actually were born into the Kingdom of Hawai'i, and others, such as Yoshida and his cohorts, were born in the earliest years of the territory.

Workers and their families frequently sought to gain a level of independence from the plantation system. Parents either came with or acquired through diligence a margin of autonomy for themselves. Shigeo Yoshida's father was a sharecropper, not a plantation laborer. The father of Masa Katagiri was a barber, then a garage owner. Dr. Shunzo Sakamaki's father was an interpreter and translator. Masaji Marumoto's father owned a store on the Kona Coast of Hawai'i Island.

For those who remained in the plantation system, the demand for skilled work created a parallel if less obvious measure of leverage. The sugar industry was just that—it was industry. King Sugar was constantly becoming more industrialized. Unlike cotton in Mississippi or colonial products such as ore, rubber, and sisal, sugar required timely processing. It required sugar mills near the harvested fields, mills that were enormous workplaces filled with intricate machines. Mechanical skills were valued, as were construction skills. In a similar vein, locomotives were tracked through the fields to haul the harvest, and water systems were carefully engineered.

Industrialization was even more advanced in the pineapple industry. Where sugar had to be processed at least into molasses before shipment, pineapple required a timely processing from field to can. As a result, the pineapple canneries developed complicated systems of mechanized coring and shelling (the Ginaca machine), work-line conveyors, boilers, packing machines, automated labelers, and the endlessly rattling trolleys on which boxes of canned product progressed to waiting ships in the harbor and from there to the world markets.

If on the surface the worker strikes seemed divisive, their real effect was arguably otherwise. The great strike of 1919–1920 seemed to have shaken the planters, catalyzing activities to lessen the distance between the workforce and the white establishment. By the 1920s, it was obvious that the Japanese community was in Hawai'i to stay (as were the Chinese before them, and as were the Koreans who had arrived in the period 1903–1905). With an influx of picture brides from Japan, the birthrate accelerated, and the birth of the Nisei generation took a leap forward.

One much-discussed aspect of this history was the campaign of Americanization aimed at the Nisei, led by a well-known Christian minister of Japanese ancestry, Takie Okumura. Like the Chinese Christian missionaries, Okumura had converted to Christianity in his country of origin, then migrated to Hawai'i to serve as a minister. Okumura was a whirlwind of energy. He built the monumental Makiki Christian Church on Pensacola Street in the image of a Japanese castle. He founded Japanese-language schools that celebrated the stories of George Washington and Abraham Lincoln. He established the Okumura Dormitory to house high school and university students in Honolulu at low cost. He went on an island-by-island sweep through the plantations, much like an old-fashioned labor organizer, preaching Nisei commitment to the United States. He brought Nisei together annually under an umbrella he called The New Americans Conference, which he held from 1928 to 1941, staging programs that encompassed newspaper editors, corporate employers, military officers, and territorial government officials. The New Americans Conference was an easy target for criticism, in that Okumura accepted subsidies from both the government of Japan and the plantations. Speakers cautioned young Japanese Americans that most of the jobs were in the sugar and pineapple industries. Such critiques notwithstanding, key individuals who actually attended the conferences thought they were interesting and beneficial.[18] Viewed dispassionately, the conferences were a face-to-face venue for inching people toward a shared viewpoint around the broad theme of Americanization. The conferences helped calm the wild talk of a Japanese conspiracy, and the Melting Pot idea advanced.

While major elements of Hawai'i worked on the incorporation of Asian immigrants, an opposite trend was occurring on the U.S. Mainland. The precedent for excluding a national group was the Chinese Exclusion Act of 1882. Subsequent exclusion policy focused on Japanese. The so-called Gentleman's Agreement of 1907 informally shut down most of the immigration of Japanese to the U.S. Mainland. Thereafter, the 1917 Congress excluded Asians from immigrating from any place other than the Philippines, which was then an American colony. It imposed literacy tests, and Japanese immigration continued to be selectively minimized by the Gentleman's Agreement. In 1921, Congress passed a National Origins Act that limited the immigration of people, other than from the Western Hemisphere, to 3 percent of their American population by country of origin. In 1924, Congress passed the Japanese Exclusion Act, which further limited immigration—to 2 percent of a group's population by national origin as it existed not in 1924 but 1890. The obvious goal was the perpetuation of an America dominated by a white population of northern European origin. In the vernacular of California, America was to be forever a white man's country. The last step, the Japanese Exclusion Act, added insult to the injury done to Japan at the Versailles conference of the League of Nations, in which Japan had been rebuffed in its quest for a declaration that all people are inherently equal.

The Exclusion Act was perceived in Japan as reducing the status of Japanese in America to that of the Chinese. No less an authority than Akira Iriye, the bilingual, bicultural Harvard historian, observed that after 1924 exchanges between American internationalists and Japanese internationalists declined sharply.[19] The influence of pragmatists and liberals in Japan who sought a modus vivendi with the West was curtailed. Protests of the U.S. immigration law occurred throughout Japan. The first day of July 1924 was called "The Day of Disgrace." Consumers boycotted American goods. The *Japan Times and Mail* described the act as a declaration of war. It "cuts the Japanese mind deep, a wound that will hurt and rankle for generations and generations."[20]

Political dominance in Japan shifted to the militarists, with disastrous consequences.

Where the impact of the Exclusion Act seems to have been widely ignored in the United States, Hawai'i again was an exception. Alarmed by the growing schism, the YMCA quickly organized a conference dedicated to improving relations among Pacific countries. The 1925 gathering resulted in formation of the Institute for Pacific Relations (IPR). Although framed in terms of engaging Pacific nations in a dialogue, at the core was the Hawai'i YMCA's concern for the rapid deterioration of U.S.–Japan relations. Scholars who have studied the IPR leave no doubt on this point—the main impetus was the Exclusion Act and fear of mounting tension between Japan and the United States.[21]

Having no formal power, the IPR was an exercise in generating "soft" power. The guiding proposition was that acquaintance mattered, that genuine exchange would follow, and that it would lead to new thinking and improved relationships.

By virtue of its multiracial (and heavily Japanese) population, and also by virtue of its Melting Pot narrative, Hawai'i was preconditioned to support the IPR. It built on the legacy of a man named Alexander Hume Ford, who had taken it upon himself to promote Hawai'i-based internationalism. Ford was the founder of an internationalist group called Hands Around the Pacific, which worked at making acquaintances across ethnic lines. The idea was to take turns speaking and listening to one another's viewpoints. Conscious communication occurred in combination with the idea of a Pacific family of nations. September 17, 1915, became the first Balboa Day, honoring Vasco de Balboa, who was regarded as the first European to behold the Pacific Ocean. President Woodrow Wilson was recruited to serve as honorary president of Balboa Day—an example of the promotional tactic at which Ford excelled. The deposed queen Lili'uokalani, in declining health, ceremonially received the flags of the Pacific nations. Event organizers announced without irony that she was again queen for an hour, and the national flag of Hawai'i flew briefly at the pinnacle of the flagpole over 'Iolani Palace.

As an extension of Hands Around the Pacific, Ford organized "3-3-3-3" clubs, bringing three people from a given ethnic group together with groups of three people from other ethnic groups. Hands Across the Pacific spread from Hawai'i to Japan, Korea, the Philippines, Australia, New Zealand, and elsewhere. In 1919, the Hands Around the Pacific clubs became chapters of a new organization, again based in Hawai'i, called the Pan-Pacific Union. The goal of the Pan-Pacific Union, its maiden publication said, was to "unite the races and countries in and about the Pacific in closer bonds of fellowship."[22] Five hundred people gathered at a conference for Pan-Pacific Union Week. The corporate sector's Frank Atherton spoke to the Chamber of Commerce about developing Pacific trade by getting acquainted around the Pacific. He described calling on businessmen in East Asian countries simply to get to know them and to tell them about Hawai'i.[23] The Filipino leader N. Dizon[24] wrote, "We Filipinos, and you Japanese, Chinese and Koreans, must draw your countries (of origin) into the Pan Pacific movement so that the prophecy of . . . war coming between the Far East and the West may not come true. It can only be done through a Pan-Pacific Union founded on love and understanding as we know it in Hawai'i." Internationalism rippled through the community, nurturing a rapid growth of Rotary Clubs and Lions Clubs, both of which were international in their orientation. As a young police officer, John Burns joined a multiracial Lions Club, through which he advocated for repealing the racial exclusion laws and replacing them with a color-blind immigration policy.

The YMCA's International Committee made a study that illuminated the contradiction of internationalism on the one hand and discrimination within Hawai'i on the other. The study asked what would happen when young Asian Americans came of age in a system controlled by a white establishment. It predicted the outcome of this situation "will radiate throughout the Pan-Pacific areas and will be felt for years to come." The Hawai'i YMCA, it contended, had a unique potential for leading a transformation "that will make for the peace, happiness, and largest satisfaction to all concerned."

Interracial contact in Hawai'i seemed to feed internationalism, and vice versa. One cannot survey the voluminous Pan-Pacific Union literature without taking it as sincere and, incrementally, somewhat effective. What was being said at McKinley High School about "The Melting Pot," what students were debating at the University of Hawai'i, and what "3-3-3-3" groups discussed, were creating a kind of echo effect.

Charles Hemenway was an internationalist. As his protégés, both Yoshida and Ching were encouraged to see the world whole, and they did so to a remarkable degree. Through the YMCA, Ching had met with people on both sides of the Pacific. Through debate, Yoshida had argued his progressive propositions throughout the West Coast and

Japan. As a student, Yoshida also lived for a time with a group of scholars and iconoclasts in the home of Alexander Ford.[25] In the moment of crisis, following the bombing of Pearl Harbor, the third member of the Morale Section, whose job it was to call on the better intentions of the Hawai'i elite, was Charles Loomis. He was the executive secretary of the IPR.

Although Hung Wai Ching and Shigeo Yoshida had taken somewhat different paths after the University of Hawai'i, their basic concerns moved in parallel across time. By 1937, the reference point of each was the Japanese army's brutal push into the heart of China. Ching's overriding concern was maintaining a good relationship between people of Japanese and Chinese ancestry in Hawai'i. Yoshida's was how Japanese aliens and Japanese Americans were to be perceived and treated in light of Japan's aggression.

Yoshida's most visible stage was a congressional hearing on the possibility of statehood, organized by the territory's nonvoting delegate to the U.S. Congress, Samuel Wilder King, a Republican. The sugar industry set the hearing's agenda, much as it had since the Treaty of Reciprocity between the kingdom and the U.S. government (1875), the Bayonet Constitution (1887), the overthrow of the monarchy (1893), and annexation (1898). Throughout, the sugar industry was driven by a desire for duty-free and quota-free access to the vast U.S. sugar market. In 1935, this access had been limited by imposition of an import quota on Hawai'i sugar, causing the planter class to seek admission to the union. In 1937, Delegate King coaxed a special committee of senators and representatives to hold a hearing on statehood in Honolulu.

In addition to the many Caucasians who testified, eleven Japanese Americans did so, forging a link between the cause of statehood and the Japanese American drive for first-class citizenship. In the process, they were met by critical questioning about loyalty and assimilation and by an underlying antagonism for accepting a state in which other than white people comprised the majority.[26] Chief among the congressional questioners were several men who later emerged as critics of Japanese Americans—Senator Guy Gillette of Iowa, Representative John H. Tolan of California, and, most notoriously, Representative John Rankin of Mississippi.

Yoshida testified near the end of the hearing in response to the anti-Japanese slant of the committee's questions. He announced that he was not testifying about statehood per se but about what had been alleged about Japanese Americans. Dual citizenship in Japan and the United States, he said, did not equate to a divided allegiance. He pointed out that Japanese Americans had not chosen to be dual citizens; also that shedding Japanese citizenship—expatriation—was extremely cumbersome. He then spoke a line that he would famously use again and again with variations: "There is only one country to which we Americans of Japanese ancestry owe allegiance, and that is the United States."[27]

Rankin of Mississippi, who was to eventually say, "Once a Jap always a Jap," attempted to lecture Yoshida on why "you people" had failed to understand the gravity of the dual citizenship issue. Yoshida ignored Rankin and pushed on: "As much as we would hate to see a war between the United States and Japan, and as much as we would hate to see the day come when we would have to participate in such a conflict, it would be much easier for us, I think, to face the enemy than to stand the suspicion and criticism, unjust in most cases, leveled against us." To this he added, "It would be easier for me to pack a gun and face the enemy."[28]

A long discussion followed on Japanese participation in the public school system as well as the language schools. Yoshida's conversance in education made for strong testimony, which he concluded by proposing that the territorial government teach Asian languages as it taught French and German. This, he said, would lessen parental demand for continuing the Japanese-language schools.

Congressman Tolan asked how Yoshida might mitigate suspicions of Japanese people. Yoshida said one way was to have people like Tolan come to Hawai'i and get the facts. Tolan responded by saying that suspicion was partly grounded in "the proposition that your people from birth are taught loyalty to the Mikado and his government." "No," Yoshida replied, such an assertion was both "mistaken and unjust." Tolan persisted. How many men did Yoshida know who had gone home to fight in Japan's war against China? Yoshida said the answer was none. He added that he did not use the word "home" for Japan, in Tolan's meaning of the word, "as it isn't 'home' to us."[29]

Representative Claude Fuller of Arkansas praised Yoshida's testimony, saying, "[From] the fine example which you yourself have presented to us, I don't think America will have much trouble about citizens of Japanese ancestry, if they live up to the impression you have made on this committee."[30]

The transcript of Yoshida's appearance ran to more than seven thousand words, which translates to about an hour of time. The following day, the more colorful excerpts were on the front page of the *Honolulu Star-Bulletin*.

The hearing was held in the throne room of 'Iolani Palace. When it was over, the congressional delegation toured U.S. military installations. Members stood around during these outings with their hands in their pockets, chewing cigars, listening intently to the generals and admirals. In one obligatory photo, the delegation was on a boat at Pearl Harbor. Yet another photograph was shot in the notch in the Wai'anae Mountains called Kolekole Pass, through which Japan's pilots eventually would fly in their bombing run to Pearl Harbor.

Following the congressional visit, Yoshida became a central figure in the movement of Japanese Americans to expatriate their Japanese citizenship.[31] In January 1938, he published an article addressed to educators, "Why and How to Expatriate." He acknowledged that the dual citizenship of Japanese Americans was a barrier to statehood but said the issue exceeded the bounds of the statehood discussion. Dual citizenship, he wrote, created suspicions that Nisei must answer by freeing themselves from the government of Japan. Further, "dual citizenship is neither natural nor desirable."[32]

The status of dual citizenship resulted from Nisei born after 1924 being registered with Japan's consulate during the two weeks following birth. Yoshida contended that many Nisei did not know they were dual citizens. Many who did know, he said, refused to petition Japan to release them because it would be admitting an allegiance that they "did not owe at any time and which they neither sought nor desired." Some Nisei, under age twenty, had been blocked by their parents from expatriating, while a small number actively wanted to retain their citizenship in Japan, primarily as a means of inheriting property.

Japan did not let go of the Nisei readily. As described by Yoshida, the first step to expatriation was either a birth certificate or a replica thereof from the secretary of the territorial government. If an applicant was under fifteen, a parent had to initiate the application. If the applicant was between fifteen and twenty, the parents had to concur in the application. The applicant then was required to produce a traditional family register, a *koseki*, from Japan. In addition, the applicant was required to submit two copies of the paperwork to a family council in Japan via the minister of the interior of the Japanese government. After six months, the applicant's name was to appear in the Japanese government's *Official Gazette*. The head of the applicant's family then was required to report the expatriation to the consulate, which in turn forwarded the information to the registry in Japan where the family originally lived, at which point the expatriation of citizenship was complete. In short, Yoshida's article was an attempt to help Nisei navigate a bureaucratic and cultural swamp. It was no wonder that families often retained attorneys to help Nisei members expatriate. Only a minority even attempted this aggravating maneuver.

In his article, Yoshida had neglected to add that with expatriation, the person's name was stricken from the record of the village of origin. This was not merely cutting the tie to the emperor but to the imagined twenty-six hundred years of Japan's descent from the sun deity Amaretsu. It meant removing oneself from the traditional record of relationships to grandparents, aunts, uncles, cousins, and even siblings in Japan.

Despite this, the expatriation movement continued doggedly, moved along by a Nisei organization called the Hawaiian Japanese Civic Association (HJCA), a group founded in 1926 under the auspices of the IPR. Young Japanese Americans went from the University of Hawai'i campus into the HJCA, which provided counseling on expatriation.[33] The HJCA reflected the desire of many Nisei to free themselves from Old World influence and to deal with life as they experienced it as Americans. As such, it was an interesting window into interwar Hawai'i. Its identity was soon to be all but lost to history, but it played an important role in its time by identifying and developing early Nisei leadership. Participants were usually older Nisei who had acquired education and established themselves in an urban environment. Yoshida, for example, appeared in a newspaper article along with other HJCA leaders, presenting a college scholarship to a young person of Japanese ancestry.[34] As part of its expatriation campaign, the HJCA circulated a mass petition to the U.S. State Department to work with Japan's government on a simplified procedure for expatriation.

In part because of the YMCA's international orientation, Ching shared Yoshida's sharp awareness of the threat of war. In 1935, he traveled to Shanghai, China, on a two-week trip. He saw corpses lying in the street, dead of starvation. At that point, Japan had long since taken over Korea, and now it was transforming the northern reaches of China into a puppet state, Manchukuo.

In 1937, Ching participated in an unusual study conducted by the IPR. Its goal was to assess how Japan's aggression was affecting the relationship between people of Chinese and Japanese ancestry in Hawai'i. The research team delved into ethnic newspapers, magazines, books, radio programs, motion pictures, language schools, temples, churches, lectures, and performances. They studied intermarriage and voting patterns. They asked people about their interethnic friendships or lack thereof.

The resulting report, *Chinese and Japanese in Hawaii during the Sino-Japanese Conflict,* delved into expressions of enthusiasm for Japanese militarism. It reported that in the first year of Japan's invasion of China, various people had contributed about $70,000 to Japan for a soldiers' relief fund. About $7,000 went directly to the war-making effort, and various rural O'ahu communities raised enough money to ship seven trucks to Japan.[35] At the family level, the study reported conflicts between the immigrant generation and the American-born generation. Where Issei sometimes took pride in the military achievements of Japan over a traditional enemy, Nisei tended to object.

The study attempted to assess the allegation that "Japanese stick together," particularly the persistent contention that Japanese Americans voted as an ethnic bloc with the goal of taking over the political system. The study analyzed a multimember House district with precincts that were disproportionately Japanese on the one hand and disproportionately Chinese on the other. By counting ballots on which voters "plunked" for only one candidate, the study concluded that "voting by national descent exists, but is not heavy. It would not swing an election, unless in a contest exceedingly close on other grounds."[36]

The study cited numerous anecdotes of positive relationships between Japanese and Chinese. It reported a 1938 gathering at Hemenway's home on the occasion of his birthday. Six couples were Chinese and six were Japanese. "When they assembled there was no need to break the ice," the study said. "There was no ice to break."[37] A second anecdote described nine schools that were asked for evidence of interethnic conflict among their students. By this time, two-thirds of the student body of McKinley High School was of Japanese ancestry. A McKinley teacher wrote, "The war in the Orient has not penetrated our fabric." She said ethnic identity was giving way to a shared American identity: "Perhaps our students are not Japanese and Chinese. The more I see of them—as the years roll round—the more I see them as Americans."

Ching appeared anonymously in an account of a campus YMCA club in which a Chinese student was nominated to lead an otherwise all-Japanese membership: "At first there was some hesitation about accepting him. The [YMCA] secretary found that the objections came from parents." Ching sought out the parents and urged them to withdraw their objections, "on the ground that the young people were all American citizens and would have to spend their lives together in Hawai'i." The Chinese student was accepted as the leader of the YMCA group.[38]

The Congregational Church of the Crossroads—Yoshida's church— had many Japanese as well as Chinese members. Its minister told the IPR researchers, "I can safely say that the activities and relationships in the church have gone on undisturbed."[39]

The study concluded that despite the war in Asia, people in Hawai'i were living in a state of "undisturbed friendliness. . . . Over against the old saw that blood is thicker than water," it said, "the role of culture or learned behavior is an incomparably stronger actor in human conduct than race." The last line said, "In particular, the contrast between immigrant and Hawaiian-born generations shows that in a new environment, culture, including national sentiments and values, can change radically in one generation."[40]

In the gloom of impending war in the late 1930s, this was an optimistic observation about human nature. It was a case for the view that learned behavior was a greater influence than ethnicity: in a new environment, culture, including national sentiments and values, *can change radically in one generation.* Such a finding was much in contrast to prevailing American opinion, as exemplified by the president of the United States, Franklin D. Roosevelt, who believed that persons of Japanese ancestry could not assimilate into American society.[41]

Obviously, the study was subjective, with Mr. Hemenway, his protégés Ching and Yoshida, Miles Cary, the YMCA, the public schools, and the Church of the Crossroads all speaking to a narrative of Island aloha and American democracy. However, it was but one of many commentaries during the interwar period suggesting an increasingly harmonious society. To a passing researcher, a cluster of Japanese informants described haole as snobs but paradoxically also said, "the ones I've met are very nice. I like them."[42] Miyamoto wrote that despite the barriers erected by the Anglo-Saxon elite, "Hawaiian existence made all people tolerant, and a spirit of 'live and let live' seemed to be the guiding motif. Whatever contrary feelings one might have harbored regarding racial equality and intermarriage prior to his arrival in the islands, he soon changed his mind about humanity. According to the Hawaiian mode of reasoning, as long as one was intrinsically good, just, and capable, he was welcome as one of the family, irrespective of his racial extraction."[43]

In July 1939 Ching, along with Elsie, led a contingent of young YMCA leaders to the World Congress of Christian Youth in Amsterdam. A list of his young charges on the trip gave a clue to his influence over the coming generation. The student Abraham Akaka was to become known globally for his spiritual definition of aloha; for his bond with Dr. Martin Luther King Jr.; and also for the fact that his brother Daniel was to become a longtime U.S. senator. It was during the Amsterdam trip, through which he witnessed the world in crisis, that Akaka devoted himself to the ministry. Mineo Katagiri (brother of Masa Katagiri) was also to become a well-known Congregational minister in whom Ching took a particular pride. A third student in the delegation was Kenneth Lau, eventually a professor and high-level administrator in various positions at the University of Hawai'i.

Ching, Elsie, and his students were still in Europe on September 1, 1939, when Germany invaded Poland, causing Great Britain and France to declare war on Germany. The group rode to Paris on a blacked-out train, where they learned the British government had commandeered the ocean liner on which they were supposed to return home. After a week of hounding American Express, Ching contacted a mysterious figure of African ancestry in Paris—in Ching's telling of the story, the "Black Eagle." Trusting the man's honesty, Ching paid him cash up front for passage out of the port of Le Havre.[44] The ship sailed on September 9, eight days into the war in Europe. It was so crowded that Elsie slept in a makeshift bunk eight persons high in the library. Hung Wai slept on deck under a ping-pong table. To avoid the deadly German U-boats, the ship zigzagged on a long, circuitous route to the north, passing Greenland. A voyage that usually took a week or less took ten days before arriving in New York Harbor. Almost immediately after his return from Europe, Ching—in response to Shivers and Hemenway—began organizing the group that was to call itself the Council for Interracial Unity.

Over the horizon of several years, Ching and Yoshida each had thought deeply about fascism and had come to fear it. Each had traveled extensively and been influenced by some of the most progressive thinkers of the period. They were the core of the group who grasped the hard fact that war was coming, and that the only question was how to respond. Each had embraced a strain of Christianity that sought to bring the races together not only in name but in fact. They embraced the aloha spirit as a matter of faith.

PART II

Under the American Flag

nies will try to divide and conquer. We must rem

tand, divided we fall". Let us all work togethel

to a living thing that will weld us to the commor

nd defending our American institutions and our hc

Hawaii there is no north, no south, no east nor

s, regardless of racial descent, speaking one lan

loving one flag, having allegiance but to one co

n Hawaii which you citizens can help us to perfec

must be all inclusive. It is true that we have

must weld these groups into one people, inspired

ave many economic classes. We must work to reduc

e classes and develop a teamwork that subordinate

our country's good. This unity must be mutual to

I know that you will do your share to make it so

-5-

Yoshida's patriotic phrasing in the U.S. Army's message to students
at McKinley High School, in mid-summer 1941, was an early draft of his
subsequent writings at pivotal moments. UH Archives and Manuscripts.

CHAPTER 3

External and Internal Security

As the United States moved toward war in the Pacific, two major issues hung over Hawai'i. First, the U.S. military's defenses were weak relative to the situation. Neither the army nor navy was ready for war. Defenses on the ground were a fraction of the strength recommended by the army, and the Pacific naval fleet was crammed uncomfortably into Pearl Harbor. Second, the military intelligence agencies had no agreed-upon approach to dealing with the large ethnically Japanese population.

A commander of the Hawaiian Army Department remarked to his staff, "Comparing this with all other military bases, Hawaii has the most apparent connection between external threat and internal security." That is, the Island Japanese community was the most obvious internal security question, and Japan was the most obvious external threat. Japan had invaded Manchuria in 1931, withdrawn from the League of Nations in 1933, and invaded China in 1937. In the fall of 1940, it had allied itself formally with the fascist states of Germany and Italy by signing an agreement to provide one another with military and economic aid and to support "a new order of things." The same year, Japan staged a propaganda event celebrating what was purported to be the 2,600th anniversary of the Japanese nation. A delegation from Hawai'i attended.

In the context of a vulnerable Hawai'i, many people thought it eminently reasonable to inquire into the prospective loyalties of the Japanese-ancestry population in the event of war. As was said over and over, nearly 40 percent of the population was of Japanese ancestry. In the 1940 U.S. Census, 110,000 were native born and therefore U.S. citizens. Another 50,000 were first-generation Japanese aliens, ineligible for naturalized citizenship by virtue of the U.S. government's discriminatory naturalization laws. Many members of the first generation and occasionally the second generation, as dual citizens, had served in

Japan's military. Most troubling to the U.S. intelligence agencies were the *kibei* (Japanese Americans born in the United States but partially educated in Japan). By the thousands, they had gone to Japan—typically at the direction of their parents—to study, practice the Japanese language, and connect with the culture.

Through the 1920s and 1930s, travel to and from Japan accelerated, as did the movement of goods. Japanese steamship companies opened lines to Hawai'i. Japanese banks opened branches in Hawai'i. When Japan's naval training ships docked, their arrival set Issei businessmen to competing for who would entertain the ship's officers. Buddhist and Shinto temples were staffed by priests sent from parent organizations in Japan. Japanese-language schools sent teachers. The national government of Japan maintained a large consulate and a network of several hundred associates, who reached out to the widely distributed immigrant population. Japan's print news, radio broadcasts, movies, and traveling performances all arrived in Hawai'i regularly, and the increasingly propagandistic wire dispatches were reprinted in Hawai'i unedited. Euphemistically, events such as Japan's slaughter of Nanking's people became part of "the China incident." Appeals were made to Hawai'i's Japanese to support Japan's field army with comfort kits, metal scraps, and cash donations.

Among the Americans who had agitated for taking over Hawai'i in the 1890s, Theodore Roosevelt stood out for his impact on history. He wrote a book about building up the U.S. Navy. He worked closely with Captain Alfred Mahan, the country's foremost advocate of sea power. Together they developed a three-pronged strategy: first, to build a navy capable of fighting simultaneously in both the Atlantic and the Pacific; second, to build a canal across the narrow neck between North and South America, facilitating a much quicker transfer of forces between the Atlantic and the Pacific; and, third, to develop secure ocean routes to the markets of Latin America and Asia.[1]

The taking of Hawai'i was the preliminary step in their plan of American expansion. With Lorrin Thurston, Roosevelt contended that if the United States failed to take over Hawai'i, Japan would.[2] Thurston quoted Roosevelt as asking, "Do you think, Thurston, that the Japanese really intend to fight in Honolulu? If they do, I hope they will do so now, and we certainly will give them a bellyful."[3]

Theodore Roosevelt toned down when he became president in 1901. He realized that the Philippine Islands were a liability. In 1905, to the surprise of many, Japan defeated Russia by moving a large attack force by sea undetected. In 1907, the U.S. War Department began developing its first plan for a war against Japan. Extrapolating from Russia's defeat, U.S. war planners assumed that Japan was capable of mounting an invasion of O'ahu with an army of 100,000 men.[4]

By this measure, the U.S. Army garrison in Hawai'i was never remotely close to being large enough.[5] As a result, the army turned to unconventional and sometimes bizarre plans of defense. A 1911 army plan drew two imaginary lines. The eastern defense line ran from Diamond Head crater at the far end of Waikīkī up toward the Ko'olau Mountains. The western defense line ran from Pearl Harbor up to the mountains. It left the plantations and their nonwhite workers outside the perimeter. Planners calculated that the U.S. Army could hold out for as long as three weeks. Subsequent plans noted that invaders could cross the Ko'olau Mountains and directly invade Honolulu and Pearl Harbor, rendering the two imaginary defense lines meaningless.

During World War I, when Japan supported the Allies, two-thirds of the regular army garrison of Hawai'i was shipped to Europe, leaving only 4,000 men. With resumption of international tension resulting from the 1924 Japanese Exclusion Act, the U.S. Army garrison on O'ahu expanded to 13,000 men. The Hawaiian Department proposed a nearly eightfold increase, to 94,000 men, a multiple far outside the realm of possibility in peacetime budgeting and politics. (In the same period, army commanders in the Philippines proposed a garrison of 125,000 men.) The inconvenient truth was that hundreds of thousands of troops were needed to defend the country's unplanned Pacific empire. The defending force, to be effective, had to be immediately available. Invaders could not be buffered by a large landmass while defending forces stalled for time, awaiting a comparatively quick arrival of reserves.[6]

"American political leaders insisted on retaining foreign garrisons and pursuing active, even confrontational policies against Japan," the military historian Brian Linn has written, "but refused to fund either the armament or the manpower required to make these policies good."[7] The Hawai'i garrison remained essentially the same until 1936, when it was increased to 19,000 and then, in 1939, to 21,500. This was still only one-fifth of the force the army believed it needed.

As a defensive alternative of a sort, the main elements of the country's Pacific naval fleet arrived in Hawai'i from the West Coast in October

1939. In April 1940, President Franklin Roosevelt announced they were in Hawai'i to stay, which meant they were nearly halfway to Japan. By this time, the evolution of aircraft and aircraft carriers had turned Pearl Harbor's three recessed deepwater lagoons into a liability. Pearl Harbor bunched many ships together tightly, unable to flee quickly through the harbor's narrow mouth.

Well before the war, the Pacific navy commander, James O. Richardson, described Pearl Harbor as a death trap. He said it was too small to accommodate so many large ships. Fearing a pileup, he tried to keep much of the fleet at sea. He told Roosevelt that moving additional ships to Pearl Harbor would have no deterrent effect on Japan. He further contended that the fleet was unready for war and should be returned to the West Coast for upgrading. He wanted, for example, to replace the wooden decking that remained in many of the U.S. ships with steel.[8]

The president repeatedly dismissed Richardson's views and then dismissed Richardson from command.

While the navy agonized over possible carrier-based air strikes, the army attempted to plan for turning back an amphibious invasion. Being perpetually under strength, the Hawaiian Army Department periodically looked at Japanese Americans as a source of manpower. At first this idea did not go well. After World War I, the army commander was dismayed to learn that three officers in the Hawai'i National Guard were of Japanese ancestry. They were investigated for indications of disloyalty, but to no avail. Nonetheless, the guard commander directed that no one of Japanese ancestry was to be commissioned as an officer or allowed to enlist.

Counter to such prejudicial thinking, the presidentially appointed governor of Hawai'i, Wallace Rider Farrington, argued during the 1920s that inclusion of Japanese Americans in the Hawai'i National Guard would promote pro-American patriotism among Nisei while diminishing the influence of first-generation Japanese.[9] The National Guard continued to enroll Nisei but in numbers that were disproportionately small compared to the Nisei share of Hawai'i's population.

In 1924, the commanding general of the Hawaiian Department, Charles P. Summerall, described the Japanese as energetic, ambitious, aggressive, shrewd, persistent, and astute. On the downside, he said they also were secretive and clannish. Tipping the scales toward inclusion, Summerall approved formation of the ROTC unit at the University of Hawai'i and also McKinley High School. One of his supervising officers claimed that ROTC was more actively welcomed in Hawai'i than anyplace in the United States. At the university, the program provided basic infantry training for freshmen and sophomores. After two years, select individuals were provided university scholarships in exchange for training to become commissioned officers.

In 1931, the Hawaiian Army Department proposed including Japanese-ancestry soldiers in the organized reserve in proportion to their numbers in the general population. Its recommendation again was couched in terms of enhancing Nisei loyalty to America. The same year, the army command admitted an ROTC graduate named Gero Iwai into its ranks as an intelligence operative. Iwai was a graduate of both McKinley High School and the University of Hawai'i. His job was, essentially, to work at assessing the security issues posed by the Japanese community and, more particularly, to keep an eye on Japan's consulate. This was a significant step, in that it reflected a belief on the part of the Hawaiian Army that, with better intelligence, they could and should work effectively with Japanese Americans.[10]

The War Plans Division in Washington rejected the idea of proportionately admitting Japanese Americans, but in an updated 1933 war plan it nonetheless took a step forward, saying that unless there was specific evidence of a person's disloyalty, the government was obligated to treat a person as loyal.[11] In 1935, the Hawaiian Army commander dismissed as impractical the idea of a mass segregation of the Japanese community in the event of war.

The pattern was for the army in Hawai'i to advocate for, or at other times to at least consider, inclusion, while the War Department in Washington opposed it. This is a confusing point, because the most notable exception has become the most widely known war plan in contemporary history, based on a paper reporting Colonel George Patton's 1935 list of 128 Japanese community leaders to be incarcerated—this, as a tactic to forestall subversive activity in the event of war.[12] Patton, then chief of Army Intelligence in Hawai'i, was to become a magnet of attention as a fighting general in Europe. His plan for Hawai'i was a hostage-taking plan, widely interpreted by contemporary historians as an index of the military's dehumanization of persons of Japanese ancestry.[13] While strong elements of racially and ethnically based distrust continued in the military, the Patton story distorts the dominant historic record of positive recommendations for an inclusive policy within the Hawaiian Department. It likewise fails to account for the changes that were at work at a community level in Hawai'i.

In the same time frame as the Patton report, the commander of the Hawaiian Department, General Briant Wells, proposed a Japanese American battalion with Nisei officers. Washington opposed his plan and directed that Nisei be assigned only to labor duties. Wells retired in 1938 and settled in Hawai'i as chief executive of the Hawaiian Sugar Planters Association. By then, he unreservedly advocated for the Nisei as soldiers and officers. He took his successor, Major General Charles D. Herron, to talk with a range of knowledgeable people, causing Herron to think Washington was out of touch and out of date with regard to the Nisei. Like Wells, Herron became a student of the Japanese community. Washington "treated Hawai'i's Japanese as a solid bloc," Herron said, "when in fact they were deeply divided between younger American-born leaders, many of them educated at the University of Hawai'i and participants in the ROTC program, and their Japan-born parents whose loyalty was to their homeland." Herron added fifty cadet slots to the McKinley ROTC unit, bringing authorized enrollment to 230 and real participation to more than 700, with a regular army staff of four.[14] He believed that in the event of war, Nisei loyalty to America would offset any upwelling of Japanese nationalism in the first generation. "Some [Issei] will adhere [to America] through conviction," Herron said, "and some because their children, their property, their business and all of their future prospects are here."[15]

Herron knew the stakes were high: "The Japanese population, by its attitude and actions, may well decide the fate of these islands in the next war." He reduced the concept of mutuality to a few words: "Until fully trusted, they will never become trustworthy."

The perception of Nisei as unused military manpower became a recurring theme in Hawai'i but was not acknowledged in Washington. When President Roosevelt expanded the country's National Guard by 20 percent, none of the new slots were assigned to Hawai'i. The territory's adjutant general, Colonel Perry Smoot, told Herron that if Hawai'i was given freedom of action, he could raise a force of 25,000 men, proportionate to military participation in the forty-eight states.[16] Herron in turn proposed that the War Department authorize a multiethnic reserve regiment that included Nisei officers. A majority of the General Staff in Washington agreed with Herron's assessment of Nisei loyalty but was concerned that white soldiers would resist serving under or alongside Nisei. The War Department chief of staff vetoed Herron's proposal.

Given the movement of the guard toward a war footing in the late 1930s, this was possibly Washington's last chance to develop a racially integrated reserve regiment that trained together and enjoyed the support of the Hawaiian Army Department. In 1940, General Herron criticized Washington's anti–Japanese American attitudes publicly. He told *Collier's Weekly Magazine,* "The Army is not worried about the Japanese in Hawaii. Among them there may be a small hostile alien group, but we can handle the situation." Prophetically, he added, "It seems people who know least about Hawaii and live farthest away are most disturbed over this matter. People who know the Islands are not worried about possible sabotage. I say this sincerely after my years of service here. I am sold on the patriotism and Americanization of the Hawaiian people as a whole."[17]

In September 1940, the U.S. government enacted a new Selective Service law instituting the first military draft in peacetime. As a result of lobbying by African American organizations, the new law contained a provision making the draft apply to all males regardless of race. It also opened military service to qualified volunteers regardless of race. The African American community's pursuit of inclusion in the military was a precursor to its wartime Double V campaign: "Let we colored Americans adopt the double V for a double victory: The first V for victory over our enemies from without, the second V for victory over our enemies from within."[18] Although the new draft law failed to address the segregation of minorities into ethnic military units, it at least removed the barrier to entry based on race.

Suddenly, hundreds of Nisei at a time were drafted into the U.S. Army. The first draft in Hawai'i was held in October 1940, and three more drafts were held in the ensuing months. The draftees were assigned to basic combat training in units of varied ancestry at Schofield Barracks. Herron observed that when other draftees headed for the showers at the end of the training day, Japanese Americans remained on the drill field practicing their new skills. While the Nisei were not yet "on the spot," many thoughtful Nisei quickly grasped that their future was at stake. Simultaneous with the peacetime draft, the War Department federalized the Hawai'i National Guard and called up its troops for a year of training at Schofield Barracks. These were the 298th Infantry Regiment, which was based on O'ahu, and the 299th Infantry Regiment, which was based on the neighboring islands. These regiments previously had been understrength units, in which Nisei had barely been represented, but now the ranks were filling with Nisei draftees. President Roosevelt's special adviser for Japanese Americans, Curtis Munson, told FDR that Nisei participation in integrated units was "a great thing in strengthening the loyalty of the Japanese in the Islands. They are beginning to feel that they are going to get a square deal." Despite Washington's opposition to Japanese American officers commanding white troops, Munson reported that the army command at Schofield had experimented with racial integration at the officer level. "The army officers confessed that they held their breath," Munson wrote. "Much to their surprise and relief, there was absolutely no reaction from the white troops and they liked these officers very well . . . the Army is going to try more."

With the Hawai'i National Guard federalized and on active duty, the Territorial Legislature in October 1941 responded by creating a second guard unit. A great deal of attention was to be paid to the Hawaiian Territorial Guard (HTG), but in fact it was a small unit established at virtually the last possible moment. It was a multiethnic organization that was to be predominantly made up of university ROTC students and, as such, the majority were Japanese American.

Two years previously, the largest group in the local guard had been Native Hawaiian and part Hawaiian (767), followed by Portuguese (320), Chinese (238), and Caucasians other than Portuguese (208). There were more Puerto Ricans (86), Filipinos (53), and Koreans (53) in the Guard than Japanese, who numbered 37.[19]

Now, in a short time, more than two thousand Nisei were armed and trained in military units in Hawai'i, counting draftees and cadets from the University ROTC.[20]

The schism in attitudes toward the Nisei between Washington and Hawai'i was taking further shape. Possibly the strangest of all situations involved young men whose families had sent them to Japan to study, the *kibei*. Although the *kibei* were of great concern to the intelligence agencies, the *kibei* of Hawai'i were nonetheless being drafted into the U.S. Army and trained in the skills of warfare. If these young men were in fact a real danger to U.S. security, then the army was compounding the danger.

It was at this point that George Bicknell, an army reservist who lived in Hawai'i, was mobilized to serve as a pivotal figure in U.S. Army Intelligence. Bicknell initially was the assistant to the chief of Army Intelligence, Colonel M. W. Marston, and he then temporarily served as Marston's replacement. That the army would entrust someone from Hawai'i to such a sensitive position was interesting in itself, because Bicknell understood and appreciated the history of the Japanese immigrants. To illustrate the ridiculousness of Washington's suspicions, Bicknell cited the Japanese hog farmers of Oʻahu who picked up swill from the military bases to feed their animals. With sarcasm, he wrote, "There was no indication that such a plan was subsidized by the Japanese government to serve as an espionage agency."

While Gero Iwai continued his solitary work on behalf of the U.S. Army, the navy developed a more aggressive approach to internal security. Its performance was episodic compared to the army, which was to become much more involved in Hawaiʻi over the years. But, on occasion, U.S. Naval Intelligence inserted itself into events to great effect.

The navy's central figure was a quixotic medical doctor named Cecil Coggins, who by vivid imagination and wide reading had transformed himself into an intelligence officer. As a teenager, he had signed on to a merchant vessel, jumped ship in Greece, and wandered into a local war zone. He was thrown into prison for not having a passport and then was rescued by a sympathetic American. After a turn through North Africa, his next stop was a banana plantation in Central America. One night a man who had been in a fight, his arm cut off by a machete, came begging at his door. Coggins failed to save him. At that moment, he said, he decided to go to medical school.

After graduation, Coggins joined the navy and was stationed at Long Beach, California, specializing in obstetrics. Soon bored, he turned to reading books such as *The Coming War with Japan,* coupled with books about spying. In the early 1930s, on his own initiative, he began inquiring into the Japanese immigrants who fished off the coast of southern California. He became convinced that certain fishing boats returned to port with more crew than they had taken out, leading him to conclude that Japan's navy was ferrying spies into the West Coast disguised as fishermen. He submitted a report to the chief obstetrician of his naval base, who sent the report to the Office of Naval Intelligence in Washington. "To my astonishment," Coggins was to say, "I created considerable concern." If the navy was so interested in what he, an amateur sleuth, had to say, he worried about the state of U.S. intelligence: "I realized the depth of the ignorance in Washington."[21]

At the navy's direction, Coggins wrote a manual on how to conduct an intelligence investigation. He also sent monthly memos to officers of the U.S. Pacific fleet. He conceived of himself as not merely an investigator but a strategic analyst. He derided FBI agents as "gumshoes" who waited for the obvious to occur, as when "some fellow falls down the steps and his violin case breaks open and it's full of information." Coggins took what he called the cheese factory approach: "Find the cheese factory. The rats are going to be in the cheese factory, not anywhere else."

In the grip of this thesis, he was assigned to Hawai'i. The navy described him as a health, recreation, and morale officer. He was appointed to the Venereal Disease Control Committee of the territorial government of Hawai'i. When he went looking for spies in the Japanese community, resident people told him there were none. He concluded that the immigrant generation no longer cared about Japan. He set out to recruit what he thought of as a counterespionage network of Nisei. "They were the cream of the crop, good, patriotic, energetic fellows," Coggins wrote. He said they were picked out by an officer of the Naval District Intelligence Office at Pearl Harbor, Howard A. Stephenson, a reservist who had practiced law in Honolulu.[22]

Coggins said the Nisei were "just itching to prove that they were good Americans." At the same time, the Nisei recruits were sensitive to the charge of being *inu* (dogs) who spied on their own people. Coggins said he had more than a hundred Nisei in his network. His estimate was later confirmed by the FBI, which said the navy investigation involved 142 Nisei.[23] How deeply and to what end they were involved at this stage of events, in 1936 and 1937, is unclear. Coggins described the Nisei as "eyes and ears," which might suggest that the relationships were superficial. After giving the recruits an orientation, he turned them back over to Stephenson, a disconnection that may account for the fact that their work seemed to have little to no apparent impact, and also for the fact that their individual identities were not to become known.

Coggins was to be remembered by only a handful of people in Hawai'i, most of whom took him less seriously than he took himself. In 1941, he was told of an "antimagnetic torpedo belt" that could protect navy ships. He searched for individuals who might be spying on it. This led him to the island of Hawai'i, where he found an attractive blonde woman named Suzanne, who was making a living as a prostitute in a small house in a cane field. Believing Coggins was indeed a venereal disease officer, she showed him her certificates of medical examination. "The place was clean as a pin," Coggins said. When a Japanese laborer came to the door, Suzanne spoke to him in Japanese. Coggins was all ears. Had she studied Japanese? he asked. "Not seriously," she said, "but I picked it up here." He recruited her to spy on the Japanese consul in Honolulu, theorizing that Japanese had a weakness for blondes. Her work came to naught, as it was interrupted by the events of December 7.

Coggins's eccentricities obscured his concrete achievements. In 1937, early in his assignment to Honolulu, he played a role in recruiting a Japanese-speaking Nisei into full-time intelligence work. This was a significant contribution, because the intelligence agencies urgently needed to expand their capability in the Japanese language. The person's name was Douglas Wada.[24] Wada was the son of a temple carpenter who had been trained in the tradition of purely wooden construction. He was brought to Hawai'i by Samuel Mills Damon, the banker son of the seaman's missionary Samuel Chenery Damon. In the family's internationalist tradition, the younger Samuel created Moanalua Gardens, which represented the cultures of the Pacific. It prominently featured an authentic Japanese temple built by Wada's father—a temple that would be destroyed by the U.S. Army in a display of wartime spite.

Douglas Wada was born in 1910 and grew up on Robello Lane in the inner-city Palama district of Honolulu. Although he was barely five feet tall and just over one hundred pounds, he went out for the football team at McKinley High School. "Do you want to get killed?" the coach asked. Wada turned to baseball. Japan was in the beginning stages of its baseball craze and, as with many things, imported talent to light the way. Through Wada's Japanese-language school, run by the Honpa Hongwanji Buddhist Mission, he learned that Doshisha University in Kyoto was looking for baseball players. Before embarking, Wada renounced his Japanese citizenship, most likely to avoid the possibility of being drafted into the Japanese army. He would most vividly recall an exhibition game in Japan against another short player, Ty Cobb. Wada was the only American who played on the Japanese side, which lost 5 to 4. After four years of study and baseball, he returned to Honolulu and enrolled in the University of Hawai'i. He played second base for UH and on the side played in the Japanese leagues for a team called the Nippons. Faced with a graduation requirement of foreign language credits, he opted for an easy A by enrolling in a Japanese-language class.

The first day of class, a tall, talkative haole sat beside him named Kenneth D. Ringle. The two chatted repeatedly about baseball. At the end of the semester, Ringle gave Wada a business card and said if Wada

ever needed a job, he should get in touch. Wada wanted to go to graduate school but needed to save money, so he made his way to Ringle's
address, Room 221 of the Federal Building. There he saw his classmate
in navy whites with officer shoulder boards. "My God," Wada said to
himself, "what is this?" A navy captain sat him down. "Sooner or later
we're going to be at war with Japan," he said, "How do you see your
bread being buttered?" It was Coggins. Wada momentarily wondered
what the bread and butter was about but then thought, "Oh-oh, it's the
loyalty question." "I expatriated in 1928," Wada replied. "My loyalty is
with the United States." Approval of his recruitment went to the top
of the navy, where his language abilities outweighed his four years as a
kibei. To his surprise, he was commissioned a second lieutenant.[25]

Wada was a rarity of rarities. He could not only speak but read and
write contemporary Japanese. He was an officer despite the navy's policy of racial segregation and also the prejudices against Japanese Americans often attributed to navy personnel. He worked in Honolulu under
cover, chronically wary that his navy affiliation would become apparent. In the process, he was increasingly isolated from other Nisei whose
circles of acquaintance were with Army Intelligence and the Federal
Bureau of Investigation.[26] Wada had two covers. One was as an insurance
salesman, which allowed him to move freely around the Japanese community. The second was as an employee of U.S. Customs, which allowed
him to search incoming Japanese ships and talk with the crewmen and
officers.[27] He also translated the Domei news service that imported news
and propaganda from Japan and was published by Honolulu's *Nippu Jiji*
newspaper, which at the time was one of fourteen Japanese-language
newspapers in the territory.

When Wada started his service, the downtown office of Navy Intelligence had a staff of seven. As the threat of war intensified, several
naval reserve officers from Hawai'i were called to active duty, and others arrived from the U.S. Mainland. Some of the white personnel were
known as "BIJ"—Born in Japan—usually of missionary parents. By mid-
1941, according to Wada, the downtown ONI office had over a hundred
people, filling the entire sixth floor of the Alexander Young Hotel.

Wada progressed from the downtown office to the 14th Naval District's intelligence section at Pearl Harbor, which was to play a pivotal
role in the war by breaking Japan's diplomatic codes.[28] He was eventually to retire with the rank of commander and lifelong had an air of
mystery about him.

The U.S. Navy's impact on the interior workings of Hawai'i from 1937 to 1941 seems, in retrospect, considerably less than might have occurred as a result of its early start and the size of its operation. Nonetheless, from deep behind the scenes, over the coming months, Coggins and his circle were to emerge at crucial moments, then vanish, as if they had never existed. There was a cloak-and-dagger quality to Coggins. He liked to use the word "counterintelligence." He set a clandestine example for Ringle, who was to become known for a black-bag burglary of a Japanese consular office in California.

The other intelligence agencies looked at the navy's intelligence shop with dismay and distrust. The FBI saw the navy as an amateurish rival. Burns never talked about the navy's operation, as if it never existed. Yoshida's papers were all but silent on the navy. Hung Wai Ching spoke derisively of Naval Intelligence. Such a judgment depended on where one looked. The navy's real task was to find out what Japan intended to do at sea, and Naval Intelligence was to succeed brilliantly in code breaking. Figuring out Hawai'i would be largely left to the army, and for that the army relied on making an alliance with the hitherto absent FBI.

The single most important individual on the domestic security side in Hawai'i would turn out to be the latecomer, Robert L. Shivers of the Federal Bureau of Investigation. Events great and small turned on his unlikely person. A military intelligence officer described him as a "soft-spoken man with an expression of utter guilelessness, the last person one would expect, at first sight, to be an agent of the Federal Bureau of Investigation."[29] Others described him as tough, shrewd, and tight lipped. A U.S. Customs agent regarded him as overbearing. On the positive side, John Burns was to eventually promote the idea of Shivers as governor of territorial Hawai'i. Hung Wai Ching, who held himself as a lesser to almost no one, spoke of Shivers reverentially. Yoshida readily worked with him on intimate terms. Finally, Hemenway served him as sounding board and counselor.

Shivers smiled in snapshots taken at home, but his formal portrait was dour. He often carried a handgun. He was above all an investigator. He probed for information and weighed it for its meaning. He analyzed individuals for their trustworthiness and cross-checked his sources. He wrote his reports in a clear, straightforward way. He made a deep impression on the people he met, and during crucial periods he held fractious interagency relationships together by force of personality.

Shivers was born the fifth of ten children in 1895, which made him forty-five by the time he arrived in Hawai'i. He was descended from a settler who walked through the Cumberland Gap into east Tennessee about the time of Daniel Boone. His great-grandfather was a slaveholder. His grandfather fought for the Confederacy. His father was the postmaster of Ashland City in Cheatham County, Tennessee. He joined the U.S. Army during World War I and was shipped to France, where he served in ordnance supply and attained the rank of sergeant. He wrote a long letter to his mother that was published in the Ashland newspaper, describing the American troops sitting inertly, staring, smoking cigarette after cigarette, waiting for news of an armistice. "The air was charged with a tenseness almost unbearable," wrote Sergeant Shivers. Then a messenger shouted, "It's all over, boys!"

With an unused pass in his pocket, Shivers left camp on his own hook and walked six miles to a regional town. He previously had seen the French as unassertive and demoralized. In victory, they were transformed: "They were a new people." Shivers pressed his way into the front rank of a large crowd in the courtyard. The band played "The Star-Spangled Banner." "'Long live France and long live America!'" people shouted. "What's more," Shivers wrote, "I found myself standing by one of the prettiest girls in France. On such a day as that, everybody knows everybody else and no introductions were necessary."

Possibly this scene was an important frame of reference for him: France and the armistice opened his eyes to the possibility of dynamic change. After a time of terrible tension, recovery followed.

Shivers was accepted into the FBI in 1923 despite having no education past high school. His entry coincided with J. Edgar Hoover's precocious rise to the top of the bureau. A faltering agency quickly had become Hoover's agency. "[Crime] is ever at your elbow," Hoover wrote in an early book, "vicious crime, dangerous crime, against which you cannot relax your vigilance for an instant."[30] Hoover inscribed a copy of his book to the field agent Shivers with all good wishes. In his narrative, gangsters, kidnappers, and booze runners were omnipresent. The identities of the hunted inflated like giant balloons: Ma Barker, Baby Face Nelson, Pretty Boy Floyd, and, best of all for the durability of his story, John Dillinger. According to a U.S. Customs agent, Shivers had been involved in tracking down and shooting it out with Dillinger.

As FBI director, Hoover quickly expanded the number of field offices from nine to thirty, which among other things created career

The FBI agent in charge, Robert L. Shivers, bridged the distance
between the U.S. intelligence agencies and the community, ultimately
allying himself with Japanese Americans. Courtesy of Sue Isonaga.

opportunities. The head of a field office was given the title special agent
in charge. In 1936, Shivers was appointed special agent in charge of
the Pittsburgh office. The next year he was assigned to Miami, osten-
sibly because of its mild climate. A year later, Hoover wrote notes of
concern to Shivers about his health. Shivers had high blood pressure
and possibly something wrong with his heart. When Hoover put him on
light duty, his symptoms abated. Hoover wrote to Shivers that he would
always have a place in the FBI, his health problems notwithstanding.[31]
Hoover's many letters to Shivers had fleeting references to his reputed

obsession with loyalty, but the main impression is of Hoover's genuine concern for Shivers. For his part, Shivers was willing to risk a difference of opinion with Hoover, but his default posture was loyalty to the chief. All in all, the relationship was strong and mutual.

The assignment of Shivers to the territory of Hawai'i made him a special agent in more than title. The FBI's crusade against gangsters largely had been won, in no small part because the gangs had derived income from bootlegging alcohol in the era of Prohibition, which ended in 1936. Hoover was at the peak of his national popularity but needed a new core mission. This he located in the mounting fears of espionage, sabotage, and what was vaguely labeled "subversive activity." In an environment of increasing national anxiety, these words and their definitions seemed to function almost interchangeably.

The first FBI initiative in this realm was directed at domestic communists and then domestic fascists. As the Tripartite Alliance of the Axis powers took shape, the bureau became more specifically focused on immigrant aliens. At first these were Germans and Italians and, only belatedly, Japanese. Like gang crime, the possibility of wrongdoing was, in Hoover's phrase, ever at your elbow.

Shivers arrived in Honolulu by airplane on August 23, 1939, with his wife Corinne, a woman with a long oval face and a warm smile. In photographs he would usually stand while she sat, or vice versa, which obscured the fact that she was taller than he. The couple received a colonial welcome. A Big Five executive rented a house to them on Black Point Road, on the flank of Diamond Head crater overlooking the ocean. Shivers rented office space in the Dillingham Transportation Building, an elegant four-story structure just off Merchant Street, across from the harbor and within walking distance of 'Iolani Palace.

Two weeks after Shivers's arrival, President Roosevelt designated the FBI as coordinator of the intelligence agencies, which may suggest that Shivers's assignment to Hawai'i was central to the overseas ascendancy of the FBI.[32] The world situation was deteriorating rapidly. Within days, Germany invaded Poland, while Japan pursued its war against China. It was then that Roosevelt stationed an aircraft carrier and a variety of destroyers, cruisers, and support vessels at Pearl Harbor. Soldiers, sailors, and construction workers began to swell the population of O'ahu.

Meanwhile, a teacher of home economics suggested that Shivers and his wife take in a Japanese American student who needed a place to board in return for helping with the housework. Neither Mr. nor

Mrs. Shivers had ever known a person of Asian ancestry, and Mrs. Shivers initially balked at the idea. The professor persisted. She recommended a young woman named Shizue Kobatake, who, she said, came from a good family and a good home on Maui.

Given what was to come, it seems germane to the story that Shizue was twice half-orphaned. Her biological father died when she was four. Her stepfather died when she was fifteen. As the fall semester of 1939 approached, she had completed a year of study at McKinley Technical School and hoped to become a cafeteria manager. She needed a place to stay and food to eat, and she welcomed becoming part of the Shivers household. First, she became close to Corinne Shivers, and then Mr. Shivers began to talk with her in the evening, after the dishes were done. Shivers wanted to know what it was like to grow up Japanese American and to attend Japanese-language school. What did the school say about the emperor? How was Christianity viewed? What was the role of Buddhism? What was the significance of Shintoism? In Shizue's responses, the American experience was central and the influence of Japan was at most secondary.

Like a sojourning schoolteacher, Bob Shivers had trouble pronouncing Shizue's name. He announced that it now would be "Sue." He gave her driving lessons. She scraped his car's bumper. He told her not to worry. Soon Shivers and Corinne integrated her into their social life. Childless, they introduced her as their adopted daughter.

People of Asian ancestry were welcomed frequently at the house on Black Point. Hung Wai Ching often visited, as did Yoshida and his wife Thelma. So did the well-known dentist and sportsman from Kapahulu, Katsumi Kometani. The attorney Marumoto and his wife Shigeko were particularly close to the Shiverses as a couple. The one Caucasian who frequently came and went was the intense young police officer, John A. Burns.[33]

Beneath Shivers's cool exterior, he struggled emotionally with the complexities of the situation. Despite the Black Point house and the downtown office, he told Hoover that the Caucasians of Hawai'i were "utterly cold" to the FBI presence. "They felt we were not needed here and were completely disinterested," he wrote. The various Asian communities "were most reticent and said nothing to indicate how they felt other than to avoid all contact."[34]

The FBI office had been at its peak functioning in Honolulu during the First World War, but then it closed. It had reopened in 1931 for three years and again in August 1937 for eight months.[35] Although Shivers was inundated by work, his staff initially consisted of only two agents and a stenographer. Nonetheless, Army Intelligence forwarded him the files of 125 individuals who they believed should be investigated.[36] The writer Blake Clark quoted Shivers as saying he believed that Army Intelligence at that point wanted a large-scale internment in the event of war, either through relocation to the Mainland, to a smaller island such as Moloka'i, or to camps deep in the rural valleys of O'ahu. This seems dubious, given the army's subsequent performance. Suffice it to say that Shivers was initially wary of the army's fact-finding and outright dismissive of Naval Intelligence. In later testimony under oath, Shivers said it was only on his arrival that he learned of the extent of the military intelligence operations. Therefore, he said, he was under their influence for several months.[37] He said by that time the army had an "A" list of arrests to be made in the event of war numbering seven hundred people, as well as a "B" list of an additional one thousand people who were to be kept under close surveillance.

Shivers next made his own tour of the Islands, talking with plantation owners, managers, and businessmen. "I got just about as many different answers as the number of people that I talked to," he wrote. "The haole population in Hawai'i was not in a position to give any accurate information about the Japanese populace because there had been very little intercourse between the two."

He decided to start from the ground up. Meeting with a group of six white businessmen, Shivers talked for the first time with Charles Hemenway. He asked if any of them could recommend individuals of Japanese ancestry he could trust unreservedly. Several said maybe they could, but they couldn't be sure—one could never be sure about the Japanese, and so on. Hemenway gave Shivers a completely different response: "I certainly can," Hemenway is said to have replied. "Any number you want—five, fifteen, fifty, or five hundred. How many?" Shivers said a half dozen would do. Hemenway said, "I'll introduce you to six Americans who are just as loyal as any one of us here."[38]

Despite the suggestion that Shivers's initial six advisers represented the Nisei generation, they were in fact all drawn from a narrow slice of the relatively privileged class of the Japanese community. All were early day Nisei leaders, all were professionals, and all were alumnae of the University of Hawai'i. They were also previously acquainted with one another. At the top of the list was Yoshida, followed by people whom Yoshida knew well: Clifton Yamamoto, Masatoshi Katagiri, Jack Wakayama, Shunzo Sakamaki, and Thomas Kurihara.

At forty-five, the oldest was Clifton Yamamoto, an insurance executive who had attended UH in 1915. He was past president of the Hawaiian Japanese Civic Association (HJCA). Katagiri, next oldest at thirty-seven, was also an insurance executive. He was a UH graduate who had worked closely with Hung Wai Ching in developing the University YMCA. He was president-elect of the HJCA. Wakayama, thirty-two, was the current HJCA president. At the time he was in the car business and later became well known as a government statistician. Sakamaki was probably the best known of the group. He was a PhD professor of Okinawan history at the University of Hawai'i, as well as an active figure in the HJCA. Kurihara was an employee of the City and County of Honolulu.[39]

They were an interlocking directorate of a sort. During the years when Yoshida dominated UH debate, Kurihara and Wakayama were also active debaters. Alongside Yoshida when he was editor of the UH annual, Kurihara served as associate editor. Wakayama was the annual's advertising manager. During this same period, Sakamaki was the editor of the student newspaper *Ka Leo*. Four of them—Katagiri, Wakayama, Kurihara, and Sakamaki—previously had worked not only with Yoshida but Ching. Through the HJCA, all had campaigned actively for the Nisei to expatriate their dual citizenship with Japan.

Although a tight little group, they represented a crucial layer of leadership that has been overlooked in written history. Hundreds were readily identifiable through a book of biographical profiles called *Who's Who: Americans of Japanese Ancestry*.[40] They shared two characteristics: they were early born Nisei, like Yoshida, and they had gained a level of autonomy from the plantation economy.

A Yaso Abe, born in Kona in 1909, had graduated from Konawaena High School and the University of Hawai'i. He was a reserve officer in the army and a member of the Honolulu Police Department. Tom Tamotsu Aoki of Hilo was a branch manager of American Savings and Loan. Ryoshin Agena was born in Honolulu but educated in Japan. On his return, he attended the Nu'uanu YMCA night school for one year. He worked at Honolulu Café for five years and then, with a Nisei partner, bought the café. George N. Amano, born in 1897 in Windward O'ahu, had attended Royal Elementary and McKinley High School. In 1917, he joined the Hawai'i National Guard. In 1920, he was employed by Andrade & Co. as a salesman and, in 1938, became the treasurer of the HJCA. Katsuji Asahara, a farmer from Kāneʻohe, Oʻahu, was secretary of his Republican Party Precinct Club. Dr. David T. Betsui, a physician and surgeon in the plantation town of Hanapēpē, Kauaʻi, was a member of HJCA, the Lions Club, and the Kauaʻi Civic Association. He also sat on the Kauaʻi draft board.

Often their Issei parents had created an opportunity on which they had expanded. John H. Fujieki, born in 1917, worked seven years in the Kakaʻako meat market of his father. He then studied meat cutting at Armour & Company in Chicago. With his older brother, he took over their father's business, which was said to have grown twelve times over as Star Market.

James S. Fukuroda was introduced to merchandising in his father's hat shop on Hotel Street. In 1931, he opened the Goodyear Dress Shop.

A number who had returned from extended stays in Japan turned to the YMCA for English-language classes. One such person, Robert T. Fujino, born in 1898 at Kealakekua on Hawaiʻi Island, was trained in cabinetry in Japan and on his return started a cabinet business. He was a member of the Japanese Contractors Association and the HJCA.

Although his age cohort was largely shut out of the U.S. military, Mack M. Fukuda, born in 1900, had enlisted in the Hawaiʻi National Guard in 1916, presumably by disguising his real age. He served fourteen months at Schofield Barracks, then attended McKinley High School, graduating at age twenty. He thereafter managed a department of City Mill. He was president of Washington Intermediate School PTA.

Thomas K. Date was a director of Troop 62 of the Boy Scouts. Akira Doi owned Doi Electric Shop in Wahiawā. Yoshio Doi was a masonry contractor in Kauaʻi. George Fukuoka, born in Hilo, founded the popular Pearl City Tavern above Pearl Harbor.

Other than Yoshida, Masa Katagiri was perhaps the most conspicuous example of the early day Nisei leaders who stepped forward when there was work to be done. Katagiri was born in 1904 in the plantation town of Haleʻiwa on the North Shore of Oʻahu. His parents had immigrated from Yanai, a port city in Yamaguchi Prefecture. His father was a barber who saved tip money from the corporate executives who rode in on the sugar train for a relaxing weekend at the Haleʻiwa Hotel. He organized a money-pooling and investment club—a *tanomoshi*—and, with two other investors, he bought the automobile garage in the nearby plantation town of Waialua.

The Katagiris sent their son Masa to McKinley High School in Honolulu, which required boarding, and then on to the University of Hawai'i,
where he was reputed to be the first university graduate from his North
Shore neighborhood. At UH, Katagiri joined the YMCA, then worked
part-time with John Young at the Nu'uanu Y. He wanted to go on to the
Chicago Theological Seminary, but his father insisted on as many of
his children working in business as possible—hence Masa began selling
insurance. He became active in the HJCA and, while advising Shivers,
was sworn in as the HJCA president in a meeting at the Nu'uanu Y. In
addition to his close ties with Ching, Katagiri was a friend and adviser to
Jack Burns, who would drop by his house for a Japanese dinner.

Before recommending Yoshida to Shivers, Hemenway asked Yoshida if
he was willing to work with the FBI station chief. Yoshida said he was.
Presumably the other five were given the same courtesy. On their first
meeting, Shivers told them, "We do not need a counterespionage organization. What we do need is information and considered opinion from
well-informed, absolutely loyal Americans. I want you to talk with me,
freely and frankly, about every aspect of life among the Japanese here."[41]
He specifically announced that he wanted their insights and not the
names of suspect individuals.

He pursued his inquiries into the Japanese community openly. He
extended himself to new friends and acquaintances of Asian and Hawaiian ancestry, as well as some of the more forward-thinking Caucasians.
He weighed his opinions, thoughts, and biases in an atmosphere of give
and take. He thought of himself as breaking down barriers on both
sides. The problem of haole isolation, Shivers said, was compounded
by the Japanese community being so closely woven together. "To a large
extent the average haole does not know the Japanese psychology," he
said. "He does not know the Japanese mind, and for that reason he
(does) not know what was going on within the inner circle of the Japanese community."[42] Obviously, Shivers believed he was learning something that most haole did not know. By conjuring and then crossing the
barrier of inscrutability with which the Japanese were stereotyped, Shivers gained confidence not only in Japanese Americans but in himself.
Other Caucasians of the time—Hemenway and Burns, for example—
similarly believed they were blessed with a special understanding of
Japanese Americans. If today this might sound odd, it reflected their
sincere interest, and it was valuable in its time. The question of making

acquaintances across ethnic barriers recurred often. An army report described Burns as a Japanese specialist. Yoshida wrote that citizenship was not merely the exercise of voting rights or bearing arms. "At heart it is the feeling of belonging to the larger American community, of participating in equal terms with equal concern and comradeship in the affairs of the group."

Yoshida sensed change coming. "The old world is inevitably gone," he wrote. "What the future shall be is partly for us to determine." It was a thought of great importance—a guiding notion that Japanese Americans in Hawai'i could become makers of history, not its victims.

By virtue of circumstance, the aggregate capacity of the Hawai'i Nisei leadership surpassed their counterparts on the U.S. Mainland in crucial ways. The Hawai'i settlement was older, more diverse, less isolated, and better connected. Hawai'i's Nisei were acquainted with one·another— as well as other ethnic groups—through the plantation camps, the public schools, the university, the YMCA and, ultimately, through the city of Honolulu. In contrast, Nisei of the Mainland were widely scattered over the vast spaces of the Western states, often in rural areas.

If at first glance the HJCA appeared parallel to the Mainland-based Japanese American Citizens's League (JACL), the comparison was superficial. The Japanese-ancestry population of Hawai'i was not only larger but had developed stronger supports. As if to underscore that fact, the president of JACL in the late prewar years was a product of Hawai'i: Saburo Kido of Hilo. Kido had attended Hastings Law School in San Francisco and then settled on the U.S. Mainland. His protégé, who was to gain national prominence, was a Mormon from Utah, Mike Masaoka. In 1941, Masaoka was twenty-six years old.

Like the circle of six Nisei advisers, the Council for Interracial Unity likely grew out of seminal conversations between Robert Shivers and Charles Hemenway. Shivers eventually wrote that he gave Hemenway "the credit for putting me on the right track."[43] Ching played a leading role in pulling the group together. In his kaleidoscopic style, Ching retrospectively attributed the group's existence to Hemenway but also said simply that he received a telephone call from Shivers and was told to show up at a meeting, where he would find out what was to come next.

Yoshida's description of the group's origins reserved a greater degree of volition to the membership. He said Ching was a major force in bringing the group together. "Mr. Shivers," he wrote, "was prevailed upon to accept the chairmanship of this [steering] committee and authorized to select its members." In either case, Shivers's support for organizing simultaneously in two modes—*across* ethnic lines and also *within* the Japanese ethnic group—reflected a sound grasp of how Hawai'i functioned. That is, while the majority of people tended to live largely within their ethnic group, a minority of pathfinders mixed with one another. Often these people were the more adventuresome and the better educated, the council members being especially so.

Once formed, the Council for Interracial Unity worked with an ever-greater urgency. Yoshida said the group met at least twice a month and sometimes more often. Shivers said it met weekly. As the resident writer, Yoshida exerted a unique influence over how the council was to be perceived. He wrote that the first objective was not only national defense but "the way the people of Hawai'i are going to live together after the emergency is over." Accordingly, from the beginning the council's thinking spanned the prewar, the anticipated war, and a vision for the postwar: "If the people here of various races can continue to live together harmoniously during the emergency, trust each other, and cooperate even more closely than they have in the past, then a basis for a still better human relationship will have been established for the future." To which Yoshida added, "The contrary will be equally true."[44]

Yoshida advocated inclusiveness in the war effort as a means of achieving both interracial harmony and a strong national defense. "We cannot afford to have a divided citizenry," he wrote, "one race set against another, or one class against another." He dwelled on the fact that Japanese aliens and Japanese Americans together made up a large part of the territory's population. "Accepted and united in purpose and action, they are an asset to the community," Yoshida wrote. "Rejected and treated as potential enemies, they are a burden, even a danger, to our security." The crux of his thesis might have been paraphrased as, "We Japanese Americans and our Japanese parents are many. Treat us decently, include us, and we will go all out in the war effort. Reject us—at your peril."

The council worked through indirect means. Yoshida said the group purposely avoided publicity, "with the result that only a few people know that it even exists." Other than Shivers acting as chair, there were no officers. There were no bylaws, rules, office space, or staff. But what the group lacked in trappings it made up for in activity.

Both the governor of the territory and the mayor of Honolulu were approached and briefed on the work of the council, as well as other governmental and civic leaders. Shivers and the two Army Intelligence officers, Marston and Bicknell, spoke to civic and business groups. The civilian members spoke with "certain key leaders of racial and other groups" and elicited promises of cooperation in the event of war. Yoshida said they additionally spoke to groups of working people, including defense workers. The council also reached into the Japanese ethnic community.

Their message returned constantly to the theme of unity through participation and inclusion. Yoshida wrote that the first of eight steps in the message was for Hawai'i's people to feel "that Hawai'i has something unique and worthwhile to preserve in the way of human relationships." Although the group was organizing for America's participation in international war, the idea that Hawai'i was special was foremost in Yoshida's thoughts.

Step two was, "Accept the idea that a united citizenry is essential to our national defense."

Step three: "Have faith in the American way of life and be willing to protect it."

Step four: Trust authority, "confident that they will treat everyone with equal fairness." The idea of fairness rested on the government dealing "promptly and severely" with acts inimical to the general welfare. To this Yoshida added, "There is no need for, and there must not be, any vigilantism on the part of any group." This was aimed at fears that, in the event of war, various Asian ethnic groups might descend on the Japanese community with violence.

Step five: "The people must overcome fear," Yoshida wrote, "fear on the part of the nationals of those countries with which we might become involved in a war that they will be mistreated and persecuted, and fear on the part of the rest of the people that these particular aliens might actively assist our enemies."

Step six: Take personal responsibility for making Hawai'i strong militarily in the face of an outside threat. This extended to aliens "who must accept the fact that they owe a certain obligation to the land in which they are now living and that they will be protected and allowed to enjoy all normal privileges only as long as they obey our laws and conduct themselves constructively."

Step seven: People must "be willing to give every loyal citizen, regardless of race, a place in the scheme of national defense."

Step eight: Loyalty was influenced by how people were treated; it did not exist in a vacuum. "Remember," Yoshida wrote, "that loyalty grows only when it is given a chance to grow. It does not flourish in an atmosphere of suspicion, discrimination, and denial of opportunities to practice that loyalty."[45] Therefore it was imperative that fear *within* the Japanese community and fear *of* the Japanese community must be dealt with simultaneously.

In addition to Shivers meeting regularly with his interracial and Nisei advisers, he chaired weekly meetings of Army Intelligence, Naval Intelligence, and other federal agencies involved in security issues, such as the Customs House.

While internal security questions were being worked out more or less coherently in Hawai'i under Shivers's direction, lines of authority were repeatedly a matter of contention in Washington, D.C. Nine months after the FBI was assigned to coordinate domestic security efforts, the intelligence agencies in Washington temporarily agreed that the FBI should take sole responsibility for investigating all civilian cases having to do with espionage, counterespionage, sabotage, and subversive activities. This agreement included Hawai'i but excluded the Panama Canal Zone, Guam, Samoa, and the Philippine Islands. As of this directive, Hoover had won the bureaucratic infight. Naval Intelligence had been confined, at least in theory, to investigating naval personnel and naval bases. Similarly, the army had been confined to its bases and personnel.

Hoover's victory was short lived. Within a month, high-level ONI officers told Hoover that Japan and the Japanese American community had been their main concern for years, and that they had accumulated a large number of Japanese informants and a large volume of information.[46] ONI accurately portrayed the FBI as handicapped by a lack of Japanese-language ability, a lack of background, "and the difficulties involved in assimilating the store of information which was a matter of record in the Navy Department." The navy insisted on regaining what it called a large share of jurisdiction over the possibility of Japanese espionage. Despite Shivers wanting exclusive jurisdiction over civilian cases, Hoover reversed his previous position, agreeing to shed the FBI's exclusive responsibility for internal security in Hawai'i, where the stakes were the highest.[47] After the fact, Shivers testified that Hoover did not want to take exclusive responsibility "for lack of knowledge concerning Japanese conditions, lack of language students, and lack of Japanese interpreters."[48] Given Hoover's reputation for defensive maneuver and self-aggrandizing behavior, it seems plausible he first sought power over the military but then protected himself from the possibility of undivided blame if things went wrong.

Eventually, the incessant muddling and reshuffling of responsibility for domestic intelligence was to become part of the poisonous national legacy of blame for the Pearl Harbor attack. In real time, Shivers held things together in Honolulu despite the jurisdictional issues in Washington. He cultivated a strong relationship with the army. He nurtured a refrain among the various intelligence agencies to the effect that many or most Nisei were both loyal and capable and that members of their parents' generation who retained some loyalty to Japan would do nothing to embarrass or compromise their children.

In contrast, the operative milieu on the West Coast was the absence of acquaintance, as well as the absence of organization, knowledge, and conviction. Lack of adequate intelligence on the West Coast resulted from not knowing much about the Nisei and not having an objective estimate of what might happen if war came. Just as knowledge and acquaintance were a form of security in Hawai'i, not knowing was a cause of insecurity in the West Coast states.

CHAPTER 4

A Swing toward Americanization

As a recently arrived world power, Japan created a prideful trajectory for its overseas emigrants. In the context of an approaching war, an American might have tightened up on reading the opening words of Emperor Meiji's rescript of 1890, which said, "Our Imperial Ancestors have founded Our Empire on a basis broad and everlasting and have deeply and firmly implanted virtue."

But who could take issue with the virtues prescribed in the second paragraph: "Be filial to your parents, and affectionate to your brothers and sisters; as husbands and wives be harmonious, as friends true; bear yourselves in modesty and moderation; extend your benevolence to all; pursue learning and cultivate arts, and thereby develop intellectual faculties and perfect moral powers; furthermore advance public good and promote common interests; always respect the Constitution and observe the law." There followed a grandiose statement declaring the ancestors' teachings to be "infallible for all ages and true in all places."

The nineteenth-century Japanese migrants to the Kingdom of Hawai'i were regarded as extensions of Japan, much as the American missionaries and whalers were regarded as extensions of the United States. Prior to allowing—and then encouraging—the first extensive migration in 1885, Japan negotiated a pact with the Hawaiian Kingdom covering work, pay, and living conditions. The agreement also provided for Japanese labor inspectors to monitor the faithful fulfillment of the labor contracts.

When it became apparent that the immigrant workers' morale was low and that gambling and prostitution were common among the mostly male workforce, the remedies from Japan included Buddhist and Shinto priests, Christian ministers, Japanese-language schoolteachers, and—most importantly—picture brides. This system of supports enhanced stability and a rapid evolution of family and community life, but it also created confusion. America refused to accept the Japanese immigrants as citizens, and Japan was disinclined to let go of them. This extended from the first to the second generation, its American birth and American citizenship notwithstanding.

The challenge for the American intelligence agencies was to accurately distinguish between the virtuous character of the growing Japanese community and the imperial behavior of Japan. Shivers did not have either the manpower or language capability to investigate the 125 case files the army had given him or the seven hundred names on the army's "A" list of potential arrests. For investigative support, he turned to the Honolulu Police Department, whose chief, William A. Gabrielson, had been consistently supportive of the Japanese community, particularly the Nisei.

It was in response to Shivers's request for help that Gabrielson assigned John Burns to supplement the FBI. Burns and a four-member team of investigators proceeded to work tediously through the list one name at a time. All of his life Burns could recite queries from the FBI, such as, "We received information that [name] has a relative who is a member of the general staff of the Japanese navy and that he has further links with the imperial government. Will you investigate his background, general reputation and activities to ascertain whether in the event of hostilities between this country and Japan his interests would be inimical to those of the United States?"[1]

Shivers, for his part, had come to think there was little factual information to support individual arrests.[2] Nowhere was there evidence of individual wrongdoing of any kind, let alone espionage or sabotage. He concluded that case-by-case investigation was too time consuming for the task at hand, and that he had to concentrate on broad strokes. It was a conclusion that led inevitably to injustices.

Shivers's main concern was that for half a century, Japan had maintained a large consulate that enlisted prominent Japanese community figures to serve as representatives.[3] Each volunteer was to confine his activities to his own residential district. If a volunteer was absent from his duties by traveling outside of Hawai'i, he was expected to notify the consulate.

The fact that agents were only appointed in outlying areas was evidence that the system resulted from the wide dispersal of Japanese plantation workers.[4] Most such individuals were on the Neighbor Islands. A few were in the outlying plantation communities of O'ahu, such as 'Ewa, Wai'anae, Waialua, Kahuku, and Waimānalo.

Through his work with Shivers and with Japanese Americans, the
police officer John A. Burns was joined to the deep history of
Hawai'i. *Honolulu Advertiser.*

Kazuo Miyamoto wrote, "To persons of the first generation . . . a man is
measured in the degree of responsibility he takes in his uttered promises
and in his willingness to devote himself to communal welfare—not the
egotistic betterment of one's lot alone." Miyamoto's fictional protagonist
had risen from fieldwork to owning a grocery store in the Makaweli Plantation on Kaua'i. He "had his prestige to look after," Miyamoto wrote. "The

Consulate General in Honolulu appointed him, without compensation, to help fill out applications from the illiterate, to interpret orders, and in general help the official Japanese representative keep the immigrants orderly."[5]

Although knowledgeable people understood the humanitarian and communication tasks performed by volunteers, their identity became enshrouded in the term "consular agents." This was an ominous pairing of words. Like the businessmen who visited Japan's training ships in the harbor, the consular agent became a repository for the accumulation of suspicion. Shivers investigated twenty such persons beginning in April 1940. He told Washington that agents were usually teachers or professors who engaged in such things as writing letters, filling out forms, claiming property in Japan, taking the Japanese census, and registering Nisei at birth for dual citizenship.[6] They also helped Hawai'i Nisei file for deferments from Japanese military service, and they assisted in a survey of commerce taken every five years.[7] More ominously, "They have been quite prominent in collecting comfort kits, moneys, and funds for transmittal to Japan." While this was not illegal at the time, fund drives were based on appeals to Japanese nationalism and militarism and otherwise exceeded the traditional role of the consular representatives.

Shivers wrote that the consular agents were required "to keep alive the Japanese spirit, and to do the bidding of the Japanese consulate." He had no evidence that consular agents were engaged in espionage, "but if used as an espionage ring they would be in a position to furnish the Japanese consulate with espionage information from every corner of the Hawaiian Islands." He said his views were influenced by his conclusion that both the consul and vice consul in Honolulu had engaged in intelligence work in their previous assignments and as such were more concerned with spying than with supporting the immigrants.

A landmark dispute followed. In September 1940, Shivers recommended to the Justice Department that the 234 consular agents be arrested and prosecuted under a recently passed U.S. law requiring foreign agents to register with the State Department. Marston and Bicknell of Army Intelligence favored the arrests, as did Captain I. H. Mayfield of Naval Intelligence. Considerably later, an ONI officer would tell a federal investigator that the navy had received an alarming tip in mid-1940, quoting an informant who said the consulate had asked a consular agent to describe the movement of U.S. ships off the leeward coast of Maui in what then was called the Lahaina Roads.[8]

The sole opponent to arresting the consular representatives was General Walter C. Short, commander of the Hawaiian Army Department. He disagreed with his own intelligence service as well as the FBI and navy. Short had a broad view, deriving from the start-up of the peacetime draft, as a result of which Nisei were excelling in combat training at Schofield Barracks. Under Short's command, the army was bringing the 298th and 299th Regiments up to strength as racially integrated (and federalized) National Guard units, with large numbers of Japanese Americans. Short argued, "If we expect loyalty from a second-generation citizen we must show the same loyalty to him."[9]

He took his arguments to Secretary of War Henry Stimson, who relayed them to the U.S. Justice Department. "We are at present engaged in a counter propaganda campaign whose object is to encourage loyalty of the Japanese population in Hawai'i on promise of fair treatment," Stimson said. "The present outlook of results of this campaign on the entire population is very favorable." Prosecution, he said, would unduly alarm Japanese and non-Japanese alike and thereby jeopardize the entire effort.[10] With Stimson's support, Short's views prevailed. That Stimson was familiar with and endorsed Short's positive attitudes toward Hawai'i was to matter downstream, because Stimson continued to be a person of great influence long after Short left the scene.

More than a year after this initial exchange, in June 1941, the U.S. attorney for Hawai'i, Angus Taylor, revived the idea of prosecuting consular agents as unregistered agents of a foreign power. Shivers called together the various intelligence agencies for discussion. The navy continued to favor it. Marston of Army Intelligence said the Hawaiian Command continued to oppose it. The U.S. attorney turned to Shivers, who deferred to the army's viewpoint. Taylor dropped the idea.[11] On only this one issue had the FBI and Army Intelligence ever disagreed, and now Shivers had signed on to the army's belief in the paramount importance of building positive relationships.

The problem of investigating large numbers of people continued to plague the counterintelligence operation. Bicknell was to write that there were too many Japanese and too little time. "It was believed that many Japanese would be loyal to the United States but there were still a large number of individuals who were decidedly on the fence," in Bicknell's view. "Their sympathies were divided and their future actions depended upon swinging their sentiments to one side or the other." The goal, he said, became "a swing toward Americanization."[12]

Although the Council for Interracial Unity maintained a low profile, its work must have been obvious to many people. Shivers became a public figure. Speaking to a group of engineers on Oʻahu, he debunked rumors of a mass internment of aliens in the event of war. He said the FBI recognized that Hawaiʻi was a melting pot of many races, and accordingly his main focus was on allaying suspicion and doubt. He spoke to Japanese groups in Hilo and Kona on Hawaiʻi Island; at Wailuku, Maui; and elsewhere on the Neighbor Islands. He quieted fears, warned against disloyalty and, in the words of a newspaper account, "[told] them what is expected of them in this national emergency."[13]

Council members spoke with government leaders, service clubs, and church groups. Meetings were held in numerous locations urging Japanese audiences to fully realize the value of the American way of life. Bicknell described the message as part promise, part threat: "The precarious position of local Japanese in case of war with Japan was frankly discussed. They were assured that as long as they lived their lives as American citizens they had nothing to fear."[14]

The high point of this campaign was a mass rally on June 13, 1941, at McKinley High School. It was held in the name of an ad hoc Japanese American organization called the Oʻahu Citizens' Committee for Home Defense, led by Dr. Shunzo Sakamaki, one of Shivers's six Nisei advisers. Two thousand people jammed the McKinley auditorium. Most were students of Japanese ancestry. The rally was chaired by Wilfred Tsukiyama, then a prominent attorney, later to be chief justice of the Hawaiʻi Supreme Court. The Royal Hawaiian Band played, followed by a singing of "America" and classical performance numbers by young Japanese Americans. Sakamaki gave a fiery introduction. "This meeting is not an end in itself," he said. "[It is] a step toward the goal of complete national unity, preparedness, and security." If war comes, he said, "we will do everything we possibly can, giving our lives if necessary, in defense of those democratic principles for which other Americans have lived and fought and died."

Anonymously, Yoshida wrote much and perhaps all of the key speech of the rally, which was delivered by Marston of Army Intelligence. The surviving text resonates with Yoshida's favorite phrases, beginning with an evocation of aloha, mutuality, and unity of purpose. "Here in Hawaiʻi," Marston would be quoted as saying, "there is no north, no south, no east nor west. We are all Americans, regardless of racial descent, speaking one language, having one loyalty, loving one flag, having allegiance but to one country—America."[15]

He said the cooperation of Japanese Americans in war preparation "has made a profound impression upon everyone in Hawai'i." The community, he said, "must be all inclusive. . . . It is true that we have many racial groups. We must weld these groups into one people, inspired by our common cause. We have many economic classes. We must work to reduce the barriers between these classes and develop a teamwork that subordinates personal interest to our country's good."

Although Hawai'i was heading into a difficult time, a crisis could give greater reality to the American motto, "Out of Many, One." Marston cited the military service of Japanese-ancestry troops in World War I, as well as the growing number of Nisei from Hawai'i in the U.S. Army. "These men are living together in the same tents and barracks, eating the same food, sharing the same training, undergoing the same hardships." Praise for Americans of Japanese Ancestry (AJA) in the federalized National Guard units was unanimous: "No group of selectees is doing its work with more intelligence, enthusiasm, and efficiency than the young men of Japanese ancestry." In the process, the Nisei soldier was being further Americanized and would spread "the gospel of Americanism among their relatives and friends. . . . The fire of this period of national emergency and any war—even a Pacific War—[can] weld our Japanese into the structure of American unity."

The speech quoted Franklin Roosevelt's famous line from his first inaugural, "We have nothing to fear but fear itself." It acknowledged that elements of the population in Hawai'i feared the Japanese Americans and that, in turn, Japanese Americans feared unfair or even violent treatment. The answer was a combination of calm and trust: "Trust breeds trust. If we in authority are to expect loyalty from our citizens of Japanese ancestry we must give them our trust in turn."

The speech clearly suggested that if the Japanese community supported the government, there would be no mass internment. "In return for [your] support, you citizens have the right to expect that your government and its armed services will do all in their power to give you the security of your liberties. Together, we cannot fail."

The address laid the basis for an understanding between the army in Hawai'i and the Japanese community. It explicitly departed from the widely held view in Washington that the Japanese community in Hawai'i was not to be trusted. It was a sea change from the army's first Orange

Plan, when the War Department had contemplated pushing people of Japanese ancestry on Oʻahu outside the perimeter of defense. It was unlike anything contemplated by army commands in the West Coast states of the U.S. Mainland. Finally, it was out of synch with the U.S. Navy and the president of the United States.

In itself, the fact that Yoshida drafted Marston's speech reflected a strong degree of trust. It also confirmed Yoshida as the foremost writer on the scene. Through interracial organization, the Council for Interracial Unity had facilitated a significant level of interaction between the community on the one side and intelligence agencies on the other. In the process, intelligence assessments of Hawaiʻi were becoming more nuanced, and the arrest lists were shrinking.

"Results of this campaign were immediately apparent," Bicknell wrote. "A new feeling of confidence in organized authority and the military establishment developed as these people became convinced that they would be treated fairly."[16] Mitsuyuki Kido, a classmate of Ching's at the University of Hawaiʻi, by now a well-liked teacher at Farrington High School, responded on behalf of the rally's audience. Kido said Marston's speech was a challenge "we cannot afford *not* to accept." "It's straight talk from the army in Hawaiʻi," the *Honolulu Star-Bulletin* said. "It has immediate and future value. It can and will be referred to whenever . . . there is an attack made on the loyalty of these citizens of the Japanese race." The *Star-Bulletin* said the speech was both assurance and inspiration.[17] Hemenway wrote an article for the newspaper concluding, "There must be no distinctions made between Americans on a basis of divergent racial ancestries." *Star-Bulletin* editor Riley Allen forwarded a copy of the speech along with Hemenway's remarks and various press clippings to Hawaiʻi's delegate to congress, Samuel Wilder King. He commended the speech as "epochal," urging its inclusion in the *Congressional Record*. He told King the reaction was good not only among Japanese Americans but also the military. He pointed out that Marston had spoken in the name of General Short. He credited General Herron for setting a "liberal policy" that Short now had amplified.[18] King told Allen he believed the atmosphere in Honolulu was much improved.

Precisely for these reasons, Hung Wai Ching was alarmed. He realized the army on the ground did not necessarily reflect the views of the War Department in Washington, D.C. The rally, he cautioned, lulled people—both Japanese and non-Japanese.[19]

* * *

Thereafter, more than a hundred Nisei youth volunteered to serve in the reserve force of the Honolulu Police Department.[20] At the time, the idea of a police reserve had more of a quasi-military connotation than it would subsequently.[21]

Japanese Americans were underrepresented in the Honolulu Police Department, but a Japanese American named Yoshio Hasegawa had worked his way up to the rank of lieutenant (and eventually would become an assistant chief). The Nisei group sought out Hasegawa to act as a go-between. Meetings followed, variously including Hasegawa, Shivers, Gabrielson, and Burns. Yoshida, Sakamaki, Wakayama, and Yamamoto were also repeatedly involved in these meetings, underscoring the central role of the Council for Interracial Unity and Shivers's circle of Nisei advisers.[22] It was decided to organize the volunteers as a community-based team called the Police Contact Group. The Contact Group was to disseminate "correct information relative to American principles and practices to members of their own race." This was none too subtly a matter of Nisei propagandizing Japanese immigrants as to what was expected of them in wartime. The Contact Group was also to disseminate information for "the protection of persons of their race from those who would prey on them due to their ignorance." Third, the Contact Group was to obtain information "of Japan and her agents and who those agents might be."[23] Contact Group members were intended to work within police beat lines, with extra members assigned to heavily Japanese neighborhoods such as Moʻiliʻili.

The volunteer group contacted Lieutenant Hasegawa in July. Meetings were held on three successive days in late August aimed at developing a volunteer plan.[24] On behalf of the police department, Burns was given primary responsibility for drawing up the plan. The Oʻahu Committee for Home Defense supplied a list of potential volunteer police numbering in the hundreds. The Honolulu Police Department (HPD), and by one account the FBI as well, began vetting names for character and reputation. The work went slowly. Why is not clear, given the atmosphere of urgency within Honolulu. Gabrielson, Burns, and Hasegawa of the Police Department met Shivers of the FBI along with Shunzo Sakamaki and Jack Wakayama to review a draft of the plan on August 25. A follow-up meeting was attended by Shivers's Nisei advisers, along with Hasegawa.[25] A final meeting to review the police beat assignments was scheduled for December 8, 1941.

* * *

Like many people born elsewhere, John Anthony Burns could recite the
exact date of his arrival in Honolulu, May 30, 1913, almost as if his life
had begun then, at age four. His childhood story centered around an
irresponsible father and a saintly mother. Harry Burns had fought in
the Spanish-American War. Assigned to the army garrison in Hawai'i, he
housed his family in a tent at Fort Shafter, then rented a house in Kalihi
between Shafter and Honolulu Harbor. Harry was a star baseball player.
Jack Burns also was to say, offhandedly, that his father was one of the
army's ten best marksmen. He was troubled. He was discharged from the
army for misuse of funds, then quickly ran through several jobs. He drank
heavily and got into bar fights. One day, he disappeared, leaving behind
a letter saying he was looking elsewhere for work to support the family.

Burns never saw him again, nor did he often speak of Harry. When
he did, it was with a mixture of suppressed resentment and a sort of
secret pride. Harry Burns was the bad boy of legendary scale in Jack's
complex makeup. Burns kept a photo in his desk drawer of Harry,
dressed in his baseball uniform.

Juxtaposed against the mythic but wayward father was his steadfast
mother. She was known in Kalihi as Mother Burns, mistress of the post
office, counselor to many, and friend to all. She organized a club for
rough and wayward kids. She was Irish and Catholic. She taught Jack
about anti-Irish prejudice. She told him about the signs in the windows
she had seen in Mainland stores, "Irish need not apply." Burns said his
mother was like the Hawaiians: "Nobody looked down anybody's nose
at anybody."[26]

"She ingrained in all of us that you don't despise or dislike a person
because of his race or his color or his creed."[27]

Burns was a rebellious student. He dropped out of high school.
He was sent to Kansas to live with an uncle, who was determined to
help him grow up. Burns would remember his youth as a Kansas farm-
worker nostalgically. He was briefly in and out of the army. He pursued
sports passionately. At one point, he played on a basketball team of high
school dropouts. They challenged a team of ex-college players. Burns
would say he was nearly ejected for rough play, which he rationalized
as being for the good for his teammates: "Somebody had to make the
rest of the guys remember that they were just as good as the other guy
was." His dropouts won by one point.[28] With a second chance at formal
education, he dropped out of college.

His enormous oral history was taken as he approached death. It was emotional and poignant and often nineteenth century or deeply local in its pidgin phrasing. It might have seemed like a collection of tall tales, save for the fact that, in Burns's life, almost everything seemed to jump the bounds of the ordinary.

His rejection of white privilege stayed with him in adulthood. "You had a haole group that believed in the haole group superiority," he was to recall. "There was one vice president of one of the companies downtown, friend of mine—I liked him. 'Jack, you gotta' admit that certain people are born to run the lives of others.' 'I don't gotta' admit nothing. I sure don't gotta' admit that. As a matter of fact, I'll deny it.'"[29] When he applied for a plantation job in the early 1930s, he said the company received him warmly, meaning as a fellow haole, until they found out he was from Kalihi, colored by association with local people and the poor.

He was attracted to the HPD in the belief that if he applied himself, he could advance on merit. Despite scoring at the top of advancement exams, he was passed over for promotion several times until finally, as a homicide detective, he made lieutenant. By 1941 he was convinced that Chief Gabrielson kept him under a watchful eye, and that his possibilities were limited.[30] "The boss," he was to say, "I think he was afraid of me."

His wife Beatrice was afflicted by polio, and he was struggling to find treatment for her and also to care for their three children. When he was caught, off duty, driving under the influence of alcohol, Mother Burns made him swear off drink forever.

Gabrielson's assignment of Burns to work with the Japanese community was something to which he would have given a great deal of thought. Despite the tension between them, he saw in Burns an officer of considerable capacity who would treat the Japanese fairly. Practically overnight, Burns became a central figure in many of the issues relating to the Japanese community, and in the process he became joined to the deep history of Hawai'i.

While the Police Contact Group was coming together, he and four investigators under his direction were assigned to work with Shivers. They were called the Police Espionage Unit. This arrangement reflected what Shivers knew firsthand in Hawai'i and what J. Edgar Hoover knew secondhand in Washington, D.C.—that the FBI did not know enough about the population of Hawai'i. Burns echoed this view. He was to say that the FBI was frustrated, that it was not getting the information it needed, and that it lacked the ability to communicate with local people.

Burns's team included three who spoke Japanese. Kanemi Kanazawa was Japanese American. The second, whom Burns identified as Chung, was a Korean American whose Japanese-language skills likely were derived from Japan's colonization of Korea. The third man, Richard Miller, was of mixed Caucasian and Japanese ancestry who had partially grown up in Japan. The fourth, William Kaina, was Native Hawaiian.[31]

The names of people to be investigated went from Shivers to Burns, who oversaw inquiries into their backgrounds, activities, and general reputations. Particularly sensitive assignments often went to Kanazawa, whom Burns held in high regard. "Kanazawa," he said, "was straight Japanese, rather old school, of American ancestry and very good education, a university graduate." Kanazawa only recently had joined the HPD. He was tall and imposing but nonthreatening in his manner. He deeply respected Burns, whom he found to be succinct and fair minded. Kanazawa liked the fact that Burns often sat by himself and read books while other policemen were chatting among themselves. Kanazawa also thought well of Shivers, describing him as "very sensitive, very concerned."

Kanazawa thought of his own father as an archetype of the first generation. His father was at one point a part of the emperor's guard. He fought for Japan against China in the 1895 war, then migrated to Hawai'i. He eventually settled in Mo'ili'ili and raised a family. He was a beekeeper. Every morning he drove a horse and buggy to the arid Koko Head Crater near the southeastern tip of O'ahu. Flower farms abounded, and his bees thrived. Although he was barred from becoming a U.S. citizen under U.S. naturalization law, he valued his new life in Hawai'i over his homeland. "You would think he would have loyalty to Japan," Kanazawa said of his father, "but he said, 'My kids are more important.'"

Kanazawa talked with the subjects of investigation informally. He recalled Burns telling him to proceed simply, "to find out what people think," and to use a "talk story" approach, as opposed to frontal questioning or interrogation. Talking to people about whether their interests were "inimical" to the United States was, Kanazawa believed, talking over most people's heads.

He found the immigrants focused on making a living and raising their families. They thought of Hawai'i as hospitable in some ways, discriminatory in others. Many of the older people had immigrated not to the United States but to Hawai'i when it was an independent country. As a result, Hawai'i defined nationhood for certain elders, while their status as immigrants in America was an unanticipated experience. "They could never become citizens, so their feeling was 'Japan,'" Kanazawa said. "But their feeling was also 'Hawai'i,' and that was their interest." As with others close to the scene, Kanazawa said the *kibei* were a primary concern. He read the letters of returning students. He checked ship manifests for returning students. He found out how long a student had been away from Hawai'i and "how Japanese they had become."

Buddhist and Shinto priests were also of particular concern, as were teachers of the Japanese-language schools. Police invasions of privacy were common and became more so. He said the part-Caucasian Richard Miller went into people's houses without a warrant and searched their effects for Japanese flags and other artifacts of Japan. Miller must have made an impression. He was exceptionally handsome. Although appearing to be predominately Caucasian, he spoke Japanese and, in Kanazawa's view, "did not think of himself as a haole." He cultivated informants who were in a position to observe Japanese people congregating—Japanese restaurant owners and bar owners and also the owners and managers of the Japanese hotels that ringed A'ala Park in the old downtown area.[32]

As head of the Police Espionage Unit, Burns acquired the reputation of a man in the know. A visiting correspondent of *Collier's Magazine*, Remington Stone, wrote that Burns was the most "intelligent and wide awake" police officer he had met.[33] "He has the reputation of having his ear closer to the ground, and of having a fuller knowledge of the acts and thoughts of Americans whose parents are foreign-born (as well as all types of aliens) than anyone else in Hawai'i."[34]

Stone credited Burns with coining the phrase "Americans of Japanese Ancestry" and with the acronym AJA that was to come into wide usage. Burns credited himself with those words as well. He had worked as a night clerk in the city room of the *Star-Bulletin* as a youth, which gave him a measure of familiarity with the press. In the month before the war started, he had written his column opposing martial law and attesting to the loyalty of the Japanese community. Now Burns wrote to the editor, Riley Allen, proposing that he consider describing members of the Japanese community in positive terms. He took issue with an editorial referring to "American-Japanese": "We have too many hyphenated organizations—Americans for

the first half, before the hyphen, and something else for the second half—
behind the hyphen. We want no more of these groups—half American
and half something else." Burns suggested Americans of Japanese Ancestry (AJA), American Citizens of Japanese Ancestry (ACJA), or American
Citizens of Japanese Descent (ACJD). Allen wrote back, "We will now try
AJA for a while and see the response."[35] AJA caught hold.

CHAPTER 5

A Climate of Fear

FIRST IN 1936 FOLLOWING HIS TRIP TO HAWAI'I, then in 1939 following Shivers's assignment to Honolulu, President Roosevelt demanded formulation of an arrest list for the territory of Hawai'i in the event of war. Throughout this period, he, the secretary of the navy, and various generals and admirals in Washington continued to regard Hawai'i's Japanese community with deep suspicion.[1]

Shivers was responsible for investigating people, then sending the files for approval of potential arrests to the recently organized Special Defense Unit (SDU) of the Department of Justice in Washington, D.C.[2] Under the growing pressure of events, this system would eventually give way to an alliance in Honolulu between Shivers and the Hawaiian Department of the U.S. Army.

Emblematic of the FBI's close relationship with Army Intelligence, the two agencies occupied offices next door to one another in the Dillingham Transportation Building. By 1941 the FBI office had sixteen agents, plus Burns and his four HPD investigators. Army Intelligence had nineteen investigators.

What Shivers was doing with the arrest lists will possibly never be indisputably clear. Either he was engaged in a deception aimed at minimizing potential arrests or he was conflicted and somewhat overwhelmed—or both. The pressure on him was immense. Although outwardly self-assured, he was in the throes of mixed views and mixed emotions. His path of least resistance would have been to put everyone on the arrest list who might in any way be regarded as suspect. In the panic of actual war, no one would have been likely to challenge him. He nonetheless proceeded deliberately, building his own base of information and intelligence.

It was not until the spring of 1941 that Shivers gave Short so much as an outline of an arrest plan.[3] It almost certainly was based on categories of people who were leaders of the first-generation immigrant community. Short approved. Shivers continued to focus on Japan's consulate. On September 8, 1941, he submitted the names of the consular agents to the SDU in Washington, D.C. These were the first persons of Japanese ancestry in the country whose names were submitted to the SDU for arrest in the event of war.[4] Otherwise, Shivers continued to equivocate over who should be arrested.

On September 17, 1941, Shivers received a list of an additional 135 people of Japanese ancestry from a "reliable contact" whose identity was unspecified. FBI agents went to work on these names, as Burns and his four investigators likely did as well. According to the FBI postwar report, an expanded "listening-post" program became operational on November 1.[5]

On November 13, 1941, the national FBI headquarters again directed Shivers to make a plan of "custodial detention" of Japanese aliens. Shivers worked with Bicknell on a response, which they presented to General Short on November 17. This version included a plan of arrests for persons of German and Italian ancestries as well as Japanese ancestry.

On November 22, 1941, Shivers and Bicknell proposed an approach to arrests based on three levels of perceived danger. Plan I assumed a war in which there was no immediate threat to Hawai'i. Plan II assumed a war in which the U.S. naval fleet in Hawai'i was threatened by Japanese raids but continued to function. Plan III assumed a large-scale war, with the fleet "absent from Hawaii waters" and with the islands in danger of invasion. Given that each scenario was different, the arrest plan for each was surprisingly similar. The largest category of planned arrests continued to be consular agents. Under Plan I, thirteen Buddhist and Shinto priests and four other persons "known to be dangerous" also were to be arrested. Additional arrests were to be made of priests if there was evidence of sabotage. Plan II expanded the arrest list by fifty-four persons. Plan III assumed "absolute martial law" and additional arrests of small numbers of German and Italian aliens.[6]

The question of violating people's constitutional rights dogged the process, albeit seemingly with minimal knowledge of or concern for the Constitution. Individuals were to be arrested without evidence of a crime. While the word for those on the arrest list was usually "alien," oblique references were made to "citizens," meaning American citizens of Japanese, German, or Italian ancestry. Plan III said that the FBI would obtain warrants before arresting Americans but did not explain on what grounds.

Generally, the intelligence agencies appear to have assumed that only under martial law could the constitutional rights of American citizens be

suspended. The main targets were *kibei*. The FBI postwar report was to say
the Hawai'i detention plan was "carried forth in anticipation of a state of
martial law being declared in Hawai'i upon the outbreak of war."[7] Accordingly, the government's fear of the *kibei*—resulting in an intention to arrest
and incarcerate American citizens—was one of the ways in which the FBI
and the army contributed to conditioning the federal government to think
in terms of martial law in Hawai'i. Arguably this thinking was related to the
fact that, during this last summer before the war, the Department of Justice
agreed that the War Department would handle the custody of people in
Hawai'i once arrested.[8] This meant that the detention camps in Hawai'i
would be military camps, unlike most of the camps on the U.S. Mainland.

In any event, there is considerable evidence that Shivers was maneuvering to make the list short. The number of arrests being contemplated was
349 out of a Japanese-ancestry population of 160,000. This contrasted with
the FBI's Japanese-ancestry arrest list on the West Coast, which was roughly
ten times larger, despite the population being smaller than Hawai'i's by
40,000 or so.[9]

A discussion of arrest procedures occurred among Short, Bicknell, Shivers, and the new director of Army Intelligence, Colonel Kendall Fielder.
Short hoped for a minimum of disturbance. He sought to "prevent a fear
and hysteria psychosis of the public mind."[10]

In this last month of peacetime, the number of people who were listening posts or "eyes and ears" ran into the hundreds. Shivers had his circle. Burns had his. ONI had its network of 142 Nisei (or 110, in a second
account), and Army Intelligence likewise had a group of watchers and listeners. Apparently none yielded information of much use, if any—likely, as
a navy officer later would testify, because there was nothing to see or hear.

In mid-November, Japan's special envoy, Saburo Kurusu, along with
Ambassador K. Nomura, passed through Honolulu. On November 25,
they met with President Roosevelt in Washington, D.C., nominally in a last-
moment effort to avert war. On November 27, the army chief of staff and
the chief of Naval Operations notified the military commands in Hawai'i
that "an aggressive move by Japan is expected in the next few days." Hoover
cabled Shivers: "Ultra-confidential. Bureau [is] advised negotiations
between United States and Japan breaking down. Government officials con-
template some extraordinary efforts on part of Japanese in United States."
Hoover ordered his field office to be especially alert to the possibilities of
espionage and sabotage. The same notice was sent to Bicknell at Army Intelligence and Mayfield at ONI.[11]

It was not until four days later, on the first day of December, that Shivers completed a revised arrest list with the help of Army Intelligence. Shivers's reliance on the army reflected his own uncertainties and suggested respect for Bicknell's familiarity with Hawai'i. Naval Intelligence long since had been excluded from the decision-making process, and now the Special Defense Unit in Washington also had been excluded. Time had run out. The joint army–FBI arrest list became the FBI's custodial detention plan. A three-by-five-inch card was made for each person, including directions on how to locate the person by the shortest route.[12]

On December 3, an FBI wiretap of the Japanese Consulate revealed it was burning its papers. On December 4, Shivers submitted his final arrest list to Hoover, supposedly to be either approved or disapproved. It now contained the names of 338 Issei aliens and 9 Nisei Americans. On that same day, an American "blueprint for total war" called Victory Parade was leaked to the national press by the military in Washington, D.C. This was a monumental disclosure that seemed to have no impact on the public in Hawai'i. On December 5, Hoover notified Shivers to prepare for making the arrests in the event of war.

Also on that day, the wiretap of Japan's consulate revealed a conversation in Japanese between Dr. Motokazu Mori (or his wife, a disputed point) and a newspaper in Japan, *Yomiuri shinbun*. The conversation revolved around which flowers were in bloom in Hawai'i. Shivers and others in intelligence suspected that the "flowers" referred to which ships were in Pearl Harbor, a view possibly put in question by the fact that an article actually was published in Japan about the blooming of Hawai'i's flowers. Motokazu Mori was the son of Dr. Iga Mori, who was a founder of Japanese Hospital (now Kuakini Hospital) and the first person of Japanese ancestry on the board of the Nu'uanu YMCA. He would be arrested and interned but never charged with wrongdoing.

On the same day that Shivers and Bicknell completed the list, Shivers called Burns into his office. Shivers said he believed the United States was going to be attacked somewhere in the Pacific within the week, possibly in Hawai'i. He asked Burns to check all his best sources for any sign of suspicious activity. His eyes filled with tears.[13]

The idea of making last-minute inquiries into obscure corners may sound more dramatic than it likely was. Kanemi Kanazawa talked with workers at Pearl Harbor, looking for signs of unusual activity that might suggest espionage or sabotage. He drew a blank. Richard Miller spoke with the insurance executive Clifton Yamamoto, who was helping to set up Burns's

Police Contact Group. Yamamoto told Miller that a few Japanese aliens with property in Japan said they wished they could go to Japan. "[They] fear reprisals from the government and rough elements of the community," Miller reported. However, Yamamoto said that most aliens with property in Hawaiʻi were content to remain in Hawaiʻi, and that they were not worried either about their treatment by the government or the security of their property. Fatalism was at work, Yamamoto said. "They have arrived at this state gradually, until now they are ready to accept anything."[14] Miller spoke with a technician at the Japanese Hospital who said Japanese in the plantation areas of Oʻahu feared retribution from Filipino workers in the event of war. A bookstore owner said some of his customers feared race riots but believed the government would curtail unlawful actions. A Japanese hotel manager, asked if anyone was trying to book passage to Japan, said the answer was no, not since early November, when the last ship out, the *Taiyo Maru,* had sailed from Honolulu.

"Rumors and talk of an internment camp are floating around the Japanese communities," Miller wrote, "but the aliens are resigned to whatever the authorities may have in store for them. They are also willing to cooperate with the Government as much as possible and have confidence in the constituted authorities."[15]

The next day, Wednesday, December 3, the same contacts said essentially the same thing, except the bookseller was unavailable. His wife had died. A new interviewee, the owner of the Kokusai Theater movie house, said some of the elderly Japanese feared "riffraff" and Filipinos. The owner of the Kobayashi Hotel said rumors were circulating among "the uneducated class" about an internment camp on Molokaʻi.

Many of the same individuals were contacted yet again on Friday, December 5. None reported anything new except Clifton Yamamoto, who had been advised by an elderly Japanese Christian minister that the United States and Japan would be foolish to make war against one another. The minister believed that such a war was just what Nazi Germany wanted. He theorized that it would weaken both countries, then Germany would take over China and also take over Japan.[16]

Shigeo Yoshida was pleased with the prewar work of the Council on Interracial Relations but was still haunted by doubt. He saw "a calmness among all people in the community which is more than might be reasonably expected in view of the international scene." He felt the McKinley rally had sunk in. He cited a "lack of hysteria among the Japanese aliens concerning their fate in case of a war" and also a "growing confidence that as long as they behave themselves and conduct themselves within the law, they have nothing to fear from the authorities." In this regard, Yoshida and Bicknell concurred. Although dismissals from work had occurred, there was no wholesale dismissal of Japanese employees. There had been no overt conflicts, no boycotts, and no cancelling of insurance policies, let alone rioting. Yoshida felt the idea of including all races in defense preparations was taking hold, although not an inclusion of Japanese aliens and Japanese Americans proportionate to their share of the population. What might happen next was an open question: "There are still many individuals and groups who are suspicious of all aliens; who feel that every Japanese, citizen and alien alike, is an agent of the Mikado and should be placed in concentration camps; who would like to take the law into their hands when the crisis comes; who refuse to have anything to do with people of other races, particularly the Orientals . . . [and] who are un-Christian and inhuman in their relationships with their fellow men."[17]

Yoshida was nonetheless ready to excavate a great result from chaos. "Hawaii may not only survive the crisis, if and when it comes," he wrote, "but actually use it constructively to establish a firm and more Christian basis of human relationship among people of diverse races." He praised Shivers and the army for their "interest in the human side of Hawaii as well as in its position as a military outpost of the nation." On the brink of war, Yoshida declined prophecy. "The seeming calmness in the Islands may be only a veneer, a thin veil of oil on a turbulent sea. The first incident in an actual war in the Pacific may turn loose all the forces of hatred, suspicion, and race prejudice in these Islands. What the future holds, no one can foretell."[18]

While work on the arrest list was moving unevenly forward, the army was devising systems for controlling large numbers of people in the event of war. In this regard, the key person was Colonel Thomas H. Green, an army lawyer. Green had arrived in Hawai'i in 1940 imagining a pleasant posting. He quickly realized a Pacific war was all but inevitable; that Japan easily could take the Philippines; and that the army's task was to secure Hawai'i as a forward bastion on the way back to victory. He was shaken to find that two-thirds of Hawai'i's people were of Asian ancestry. At first, he couldn't tell a Japanese from a Chinese or a Chinese from a Korean. He jumped to the conclusion that when the war came, the public could not be controlled by the administration of civil law, so he set out to change the law.[19]

Green was vaguely influenced by the thought that military involvement in civilian affairs smacked of undue meddling. He at first kept his own counsel, but he then was befriended by an ex-army officer, Edward Massee, a retired federal judge. Like many older people in this period,

As staff judge advocate and then as executive officer, Thomas H. Green played a key role in shaping martial law in Hawai'i. He credited Ching, Yoshida, and Charles Loomis for constantly bolstering his faith in Japanese Americans. Ann Arbor Public Library/*Ann Arbor News* donation.

Massee's life experience was rooted in the Spanish-American War, first in Puerto Rico, then in the Philippines.[20] Green and Massee shared lunch several times. Sensing a like mind, Green began to talk about how the military might suspend the public's constitutional rights in the event of war. Green next talked to the Hawaiian Army Department commander, General Herron, whom he was later to quote as encouraging him to develop approaches to martial law.

Green helped shape the territorial legislation, known as the Mobilization or M-Day Law, that was intended to maintain civilian government but impose tight security and suspend the citizenry's constitutional rights. Drafts were first introduced in early 1941, but the bill was shelved in the regular legislative session. Green then worked with the appointed territorial governor, Joseph B. Poindexter, an attorney who had served as a federal judge on the Mainland, then moved to Hawai'i to practice law. After ten years of residence, Poindexter had been appointed to high office by Roosevelt. Poindexter called a special session of the legislature, which in October 1941 passed the M-Day Law in an atmosphere of impending crisis.

Initially, Green liked the M-Day approach. He believed it would put the onus of authoritarian control on the civilian government and free up the army to fight the war. However, the longer Green talked to individuals in the territory, the more he was inclined to think that the military would be unable to manipulate a civilian government to its satisfaction. He began to imagine outright military rule. Priding himself on his research, Green looked for legal definitions of martial law. "I concluded," he wrote, "that martial law is not a law nor are the limitations or the responsibilities well defined anywhere."[21] In other words, martial law was, in his view, a set of powers without definition and, by extension, was what the army would make of it.

Green was familiar with the Alien Enemies Act of 1798, which allowed for aliens from an enemy country to be "apprehended, restrained, secured and removed," provided the president of the country proclaimed that a "predatory incursion" was either threatened or perpetrated.[22] Green also seized on Section 67 of the Organic Act by which Hawai'i had been incorporated into America. Section 67 empowered the appointed governor "in case of rebellion or invasion or imminent threat thereof" to suspend the writ of habeas corpus and place the territory under martial law. Section 67 in turn had been lifted from the faux Republic of Hawai'i's Constitution of 1895, which had provided for putting down a rebellion of Native Hawaiians against the Provisional Government. For Green's purposes, Section 67 of the Organic Act was an antecedent that not only addressed the threat of foreign invasion but the threat of an uprising by the local population. Green concluded it would "meet every emergency."[23]

He held regular meetings with his army associates and subordinates to keep them abreast of his views and activities. Having a long while to draft General Orders, Green devised what Bicknell was to describe as the most undemocratic system in American history. While Green labored, General Short arrived to replace Herron. "General Short had one of the fastest minds I had ever encountered," Green wrote, a bit of flattery that he freely gave to high-level people who agreed with him.[24] He then met with Governor Poindexter, another smart man in Green's view.

From this determined maneuvering, Green emerged as the primary author of a martial law plan. That said, he was far from the only person who thought in terms of military rule. At the height of the Massie case in the early 1930s, a cry had gone up around the country for Hawai'i to be governed by a military commission. As war approached, Mississippi congressman John E. Rankin, a member of the 1937 congressional committee on statehood, proposed martial law for Hawai'i. In the weeks leading up to December 7, talk of martial law continued in the air.

In what would become a foundation stone of John Burns's political future, Burns published an article in the November 18, 1941, *Honolulu Star-Bulletin* headlined, "Why Attack the People of Hawai'i?" It was an argument against Rankin and martial law. Burns likened the ethnic communities of Hawai'i to enclaves in such places as Pennsylvania and Minnesota that "preserved intact their old-country traditions [and] methods of speech." Although it was the threat of martial law that moved Burns to write his article, it would mainly be remembered for saying his investigation had "not found facts which would indicate or prove disloyalty but rather the reverse."[25]

Colonel Green influenced events across a horizon of several years. Although a hard-liner for order, he was affected by his experiences in Hawai'i. He liked what he saw. Family life was strong. There was no juvenile delinquency in the Japanese community—this deeply impressed him. They were courteous and orderly. On Saturday night, they might drink sake and sing, but they quietly went home at eleven o'clock. Many were skilled craftsmen, and some were doctors and lawyers. They dressed nicely.

Green worked himself into a bind. Originally seized by anxiety in response to the sea of nonwhite faces, he had come to see people of Japanese ancestry as real people. He was further influenced by Caucasians who had a parallel experience—most notably Shivers and General Short. Further, he made the pragmatic connection that a wholesale evacuation of the Japanese-ancestry population would tie up shipping and remove skilled tradesmen. He concluded that mass removal was not only wildly impractical but unjust and probably illegal.[26]

While the arrest list was slowly moving forward in Hawai'i, President Roosevelt was assembling advisers whose principal emotion was fear and whose main response was to crack down and control. Their story begins with the fact that during the run-up to war, public opinion across America was heavily isolationist and antiwar. Nonetheless, Roosevelt had declared a "limited" state of emergency in 1939 in response to Germany's aggression in Europe and Japan's in East Asia. In 1940, he formed the bipartisan cabinet, effectively a war cabinet, that prominently included Henry Stimson as secretary of war. Stimson was by then seventy-three, a Wall Street lawyer who had served as both war secretary and secretary of state under Republican presidents. For assistance, Stimson brought in the much younger John J. McCloy, also a Wall Street lawyer, first as a consultant and then as his assistant secretary of war.

More than any other federal official, John McCloy was to become preeminently influential in the areas of internal subversion, internment, the fate of Japanese Americans, and the question of how the national government was to handle Hawai'i. The cross-currents, contradictions, and hypocrisies of these several subjects all ran through McCloy.

McCloy's appointment reflected the administration's preoccupation with the imagined enemy within and specifically with sabotage. He was just old enough to be connected to the U.S. Army's frontier experience. As a college student, he had attended a private military camp in upper New York State run by a retired army general, Leonard Wood. Wood originally was an Indian fighter, then was commander of the Rough Riders in Cuba, with Theodore Roosevelt his second in command. Theodore Roosevelt, in his old age, was a guest speaker at Woods's military camp. McCloy subsequently served in World War I as an aide to General Guy H. Preston, who had participated in the Wounded Knee Massacre of the Sioux Indian tribe. As an aide to Preston in Europe, McCloy made the acquaintance of people who were to be of great influence

Assistant Secretary of War John J. McCloy simultaneously pushed the West Coast internment while taking a fundamentally different tack in Hawai'i. McCloy Archive/ Amherst College.

in World War II, such as George Marshall, Douglas MacArthur, and William Donovan.

McCloy's emergence into public life was linked to the sensational explosion during World War I of an arsenal on an island in New York Harbor. The bang was heard around several states. It became known as the Black Tom (Island) incident. Thereafter McCloy spent nine years litigating on behalf of corporate clients in the Hague World Court and elsewhere, aiming to prove that the damage was the work of a German sabotage ring. McCloy's biographer, Kai Bird, described the event as McCloy's "Wilderness of Mirrors." "Having proved the existence of the German spy ring responsible for Black Tom," Bird wrote, "McCloy was now psychologically prepared to be a ready believer in all spy rings."[27]

McCloy's enduring role as a representative of the aging Stimson was fundamental to his influence. A track coach once told him that if he ran with the swift, he might come in second. In the coming years in the War Department, while a nominal number-two man, he ran with the swift. Moving from New York to Washington, D.C., he quickly became an insider who served as legal adviser, crisis manager, mediator, and emissary to distant outposts. A critic said McCloy had his nose in everything. Most consistently, his nose was in questions of order, and it was in pursuit of order that he teamed up with a young lawyer named Karl Bendetsen.

Karl Bendetsen was an army reservist from the state of Washington who had been bitten by the prospect of impending war. In a visit to Washington, D.C., Bendetsen helped lobby for extension of the peacetime draft. The significance of his volunteer lobbying could not be discounted, in that extension of the draft passed the U.S. House by only one vote. Bendetsen went on active duty in 1940 in the Judge Advocate General's Office. He soon was rubbing shoulders with people whose rank was far above his own.

According to McCloy's logbook, Bendetsen began working with him on May 2, 1941, seven months before the war. The subject of their meeting was labor unrest at the North American Aviation plant outside of Los Angeles. The plant was of great strategic importance—manufacturing bombers, fighters, and pilot-training aircraft. They talked about the possibility of the president taking control by declaring a full-blown statement of emergency, as opposed to the limited emergency of 1939.[28] Following a disputed union election at the plant, the United Auto Workers won the right to bargain on behalf of the workforce, which led to a strike. This was of particular concern to the Roosevelt Administration because of its war preparations and because it was supplying weaponry to beleaguered Britain, in the hope that Britain could withstand Germany's air attack.

By the third week in May, McCloy was bearing down; as the strike situation at North American was coming to a head, Roosevelt declared an *unlimited* national emergency that had been at the heart of McCloy and Bendetsen's discussion. Roosevelt conjured a world ruled by Adolph Hitler. He said all military and civilian defenses must be readied to repel aggression "directed toward any part of the Western Hemisphere."

Immediately thereafter, McCloy met with Secretary of the Navy Frank Knox and Stimson about how they might track down enemy agents operating in the United States. It is a logbook entry rich with possibilities in light of McCloy's role in combatting sabotage and espionage. The move toward war had reached a turning point. What had begun as a discussion of threats to aircraft production had become a declaration of unlimited emergency. This in turn was joined to searching for subversive elements not only in the North American aircraft plant but countrywide.

Among Roosevelt's top advisers, McCloy was the most active. In late May 1941, he engaged in a flurry of meetings with the apparent aim of developing a more organized system of intelligence. He had lunch with Knox and Stimson at the home of William Donovan, who at that point was a retired army officer on friendly terms with Roosevelt. Thereafter he huddled with Donovan on four successive days and also met frequently with Knox and J. Edgar Hoover. On Thursday, May 29, he met over lunch at Donovan's house with Knox, and two days later he held yet another such meeting there. That afternoon, he discussed a "possible delegation of wider powers to FBI."[29] In what was surely an evolution of this elaborate round of conversation, Donovan called McCloy on June 3 to talk about entering the government. Thereafter, the president appointed Donovan to head the new Office of Coordination of Information, the precursor to the Office of Strategic Services (OSS), which eventually became the Central Intelligence Agency (CIA).

McCloy was running with the swift.

He next met with the president at the White House, where he gave Roosevelt a draft statement directing the army to seize the North American Aviation plant. McCloy then engaged in a last-minute round of meetings and telephone calls. He spoke with more than a dozen contacts on Saturday and nineteen on Sunday, capped by dinner with Donovan and members of Congress. In the early morning of Monday, June 9, the discussion moved to the president's yacht, then to the White House. Roosevelt declared North American Aviation to be essential to national defense. Army troops took control of the plant and ended the strike.

Throughout, Karl Bendetsen was intimately involved. On an army form describing his career experience, he would write, "Conceived and drafted Executive order and precise operating instructions for seizure of North American Aviation plant in spring of 1941."[30] The working relationship between the high-ranking McCloy and the midlevel attorney Bendetsen continued. Over the following two days alone, they met three times. They were just getting started.

McCloy told Bendetsen to explore questions of detention and internment for security purposes in the event of war.[31] Repeated conversations
on security ensued in the weeks and months following. In addition, two
more federal takeovers occurred over the summer, one in an airplane
parts plant and one in a shipyard. In both, Bendetsen served not only as
legal adviser but director of events on the ground.

Through the persons of McCloy and Bendetsen, the takeover of war
plants and the potential mass internment of people became intertwined.
The seizing of plants and the internment of people had one painful feature in common, which was the extraordinary use of power (or abuse
thereof, depending on one's viewpoint) by the federal government.

Strikebreaking brought together the president with his other security and intelligence people, such as Stimson, Knox, and Donovan, along
with a general soon to be provost marshall, Allen W. Guillon. Their
convergence was a crucial step in the formation of a national-security
apparatus that was to become a permanent feature of the U.S. government. Their collective prewar behavior foreshadowed their belief that
military matters rationalized preemptive executive action and that constitutional rights could be suspended in the name of national security.

In a discussion of detaining U.S. citizens without due process, McCloy
soon would tell the attorney general, "If it is a question of the country
[or] the constitution of the United States, why, the constitution is just
a scrap of paper to me."[32] Similarly, Bendetsen would write to a mentor
who was studying civilian rights in time of war that "a sovereign power
can do whatever is necessary in a moment of urgency to protect itself."[33]

As Bendetsen rose in prominence, he was reassigned from the Judge
Advocate's Office to General Guillon, with whom he organized the
Office of Provost Marshall, which was put in charge of military policing,
prisoners of war, prisoner exchanges, and, not least, internment. In this
context, Bendetsen pursued the question that McCloy had raised in the
spring: In the event of war, how would the government go about arresting and detaining people?

Pursuant to an order from the secretary of war, Bendetsen undertook
a tour of existing detention camps run by the Immigration and Naturalization Service (INS). He conferred with INS officials about how to
administer camps and how camps could be expanded quickly if need be.
He traveled to obscure way stations, which at that point were mainly used
to hold nonmilitary German and Italian sailors who had been marooned
in U.S. ports as a result of the war in Europe. At the end of August, he

visited Fort Lincoln, North Dakota, then Fort Missoula, Montana. He stopped briefly at Fort Lewis, Washington, then flew on to Hawai'i.

In Honolulu he met with General Short, Colonel Green from the Judge Advocate General's Office, and a representative of Army Intelligence.[34] He went not only to army headquarters on O'ahu but also to neighboring islands, including a well-documented inspection of the army's Camp Kīlauea on Hawai'i Island, near the famous volcano. A handwritten entry on Bendetsen's trip notes struck a tone of dark suspicion: "Jap vote controls this very political island. Therefore good Americans who depend on Jap business and votes may give Japanese the

Major Karl Bendetsen, McCloy's point man in creating a system of incarceration, unsuccessfully promoted a mass internment scheme to the U.S. Army in Hawai'i. Stanford/Hoover Institution.

n the early fall of 1941, General Gullion, The Judge

l, sent one of his officers to Hawaii to acquaint us

Coast Plan" for the evacuation of the Japanese in tl

:h Japan. When he reported to General Short, I was

ference. The "West Coast Plan" contemplated the r

Japanese ancestry from their homes on the West Coa

ng them in detention centers. The emissary recomn

1 be paralleled in Hawaii. When my turn came to e

: made strong objection to the suggestion, statin;

miliar with the suggested plan, that I had consic

Green's description of the "West Coast Plan" coincides with the records of
Bendetsen's travel to Hawai'i in his papers at Stanford University. Green
autobiography, online.

benefit of the doubt." That was to say, Bendetsen not only distrusted people of Japanese ancestry in Hawai'i but also distrusted otherwise "good
Americans" who worked with them. He stayed ten days in Hawai'i, from
September 7 to the 16th.[35] Thereafter his pursuit of where and how to
detain people continued. Stopping at the Presidio in San Francisco, he
made an ally second in importance only to McCloy. This was General
John DeWitt, the head of the Western Defense Command. He also visited Fort Stanton, Texas. His network of contacts was in transition to a
network of de facto prison camps. In a letter following up on Missoula,
for example, he wrote approvingly of a blueprint to expand the capacity
of the INS station from several hundred to one thousand prisoners.[36]

Bendetsen remained intent on Hawai'i becoming a part of a mass
removal and detention system. In late November he returned to
O'ahu. Green, in his unpublished autobiography, described a visitor
at this time from the army's West Coast headquarters who almost certainly was Bendetsen.[37] "The emissary," who served on Guillon's staff,
described a plan to relocate all persons of Japanese ancestry inland

from the West Coast states in the event of war with Japan. Green called in General Short to hear this scheme firsthand. According to Green, "The emissary recommended that the 'West Coast Plan' be paralleled in Hawai'i." Green wrote that he made "strong objection," arguing that mass evacuation was inappropriate for Hawai'i. He said he questioned its justice, effectiveness, and legality, and that Short shared his views.[38]

Bendetsen's telling of the story meshes with Green's in key respects. While Bendetsen skirted an outright description of internment, he did talk about his mission being highly sensitive and about meeting with the army command, the FBI, Army Intelligence, and ONI.

Along the route of Bendetsen's travels, the subjects of detaining people rounded up in FBI arrests and a larger internment had become inseparable. The question was scale.

Read together, this chain of events places planning for internment in a new time frame and a new light—namely, *the internment originated in prewar planning*, not the widely cited "wartime hysteria" following Pearl Harbor.[39] The principal collaborators had converged in the army's strikebreaking takeover of North American Aviation. The possibilities advanced when McCloy asked Bendetsen to study INS detention centers, which Bendetsen did. In pursuit of this goal, Bendetsen left evidence of his intentions in his unsuccessful attempt to sell the Hawaiian Army Department on the "West Coast plan."

Importantly for the future of Hawai'i, General Short and Colonel Green's rejection of Bendetsen's plan foreshadowed a pattern that was to take on a life of its own.

PART III

Inside the War Zone

URGENT -:- WARNING -:- URGENT

"BLACKOUT ENEMY" Planes will Simulate Attack on Your Island, Thursday Night, May 23rd, 1940, sometime between 8:30 and 9:00 p.m. When warning bells are rung or sirens are sounded, IMMEDIATELY put out all lights, inside and outside. TURN OFF ALL SIGNS. Don't use flashlights, matches, etc.

BLACKOUT COMPLETELY.

While this raid is only make-believe, do your part in this rehearsal
for an event we hope will never come.

"OUTBLACK THE LAST BLACKOUT"

燈火管制についての警告

来る五月二十三日(木曜日)の晩八時半より九時までの二十分間慘敵國の飛行機が貴島を襲撃する、その時には警報としてサイレン又は鐘を鳴らす、同時にすべて内外の點火を消す事、店のネオン・サイン、飾窓の燈火も消す事、フラッシ・ライト及マッチも使用せぬ事、完全に消燈すべし

この點燈は元より假裝なるも市民は實際の時さ同じ氣持にて共力せられん事を望む、去年の燈火管制より向一層真暗にする事

布哇縣燈火管制委員
ホノルル郡委員長
ベン・エフ・ラッシュ
布哇郡委員長
エ チ・シ ウ ォ ル タ ス
馬哇郡委員長
ロバート・イー・ヒューズ
加哇郡委員長
ウ イ リ ア ム・エ リ ス

重要警告

本島定於五月二十三號(卽禮拜四晚)。由八點半至九點鐘。舉行防空演習。施行燈火管制。屆時以鳴鐘或響笛爲號。無論內外燈火。及各種電招牌。皆須立刻熄滅。甚至電筒火柴等。均在受管制之列。務使完全照暗。切切至要。

[黑暗比前次更黑暗]
山疆省燈火管制委員會啓

(防空演習時間内。諸各盡職責。惟望真正空襲。永不來臨)。

NAINGET -:- PAKAUNA -:- NAINGET

"PANAGSIPNGET KABUSOR" NGA AIROPLANOS KASDALA RAOTEN DAYTA ISLA NGA YANMO INTON RABII TI JUEVES, MAYO 23, MANIPOD ORAS TI LAS 8:30 INGANAT LAS 9:00 P.M. INTON MANGNGEGYO DAGITI CAMPANAS NGA AGAWENG KEN PANAGTIMEK DAGITI SILBATOS, IDDEPENYO A DAGOS DAGITI SILAWYO ITI UNEG KEN RWAR. IDDEPENYO AMIN DAGITI MARKA NGA NASILAWAN. SAANKAY NGA AGGAMIT ITI LENTE, GURABIS, KEN DADDUMA PAY NGA UMAPOY. PAGBALINENYO NGA NASIPNGET.

(No man pay daytoy nga iraraot saan nga napaypayso, aramidenyo ti rebbengenyo iti daytoy a panagpadas tapno masagsaganakayo iti aniaman a dumteng, sapay koma to saan met la a mapasamak.)

"NASIPSIPNGET PAY KOMA NGEM ITI DAYDI NAUDI A PANAGSIPNGET"

TERRITORIAL BLACKOUT COMMITTEES:

Ben F. Rush, General Chairman, Honolulu County;   H. C. Walters, General Chairman, Hawaii County;
Robt. E. Hughes, General Chairman, Maui County;   William Ellis, General Chairman, Kauai County.

Where war was to hit most of the country in the shock of a day, war came to Hawai'i in slow motion. In this 1940 poster, residents were coached on how to perceive mock air raids. *Hawaii in the World War*, Ralph S. Kuykendall

CHAPTER 6

Resetting the Clock

THE *HONOLULU STAR-BULLETIN* OF DECEMBER 6, 1941, devoted an entire page to chitchat about the military on Oʻahu. Captain Howard B. Simpson was now in charge of the recreation program at Hickam Field, where, it was mentioned in passing, five thousand personnel were stationed. An army major, surely one of the army's oldest, Darwin D. Martin of Detroit, once had pursued Pancho Villa along the Mexican border, and now he was in command of Coastal Artillery Intelligence at Fort DeRussy in Waikīkī. There were attempts at humor: "Wahiawa Wanda swears she's never been kissed by a soldier—in fact that's why she swears!"

The evidence of impending war was widespread. Pearl Harbor teemed with ships and shipyards. Twenty giant oil storage tanks—each the size of a twenty-story building—were being constructed under Red Hill, between Pearl Harbor and urban Honolulu, bringing thousands of civilian workers into the island of Oʻahu. Navy secretary Frank Knox and the U.S. chief of staff, General George C. Marshall, lately had made inspection tours in Hawaiʻi. While in Honolulu, Knox told a Chamber of Commerce luncheon "of having so much money poured into my lap for national defense purposes, that my concern, my grave anxiety, was whether I could actually spend it."[1] The Territorial Legislature had passed its M-Day disaster plan. Finally, the Council for Interracial Unity had gone public in midsummer, most visibly at the McKinley High School rally.

Despite a certain nervousness, the idea of an American Gibraltar was deeply embedded. Someone as learned as Dr. Romanzo Adams, founder of the university's sociology program, as late as November 25, 1941, reassured his two brothers in Wisconsin that an attack on Honolulu was implausible: "Its defenses are so strong that no enemy is likely to run the risk of a long voyage and a battle far from its home base."[2]

When the bombs fell, people across the country were to remember the line, "This is the real McCoy!" It was widely taken as engaging slang. Actually, it was an attempt by the broadcaster Webley Edwards to shock an island populace that had become accustomed to mock air raids. Numerous residents who saw the attack planes thought they were U.S. Army planes, painted with the rising sun of Japan on the wings and tails to add realism. A witness who saw smoke billowing from Pearl Harbor wrote, "They are even using smoke screens in this maneuvering."[3] Thomas Higa, a *kibei* who had been drafted into the U.S. Army, was at home in the windward Kahaluʻu Valley on a weekend pass. He awoke on December 7 to the sound of explosions at the new air base on the opposite side of Kāneʻohe Bay. Having previously been interrogated by the secret police in Japan and also by the FBI in Hawaiʻi and having undergone basic combat training at Schofield Barracks, Higa was no stranger to the idea of impending war. Yet he first thought of December 7 as the most imaginative drill to date. A shell exploded near him. "I became angry, thinking it was dangerous to simulate actual war in populated areas," he recalled. Finally, he admitted to himself what had happened. "I became dizzy and was thrown into an indescribable terror, as if being pulled into a bottomless abyss."[4]

Just before the *Honolulu Star-Bulletin* went to press, the mangled bodies of two young girls arrived at an emergency hospital. One girl, nameless at press time, was thought to be Portuguese and about ten years old, dead as a result of a puncture wound to her left temple. A Japanese girl, about nine, wearing a fur collar on her coat, was dead. Mrs. White, forty-four, of Dowsett Tract, a wealthy neighborhood in the Nuʻuanu upland, was dead of a puncture wound to the chest. Toshio Tokusaki, age five, of Peleula Lane, was dead. Patrick J. Chong, thirty, of 1457 Fort Street, was dead.

Young Daniel K. Inouye, a student at McKinley High School, recalled swearing at the sky, "You damn Japs." He had taken first aid training. He came across a wounded infant, rushed it to a first aid station, and asked a woman, who happened to be Yoshida's wife, Thelma, what they should do. She took the baby from him and said nothing could be done—it was dead.

The instantaneous struggle with denial in Hawaiʻi foreshadowed denial of a different sort that swept across the country. It was a denial that Japan, unaided, could have dealt America such a blow. For the wounded mind, the answer was all but ready-made. It was that the people of Japanese ancestry in Hawai'i had aided Japan. Presumption reigned, both in and out of the national government. An intelligence estimate prepared in early 1941 had said if an attack came, "sabotage is first to be expected and may, within a very limited time, cause great damage." A September 1941 assessment rated sabotage along with submarine warfare as the most likely threats to O'ahu.[5] General Marshall was to say he had expected "a terrific effort to cripple everything out there by sabotage."[6]

Most Americans never realized that sabotage was not the problem, but rather it was the misplaced fear of sabotage that had contributed so greatly to the disaster. In the week before the attack, Marshall had ordered the army in Hawai'i to cluster its fighter airplanes together in the belief that they could be guarded efficiently on the ground and thereby kept safe from sabotage. General Short complied. He was to tell investigators that, like Marshall, he had feared sabotage more than anything.[7]

Japan assigned 60 percent of its first wave of attackers to destroying the clustered airplanes.[8] Everywhere the Japanese pilots found American flyers struggling to untangle and get into the air to fight. For the most part, the Japanese pilots destroyed the air fleet where it sat. Thereafter Pearl Harbor was largely defenseless.

An indiscriminate cry for revenge followed. The president, posters, lapel pins, matchbooks, plays, and movies exhorted people to remember Pearl Harbor. December 7 reordered Americans' shared awareness of elapsed time. It reset the American clock. *Where were you on December seventh?*

Robert Shivers had planned to meet with his Nisei advisers and Hung Wai Ching at his house on Black Point. Corinne Shivers and their "adopted daughter," Sue Kobatake, were cooking a big breakfast. When Shivers was notified of the attack, he told his wife, "Watch out for Sue." He then left home, not to reappear for a week. Ching called Yoshida and informed him of the bombing. He then called Shivers's house and was told they might as well come over and eat their breakfast. Ching, Yoshida, and four other Nisei did so, then followed Shivers to the FBI office. Mrs. Shivers drove Sue to a house in the mountains that was less exposed than their house on Black Point. A number of Caucasian women were gathered. Mrs. Shivers felt that some were staring at Sue, at which point she moved her to a more welcoming house.[9]

Shivers told Yoshida and the other Nisei to disperse and report any suggestion of subversive activity. He told them to contact one hundred "listening post" people. How this worked out went unrecorded, but by inference it helped reassure Shivers that no sabotage was afoot. Shivers told Ching to check out several areas in the city where fires were burning. One was in the Liliha district on the Pearl Harbor side of downtown Honolulu. A second was in the McCully district beyond Honolulu. Ching reported that the fires were under control, the situations were manageable, and calm prevailed. That night, Ching's wife Elsie, seven months pregnant, went into labor. Ching drove her through the blackout, his car lights off, to Kapiʻolani Hospital, where she gave birth to a son.

Bicknell had witnessed the attack from his home in Aiea Heights overlooking Pearl Harbor. He provided his office with blow-by-blow accounts of which ships had sunk, which were listing, which were on fire, and which were still intact.

Jack Burns was driving in his car, out to buy ice cream for his daughter's seventh birthday party. When he saw the Kāneʻohe Air Station was on fire, he called in a report to the FBI office, then drove there, leaving his daughter to wonder what had happened to her ice cream.[10]

Burns, Bicknell, and Shivers, who among themselves had brought the individual investigations in the Japanese community forward, were now in the same room.

Around noon, Shivers got his first call from Poindexter, who had a reputation for equivocating. House Speaker Roy Vitousek wrote of him, "It was very difficult to consult with [Poindexter] and feel that you had any results."[11] Poindexter asked for advice: should he activate the Territorial Legislature's emergency restrictions? Shivers said yes, he should. An hour later, Poindexter called again. This time he asked if he should declare martial law. Shivers said yes, he should.[12] By his second telephone call, Poindexter was face-to-face with the U.S. Army, in the person of Short and his lawyer, Colonel Thomas Green, who over the preceding months had developed not one but two plans for what should happen in the event of war.

At the Dillingham Transportation Building, three short blocks from ʻIolani Palace, Shivers took charge of internal security. About 2 p.m., he was given a letter from Short authorizing execution of the arrests. The margin between personal freedom and incarceration now hinged on such subjective factors as personal acquaintance or who knew whom. Shivers, Bicknell, and Burns sat down and went through the card file. Burns said he would come to names of people he knew and he would say, "I think so-and-so is a damned fine American." Burns said when an arrest was contested, the three would vote. He believed that he and Shivers were the best informed about people in the community and that usually their votes aligned.

The army vehicles that were supposed to have been set aside for the arrests were not available. The Honolulu Police Department then provided men and squad cars. Burns divided the arresting teams by districts. When officers arrived at the homes of those to be arrested, they sometimes found that an individual in question already had packed a bag. After having been interviewed repeatedly, this was only logical. These were awkward, sad moments. One member of the police force, a tall, athletic man of Japanese ancestry, was mortified when he was required to arrest a frail, bent priest in the distant leeward district of Wai'anae.

Plan III conditions prevailed—that is, Hawai'i was under attack, and much of the American naval fleet was "missing," meaning it was on fire or sunk. However, Shivers led a Plan II response. He stuck to the shortest arrest list, meaning the "A" list of people who were alleged to be the greater threat, as opposed to the larger "B" list and the much larger "C" list.

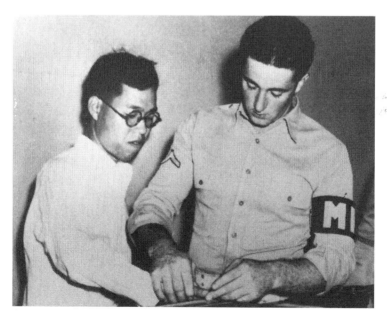

Approximately five hundred people on the FBI/Army list were arrested and booked in the first two days of war. Japanese Cultural Center of Hawai'i.

On Oʻahu, persons of Japanese ancestry were arrested on December 7, and Germans and Italians were arrested on December 8. Shivers also made telephone calls resulting in arrests on the neighboring islands, including Molokaʻi (four arrests) and Lānaʻi (two). During these first two days, 391 people of Japanese ancestry were arrested, along with 93 people of German ancestry and 13 of Italian ancestry, for a total of 497.

The consular agents were arrested, as were the keepers of the Shinto temples and many of the priests of the Buddhist temples, leaving the majority of the Japanese community without spiritual support in their daily lives or in instances of peril or death. Language-school teachers were arrested. Wholesalers and retailers whose business caused them to travel to Japan or to stockpile goods from Japan were particularly vulnerable. So were fishermen. The Japanese fishing fleet was assumed to pose a danger, even though the FBI investigated the fishermen after December 7 and found them blameless. The publisher, editor, and news reporters of the *Nippu Jiji* were arrested, as were various additional newspaper men of Japanese ancestry.

The police department commandeered the Yokohama Specie Bank, which was located in the heart of downtown on Merchant Street directly across the street from the HPD. It was used to book, fingerprint, and interrogate those who had been arrested. It was one of three Japanese banks taken over, along with Pacific Bank and Sumitomo Bank, none to ever reopen.[13]

After the arrests of December 7 and 8, the number of arrests began a slow creep upward. By December 16, the total was 543. As a group, those arrested represented much of the traditional leadership of the Japanese community. The underlying concept was to neutralize the first generation. Even Burns, renowned as an advocate for the Japanese, said that in the heat of the moment, he bought into the idea of "taking the leadership." They were described as enemy aliens, even though many had become more attached to Hawaiʻi or the United States, or both, than to Japan. They had been barred from becoming naturalized citizens of the United States, which left them "alien" in a narrowly legalistic sense, as various observers frequently stated.

A number of Americans of Japanese ancestry who had been extensively educated in Japan were also arrested. Their identity and legal status were obscured by the word *kibei,* which referred to returning home. When Shivers first met with his inner circle of six Nisei advisers, his primary subject of discussion was the *kibei*. He and other key figures in intelligence remained convinced that *kibei* posed a security threat to America in wartime. Their arrests crossed the line into the incarceration of American citizens without a semblance of due process.

None of these people—consular agents, priests, teachers, businessmen, journalists, or *kibei*—was ever charged with a wrongdoing. No specific evidence was ever presented against anyone. Rather, as noted, the arrests were made because of an individual's social, cultural, educational, linguistic, religious, or economic proximity to Japan. Needless to say, this metric was highly subjective and in violation of the subject's constitutional rights.

Families were not notified in a timely way of the whereabouts of their loved ones. With the civilian courts closed and habeas corpus suspended, those in custody had no representation and no legal means by which attorneys could demand their appearance in court. It was a matter of judgment without trial. With all powers vested in the military government, the legal status of the prisoners was thrown into a limbo of lawlessness.

Some of the arrested Issei absorbed the blow with equanimity. Some were scarred. Some whispered the epithet *inu*—dog, spy—to insult Japanese Americans who worked with the intelligence agencies and who, despite the protestations of Yoshida and others, inevitably were suspected of naming names.

Taken together, the FBI arrests and the declaration of martial law marked the beginning of the country's abandonment of constitutional government during World War II.

When Japan bombed Pearl Harbor, Green was living at a small hotel on the edge of Waikīkī. Hearing the explosions, he grabbed his sidearm and drove as fast as he could to his office at Fort Shafter. He was suddenly overwhelmed by a notion that he was not really a lawyer but, at heart, a line officer. He threw a book at the wall, enraged, then rushed on to Short's office, where he found the commander in shock. He next went to Pearl Harbor and the contiguous Hickam Air Field, witnessing horrible casualties. Returning to headquarters, he asked if anyone had reported to General Marshall. No one had, so he placed a call. According to Green, Marshall said, "Bombed? What do you mean bombed?" After listening to the explosions, Marshall then said, "Oh my God," and hung up.[14]

General Short then drove with Green to 'Iolani Palace in downtown Honolulu to talk with Poindexter. They insisted that Poindexter abandon the territorial government's M-Day law in favor of an outright declaration of martial law. In the heat of the moment, Green's backup plan suddenly had become Plan A. He took a declaration of martial law from his briefcase and placed it in front of Poindexter. Poindexter rambled. He said a bomb had gone off in front of him on his way to the Palace.[15] Short expressed concern. Poindexter shrugged, saying he had lived a long life. Poindexter asked if the Japanese were going to attack again. Short said he was preparing for the worst.

Poindexter worried that the Honolulu Police Department did not have enough officers, and that some were of Japanese ancestry. He said Filipinos and Chinese might turn on the Japanese and slaughter them, or that "the Japanese might go over to the enemy, and that in any of these events the local police would be virtually helpless and that thousands of innocent people might be injured or killed."

To this terrifying description, Green later would add, "[Poindexter] said that he already had unconfirmed reports of Japanese insurrection," which were false. Poindexter wondered aloud whether the Japanese community would remain loyal to the United States. Short and Green said they didn't know. Poindexter walked out onto the lanai of the palace, where Queen Lili'uokalani once had watched the American soldiers take up positions in a show of support for the missionary-descended insurrectionists of 1893. The governor stared at a hole in the palace lawn, where a shell had exploded. He was silent for several minutes, then motioned for Short and Green to join him. They talked about the hole. Green quoted Poindexter as saying to Short, "General, I have thought it through. I feel that the situation is beyond me and the civil authorities and I think the safety of the Territory and its citizens require me to declare martial law." The meeting recessed. Poindexter spoke with Shivers a third time by telephone.

When Short, Green, and Poindexter reconvened, Poindexter signed the draft declaration. They shook hands all around. "I wish you luck," Poindexter said. "You people are in charge now and you have my sympathy." Thereafter, Poindexter continued to preside over various functions of domestic government, but in effect he became window dressing in the U.S. Army's exercise of power over Hawai'i. Governmental administration, lawmaking (in the form of General Orders), the interpretation of laws, and punishment for breaking laws—all were now in the hands of the Hawaiian Department of the Army. The constitutional rights of the citizenry were suspended, including habeas corpus, the ancient right of an imprisoned person to appear before a judge. Likewise, the right to a trial by a jury of one's peers, the right to freedom of assembly, freedom of the press, and free speech, were suspended.

In the moment of crisis, no one protested the loss of constitutional government in Hawai'i. With Green as the point man, General Short became military governor.[16] Green immediately moved into the palace and stashed a rifle behind a curtain, determined to shoot it out in case of an uprising by the Japanese population. In addition to declaring martial law, he issued the first thirty-one of his previously drafted General Orders, with more than a hundred yet to come.

General Order Number One directed formation of a six-member civilian advisory committee that included Charles Hemenway. General Order Number Five addressed persons of Japanese ancestry. It restated the position of Army Intelligence at the McKinley High School rally, promising that if people complied with security regulations and the law, "They shall be undisturbed in the peaceful pursuit of their lives and their occupations and be accorded the consideration due all peaceful and law-abiding persons." Contrary to what lay ahead on the West Coast, the phrasing borrowed from the limitations on wartime internment as had been proclaimed by President Wilson in World War I.

Looking back from a conventional wisdom that now regards the internment as reprehensible, we might ask what people today might have done? One such person who asked that question in the moment was the writer Blake Clark, a young teacher who was living on Punahou Street in the home of one-time territorial governor Walter Frear. Frear's gardener, Yamato, and his maid, Hatsu, were aliens. Their wages supported the education of their son in Japan. Clark prided himself on believing in their trustworthiness, but of December 7 he wrote, "I had more hope than conviction that I had been right." That night, after a day of witnessing bomb craters and dead bodies in the streets, he struggled to sleep. "I remembered all the horror stories I had heard about yard men being prepared to cut off the heads of their employers," he wrote. "Absurd, but as I groped around in the dark I thought of Yamato and his efficiency. Ashamed to let anyone else know what I was thinking, I slipped downstairs and brought in the outside keys to the front and back doors."[17]

Following the bombing, the Council for Interracial Unity went into action on its own authority. Members regrouped within minutes. As if scripted, it was Hung Wai Ching who telephoned Shigeo Yoshida to tell him about the bombing. Yoshida recorded five aspects of his reaction. The first four were fear, anxiety, uncertainty, and anger. He was angry at Japan, and he was flooded by fear that someone who shared his Japanese ancestry might engage in sabotaging the U.S. military. He was reasonably confident that he, Ching, and their cohorts had done their prewar work well, but no one could be certain. Even one instance of sabotage, he knew, might cause the strained social relations of Hawai'i to come undone. Yoshida's fifth reaction was hope that out of the war might come a better future.[18]

In the immediate aftermath of the bombing, Hawai'i's people responded well. Yoshida initiated numerous meetings with schoolteachers and principals. Ching met with church groups. Various individuals talked with Japanese immigrants who spoke little or no English. The message was to stay calm, trust authority, and support the war effort.

Calm did prevail. Interracial friction was largely absent. There was no violence. People worked energetically to meet the many problems brought on by the bombing. There was no sabotage.

Although formal jurisdiction over internal security shifted from the FBI to the army's martial law government, the effective exercise of authority was unchanged. Two days after the bombing, General Short issued an order saying that no one would either be detained or released except on Shivers's signature. Short thereby assigned the most key security function to a public official (Shivers) who was widely acquainted with the Japanese community—the person who was advised by Hemenway, Ching, Yoshida, and circles of Nisei, including, at his home, the student Shizue Kobotake.

Through Shivers's restrained approach, an informal process of vouching for a person's loyalty occurred. Burns believed that by vouching to Shivers for individuals on the arrest list, he saved many people from the initial detainment. Ching said he got several of his friends out of internment. One was a high school friend who worked for the Kodak photography laboratory, a form of employment that attracted scrutiny. "I told Bob [Shivers], 'No way this person was dangerous,'" Ching recalled, "and Bob let him out, just like that." The attorney Masaji Marumoto visited the Sand Island camp on Christmas Eve and secured the release of several more individuals. Yasutaro Soga, editor of *Nippu Jiji*, wrote that at least ten were let out in the first days or weeks from the Sand Island camp. He attributed most of these to circumstances such as illness or advanced age. Those released included a fisherman, two bankers, an accountant for a Christian church, and two Christian ministers.[19]

It is debatable how many individuals were released from confinement as a result of vouching. Undoubtedly, it influenced the resulting narrative.[20] It was a counterweight against fear indiscriminately sweeping the vulnerable into an ever-widening roundup. During the initial period of fewer than five hundred arrests in Hawai'i, seven times that number were arrested in the Pacific Coast communities. The contrast suggests that internal-security arrests were significantly the result of local dynamics playing against the pressures and prejudices of the federal government, as opposed to being the direct result of federal policy. While it is true that anti-Japanese sentiments existed in Hawai'i, the main threats to the Japanese community were not from within but from the president of the United States, the secretary of the navy, and the actively anti-Japanese bigots of the West Coast states.

In the lead-up to the war, the commander of the Hawaiian Army Department, General Short, had spelled out the idea that trust builds trust. He had guided Shivers and the national government away from prosecuting the community representatives of Japan's consulate. He had engaged with the community in the McKinley High School rally. He had supported the Nisei draftees. He had articulated a far-sighted army policy toward the Japanese community that otherwise eluded the War Department as well as Americans high and low.

Memory of his positive contributions was swept away by a day that, in President Roosevelt's appositive phrase to Congress, would live in infamy. The fixation of history became the Pearl Harbor attack. Along with the naval commander, Admiral Husband Kimmel, Short was blamed for a lack of preparedness. In addition to his clustering the air fleet (on Marshall's order), Short was haunted by an incident on the evening of December 6, in which Shivers and Bicknell alerted him to the FBI's intercept of the Mori telephone call to Japan. Short thought that, as evidence of an impending attack, the conversation about what flowers were in bloom was unconvincing. This and many other recriminations about Pearl Harbor were to reverberate for decades, the subject of no fewer than eight federal investigations. Ten days after the bombing, Short was dismissed from his post.

His successor, General Delos C. Emmons, arrived in Hawai'i on December 16. For three days prior to his arrival, Secretary of the Navy Frank Knox had toured Hawai'i, loudly blaming Japan's success on O'ahu's

Japanese-ancestry population. Knox had demanded retribution. Returning to Washington, D.C., on December 19, he proposed to Roosevelt that the U.S. government remove and incarcerate all Japanese aliens from O'ahu. Roosevelt agreed.[21] Accordingly, only twelve days into the war, the commander in chief was in the Knox camp, if not yet publicly.

Clearly, Emmons was under immense pressure to quickly figure out a course of action. For this, he was an interesting choice. He had learned to fly an airplane only thirteen years after the first flight of the Wright Brothers. He was a contemporary of the famous William "Billy" Mitchell, who had led the American bombing raids in World War I and who was later court-martialed for too aggressively insisting that the air service be made a coequal branch of the military. He enjoyed a close relationship with Mitchell's successor, Harold "Hap" Arnold, who had systematically built up the Army Air Corps after Mitchell's departure. Between 1934 and 1936, Emmons had commanded the Army Air Corps in Hawai'i. When an eruption of the Kīlauea volcano on Hawai'i Island threatened Hilo, he personally had bombed the river of lava to divert it. He could recite the time required by various aircraft to fly to strategic destinations, such as the airstrip on Midway Island, at the far northwestern end of the Hawaiian archipelago.

Prior to his reassignment to Hawai'i, Emmons had served as the executive officer to the chief of the Army Air Corps and also as chief assistant for air to the assistant secretary of war, Robert A. Lovette. In 1939 he headed the Army Air Force combat command, which included defense of the air space over Washington, D.C. In 1940, he was one of three American military officers sent to London to consult with the British during Germany's massive aerial bombings. In addition to being a pilot, he was a scholar, earning a doctorate degree at Marshall University.

Despite the controversy over how air power should be organized, Emmons conspicuously adhered to the concept of unity of command. Because a lack of coordination between army and navy was partly blamed for the Pearl Harbor disaster, acceptance of a unified command was a paramount value in the moment. It meant that Emmons would cooperate closely with the new five-star admiral of the Pacific fleet, Chester W. Nimitz, and that he would subordinate himself to Nimitz's overall leadership in the Pacific theater of war.

For all of these reasons, Emmons was a good fit. To succeed in his assignment, he had to get along with the navy, the army chief of staff, the War Department, and the president of the United States. He also

General Delos Emmons arrived on December 16 to take charge of Hawai'i. He was quickly surrounded by advisers who believed in the loyalty of Japanese Americans and their potential contribution to the war effort. Library of Congress.

had to repair the ruins of the island's aerial defense while contributing to plans for counterattacking Japan. At fifty-three, he was in an optimal age range. Given the risks that he soon was to take, his strong résumé would be crucial to his survival.

Simultaneously with Emmons taking command, the role of the Council for Interracial Unity was being defined. A *kama'āina* business executive, Frederick Simpich Jr., hosted a community-level meeting at 'Iolani Palace on December 15 in his capacity as director of the Office of Civilian Defense.[22] The meeting prominently included Hemenway, Yoshida, Ching, Masa Katagiri, Dr. Miles Cary, and Charles Loomis. The latter then was general secretary of the Institute for Pacific Relations. The meeting focused on incorporating community advisers into the martial law government. Simpich was mainly concerned with ways to reduce public panic. He asked the committee to designate one of its members to work as a full-time volunteer in Civil Defense. By virtue of General Order One, Hemenway was a member of the government's six-member civilian advisory group and the only adviser who was not a public officeholder. The other five were the civilian governor, the territorial secretary, the chair of the Board of Agriculture and Forestry, the acting attorney general, and the mayor of Honolulu.[23] Green was to say, with a certain smugness, that the group met only once. If so, it was enough time for Hemenway to make effective recommendations to the army on how the community should be represented in the martial law system.

Along with Yoshida and Ching, Loomis of IPR became the third nominee for working in the Civil Defense agency. It seems likely it was at this point that Yoshida wrote the four-page history that described the work of the Council for Interracial Unity as it thus far had unfolded after December 7. "The office," he wrote, "was determined to deal with not only the emergency but with how people were to live together over the long term." Its purpose was to maintain relationships "in the spirit of unity" among the various racial groups. "The office feels this to be its function because it already has lanes open through the community."[24] He claimed legitimacy for the group because it created an atmosphere of inclusion among a wide diversity of people: Filipinos, Japanese Americans, alien Japanese, Chinese, Koreans, long-settled Caucasians (*kama'āina* haole), newcomer Caucasians (*malihini* haole), the army, the navy, the Chamber of Commerce, public school educators, churches, temples, labor unions, civic associations, fraternal groups, the American Legion, and the Hawaiian Sugar Planters' Association pickup.

Hemenway met with Simpich on December 16, the second day running. He submitted Yoshida's memorandum along with two letters in draft form. In response to Simpich's request for one volunteer, one of the letters gave only the name of Loomis, who was likely a reassuring figure to Simpich. Loomis was older, and his work in the IPR and YMCA

connected him with influential Caucasians. The second letter named
Loomis, Yoshida, and Ching. The following day, the second letter was
accepted. This decision, favoring a three-member group, was crucial
even in the short run. It legitimized the roles of Yoshida and Ching, and
it made for an explicitly interracial Morale Section that served as an
emblem of inclusiveness.[25]

The December 18 *Honolulu Star-Bulletin* carried a front-page
announcement of Yoshida's eight steps, the most key step being that
"every loyal citizen, regardless of race, [will] be given a place in the
scheme of national defense." The announcement specifically addressed
aliens "who must accept the fact that they owe a certain obligation to
the land in which they are now living." If they did so, "they will be protected and allowed to enjoy all normal privileges [but] only as long as
they obey our laws and conduct themselves constructively." The final
point of the mission statement was, "Make clear to the people that loyalty grows only when it is given a chance to grow. It does not flourish in
an atmosphere of suspicion, discrimination, and denial of opportunities to practice that loyalty."[26]

The interracial composition of the Morale Section would be a key
to its survival. The reason was that the army tended to ignore the white
oligarchy. *Kama'āina* Caucasians who had volunteered to serve in the
martial law government became isolated, Simpich among them. By himself, Loomis probably would have been treated similarly. But Loomis,
Ching, and Yoshida, along with their numerous community connections, became more important than the sum of their parts.

Following a logic of urgent interests, the Morale Section was quickly
reassigned from Simpich's Civil Defense office to Army Intelligence. This
was another step toward effectiveness, because it put the Morale Section
at the heart of the twin questions of loyalty and participation in the war
effort. Clearly the word "morale" was about much more than public esprit
de corps. It was a crucial aspect of internal security. It was not about feeling good but rather about the deeper security that results from groups
and community forces having trust and confidence in one another. A
new description of the Morale Section said it acted as a liaison between
government and community on "general adjustment to war." It listed the
ingredients of morale as good health, economic security, psychological
security, confidence in associates, loyalty, and common purpose.[27]

The new head of Army Intelligence, Colonel Kendall Fielder,
emerged as a sympathetic ally. Fielder was from Georgia, yet another

southerner who became an advocate for the Nisei in Hawai'i. He had
worked with Nisei soldiers in the field in an earlier post as commander
of the 298th Regiment of the Hawaiian National Guard. As a result, he
spoke from experience about the Nisei soldier. He further attributed his
views to Short's thesis that loyalty was a two-way street. He named Ching,
Loomis, and Burns as major influences.[28]

Following the bombing, Fielder went with Ching to the plantations of
O'ahu, where they talked to the Filipino workers about getting along with
the Japanese workers. Fielder was an amateur magician, and he liked to
tell jokes. He would start his plantation presentations with card tricks,
tell a joke, and then deliver a stern statement about patriotism. He urged
the Filipinos to distinguish between Japanese Americans and "Japs" in
Japan's military. He then would turn the program over to Ching.

Fielder was the Morale Section's direct connection to the top of the
army command. Under the intense pressures of the war, egos seemingly
were submerged. It was apparently not a problem that Ching remained
under Shivers's sway and that he would say he worked under Shivers's
control. What mattered was that the threesome of Ching, Yoshida, and
Loomis seemed always to work together smoothly.[29] Although Loomis was
a presence and the nominal head, it was Ching who had the visceral drive
for leadership. In this configuration, Yoshida was Ching's partner and
guiding strategist. "Shigeo," Ching would say, "was my spiritual brother."

In the division of work between inside and outside activity, Ching was
the natural outside man. He knew people of many shades and accents.
He was acquainted with corporate executives, society women, liberals,
labor organizers, and leftists. He boasted of drinking with the wife of
the tycoon Walter Dillingham, and he was on friendly terms with the
socialist labor leader Jack Hall. As a result of his ROTC experience,
by 1941 he was a U.S. Army Reserve captain and soon would be a lieutenant colonel. He was self-assured with army people. He knew their
language. Some called him "Generalissimo," or "Gitmo," for Chiang
Kai-shek, the warlord who ruled China. Ching didn't mind. The United
States needed Chiang Kai-shek, and it needed China to survive Japan's
onslaught. With a high-level security clearance, he could travel wherever he wished, and he was about to access the War Department and the
White House.

Yoshida's role was narrowed by his Japanese ancestry. With no security
clearance, he was left to lead by the force of ideas. His speaking and

writing skills impacted people's thinking. He was capable of both a sharp focus and a wide peripheral vision. He saw the moment, which he lived with intensity, while holding within himself the burden of history and the possibilities of the future. He was outwardly calm but, understanding the stakes as he did, he was relentless, sometimes to the point of desperation. He did not suffer small talk gladly, but he accepted the necessity of repeating himself for the sake of effectiveness. The barriers of race and class erected by the white elite irritated him. When he became frustrated, he would lecture himself on the importance of equanimity. Shivers called him "The Samurai"—this at a time when things Japanese were toxic. Whether Yoshida merely smiled, or whether he told Shivers about the two family swords in his closet, was never recorded.

Yoshida's incessant linking of the wartime with a postwar world to come—"How we get along during the war will determine how we get along when the war is over"—was not his alone. But he was particularly eloquent. He burned this sentence into the minds of others. What was more, he was the only person of Japanese ancestry who directly advised the martial law government.

With Ching, Yoshida, and Loomis inside the door of martial law, the center of gravity shifted. It was no longer the Big Five and the sugar planters alone who had a place at the table but the network of people who had worked together through the public schools, the university, the YMCA, and the IPR.

As an exercise in crisis management, Hawai'i's nonvoting delegate to Congress, the Republican Samuel Wilder King, flew in from Washington, D.C., and convened a meeting with local business executives in the Throne Room of 'Iolani Palace. The meeting went on day after day. These were men who were accustomed to having their way, but Green was not convinced of their capacity to cope with the crisis. The day Emmons arrived, he called King and the assembled executives upstairs to Emmons's office, the one-time office of the monarch. King said they had agreed the civilian sector could not manage things in Hawai'i as before. He asked what the army could do. Green audaciously laid out a plan for the army to oversee food production, labor supply, shipping, ground transportation, and the setting of priorities. When the assembled executives began debating who should be in charge of setting priorities, Emmons asked (at least in Green's account), "Can't you birds agree?" Green volunteered to become what he called the director of planning and priorities, whereupon Emmons endorsed Green's proposal. "The visitors were excused," Green wrote, "and filed out like a lot of school boys."[30]

Thereafter, Emmons functioned as military governor, Green functioned as his executive officer, and an army officer designated by Green, Major Bertram Hagford, directed planning and priorities. Only beneath these three layers did haole executives serve as volunteers to guide local affairs. Through such maneuvers, their influence waned sharply, and military control tightened.

Between Emmons's mid-1930s posting and his return in 1941, he found that community figures in Hawai'i were more inclined than previously to show support for the Japanese community. His predecessors, Short, Herron, and Briant Wells, all vouched for the Nisei. Nisei were serving ably in the army, and Nisei community leaders were more confident and assertive. In some settings, an ease of relationship occurred. Dr. Isaac Kawasaki, an army medical doctor, played golf with Emmons shortly after his arrival. Emmons asked what he should do about the Japanese. Kawasaki said he should leave them alone to go about their lives.[31]

A discussion quickly got underway around the idea of Emmons making a reassuring radio broadcast to the people of Hawai'i. The Morale Section argued that an indiscriminate evacuation and relocation would be folly.[32] Loyalty was a two-way process, and the smartest thing the government could do, they advised, was reinforce people's positive feelings about America. Further, they warned that the arrests, although limited in number, were causing anxiety and fear.

After Emmons confirmed with Shivers that neither espionage nor sabotage was at work, he agreed to speak to the public by radio on his fourth day in Hawai'i. Ching said he was asked to write a seven-minute speech aimed at calming the listening public. He turned to Yoshida, who quickly produced a draft that ran exactly seven minutes. Yoshida's central role in the writing process was the irony that so delighted Ching and moved him to exclaim, "Me, write that speech? I didn't write that speech! Buddhahead wrote that speech! Shigeo Yoshida!"

Emmons called for an inclusive approach to the war. He took notice of the fact that some people had been let go from their jobs because of fear and suspicion. He praised employers who had calmed down after their initial panic and rehired laid-off workers. "[If] the courage of the people of these Islands is to be maintained and the morale of the entire population sustained," Emmons said, "we cannot afford to unnecessarily and indiscriminately keep a number of loyal workers from useful employment." He acknowledged that some people had been taken into custody. He said they were to be thought of as detainees, not prisoners of war, and would be treated humanely. He promised that family visitation with detainees would occur shortly.

He repeated the central theme of the McKinley rally: "As you have been told before, there is no intention or desire on the part of the Federal authorities to operate mass concentration camps." Despite Japan's attack, "we must remember that this is America and we must do things in the American way . . . [and] we must not knowingly and deliberately deny any loyal citizen the opportunity to exercise or demonstrate his loyalty in a concrete way."

Although he echoed the widespread misimpression that sabotage had occurred, he downplayed its importance. He said there had been "very few cases of actual sabotage," a phrasing he later was to refute altogether. He ended by recalling his two years of residence in Hawai'i in the mid-1930s. "I feel that I know the people here," he said, "their loyalty to the American way of life and the extent to which they can be counted on to help our mutual defense."

The speech dealt with both avoidance of a mass internment and inclusion in the war effort, the same themes, rendered in the same style, as the speech that Yoshida had written in midsummer for Marston of Army Intelligence. In the aftermath of the radio broadcast, Yoshida wrote a report to Army Intelligence saying that the speech had a "reassuring effect among the enemy aliens and their children." Accordingly, Yoshida not only had advocated for the speech and written it, but then advised the army command that it had gone over well.

Emmons's broadcast was yet another marker of the divergence of views between Honolulu and Washington, D.C. As the door of national life was slamming shut on Japanese Americans, the interracial movement in Hawai'i had put a foot in the door. Hemenway, Yoshida, Ching, Loomis, Burns, Katagiri, Marumoto, and Miles Cary, with the collaboration of their converts, prominently including Shivers, Emmons, Green, and Fielder, had entered into a widely publicized agreement that there would be no mass roundup.

Green credited the Morale Section with holding him to his opposition to mass internment in the heat of war. He confessed to moments of doubt but wrote that he relied on the three men for reassurance that his faith in the Japanese community was justified. Green described

Yoshida, Ching, and Loomis as they were being honored by the martial law government.
Courtesy of Ching album.

Loomis as "a highly personable and diplomatic Caucasian." Of Ching,
he wrote, "He had the ability to present a seemingly unperturbed coun-
tenance, regardless of adverse circumstances. His exceptionally keen
mind matched his affability." And of Yoshida, he wrote, "He was a man
of fine educational background and experience . . . a clear thinker and
a person of unusual intelligence."[33] Green was further assured by the
fact that the Morale Section worked smoothly with Army Intelligence
and Naval Intelligence, the FBI, and the Honolulu Police Department's
Captain Burns, whom Green described as "a specialist in dealing with
Oriental affairs." "In this manner," Green wrote, "all their efforts were
coordinated."[34]

Green thought of the Morale Section as a go-between with a crucial degree of autonomy: "The section operated with little supervision
from us for the reason that the activity was as much a representative of
the peoples concerned as it was of ours."[35] Green's acceptance of the
Morale Section's autonomous features was a seeming paradox, insofar
as his reputation was about control. What mattered was the Morale Section's role as an honest voice, an honest broker. The YMCA's Nuʻuanu

Branch provided its office space. Loomis was paid by the IPR, Ching was paid by the YMCA, and the Department of Public Instruction paid Yoshida.

For people from the U.S. Mainland such as Green, multiracial Hawai'i was substantially different from anything they previously had seen. For the outsider, the contradictions and injustices of Hawai'i were not so apparent as the atmosphere of diversity, tolerance, and inclusivity. Hawai'i was modeling practices that were all but absent from the American imagination. Hawai'i was suggestive. How far its suggestions might travel, only the months and years of war would reveal.

CHAPTER 7

The Cry of Sabotage

ALTHOUGH THE PEOPLE OF HAWAIʻI WERE the direct victims of Japan's attack, they mainly responded with a rational understanding of the facts, rather than falling into the grip of rumors. In contrast, America's millions of people experienced the event via news clips and mainly responded by embracing falsehoods. Across the country, rumors of an enemy within overran reality—a phenomenon eventually to be ascribed to wartime hysteria and a failure of leadership.

A deeper history flowed not from panic in the moment but from a longtime fear of sabotage. At the center of this legacy was President Franklin Roosevelt, who in many ways embodied the accumulated fears of the country. Roosevelt came of age preoccupied with national security. As a schoolboy he first had become acquainted with his distant cousin, Theodore Roosevelt. Surely it was a proud moment for Franklin when the *former* president Theodore Roosevelt spoke to his prep school class. At Theodore's urging, young Franklin repeatedly read Captain Alfred Mahan's *Influence of Sea Power Upon History*. When the adult Franklin entered public life, his first step was to secure the post that Theodore first had held, assistant secretary of the navy. In this capacity, Franklin served Woodrow Wilson's administration from 1913 to 1920, encompassing World War I. He was intimately familiar with the fact that Germany had attempted to forge passports, incite labor unrest, disrupt munitions production, and plant bombs within the territorial United States on bridges, canals, and merchant marine ships.[1] The U.S. Secret Service warned Roosevelt that German agents were plotting to assassinate him, and for a time he carried a revolver. Although President Wilson minimized the internment of German aliens and German Americans, he told Congress as early as 1915 that immigrants "have poured the poison of disloyalty into the very arteries of our national life." During the war, Wilson established a Committee on Public Information that consistently stoked anti-German sentiment.[2]

Thereafter Franklin Roosevelt ran for elective office, winning the governorship of New York State, as had Theodore, and then winning the presidency in 1932, a mere twenty-four years after Theodore. Shortly after taking office, Franklin remarked that war with Japan was inevitable, and that it might as well come soon. When he visited Hawai'i in 1934, his trip was widely interpreted as a warning to Tokyo. His ship docked with a flourish at Pearl Harbor, which he studied intently. He conferred with his military commanders, reviewed troops at Schofield Barracks, and watched a live gunfire demonstration.[3]

The *Nippu Jiji* newspaper made an original portrait of Roosevelt that became the centerpiece of its front-page welcome. When he went fishing on the Big Island, the Japanese Fisherman's Association wished him, via a newspaper advertisement, "Good Fishing." Others in the Japanese community similarly attempted to pay their respects and communicate their fealty to America, but he ignored them all.

What most impressed him were stories of the Issei businessmen who visited Japanese ships in port and entertained Japanese sailors. In 1936, a mere eighteen years after the Anglo-Japanese alliance of World War I, Roosevelt wrote a memorandum directing the construction of "concentration camps" in Hawai'i in the event of war. These were to incarcerate anyone of Japanese ancestry who had played host to the ships.[4] Further, he gave a joint army-navy board a vague but ominous directive to "adopt plans relating to the Japanese population of all the Islands." In such thinking, he reflected a national fear of an enemy within that had been magnified by newspaper journalism, books, and movies.

The Presumptive Fifth Column

The threat had reference points in fact. With the rise of Fascism, the German inclination to engage in sabotage and espionage was repeating itself. Germany organized Fifth Column movements in Latin America. It also subsidized propaganda within the United States aimed at reinforcing American isolationism and undermining Roosevelt's 1940 campaign for reelection.[5] On May 27, 1940, Roosevelt broadcast a warning against "the Fifth Column that betrays a nation unprepared for treachery." "Spies, saboteurs and traitors are the actors in this new strategy," Roosevelt said. "These dividing forces are undiluted poison. They must not be allowed to spread in the New World as they have in the Old. Our moral and mental defenses must be raised up as never before against those who would cast a smoke-screen across our vision."[6]

His 1940 Fifth Column broadcast was part of putting the country on a war footing. The first of the Republicans brought into his war cabinet was Secretary of the Navy Frank Knox. Knox was yet another influential figure whose understanding of the world began with the 1898 Spanish-American War. At age twenty-two, he had ridden a bicycle more than a hundred miles to volunteer with Theodore Roosevelt's Rough Riders for the invasion of Cuba. Thereafter he became a newspaper reporter and then a publisher. In 1927 he began a four-year tenure as general manager of the twenty-seven newspapers of the notoriously manipulative Hearst newspaper chain, which had fanned the flames of the Spanish-American War, then over decades had done much to create a poisonous anti-Asian and anti-Japanese climate in America. In 1931, Knox became publisher of the *Chicago Daily News*, where he ran front-page editorials attacking Roosevelt and the New Deal. He raised money for the Republican Party and in 1936 became the Republican nominee for vice president on the ticket of Kansas governor Alf Landon, whom Roosevelt easily defeated for his second of four terms in office.

Although Knox opposed Roosevelt's domestic agenda, he agreed with Roosevelt on the potential threat of the Japanese population in Hawai'i. As early as 1933, anticipating actual war by nine years, Knox advocated evacuation and removal of Hawai'i's Japanese community "before the beginnings of hostility threatens."[7] Although the navy of the mid-1930s did not respond to Roosevelt's directive to build concentration camps in Hawai'i, Knox well might have done so if he had been in office.

Knox was important not only because he was navy secretary but because of his close association with William Donovan, a confidant of the president. At the urging of Knox, Donovan had written a series of four articles for the *Chicago Daily News* about Fifth Column activity in the European War. These were the product of an assessment he had made in Great Britain for Roosevelt, weighing the likelihood of Britain holding out against the German blitz. During this period, Donovan was also consulting with Roosevelt on the sort of intelligence problem that was playing out in Hawai'i—the problem of the FBI, Army Intelligence, and Naval Intelligence shuffling uncertainly around one another without clearly delineating their roles and coordinating their efforts.

In September 1940, Knox and Donovan traveled to Hawai'i on an inspection trip. High-level navy, army, territorial, and business figures gathered over lunch at the Royal Hawaiian Hotel to meet them, in a session chaired by Hemenway. The names present were a roll call of the territorial establishment, including Frank Atherton, Leslie A. Hicks, Vitousek, Poindexter, Generals Herron and Richardson, Admiral Kimmell, and retired General Briant Wells.[8] Knox resurrected the navy's opposition to the Pacific Fleet being based in Pearl Harbor. He articulated the fleet commander's fear that Pearl Harbor was a tight space within reach of Japan's blue water navy. He said the security of the fleet again was under study, particularly in light of Japan's successes with aerial bombing and torpedo attacks from the air. "If war eventuates with Japan," Knox wrote, "it is believed easily possible that hostilities would be initiated by a surprise attack upon the Fleet or the Naval Base at Pearl Harbor."[9]

Knox predicted that an aerial attack by Japan would be accompanied by people of Japanese ancestry engaging in acts of sabotage. "Irresponsible and misguided nationals," Knox wrote, might sink their boats or lay mines in the mouth of Pearl Harbor. In response to his fears, the navy installed iron nets across the harbor entrance, and mine sweepers began patrolling the harbor. Knox wanted more of everything—more air raid drills, more anti-aircraft gunnery, more reconnaissance aircraft, and more hot-pursuit planes, as well as barrage balloons to foil enemy aircraft and smoke-screen pots to hide ships in the event of an aerial attack.

The actual bombing on December 7 made Knox a prophet. When he immediately asked Roosevelt to send him back to Hawai'i to assess the damage, Roosevelt agreed. Again accompanied by Donovan, Knox arrived in Hawai'i on December 11. Robert Shivers's wife wrote a letter describing Knox's visit to a hospital ward filled with the wounded. She said Knox attempted to give a word of solace but was overcome with emotion and left abruptly.[10] Knox almost certainly heard an allegation of a Fifth Column sabotage from the commander of the naval forces, Admiral Husband Kimmel, who on December 12 claimed that confusion caused by the Fifth Column had greatly aided the attack.[11]

Knox told Kimmel that he, Kimmel, had been caught unaware. Kimmel did not disagree. Knox told General Short the same thing. Short did not disagree. Knox returned to Washington three days later, quoting these two conversations to the president and urging removal of the two men. The next day he spoke to the press. Asked if he had seen Fifth Column activity in Hawai'i, Knox replied, "It was the most effective Fifth Column work that has come out of this war except in Norway."[12]

His choice of words was inflammatory beyond present imagination. The "Fifth Column" had entered the American vocabulary by way of the Spanish Civil War. As an invasion force of the Falangist (or Fascist) Army approached Madrid, the Falangist commander boasted of having four columns of troops under his direct command. A fifth column, he said, awaited him inside the city, ready to rise up and subvert the government from within. America's most widely read writer, Ernest Hemingway, was covering the Spanish Civil War as a correspondent, an experience that inspired such classic works as *For Whom the Bell Tolls*. With his hotel under bombardment, Hemingway wrote a play, *The Fifth Column*, which was later the title of a book of short stories. A Fifth Column was the enemy within. When Hitler launched the invasion of Europe, the rapid fall of various countries—Austria, Czechoslovakia, Poland, the Netherlands, France, Finland, Norway—was attributed in part to Fifth Columns of Fascist sympathizers, particularly ethnic Germans who resided in borderlands.

After Pearl Harbor, the conditioned fear of Germany was projected onto Japan. When Knox asserted that Japan's success resulted from Japanese-ancestry people in Hawai'i, he offered no proof. None was asked for. At his first press conference on returning to Washington, reporters failed to ask a single question about what evidence he might offer to back up his assertion. In his report to Roosevelt, he actually began to hedge his claim—apparently unnoticed—by shifting from the tangible act of sabotage to the unseen act of spying; he said "intelligence work" done by a Fifth Column before the attack provided the Japanese Navy with exact knowledge needed to plan the attack. Knox described a non-existent attempted landing on the leeward Waianae Coast by Japanese fifth columnists. Their goal, he said, was to lure U.S. ships at sea into "a submarine trap." Fortunately, he said, the quick-witted command had seen through the ruse before torpedoes struck. What this jumble of words actually meant was altogether unclear, but Knox was undeterred by critical inquiry.

He told Roosevelt that the use of Pearl Harbor should be restudied. Until then, he wrote, "no large concentration of Naval vessels can be permitted at Pearl Harbor."[13] Accordingly, his offhand allegation of a Fifth Column in Hawai'i merged with the toxic—now historically obscure—question of whether Roosevelt should have based the fleet at Pearl Harbor in the first place.

The day of Knox's press conference, the *Christian Science Monitor* asked, "Why was the Japanese 'fifth-column' espionage so successful in Hawaii, as Secretary Knox reports?"[14] The *Cleveland Plain Dealer* said the government "must determine how far into American life the fifth column might have bored." The *Buffalo News* of December 17 said, "One would think that somewhere in the vast ramification of fifth column activity which must have preceded the attack, some inkling would have been discovered by the Army and Navy intelligence services or the civil and military authorities of the islands." Truth was not at issue, even in prestigious publications such as the *New York Times,* which soon would report, in error, "Whites in Hawaii Arm for Defense in Fear of Japanese."[15]

Nine days after the bombing, on December 16, the same day as Knox's press conference, Roosevelt was presented with a fact-based view by a personal adviser, John Franklin Carter, based on reports from the field by a roving observer, Curtis Munson. The first bullet point of Carter's memo was, "No substantial danger of Fifth Column activities by Japanese." Further, he urged the president to make a reassuring statement addressed to loyal Japanese Americans and Japanese aliens. "This is doubly necessary following the Knox 'Fifth Columnist' statement," Carter wrote. He perceptively summarized the quality of internal-security intelligence from Hawai'i: "Navy intelligence poor at Honolulu; F.B.I. excellent; Army Intelligence pretty good."[16]

In other words, as Knox was making headlines about the imagined Fifth Column, Roosevelt was being told by personal advisers that it was untrue, and that the Navy Department's information was unreliable.

On December 18, on the recommendation of Knox, Roosevelt formed a commission to investigate the attack. On the same day, he fired General Short and Admiral Kimmel on Knox's advice. It was on the next day, December 19, that Knox recommended removing from O'ahu all Japanese aliens—about forty thousand people—and putting them in a camp on a neighboring island. Roosevelt agreed. Knox also recommended forming a national commission to apportion the blame for Pearl Harbor. Roosevelt again agreed.

Five years had passed since Roosevelt had directed the construction of concentration camps in Hawai'i.[17] Now his fears were reactivated.

Thereafter, periodically stirred by Knox, Roosevelt's suspicions about the Japanese community of Hawaiʻi would flare.

Eight different investigations were to be conducted by the federal government into the disaster at Pearl Harbor. Of these, the first two were conducted while national policy toward people of Japanese ancestry was being formulated. Accordingly, these first two investigations not only sought to explain what happened but were instrumental in shaping what was to happen. The first investigation was chaired by Owen J. Roberts, an associate justice of the U.S. Supreme Court, whose appointment had been recommended to the president by the ubiquitous McCloy.[18] Roberts's job history was obscured by his black robe. He previously had been a special assistant U.S. attorney assigned to prosecuting espionage and sabotage cases. He also had served as a special judge or "umpire," reviewing the Black Tom arguments that McCloy had made to the international Hague Court and ultimately ruling that Germany had perpetrated the sabotage.[19] With such a background, Roberts was a good candidate for the Fifth Column phobia.

Four other members of the Roberts Commission shared the history of America's entry into the Pacific. Two commissioners were from the army and two from the navy. A recently retired naval officer, Joseph M. "Bull" Reeves, had fought in the Philippine American War that had ensued from the Spanish-American War. William H. Standley, also recently retired, had fought in both the Philippines and Cuba. Frank R. McCoy, a retired army general, likewise had served in both Cuba and the Philippines, part of that time as an aide to General Leonard Wood and also as an aide to Theodore Roosevelt. Only the fifth commissioner was of less than advanced age and more useful to the war effort, Brigadier General Joseph T. McNarney.

The Roberts Commission convened overnight on December 18 in Washington, D.C., then quickly moved on to Hawaiʻi, where it spent several days each at army and navy headquarters. On January 6, 1942, a month into the war, the commission began taking testimony from witnesses at the Royal Hawaiian Hotel on Waikīkī Beach. The commissioners heard from 127 witnesses. All sessions were closed and the testimony classified.

The most obvious agenda was fixing blame on the Hawaiian army and navy commands. The recurring and closely related subject was blaming the imagined Fifth Column. Failing to develop evidence that local "Japanese" had sabotaged the U.S. military during the attack, the commission turned to espionage. It was much as Knox had done in his public pronouncements, shifting the subject from the potentially visible act of sabotage to the hidden treachery of espionage. The commissioners' questions often began with a preamble to the effect that Japan's attack was based on "perfect information," and that it must have been derived not only from professional spies but from Japan's network of consular agents. *Kibei* were a frequent subject of accusatory questioning, as was the recent influx of Nisei into the U.S. Army and the Hawaiian Territorial Guard. Japanese aliens, Japanese American civilians, and American soldiers were discussed as a single subject, often in context of a feared second attack on Hawai'i.

Certain local witnesses stood fast against the commission's rhetorical questioning. Lester Petrie, the elected mayor of Honolulu, said he had been brought to Hawai'i as a two-year-old and first had worked alongside Japanese on the railroad. "I have practically grown up with them," Petrie said, "and I know a great many of them." The younger generation, he said, "are pretty well Americanized." As to the aging Issei, he said, "I think they are looking for peace." An executive of the Maui Pineapple Company, Bernard J. Butler, said he was born in San Francisco in an atmosphere of anti-Japanese prejudice. When he moved to Hawai'i, "I didn't want to have anything to do with them." However, as an executive in the pineapple canneries, Butler found himself differentiating among individuals. "I have found myself no longer generalizing," he testified, "and I have found now that there are Japanese whom I have implicit and utmost faith in, and there are ones I wouldn't trust around the corner, just as there are white men I wouldn't have faith in and I wouldn't trust around the corner."[20]

Justice Roberts asked the retired Hawaiian army commander Briant Wells if he had been worried about sabotage or espionage prior to December 7. Wells replied he was aware of dire predictions that the docks would be burned and the waterworks would be blown up. "I never believed these things," he said, "[and] none of these things ever happened." Wells specifically struck at Knox's charge that Hawai'i had experienced an unparalleled Fifth Column. "This is slanderous," he said. "It is not true." Not to be deterred, Roberts asked what Wells knew about consular agents. Wells said he had concluded from investigation they were not espionage agents but "just Japanese desiring to keep in touch with their people," and, further, they were reliable individuals who worked for a living. Did Wells favor rounding up the Japanese community and deporting them to a single, guarded island? Wells said mass evacuation was an outlandish notion that he had discarded years ago. The commissioners persisted: What if Japan's military attacked Hawai'i a second time, would members of the Japanese community engage in sabotage? Wells replied: "I cannot imagine a more favorable opportunity for sabotage than that which was here on December the seventh, and nothing happened."[21]

Among Naval Intelligence officers who testified, Lieutenant George P. Kimball stood out. He was one of the several Hawai'i residents who had been activated from the Naval Reserves, along with the attorneys William Stephenson and Samuel P. King, son of Delegate to Congress Samuel Wilder King. Of the navy's Nisei network, Kimball said, "I think they were as much in the dark . . . [as] the rest of us." The navy's district intelligence officer, Captain I. H. Mayfield, presented a curiously ambiguous testimony that came close to describing the real history of Axis spying in Hawai'i. He said no one really knew anything except that a single German national, Otto Kuehn, had been caught spying for Japan. Were Japanese Americans of any help to him? Very little, Mayfield said, echoing Kimball, because Japanese Americans knew nothing more than anyone else.

U.S. District Attorney Angus Taylor was unequivocally antagonistic toward the Japanese community. He said the consular agents' loyalty to Japan had been known a long while, and no one had done anything about it. Taylor took the opportunity to criticize Shivers for consulting with Nisei such as Yoshida and Marumoto. He said such relationships resulted in testimony for the loyalty of the Nisei that then was handed up through the hierarchy to the heads of intelligence agencies, who erroneously concluded that Nisei were loyal to the United States.

No one went so far off the deep end as a navy captain, Elias Zacharias, who as a young officer had served and studied in Japan and regarded himself as profoundly knowledgeable of the Japanese mind. Zacharias had just come in from a tour of duty at sea. He previously had served in the Office of Naval Intelligence (ONI) and soon was to return to ONI as its acting head. He described the Issei as likely enemy agents. The *kibei*, he said, were so tainted by intimate contact with militarists in Japan as to be even more dangerous. Nisei who had never been to Japan were also a potential danger, in his view, as a result of contact with visiting naval officers and dignitaries. Zacharias said he recently had tried unsuccessfully to find Nisei in San Francisco to spy on Japanese in the Bay area, which by a twist of logic he found to be further evidence of their disloyalty. General McNarney said if the situation on the U.S. Mainland was so bad, the situation in Hawai'i must be worse. Zacharias agreed, saying that Japanese in Hawai'i "have been subjected to real racial discrimination, which is nonexistent on the West Coast." His evidence was that wealthy Japanese had access to certain golf courses on the Mainland but not in Hawai'i. On parting, Justice Roberts told Zacharias he was deeply obliged to a person of such vast experience.

His performance before the Roberts Commission might be dismissed as a historical curiosity of misinformation, except that as the head of ONI he later was to play a major role in the federal government's handling of Japanese Americans in the detention camps.

The Roberts Commission spent sixteen days in Hawai'i. It then worked another twelve days in Washington, D.C., and hurriedly authored its findings. Even for this fear-ridden period, the report was oddly contorted. It began by saying there was an understandable deficiency of war matériel, a point that had nothing to do with the issues at hand. It next called up Knox's contention that the U.S. Pacific Fleet should not have been based in Pearl Harbor but then dodged the question by saying this was not their business. In its main reference to internal security, it cited the navy's suspicion of consular representatives, Shivers's investigation, and General Short's opposition to their prosecution. By implication, this was a strike against the judgment of Short, who by this time had become a national scapegoat. The report also erroneously recounted the confusion of responsibility among the intelligence agencies, saying that the FBI had total responsibility, thereby relieving the navy from its own failings. It said that while the FBI had tried to uncover espionage, it had not done so. Nonetheless, Roberts reported that espionage was conducted by the two hundred–plus consular agents. In only this one vague yet insidious way, the report conjured the idea that persons of Japanese ancestry in Hawai'i had contributed to the "perfect information" that guided Japan's attackers.

The commission said that in the interest of national security in wartime, it could neither divulge its evidence nor its reasoning, which would not have been possible, since it had neither uncovered evidence nor produced reasoned conclusions.

In the aftermath, no one was ready to say that Japan's intelligence could have been gathered by almost anyone. Only later would General

Herron be quoted as saying, "Pearl Harbor is a goldfish bowl." And Gordon Prange would write in his famous work, *At Dawn We Slept*, "Missing Pearl Harbor from the air over Oʻahu would be like overlooking a bass drum in a telephone booth."

After the Roberts Commission finished work in mid-January 1942, Roberts immediately talked at length with Roosevelt, then Stimson, then again with Roosevelt.[22] Stimson wrote in his diary that Roberts doubted whether Shivers had gotten "under the crust" of the thoughts of Japanese. Roberts also voiced alarm over the Nisei in the U.S. military who were standing guard in Hawaiʻi. Nowhere in the report was there reference to the many positive testimonies that had been given to the commission in Hawaiʻi on behalf of the Issei and Nisei.

On the day of Roberts's second meeting with the president, the commission report was released to the media. Despite the vagueness of its wording, "in the feverish anti-Japanese atmosphere of California it was taken as positive proof of Japanese American disloyalty that legitimated all the previous rumors."[23] News stories of espionage, sabotage, and subversion at work in the Pearl Harbor attack raced throughout the country, fueling the bonfire of blame.

The Roberts report immeasurably strengthened the hand of the two individuals—General Guillon and Major Bendetsen—who were the entering wedge into the plan for mass internment. Their agitation for a mass evacuation initially had been met with uncertainty by General DeWitt, who was responsible for defense of the West Coast. But following the Roberts report, DeWitt signed on to the idea of a forced evacuation. With sabotage treated as a certitude, proposals for evacuation spread like a contagion. On January 27, 1942, DeWitt met with the governor of California, who also had been undecided. The two agreed to support a mass uprooting of the Japanese community. Immediately the attorney general of California, Earl Warren, endorsed the idea and became its most effective advocate. Warren professed to believe that if Japan attacked the West Coast, a Fifth Column would arise with devastating consequences. As examples, he cited France, Denmark, and Norway.[24]

At the next level up, McCloy set aside his legalistic reservations and embraced the forced evacuation. Secretary of War Stimson, previously uncertain, endorsed it as well. In the several months following Pearl Harbor, the California public had been transformed by outright lies and incessant misreporting of facts in the West Coast newspapers, in particular by the Hearst and McClatchy newspapers, into mean-spirited seekers after revenge. In the message of Roberts, their vitriolic views were now on the desk of the president of the United States.

Against this tide, Roosevelt had been advised repeatedly that the Japanese immigrant population was not a threat and that Japanese Americans were overwhelmingly patriotic and eager to participate in the war. He had the evidence of uniformed and armed soldiers of Japanese ancestry performing flawlessly on the ground in Hawai'i. He had assurances all around that everything in Hawai'i was under control.

All that was left was the response of Roosevelt.

On February 19, 1942, he signed Executive Order (EO) 9066, which Bendetsen and McCloy had drafted. EO 9066 licensed the forced removal of anyone anywhere under U.S. jurisdiction, alien or citizen. It specifically authorized military commanders, such as the Western Defense Command and the Hawaiian Army Department, to remove any and all persons from their areas of operation. The question after February 19 became how EO 9066 would be used.

The Tolan Committee

The most publicized forum for publicly debating the use of EO 9066 became a roving congressional committee chaired by a California congressman, John H. Tolan.[25] After the Roberts Commission, the Tolan Committee emerged as the second investigation in the wake of Pearl Harbor.

One of the bitter ironies of the Tolan Committee was that its original mission was to investigate the domestic migration of the unemployed. Tolan was a New Deal Democrat, elected in 1936, and as such his committee was nominally concerned with the impoverished and dispossessed. With EO 9066, the Tolan Committee refocused onto the question of a forced "migration" of the Japanese-ancestry population. Proposals ranged from evacuating aliens living near defense facilities to what originally was taken as an extreme view—evacuating all people of Japanese ancestry from the West Coast states. The committee explored whether Japanese American citizens as well as aliens should be evacuated and, additionally, whether evacuations should be voluntary or mandatory.

According to the renowned reporter of California history, Carey McWilliams, the California congressional caucus pressured Tolan to

hold the hearings, with the goal of promoting a far-reaching evacuation.[26] A second observer, Morton Grozdins, believed the idea originated with high-level attorneys in the U.S. Justice Department who
viewed themselves as moderates on the evacuation question. In Morton's telling, the Justice Department lawyers thought of the hearings as
a way to "blow off steam" and expose the financial motives and racism
of the anti-Japanese lobby.[27]

As its tortuous life played out, the Tolan Committee became an
echo chamber for conflating the allegation of sabotage in Hawai'i
with threats to the West Coast. At the outset, committee members were
shown numerous photographs from Hawai'i—over a hundred such
photographs, according to one account—purporting to prove that local
Japanese had clogged the roads in and out of Pearl Harbor. Tolan then
opened a hearing in San Francisco on February 23, four days after Roosevelt's EO 9066.

In their questions, most of the Tolan Committee members treated
the allegations of espionage, sabotage, and subversive activity in Hawai'i
as a given. For example, Tolan prefaced a question to the president
of the San Francisco Japanese American Citizen's League (JACL) by
announcing, "The sabotage at the time of the attack on Pearl Harbor
and the disloyalty of the Japanese there was so widespread that the
details have never as yet been fully given to the public."[28]

In the glare of publicity created by the Tolan Committee, California's attorney general, Earl Warren, made a case for a mass mandatory
evacuation. Warren was soon to be elected California's governor and
thereafter was appointed chief justice of the U.S. Supreme Court, where
he would be remembered as a great liberal. By way of introduction,
Tolan thanked Warren profusely for his appearance. He said, "We shall
give you the widest latitude," and he did so.

The preceding month, Warren had mapped the farmlands and
homes of Japanese aliens and their American offspring. In this, he led
a statewide effort involving numerous county district attorneys, sheriffs,
tax assessors, and agricultural commissioners. Warren said that for security reasons, his maps did not show defense facilities, but he assured the
congressmen that they comprehensively included landing beaches, air-
fields, railroads, highways, powerhouses, power lines, gas storage tanks,
gas pipelines, oil fields, water reservoirs, pumping plants, telephone
transmission lines, radio stations, and other items. Such infrastructure, he said, usually had a considerable number of Japanese in their

immediate vicinity. He claimed he was not suggesting "some vast conspiracy to destroy our State by sudden and mass sabotage." He acknowledged that some of his map information was simple coincidence. But, he added, "it would seem equally beyond doubt that the presence of others is not coincidence." For example, he described the roadways approaching Camp Cooke north of Los Angeles as flanked by Japanese farmers. Warren went on: "To assume that the enemy has not planned fifth column activities for us in a wave of sabotage is simply to live in a fool's paradise."[29]

He then turned to tarnishing Japanese community leadership, which he described as an interlocking directorate ideally suited for a "plan of mass sabotage." While investigation of subversion had been left to the FBI, he said, "the interrelationship of the many Japanese associations and their control over the Japanese population of the State has been a matter of general knowledge."[30] As related evidence for mistrust, he said that Japanese American leadership throughout the state had been asked for names of the disloyal but had failed to produce any, thereby echoing the testimony of Zacharias. However astonishing Warren's presentation may seem in light of his eventual Supreme Court role as the champion of civil rights and civil liberties, he apparently suffered no doubt that he was right in his early 1942 testimony.

A handful of Japanese American witnesses attempted to defend themselves. Mike Masaoka, field secretary of JACL, began with a bit of drama: "We, too, remember Pearl Harbor." Tolan, unmoved, demanded to know, "What about your people at Pearl Harbor? . . . Did they remain loyal Americans?" Masaoka fumbled, erroneously stating that Secretary Knox believed some Japanese had turned their guns on Americans, but that "the reports would seem to indicate another thing—sabotage." Masaoka asked Tolan to understand that Mainland Japanese Americans were further removed from the influence of the Imperial Japanese Government than their Hawai'i counterparts and were, by implication, less likely to exhibit any taint of loyalty to Japan.[31]

Henry Tani, executive secretary of the San Francisco JACL chapter, submitted data stressing the small size of the Japanese community in comparison to the whole population—under 2 percent in California compared to 37 percent in Hawai'i.

At this point, discussion in the committee hearings veered briefly to immigrants and descendants of Germany and Italy. Tolan told an Italian American witness, "Tell us about the DiMaggios." There could

hardly have been a finer talking point than the baseball heroes of San
Francisco. Joe DiMaggio played for the New York Yankees and had won
batting titles the previous two years. Brother Dominic played for Boston, and Vincent played for the Pittsburgh Pirates.[32]

In contrast to the Roberts hearing in Hawai'i, only a few people
came forward in California to support Japanese Americans. The most
outspoken was the leftist union leader Louis Goldblatt, who was soon
to become a major figure in coordinating the work of the International
Longshoreman and Warehouseman's Union (ILWU) in Hawai'i. Where
most of the trade unions were anti-Japanese, Goldblatt tore into the
arguments for evacuation. He said the Hearst newspapers had created
an atmosphere of race hatred and, further, that the State of California had failed to provide accurate information to correct the situation.
"This entire episode of hysteria and mob chant against the native-born
Japanese will form a dark page of American history," Goldblatt said. "It
may well appear as one of the great victories won by the Axis Powers."
Goldblatt's testimony set off a tirade by Chairman Tolan, who said the
FBI had failed to control Hawai'i, resulting in "the most perfect system
of espionage and sabotage ever in the history of war."[33]

Galen Fisher, an associate of the Hawai'i-based Institute of Pacific
Relations, took an internationalist line that was beginning to resonate
in intellectual circles. He said treating Japanese in America harshly
would play into the hands of enemy propaganda that claimed Japan
was the protector of nonwhite people. Fisher went on: "The Nazis have
already made much of our maltreatment of the Negro. If we violate in
any degree the equal rights of our fellow citizens of Japanese stock, we
mock our pretensions of fighting to defend democracy."[34]

Fisher spoke for the Fair Play Committee of California. Both the
timing and position of the Fair Play organization revealed the feeble-
ness of its effort. By one account, the committee had begun organizing
only in August 1941; by another account, only after the Pearl Harbor
bombing. In either event, the Fair Play Committee ran many months
behind Hawai'i's Council for Interracial Unity.[35] Neither did it have the
authenticity of being interracial. The enduring core of the organization was Caucasian, consisting of Fisher as secretary and Harry Kingman of the University of California–Berkeley YMCA and his wife, Ruth.
The presidents of both UC Berkeley and Stanford University were somewhat active, but many of the members were window dressing. They had
been hurriedly recruited for use of their names but had not developed

a dialogue or action plan among themselves. The honorary chair was Governor Culbert L. Olson, who with General DeWitt had just cast his lot behind a mass evacuation. Masaoka was to say that the Fair Play Committee was "as ineffective as an earthen dam before a flood."[36]

Hawai'i's nonvoting Delegate to Congress, Samuel Wilder King, was distraught by the misinformation about sabotage that the Tolan Committee took as gospel. Early on, King had grasped the centrality of the Hawai'i sabotage allegation as it ate away at public opinion on the West Coast. Accordingly, he demanded the U.S. attorney general give an accounting of what the U.S. security agencies knew to be the truth. His demand was ignored.

On the night of the first Tolan hearings, the national president of JACL, Saburo Kido, wrote King a desperate letter, saying that government representatives constantly referred to sabotage at Pearl Harbor as the basis for "their various plans for singling us out." Kido and Mike Masaoka had thought of the Tolan hearings as a means of telling their story. They had worked hard on their prepared testimony but were blindsided by EO 9066 and the fury of the anti-Japanese agitation at work inside the hearings.[37] "Tolan Committee claims they have over one hundred pictures purporting to show Nisei trucks and automobiles blocking the highways leading to the airports, etc.," Kido wrote to King. "We need facts on the matter if we are to avoid . . . persecution and recrimination. We are appealing to you as our last resort to retain our status as American citizens. We trust that you will not fail us."[38]

On the second day of the San Francisco hearing, Sam King wired Tolan asking that he hold a hearing in Honolulu as a matter of fairness to the good reputation of Hawai'i's citizenry. Knowing there had been no sabotage, King said the loose talk about a Fifth Column should either be substantiated or refuted. If the committee was unable to travel to Honolulu, he said, Tolan at least should elicit sworn statements from Poindexter, Emmons, Fielder, Mayfield, Shivers, Mayor Petrie, Police Chief Gabrielson, Briant Wells, Vitousek, and Leslie Hicks, as well as editors, publishers, and others.[39] Tolan ignored King's plea. He continued on his course, holding a third day of hearings in San Francisco, then moving on to Seattle and Portland.[40]

On February 28, on the ninth day of EO 9066, King again wrote to Tolan, this time referring to Saburo Kido's appeal to get the facts straight. He said, "What is supposed to have happened in Hawai'i is being used to their detriment in California." He enclosed the Emmons speech of December 21—the far-reaching statement drafted by Shigeo Yoshida. Nonetheless, the accusatory tone of the San Francisco hearings continued. Time-wasting exchanges ensued between King and Tolan around the question of securing credible testimony from Honolulu without going there. King again pleaded for Tolan to solicit statements from community figures. Tolan countered by asking King to generate the statements, and King asked Vitousek to work on them. An attorney in San Francisco, Herman Phleger, talked with Tolan several times on King's behalf. Tolan told Phleger that various congressmen had believed the sabotage story because of the Pearl Harbor roadway photos they had been shown in Washington, D.C. This was disingenuous, in that Tolan himself believed the sabotage story—or at least purported to as reflected in his rhetorical questions in the hearings. Tolan assured Phleger that he would keep the record open until King's material arrived. Meanwhile, Tolan wrapped up the hearings in Los Angeles and moved his committee back to Washington, D.C., where the sabotage story was thriving.[41]

Precious days passed. Most ominously for the Japanese community, the staff director of the Tolan Committee, Robert K. Lamb, and on one occasion Tolan himself, talked with McCloy, who was gauging the political temperature of the country relative to a mass internment.[42] Contrary to the naïve hopes of the U.S. Justice Department attorneys, the Fifth Column story was travelling unmanageably into far-flung nooks and crannies. On February 27, a national magazine ran an article headlined, "Fifth Column in U.S.—Fighting the Foe Within."[43] The article claimed, "Evidence that a tightly knit Fifth Column exists in the United States is being uncovered daily by the Federal Bureau of Investigation." This was followed by repetitions of rumors that had been debunked in Hawai'i, such as the arrow-in-the-canefield story. A Democratic senator from Iowa, Guy Gillette, was quoted as saying Japanese might dynamite infrastructure and defense plants, echoing Warren. Gillette said a long-standing conspiracy explained why Japanese settlements were often located near strategic resources. To this, the article added, "The Iowa senator's suspicions were first aroused in 1937 during joint congressional committee hearings on Hawai'i's application for statehood."[44] Gillette pursued his theory despite having met Yoshida face-to-face, as well as the other eleven Nisei witnesses in King's statehood hearing.

Such articles skipped from one unexamined allegation to the next. The *Seattle Times* located a navy wife who had been evacuated from Hawai'i after the bombing, quoting her at length on the allegation that downed Japanese pilots wore McKinley High School rings. From there the story rambled into other allegations, never returning to or offering proof of the McKinley tale. A column in the *Washington Times-Herald* said white citizens of Hawai'i remembered what everyone else had forgotten, that Japan had poured colonists into Hawai'i in the 1890s as part of a plot, and that only by heroic effort had Hawai'i been saved from Japan by the forced annexation. Lying outlandishly, the column used the figure of twenty-four thousand Japanese immigrants a year. "The question of ownership [of Hawaii] was never settled," the column went on, "and the Japanese claim to legal ownership of the Hawaiians, they have insisted over and over, is still a living document."[45] This was one of several articles in which various media resurrected the pseudohistory of the 1898 takeover of Hawai'i as a matter of brave American settlers rescuing a mid-Pacific outpost from Japan.

On March 2, the meaning of EO 9066 began to descend in an eerie slow motion. General DeWitt, in his capacity as the Western states' defense commander, issued a proclamation—licensed by Roosevelt's executive order—saying "such persons as the situation may require" would be excluded from the area of his command. It ordered all German and Italian aliens and all Japanese regardless of alien status or American citizenship to register their forwarding addresses at a post office if they moved.

Delegate King, meanwhile, continued with his attempts to tamp down the passions that threatened his constituents in Hawai'i. At his urging, Honolulu Police Chief Gabrielson wired Tolan on March 14 saying there had been no sabotage. The Associated Press accurately quoted him to that effect and said his statement "coincided with frequent public utterances by Hawaii's congressional delegate, Samuel King."

Although King never shrank from speaking his mind, he obviously felt hampered by his lack of status as a nonvoting representative of an overseas territory. He again urged Tolan to hear testimony in Hawai'i. Barring that, he repeatedly told Tolan that long-distance submittals from Hawai'i would be taken more seriously if solicited by him, Tolan, and also if submittals were gathered by a federal agent as testimony sworn under oath.

Vitousek likewise kept pushing. The committee staff told him on April 1 that Tolan was shutting down the committee's operation within the week. Nonetheless, Tolan continued to say he would accept any additional input from Hawai'i. Vitousek then coordinated the development of eleven sworn affidavits, which he forwarded in a transmittal letter dated April 10, 1942.[46] The affidavits dissected the most prominent features of the sabotage allegations, starting with the committee's hundred photographs that purportedly showed Japanese drivers jamming the roadways.

Chief Gabrielson wrote that he made a habit of dropping by the Honolulu police station every Sunday around 8 a.m. When he did so on December 7, he was told that Pearl Harbor had been bombed. He held over the outgoing watch of police officers, doubling the available manpower. He talked with the Pearl City station about the bombing in progress, then drove toward Pearl Harbor on Dillingham Boulevard. By 8:22 a.m. he noted that HPD officers were directing traffic at Middle Street and there was no congestion. He met eight officers at a housing area, Damon Tract, adjacent to the airport. Frightened residents were beginning to flee. Satisfied that this situation was adequately supervised, Gabrielson drove on Kamehameha Highway to a point above Pearl Harbor, where he pulled over and watched the bombing. He then backtracked, set up another traffic post closer to the airport, and expanded the traffic detail at Middle Street in response to growing congestion. Military police augmented the HPD, and Gabrielson set up additional traffic stations in the corridors between Honolulu and Pearl Harbor. Roadway access was restricted. This went on all day and night. Gabrielson roamed, checked, and supervised his field officers until 1 a.m. Monday. He fell asleep at his desk for four hours, arose, and resumed work.

The captain of the patrol division, Dewey O. Mookini, further described traffic management, including his supervision of a lane devoted exclusively to evacuation of the wounded. He pointedly went on to say that as a lifelong resident, he had no problem with recognizing people of Japanese ancestry. "Many of the vehicles were being driven by persons of Japanese ancestry safely, neither fast nor slow," Mookini said, "[with] no driving behavior of any kind that might cause confusion or panic." Other officers, including Hung Wai Ching's oldest brother, Hung Chin, added detail.

Stafford L. Austin addressed the allegation that workers had cut arrows in the cane fields pointing the way to Pearl Harbor. Austin was an old hand, having worked in the sugar business since his days as a young boy in the Kingdom of Hawai'i. His testimony was particularly significant in that he chaired civil defense for all of rural O'ahu. Secondly, he managed the six thousand acres of the Honolulu Plantation Company overlooking Pearl Harbor and Hickam Air Field, along with 1,100 employees, of whom 480 were of Japanese ancestry. When Austin realized Pearl Harbor was under attack, he ordered all of his workers to their civil defense posts, in accord with previously practiced plans. He personally was on the road as a matter of fulfilling his civil defense duties. Plantation trucks were mobilized for firefighting, ambulance service, repair of utility lines, and demolition. Plantation trucks and attendant crews were sent inside the naval base. Various station wagons owned by the plantation went on patrol, usually with an army man aboard. Part of the manpower was of Japanese ancestry, including drivers, who worked no differently from others on the scene. At no time was there a question of cane being cut or burned as a signal. At 8:30 a.m., one of Japan's airplanes crashed in a field about two miles from the plantation mill, starting a fire. The plantation's fire crew, including men of Japanese ancestry, quickly extinguished the blaze. For the next month, Austin sent out two thousand men daily to create defenses above Pearl Harbor. Many were of Japanese ancestry. A large number of the skilled carpenters were first-generation aliens, and their hard work had been "accepted gratefully and without question by the Army authorities."

Perhaps the most remarkable affidavit was by police captain Burns, in that he directly addressed loyalty *and* internal security.[47] He began by reciting his experience as head of the Police Espionage Unit and the Police Contact Group—the sort of credentials that caused Colonel Green to describe Burns as an "Oriental expert." Burns then recited his birth history and ethnicity, as if he had been prompted to assure the readers that he was a truthful person. His mother was of Irish descent and his father was mixed German and Irish. He was born at Fort Assiniboine, Montana, in 1909 and had lived on O'ahu since the age of four. He had joined the police force in 1934 at age twenty-three, along with his older brother Edward. In the ensuing eight years, he had served in quick succession as a foot patrolman, motor patrolman, sergeant, general detective, homicide detective, and captain of the vice squad. Beginning on January 1, 1941, he had worked with the FBI investigating for potential espionage. From November 28 to December 7, he and his team had combed O'ahu for signs that local Japanese knew the war might start at any moment, but the investigation had turned up nothing. Since then he had served as HPD liaison to both Army Intelligence and the FBI.

Burns reported investigating numerous allegations of sabotage and subversive behavior, including rumors of flares, signal lights, sniping, paratrooper landings, unauthorized short-wave radio transmissions, the stockpiling of guns and ammunition, and underground plotting against the government. These he debunked one by one.

He described directing a search of elaborate scale in which 132 men combed an area of heavy Japanese population for eight hours. They found nothing of significance.

There were seven more similarly detailed affidavits from Hawai'i, each refuting some aspect of the allegation of subversive behavior.

The *San Francisco Chronicle* ran an Associated Press story about Gabrielson's testimony on its front page. It prefaced the story by saying it would be "surprising to thousands of Americans in view of the uncounted rumors prior to and since the Roberts report." The lead paragraph said, "All reports to the contrary, no acts of sabotage were committed in Honolulu or at Pearl Harbor on December 7 nor have any been reported to the Honolulu police department since that date."[48] This was a rare example of how the truth of Pearl Harbor might have spread, if newspapers around the country similarly had reported responsible sources accurately.

Forced evacuations and inevitable incarcerations proceeded throughout the Western states. Although these would come to be remembered in history as a single event called internment, they actually occurred piecemeal, as a result of proclamation after proclamation. After twenty preliminary proclamations restricting personal freedoms, DeWitt issued the first order for a community to evacuate. This was the Japanese community on Bainbridge Island near Seattle. The Bainbridge evacuation notice was posted on March 24—thirty-three days after EO 9066—with a deadline for evacuation of March 30.[49]

Obscured in the record is an astonishing admission by U.S. war leaders that the sabotage story was baseless. This was not after the fact but just as the internment was starting. The day of the Bainbridge notice, Secretary of War Stimson wrote to Tolan in response to a query: What did Stimson know about sabotage in connection with the Pearl Harbor bombing? Stimson replied, "The War Department has received no information of sabotage committed by Japanese during the attack on Pearl Harbor."

Secretary of the Navy Knox—who first had lit the Fifth Column flame—responded similarly, if not wholeheartedly: "There was very little, if any, sabotage by the Japanese residents of O'ahu during the attack on Pearl Harbor." Knox nonetheless clung to his insistence on espionage prior to the attack and his fallacious contention that radio traffic had confused American forces while the Japanese pilots returned to their carriers. "However," Knox wrote, "during the actual attack . . . there was little to complain of in the way of sabotage." Undaunted by this halting if imperfect confession of fact, Knox nonetheless continued to urge the removal of everyone of Japanese descent, if not to the Mainland, then to a remote outlying island. Like Stimson's, his letter was dated March 24, 1942.

Assistant U.S. Attorney General James Rowe Jr. responded on behalf of Attorney General Biddle, who had remained silent when Sam King had implored him to tell the real facts regarding Pearl Harbor. Rowe wrote that the FBI had advised the Justice Department, "there was no sabotage committed there prior to December 7, on December 7, or subsequent to that time." The statements of Stimson, Knox and Rowe were published along with those of the Hawai'i affidavits in May 1942 by the U.S. Congress on pages forty-eight through fifty-seven of the Fourth Interim Report of the Tolan Committee. Not only were the facts about Hawai'i ignored prior to publication of the Tolan Committee report but also after publication. By then, tens of thousands of people had been uprooted and herded into makeshift aggregation centers.

The rumor of sabotage by Hawai'i's Japanese community at Pearl Harbor had circulated so widely that many people in the highest reaches of government and society took it as an article of faith. Even First Lady Eleanor Roosevelt, who had pleaded for mercy and reason, had internalized the story. Possibly what Mrs. Roosevelt believed, at the time, didn't matter. When she approached the president to discuss the mass removal, he declined to speak with her. The fact was, his order, if obliquely, had given the go-ahead to the ensuing mass action.

The first clause of EO 9066 said success in the war required "every possible protection against espionage and against sabotage." It directed commanders to take whatever steps they "may deem advisable" to enforce their new powers, including the use of federal troops. It empowered military commanders "to prescribe military areas in such places and of such extent as he (the War Secretary) or the appropriate Military Commander may determine, from which any or all persons may be excluded . . ."

The fact that Roosevelt did not spell out who was to be removed, and from what areas, helped preserve his image as the benign leader who, at worst, was given bad advice about mass internment. The truth of Roosevelt's views was fully known only to a few key people, one of whom was McCloy. The president had remarked to him, "We don't want any more Black Toms."[50] Seeking guidance on how to apply EO 9066, McCloy sat with Stimson during a crucial telephone call to the president. "(I) fortunately found that he was very vigorous about it," Stimson confided to his diary, "and told me to go ahead on the line that I had myself thought the best."[51] Afterward, McCloy called Bendetsen in California and said, "We have *carte blanche* to do what we want to as far as the President is concerned."[52]

One of the gruesome facts of the internment project was that nearly eleven weeks passed between the Pearl Harbor bombing and EO 9066, and another nine weeks passed before the actual start of evacuation. If any members of the Japanese community had been a danger to military security as alleged, that danger would surely have manifested itself during this militarily crucial time period, when the possibility of an invasion by Japan ran highest.

As part of getting the evacuation underway, McCloy headed west to make a firsthand assessment of the situation. He arrived in San Francisco in the wake of Tolan's San Francisco hearing, while the Japanese American Citizen's League was holding a three-day conference on what if anything they could do. By this time, Saburo Kido saw no way out of a mass removal. He said, "We are gladly cooperating because this is one way of showing that our protestations of loyalty are sincere."[53] McCloy addressed the JACL on the last day. He said he wanted to minimize the financial losses of evacuated families and also to see they were treated as humanely as possible. "Above all," McCloy said, verbalizing what was perhaps the ultimate hypocrisy of the project, "we want to give you protection." It was a construction of events by which the racism of the internment lay not in the government but in the public's prejudices. McCloy in fact had virtually no direct knowledge of Japanese Americans and was merely deferring to the prejudices of the West Coast, as subsequent events were to prove.

Following his JACL speech, a Nisei named Masao Satow invited McCloy to join the group for noodles in San Francisco's Chinatown. McCloy thought Satow was kidding. "Aren't the Chinese hostile toward you fellows?" he asked. "Aren't you afraid to go down there?" "No sir," Satow replied. "They're Chinese and we're Japanese but we're all Americans."[54]

While on the West Coast, McCloy received a briefing from the Kenneth Ringle who had recruited Douglas Wada in Honolulu into ONI. Ringle counseled against a mass internment. He said that in overwhelming numbers, the Nisei were patriotic and loyal citizens of the United States. McCloy was said to be genuinely impressed by Ringle, but he nonetheless put the single-minded Bendetsen in charge of implementing the evacuation. This included giving Bendetsen the power to suspend all rules and regulations of the army command and to direct the work of civilian agencies of the federal government to implement a mass evacuation. Previously known only in high-level internal-security circles, Bendetsen now had an authority akin to martial law within DeWitt's Western Defense Command. In the process, he became a public figure, promoting the most draconian uses of Roosevelt's Executive Order. In a speech to the Commonwealth Club in San Francisco, he acknowledged that while many of Japanese ancestry were loyal to the United States, "It is also true that many are not loyal. We know this." As proof of his thesis, he said that no person of Japanese ancestry had reported the disloyalty of another, repeating the previous illogic of Earl Warren and Zacharias.[55]

McCloy flew off to Honolulu, arriving on March 12. The war news was bad all around, and anxiety was high. "Unidentified elements" at sea had triggered an air raid warning that sent people to their bomb shelters, trenches, and basements for sixty-seven minutes, the longest air raid alert since December 7. Civil Defense published a plan for evacuating Honolulu in case of a second bombing raid. A Big Five freighter, the *Malama,* owned by Matson Navigation Company, was lost at sea. The oil-rich Dutch East Indies had fallen to Japan. Twelve Allied ships were lost in the battle of the Java Sea. An Australian naval cruiser had gone down with over eight hundred persons aboard. Bangkok fell to the enemy. Manila fell. The Associated Press reported a meeting between Hitler and Hirohito in which, it was said, they agreed on a plan to rule the world.

The pressure on Hawai'i's Japanese community had reached a horrific intensity. If espionage, sabotage, and subversion had opened Japan's way to Pearl Harbor, it followed that Hawai'i's people of Japanese ancestry were a far greater danger to U.S. security than their Mainland counterparts. If this was so, the question was: Who among "the

Japanese" should be arrested and shipped out first? In comparison to the forced evacuation plan for the West Coast, the absence of a parallel plan for Hawai'i was becoming ever more of an anomaly. If the alleged sabotage of Hawai'i could be used in the Western states to justify a mass removal, then what should be done with the proportionately much larger population of Japanese in Hawai'i?

Contrary to the allegations McCloy had heard about sabotage, he was greeted by layer after layer of people who operated from a position of trust for the Japanese community. What he was to witness in Hawai'i was to be a fork in the road.

CHAPTER 8

The Threat of Demoralization

FOLLOWING THE CALM THAT WAS ACHIEVED during the first two to three weeks of the war, most observers agreed that morale in the Japanese community began to slide. From numerous small group meetings, Shigeo Yoshida wrote assessments that were submitted to the government through Army Intelligence.[1] Soon he was describing the Japanese aliens as increasingly withdrawn. Some were gripped by a feeling their mother country had betrayed them. "[Others] are deeply humiliated by the treacherous way in which Japan has started this war," Yoshida reported. "They feel they have 'lost face.'" Yoshida believed that discrimination against people of Japanese ancestry was on the increase, particularly in the job market: "Many Japanese, aliens and citizens alike, [are] becoming increasingly depressed because of inability to get and to hold jobs."[2] Although workers were needed desperately in the war effort, layoffs or fear of layoffs were reported repeatedly to the Morale Section. An additional source of friction and resentment was a requirement that Japanese who worked in U.S. government jobs were required to wear black identification badges.

These were aspects of demoralization that Ching and Yoshida most feared—a syndrome of isolation and alienation, followed by people becoming increasingly embittered and, in their hurt and anger, some significant number turning for solace to Japan.

The concern for inclusion could readily be dated to the 1919 worker strike, after which influential elements in Hawai'i had become more seriously engaged in Americanizing (the widely used word) its large Japanese-ancestry population. Such diverse elements as the YMCA, the public education system, the IPR, Hands Around the Pacific, and the New American Movement all had participated in educating, proselytizing, mentoring, hectoring, warning, and sometimes threatening ("you are on the spot") the Japanese community, with a focus on the Nisei.

Where the national government asked simple questions about loyalties, the threesome of Yoshida, Ching, and Loomis dealt with complexities. All had scholarly backgrounds, which enhanced their ability to aggregate and assess large amounts of information from many sources and viewpoints.[3] Their definition of reality was fluid. "The Japanese" of Hawai'i were many and varied. The future was not foreordained but was to be claimed and shaped.

The work of the Morale Section was supported by the University of Hawai'i Sociology Department, which had flourished since its founding in 1920. The founder of the department was from the University of Chicago, Romanzo C. Adams, who was followed in 1927 by Andrew H. Lind who also was from Chicago. During this period, prominent figures of American sociology frequently were attracted to Hawai'i, particularly sociologists of the Chicago School, which played a major role in defining and propagating the discipline.[4] Pioneering scholars such as Robert E. Park had traveled to Hawai'i repeatedly to study intermarriage, mixed ancestry, and multiculturalism.

In a memorandum to the martial law government written less than a week after the bombing, Lind identified himself as a longtime observer of the Japanese community in Hawai'i. He wrote that the Nisei were badly shaken by Japan's bombing and were eager to do something in response. He said that Hawaiian tradition called for an inclusive approach. In the vein of Yoshida, he proposed approaching the war as a means of transforming Hawai'i into a genuine democracy.

Lind said the Issei were not so wedded to tradition as they might appear. Immigrant lifestyle, he suggested, inevitably formed around a shared desire to maintain practices from the old country, but these same practices had been adapted over time to the new surroundings. He positively framed the Japanese-language press, the language schools, the Buddhist temples, and Japanese neighborhood organizations (*kumiai*) as conduits for informing immigrants on how to adjust to their new lives in Hawai'i. Lind urged the military to keep the institutions of the Japanese community open and functioning. He recommended that communication through Nisei channels be restored by reopening the public schools and the University of Hawai'i as quickly as possible.

The ethnically Japanese population, Lind wrote, "needs to be conceived, for certain morale-building purposes, not as a single unit but as a congery of groups—the Okinawans, with their traditional feelings of distance from the other Japanese, the first-generation Buddhists, the first-generation Christians, the first-generation Nisei nurtured within a Japanese ghetto, and the Nisei whose outlook is primarily American. What is effective strategy for one group may have a negative or neutral effect upon another group."[5]

Lind assigned and hoarded student papers of three types. The first was what students thought about themselves; second, what students experienced in their families; and, third, what they saw happening in their communities. These inquiries revealed young people with hopes of a better future but with mixed and sometimes despairing expectations. Likely they had been educated in a public elementary school, supplemented by additional study at a Japanese-language school. They had benefited from Hawai'i's growing number of high schools, of which McKinley High School in Honolulu was the centerpiece. Males likely had grown up playing baseball. Untold thousands had participated in YMCA fellowship as well as leadership development groups. If they showed drive and academic ability, their families supported their advanced studies at the University of Hawai'i. Both high school and university students had participated in the mandatory Reserve Officer Training Corps program dating to 1923.

On graduation, Nisei headed for the world of work in a small economy dominated by the Big Five corporations. Racial discrimination limited opportunity, and employment often was disappointing. Fortitude and determination were at a premium.

Lind filed away the paper of a student named Tom, last initial M (TM), who worked in a library. TM asked his supervisor about going to a university on the U.S. Mainland for advanced training. She told him "it was of no use" but in contrast often encouraged white students to seek advanced training. "Such reply hit me like a lightning," TM wrote. After nine years in the library, he asked about advancement but was told that he had gone to "maximum classification" and could go no further. He no longer liked to think about the future of his work: "Such has killed all the fight in me."[6] TM's library job often took him to plantation schools. He reported students remarking, "Waste time read, more better work. I can make a dollar fifty a day."

A second student, GM, wrote, "Many Orientals are given a lot of responsibility but are not given the same pay with the haoles." GM was perplexed by the awkwardness of interaction between haole and Japanese. "The haoles expect us to make the first move [and] we want them to make some form of move, yet we both hold back." His prescription for the future was, "The Japanese must come out from this shell and must show more enthusiasm for citizenship, etc. and the haoles should meet Japanese 50-50 and try to understand their makeup, which has come with them through many generations."

A third Nisei student, WK, felt inhibited by the Issei in his desire to become fully American. "The Nisei want to be American citizens," he wrote, "but their parents will hang on to their old order and will not give their children release."

With a critical eye on both America and Japan, JN wrote about job discrimination. He thought of long-settled haoles as having a better understanding of Asian culture than newcomers. In comparison, he regarded recent white arrivals from the U.S. Mainland as having no notion of what made Hawai'i tick. To him, the *malihini* were like the Japanese who flocked to Korea after Japan's 1905 takeover: "These Japanese didn't understand the Korean culture and people and these Japanese felt they could grab anything. Haoles, it's the same thing."

"Why do the haoles pick on Orientals?" one student asked. "Why do they ask us to expatriate? . . . I'm confident about myself being a good American citizen. The only time we get jittery is when the haoles raise a fuss about distrusting the Orientals." This particular student had caught wind of the U.S. intelligence investigations. "I get darn burned up when they question us. I'm just as good an American as any haoles here. I feel I'm a real American. I was born, raised here, and I intend to die here. When those haoles question us, it makes me sick."

SW thought of Nisei as uncertain and confused. Some were, in his opinion, fatalistic and indifferent. The fatalists, he thought, "have a strong conviction that Pearl Harbor [Shipyard] will never hire them; that good advancement in governmental jobs will never be opened to them; that Japanese will always be looked down upon as Japanese." WK wrote that the Big Five was undoubtedly a "monster," but nothing could be done to curtail their power. He thought of older Japanese as being resigned to their fate as laborers while younger Japanese were disorganized and "lacking the punch and initiative to do things."

Ed K was angry. "Racial equality in Hawaii is a lot of bunk," he wrote. "We Orientals are foolish if we think we can win the admiration of the haoles by breaking into their circle. We must accept the fact that the haoles are in the driver's seat while we are only their passengers. They take us where they please; if we complain, they can make us walk." To this he added, "To hell with the haoles."

In their numerous student papers, Nisei yearned for greater autonomy, both in relation to their parents and to societal dominance of haoles. For a generation that would become known for dramatic action, there was extensive evidence of indecision in the early months of the war. Select students moved from personal essays to journal writing.[7] DS, age twenty-one, described himself as inexperienced and uncertain about the future. He was from the country town of Wahiawa on the central plain of O'ahu. He lived with twenty-eight other young men next to the UH campus at Student House. Most were of Japanese ancestry. On December 4, he had gone to philosophy class and nearly fallen asleep. Afterward he wrestled with whether to study or take a nap. He took a nap. During the summer of 1941, he had worked at a pineapple cannery in the Iwilei district near the Honolulu waterfront, then gotten a job in a mailroom. He wanted to move out of Student House but couldn't afford the rent outside. Despite being "dozy all the way," he had made almost straight As in his classes. He was particularly interested in sociology. He thought of studying the people of Okinawa, the island of his ancestors.

The second entry of his diary was six days after the Pearl Harbor bombing. He wrote that he was "just living." His routine was work and card playing. "Study is almost impossible in that no light is allowed for fear of air raid." DS wrote that his fellow students' thoughts of developing a career through higher education had been instantly put on hold. Many of his acquaintances had abandoned school for war-related work. He worried about his younger sisters, whom he regarded as unprepared to cope with the wartime environment. He resolved to save as much money as he could for them against the time he anticipated being drafted into the military. His spirits recovered for a time, but by late February he again felt low. He was disgruntled by his habit of incessant card playing.

DS decided to become a social worker, believing that when the war ended "there will be a lot of social personal problems." He vowed, "I shall strive for a better life. More active, mentally and physically." He berated himself for spending money needlessly, especially on soda, which sold for 5 cents a bottle. He returned to other items of self-criticism: not sleeping regularly, not exercising regularly, not providing more guidance to his younger sisters, and not writing more systematically in his diary. In early spring, his morale hit a new low, but he then rebounded: "Though the future promises nothing, I am facing it with thumbs up." He found a young friend he could talk to, a freshman majoring in agriculture. They drank cokes and talked late at night: "Would we the American citizens of Japanese ancestry be discriminated against in Hawaii after the war?" They cited a lecturer who said discrimination on the basis of race would be stooping to the level of the enemy, Germany particularly. "And so we both agreed and hoped that everyone will be judged as a person."

A student with the initials RSS tracked the ebb and flow of all twenty-eight of the Student House residents. His journal was so systematic as to raise a question of why his notes would end up in Yoshida's files. The most likely explanation is that his diary was encouraged as a window on student morale. RSS gave every resident a number to preserve their anonymity. No. 1 was a UH junior majoring in accounting. Every day he went out looking for an accounting job and every day he was turned down. No. 6 worked as a bus driver and neglected his studies. In his nonworking hours, he became obsessed with playing cards and listening to phonograph records. "Morale low," RSS wrote of No. 6. "Was given a 'raw deal' by someone in the past and has not forgotten it yet." No. 11 was exceptional: "Morale high. Partly due to the many girl friends that he has 'on the line.'" No. 11 was later shocked to be diagnosed with tuberculosis and confined to an institution. Nonetheless, his will to recover was strong.

RSS was disconcerted by the personality swings that he saw occurring around him. Of No. 13, he wrote, "Last week he was an orator. This week he hardly answers a direct question." No. 17 exhibited high morale for several months but suddenly announced that since Pearl Harbor he regretted living. One previously quiet, retiring person had been given responsibility as a trustee of Student House. His new authority "changed his whole personality." He became domineering. Most alarming to RSS was the behavior of No. 27: "Shows no interest or enthusiasm in anything." He neither studied nor worked. "Doesn't dress at all, hair hanging over eyes, walks and speaks like one who is very aged." By mid-May, the members of Student House had voted to have him move out. Both RSS and DS disagreed with this decision but learned to their dismay that they were his only defenders. "Others approached us only to warn us against being 'demoralized' by him," RSS wrote. "He assumed no responsibility, lacked cooperation and wasn't sociable enough even to say 'Hello.' In fact, he lacked the 'fight' to live."

By the author's count, the majority avoided talking about the war, while the minority followed it with intense interest. In their spare time, they dug a bomb shelter. Obviously, they thought of it as make-work.

It was not completed until May. By then, three-fourths of the Student House residents had dropped out of school and taken jobs, in which they were frozen by martial law orders. If they were absent from work, they were in danger of being taken into military court and subjected to fines and jailing at hard labor.

The theme of demoralization that recurred in the self-examination of Nisei ran in parallel to the anxiety experienced by first-generation families in the wake of the bombing.

Reports of a never-publicized profiling project of the Honolulu Police Department, under Captain Burns's supervision, survived in the files of the Morale Section. It recorded a startling picture. Described as the "Special Unit," two-man teams of police officers paid visits to hundreds of homes of people who were regarded in some way as suspect or in need of instruction or screening.[8] Each team had one officer of Japanese ancestry and one of a second ancestry. The officers engaged in a combination of encouragement, probing, coaching, and criticizing. Subjects sometimes were given blunt directives. Occasionally they were threatened with arrest or some other form of punishment.

Mrs. A, thirty-eight, had migrated to Hawai'i twelve years previously with four children, the first born when she was fourteen.[9] Six of her siblings farmed rice in Kumamoto Prefecture in southern Japan. The seventh was a yard boy in a wealthy haole home in Mānoa Valley. By the time of the police visit, she had eight children. She said she had been too busy raising children to study English, and also that English was not a necessity because she was surrounded by so many Japanese-speaking people. A policeman told Mrs. A that only the Japanese did not learn English, and "their speaking only Japanese would only tend to leave a Japanese feeling in their minds and they would never become Americanized. . . . If they were going to think like a Japanese, it would only hurt the whole Japanese community and we would show no mercy for such people." Mrs. A and her husband had bought $300 worth of U.S war bonds. She had donated blood. Nonetheless, she could not say that Japan was wrong any more than she could say that the American government was wrong. Among the many reasons she gave for gratitude to America was her government-issued gas mask. She hoped the war would end soon.

Mr. O was from a farm family in Niigata Prefecture on the northwest coast of the main island of Honshu. He had nine years of education in Japan and had studied English at the Nu'uanu YMCA at night for seven years. "Japan was his Mother country and the U.S. was his Father country," the police wrote. "[He] likes, and appreciates, this place very much. As far as the War is concerned, he . . . wanted both sides to shake hands and become friends again." Mr. O said prior to Pearl Harbor he had refused to donate to Japanese war relief because he was a Christian.

Mrs. UW, age thirty-two, and her husband, a priest at the Hongwanji Buddhist Mission, had bought a $50 U.S. war bond after the bombing. Nonetheless, he had been taken into internment. She was caring for their three children, ages six, four, and nine months. Her husband's mother was confined to the territorial hospital, and his disabled sister was confined to a home for the feebleminded. The family subsisted on $58.50 a month from the Red Cross. When Mrs. UW said she was grateful for everything the government had done, she burst into tears. The police reported that Mrs. UW was accepting of her husband's internment. She "understood it to be for the best, and as a precaution to safeguard this Democracy, even though he did not have any intentions to undertake any Anti-Democratic activities."

A Mr. K told the police that as a twenty-one-year-old in Japan he was called by his draft board to take a physical examination but was never drafted. He returned to Hawai'i and worked on a plantation on the island of Maui for two years, then at Maui Soda Works for ten years, at Maui Sake Brewery for four years, then for a dry goods store for nine years, after which he moved to Honolulu, where he worked as a yard boy and in a Japanese store. Between 1933 and 1937 he tried to develop a business based on dying cloth but went back to work as a yard boy. He had first returned to Japan in 1933 to visit a sick sister. He returned a second time in 1939 to clear up family property issues after both of his parents had died. He had three sisters in Japan, all married to farmers on the southern island of Kyushu. His wife had five siblings in Japan who also were farmers. He said he had lived in Hawai'i a long while and had forgotten Japan. He was grateful for "the good treatment, the education of his children, and their being able to carry on a successful life." No place, he said, could compare with the USA.

WBK was an American citizen. He had served in the U.S. Army in France during World War I, a rarity. He then served in the U.S. Army for fourteen years. His wife's father, a Japanese alien, was paralyzed and had moved from a hospital into their home. The invalid father-in-law listened to a small radio but not to broadcasts from Japan. Their second radio did not work. The police reprimanded the couple and advised

them on how to disable their radios so as to not be in violation of martial law orders. "We feel that the arresting of such cases would be unjus-
tifiable. Even though ignorance of the law is no excuse, we feel that
punishing this type of people would do them no good, and in fact would
create ill feeling toward the (Police) Department."

RT was a carpenter, age forty-seven. Although he was subdued in the
interview, his daughter Joan "did not like our intrusion and resented,
very much, our checking the place. She later left the room, due to being
scared, we presume." The police officers explained they were only doing
their job, that the daughter's attitude was not good, and "if she were
going to be sarcastic we could make a very bad report about her." Joan,
as it turned out later, was doing volunteer war work, as was her sister. As
to RT, "after speaking to him, we were led to believe that there still was
Japan left in him." The officers condemned the Japanese people for
isolating themselves from the other races, speaking Japanese, sending
money to Japan, doing business with Japan, visiting Japan only, and all
in all, acting and thinking "in an un-American way." When the HPD
officers told RT that Japan would lose the war, he said nothing. The
interviewers regarded RT as too tight-lipped, even though he volunteered that after December 7 he had burned his photos of the emperor
and empress and his Japanese books. In a self-deprecating vein, he also
said he regretted not studying English, thinking he did not have the
brains for it. He wanted to know if he could go out in the cool air of his
yard at night as long as he did not go out on the street. The police said
he could.

Reflecting on the morale of the Japanese alien, the sociologist
Yukiko Kimura of the YWCA's International Institute wrote that immigrant Japanese had become the most isolated people in Hawai'i: "An
extreme degree of fear was present. Their first reaction to a stranger was
fear—fear of being questioned, fear of being suspected, fear of being
accused of being Japanese." Kimura paraphrased an Issei as saying, "If
we go out, we will be the focus of hate and revenge. So we stay in the
house."[10]

Rumors of a mass evacuation to the Mainland caused a run on warm
clothes and suitcases. Superstitions revived. A half-human animal of
Japanese mythology was said to have appeared. Certain families began
eating their rice with red beans—a prescription of Japanese folk culture—to protect themselves from this sinister creature. As a result of the
December 7 internment of the priests and language teachers, Kimura

wrote that for older Japanese, "domineering control and guidance is greatly missed."[11] "They felt as never before that they would have to live and act like Americans."[12] Kimura described an element of traditional Japanese who transferred their loyalty from Emperor Hirohito to President Roosevelt, resulting in their regarding FDR as being "more like a god than a person." The respect that was traditionally accorded to advanced age was often withdrawn. Now the young tended to dominate the old: "After December 7, the parents had to obey their children."[13]

The stress of wartime tore at families and communities in varying combinations. One writer, RM, was eighteen years old. His family consisted of his immigrant mother and four siblings, all of whom were American born, as well as a sister-in-law who had been educated in Japan along with her two small children. They lived in the "Japanese camp" in the inner-city Pālama neighborhood. He said the Japanese enclave of Pālama had gradually diversified ethnically, yet it had remained "pure Yamato." Of himself and his brothers and sisters, RM wrote, "We strive to do everything the 'American way.'" His brother sat up at night building models of American airplanes, and his sister learned how to make spaghetti. He often discussed serving in the "American Army."

The siblings campaigned for their mother to give up wearing *geta* (Japanese clogs) and, on Sunday, wearing a kimono that previously she had cherished. Inwardly, she resisted. RM believed she actually had become more Japanese, not less, turning to other immigrants to protect herself psychologically from her children's strident Americanization program. When they cursed the emperor, she predicted that something terrible would befall them. Far from seeing the war as a transitional opportunity, she believed that when the war was over, Japanese would be the objects of contempt and hatred.

While the investigations into the Japanese population of Honolulu yielded a mixed picture, the condition of the Japanese community in plantation areas of O'ahu seems to have been more unambiguously strained. An extensive student analysis of the plantation town of Waipahu, west of Honolulu, described the plantation manager as dictatorial. Interaction between haole in high management positions and Japanese in lower-level and laboring positions was minimal to nonexistent. The student writers described this as long-standing and little changing. As a matter of plantation policy, the different ethnic groups were segregated from one another, and the war made no dent in this pattern. By design, the barrier was particularly high between the Japanese and Filipino workforces. According to the author, Japan wielded extensive influence prior to the war. The Japanese sectors of Waipahu were a "little Tokyo" of language schools, temples, and Japanese social clubs. "Homes are furnished and decorated with Japanese ornaments, trinkets, pictures, etc." Prior to the war, celebrated visitors from Japan often made their way to Waipahu. Movies from Japan drew big crowds. The Buddhist temples controlled language schools, exerted a heavy influence on the American born, and had "taken advantage of their positions to influence the minds of their young charges with the notions of cultural and military superiority of the Japanese over the Americans."[14]

The student analysts believed that the isolation of the Japanese community lent itself to effectively promoting pro-Japan propaganda. "Deprived of an outlet by [white] social snobbery and an economic caste system, the Japanese people have been forced to organize a social group for their own outlet."

In this setting, the public schools—widely regarded as agents of Americanization in Honolulu—were described as less effective in Waipahu. The writer cited the fact that the public schoolteachers did not live in the community alongside students and families. Further, social and economic democracy were "preached theoretically but never practiced in this community." Although Japanese Americans had been drafted into the army in large numbers prior to December 7, discrimination on defense projects was particularly grievous: "To this the aliens would say, 'See, they may call you an American when they want you, but you are still a Jap if they don't want you.'"

From the information in Lind's files, from Burns's reports, and from personal observation, clearly the Morale Section was addressing a difficult and worsening situation. Nisei were afflicted by aimlessness and despair. Issei were anxious and fear ridden.

As the word "morale" was used at the time, it was about a great deal more than feeling upbeat or downcast. Morale was about cohesion, determination, and mutual trust. The question of whether the downward arc could be reversed was a morale question. Whether Hawai'i could withstand a second attack was a morale question. Whether Hawai'i, with its numerous ethnic groups, could navigate through the conflict was a morale question. It was not only the Morale Section that was worried. Green would write that rumors of sabotage and spying intensified alarmingly in a short while.[15] Coggins, ever given to overstatement, wrote,

"Bloody race riots were a distinct possibility." Shivers, in much the same vein, would tell an investigative committee he feared an element of Issei might revel in Japan's military success, causing "a general riot."[16]

With a preconceived understanding of their roles, Hung Wai Ching turned immediately to church groups and Shigeo Yoshida to the public schools. Yoshida sent out a circular to teachers throughout the territory with a call for addressing fear. Everyone "regardless of race, color or creed, must be given a place in the scheme of national defense," he wrote. "Make clear that loyalty grows only when it is given a chance to grow."[17]

While Ching and Yoshida both had a history of cooperating with others across ethnic lines, they turned to ethnic-level organization as the realistic means of quickly reaching large numbers of people. Ching had led the Chinese Student Alliance at UH and defended it as socially relevant in light of continued racial discrimination. Yoshida, in contrast, believed that ethnic identities should be obscured in favor of building an integrated community. Nonetheless, he became the central figure in numerous discussions with Japanese aliens and Japanese Americans. His first step into communicating with the Japanese community was a series of twenty meetings in Honolulu and outlying areas. These ranged across many groups, such as doctors, dentists, teachers, clerks, farmers, students, plantation workers, and housewives.

Initial attempts to influence people in the Japanese community were difficult. Contrary to the stereotype of uniformity, they found the audiences to be splintered. Yoshida felt that in response to the dire problems they faced, every leader "has his own point of view as to what should be done and how to do it." Yoshida wrote to General Emmons on February 13, 1942, nearly a month after the Morale Section had been announced in the press. His letter had a desperate tone, as if both the Japanese community and he himself were being marginalized. Referring to widespread fear of a much larger roundup, Yoshida said, "We anticipate drastic action affecting the civilian population of the entire Territory."[18]

In early February 1942, the Morale Section brought together the first of many advisory committees. They formed a seven-member executive committee called the Emergency Service Committee (ESC) to work in the Japanese community. Most ESC members were familiar figures in the prewar and early wartime interracial movement. Shivers's close friend, the attorney Masaji Marumoto, became the first chairman.

Yoshida was vice chairman. Masa Katagiri and Jack Wakayama were recruited from the Japanese Hawaiian Civic Association, along with Dr. Katsumi Kometani and Dr. Ernest Murai. An agronomist who was active in increasing the local food supply, Y. Baron Goto, was the seventh member.[19] The ESC opened a small office at the Nu'uanu YMCA and began developing a public identity for itself. Despite the blackout, and despite restrictions on travel and public assembly, the ESC reported holding three hundred meetings during its first three months of existence. These reached an estimated six thousand people.[20] Assuming a general accuracy, this meant that on any given day several meetings were in progress involving groups of twenty to thirty people, week after week for several months.

The ESC attempted to promote interethnic unity and displace fear with accurate information. People were urged to give blood, buy bonds, follow the general orders of martial law, and stay calm. If Japanese encountered hostility, they were expected to "take it on the chin."

Hung Wai Ching eventually would say that, among various initiatives set in motion on December 7, the Morale Section and its affiliates such as the ESC only slowly gained wide acceptance with the public. At least three other organizations with similar goals were active in the Japanese community in the early war months. These were the Hawaiian Japanese Civic Association (HJCA), which previously had served as a Nisei leadership development organization; the Honolulu Japanese Chamber of Commerce, primarily a first-generation organization of business interests; and a revived Police Contact Group under the leadership of Burns.

The HJCA sent out a mailing to its members over the signature of its president, Jack Wakayama, urging the Nisei generation to take "active and aggressive control" of their parents to assure conformity to the American way of life. The HJCA letter announced it would not try to tell people what to do. This was followed by a list of what to do: donate blood, contribute to the Red Cross, volunteer for Civilian Defense, avoid repeating rumors, and so on. People were told to work diligently at their jobs: "Anyone who keeps himself deliberately unemployed should be considered a slacker during these times." Also, the letter said to report any subversive activity to the FBI. It ended with an admonition: "Let us be calm, realistic and determined. This is no time for discouragement."

A second campaign was conducted by the executive secretary of the Honolulu Japanese Chamber of Commerce, Tetsuo Oi, an immigrant from Japan who had earned a degree from Stanford University.[21] Oi worked nearly around the clock to bolster the Japanese immigrants, sleeping only a few hours a night on his desk. He focused on the linguistic problems of recently arrived Japanese. Two months into the war, he reported distributing fifteen thousand government forms to the community, as well as overseeing the training of seven hundred people at a dozen first aid centers.[22] Concerned for those who had been thrown out of work, Oi set up a kind of ad hoc employment agency.

Oi's reach via the Japanese Chamber of Commerce reflected the ubiquity of Japanese business, particularly neighborhood groceries. He wrote that the chamber was divided into forty-three districts with 390 subsections. This resulted in his being able to contact well over nine thousand families who, he wrote, represented forty-six thousand people. In essence, he was claiming to reach a large portion of the immigrant community by way of Japanese businesses. Because of his active role in the Japanese business community, he was particularly vulnerable to arrest and, in fact, many of his business acquaintances were sweltering in the heat of the detention camp at Sand Island, in the middle of Honolulu Harbor. Despite his patriotic work, Tetsuo Oi was later interned.

The Police Contact Group, initiated by Nisei as a result of the mid-1941 McKinley High School rally, had been put on hold as a result of the December 7 bombing. The selection process was revived in early 1942, and the Contact Group went public in April 1942. It had sixty members and functioned both in Honolulu and in outlying areas of O'ahu. Like the other groups, its work was about outreach, communication, and quieting fears. In the press statement, it was said to have conducted 161 meetings in the Japanese community in the aftermath of December 7.

Captain Burns had a security clearance and a car, which gave him both mobility and visibility. Young Ted Tsukiyama would vividly remember Burns picking him up at Schofield Barracks to address a night meeting of Japanese working people in Waipahu. They drove through the dark on cane haul roads, guided by the car's small slit headlights. Burns apparently took great pains to coordinate his work with the Morale Section and the ESC, as well as the FBI and Army Intelligence. By May 1942, Yoshida was singling out Burns's operation for its contribution to reinforcing loyalty to the United States.[23]

In addition to these centers of activity, the Swedish consul provided humanitarian support to citizens of Japan. Its work was one of the unusual aspects of the war front in Hawai'i. It stemmed from a prewar agreement between Japan and the United States to communicate with one another, in the event of war, through third-party governments known in diplomatic parlance as "protecting powers." Immediately after the bombing, the United States turned to Switzerland as its communication channel to Japan, and Japan turned to Spain. These were logical go-betweens in that Switzerland was a noncombatant democracy and Spain was a noncombatant dictatorship. The initial focus was on swapping diplomats, including the consulate staff in Honolulu. Amazingly, the United States broached the idea of an exchange the day after the bombing occurred. Thereafter the process came to be used by both sides as they bickered over the status and treatment of internees.[24]

In Hawai'i, the Swedish consul played the role of protecting power in the absence of a Swiss consulate. The honorary consul of Sweden, a hospital administrator, delegated day-to-day work to a young Nisei woman, Shimeji Ryusaki, the daughter of immigrants who had settled in the Waimea District of the Big Island. Ryusaki was twenty-six years old and strikingly beautiful. The oldest of eleven children, she had experienced her younger sister dying at age twelve. From this she distilled a Buddhist sense of the impermanence of life and the injunction to serve others with no thought of return to oneself. She was bilingual, and she quickly took on ever-greater responsibilities. She worked at the former Japanese consul's desk and traveled in the consul's chauffeured black sedan with its mobile telephone. She inspected internment sites and transport ships carrying Japanese internees. She tended to the needs of people returning to Japan (repatriation) as well as people who wished to renounce their Japanese citizenship (expatriation). If the loved one of a Neighbor Island family died in Honolulu, she would represent the family at the funeral. Because of the internment, several hundred women were without spouses at home, and their children were without fathers. They were sometimes shunned socially. Many spoke little or no English. Each morning when Shimeji went to work, she walked through a line of callers. Often they burst into tears. She would begin these encounters by holding the women in her arms. When they wept, she wept.[25]

Taken together, these efforts reveal a combination of Japanese Americans helping themselves and others coming to their aid. Among the several initiatives, it was the Morale Section that served as the instigator, coordinating force, and go-between to the martial law government. Other than the Japanese community, the Morale Section's most pressing problem was Filipino field workers. Hung Wai Ching was among those who were concerned about potential violence, and so was Green. As news of Japan's invasion of the Philippines became progressively worse after December 7, concern heightened.

Within a few days after December 7, the Filipino American N. C. Villanueva was added to the advisory committee of the Morale Section. Thereafter an all-Filipino committee was formed, consisting of ten members under Morale Section auspices. The members asked that a previously existing Filipino hour on radio be revived as a communication clearinghouse, and the Morale Section got it reinstated. A January 20 report said that Filipinos were confident the war would be won, "but there is no doubt they are depressed at present." Although the subject of speculation, actual violence by Filipinos against Japanese was never documented—whether to the partial credit of the Morale Section is impossible to say.

Ethnic Koreans similarly harbored an abiding hatred of Japan. Virtually the entire Korean community had arrived in Hawai'i between 1903 and 1905, after which the Japanese government had tightened its grip on Korea by shutting down Korean migration to Hawai'i. Following years of Japan's encroachment, Korea was colonized outright by Japan in 1910. Korean nationalism was brutally suppressed. In response, the small but vital group of first-generation Koreans in Hawai'i and elsewhere in America served the homeland as overseas patriots who kept the idea of an independent Korea alive. They paid taxes to patriotic associations and supported émigré nationalists in their midst, such as Syngman Rhee and Ahn Chang Ho. Commencement of all-out war with Japan revived their hope that Korea's national sovereignty would be restored. One Morale Section report said that a faction of the Korean community was attempting to "assist" authorities by carrying on its own investigation among the Japanese. Apparently, this was ended quickly.

Expressions of Korean patriotism were complicated by frustration and fear. As first-generation aliens from Asia, Koreans were excluded from naturalized American citizenship, which in legal terms meant they continued to be citizens of the Japanese Empire. Accordingly, some feared the U.S. government crackdown on Japanese aliens. One family of Korean nationalists had stockpiled guns intended to support a Korean uprising *against* Japan. On December 7, they buried the guns out of fear that if found out they might be arrested by the government as *agents* of Japan. As with the Filipinos, Yoshida and Ching organized a steering committee of Korean leaders to sort out their problems and chart a course. Its first chairman was a man named Jacob Dunn, eventually to be regarded as national hero of the revived Republic of Korea. Yoshida's report grasped the significance of Korean nationalism and accurately predicted that as long as it was respected, Koreans would actively support the war effort.[26]

A brief note on the Chinese community described them as content with their status and welfare.[27] The Chinese organized a five-man steering committee chaired by Hiram Leong Fong, a classmate of Hung Wai Ching's at McKinley High School. Fong by then was a Harvard Law School graduate and eventually was to be a long-serving U.S. senator. In terms of citizenship, Chinese in Hawai'i were victims of the Chinese Exclusion Act of 1882. With Japan as the common enemy, China nonetheless was a major U.S. ally in the war, and the Morale Section cautioned that the Chinese in Hawai'i expected to play a significant role on the home front.[28] Nonetheless, Chinese community leadership apparently was soon to feel rebuffed and insulted by being relegated to secondary roles in a white-dominated businessman's militia.

Native Hawaiians seemingly were regarded as free of the war-related problems of Asian immigrant communities. So far as their country of origin was the Kingdom of Hawai'i, they were not at war with anyone else's country of origin. The Hawaiian Civic Club invited the Morale Section to talk about community problems. When the Hawaiians were asked to appoint a liaison person, they designated a rancher from Hawai'i Island named Eben Low, whose life was intertwined with the Hawaiian *ali'i* and also with Sanford Dole, who at the beginning of the century had served as the front man for the white oligarchy's takeover of Hawai'i.

In general, the fear of interethnic conflict in Hawai'i proved baseless. The YMCA's 1937 study of Chinese and Japanese relations was prophetic. The ties between and among the various Asian ethnic groups held, despite the conflicts generated by Japan's aggression in Asia. The positive contribution of the Morale Section on this level was a testimony to its work. More broadly, the good result was testimony to the evolving values of aloha and grassroots democracy.

The Morale Section's organization of the Asian ethnic groups was the easy part. The hard part would prove to be getting Caucasians to recognize that they, too, constituted an ethnic group, and that they needed to more actively help deal with the crisis.

PART IV

From the Inside Out

Hung Wai Ching Tells Mrs. Roosevelt About Hawaii's Role In War

Americans of Japanese Extraction Are Being Released for Work on Farms and in Cities

Star-Bulletin Bureau.
Washington, D. C., May 7—

Mrs. Franklin D. Roosevelt received Hung Wai Ching with Delegate Joseph R. Farrington Thursday afternoon and heard Mr. Ching discuss the contribution of residents of Hawaii to the war effort.

Mr. Ching later described his reception as "cordial and gracious."

Mr. Farrington said he was pleased with the attention the first lady gave the Honolulu resident discussing the contribution his part of the country is making to the war endeavor.

In connection with this situation it was announced that the war relocation authority has a graphic press release revealing how Americans of Japanese extraction held in reallocation camps for more than a year are being returned to normal life on farms and in cities.

These west coast evacuees, two

Japanese Driving On Hunan Capital

CHUNGKING, May 7. (AP)—A strong Japanese force which crossed Tungting lake by launches under airplane cover, effected a lodgement on the southern shores of the lake, Chinese headquarters announced tonight.

The announcement indicated another Japanese drive on Changsha, capital of Hunan, is underway.

WELLES IS REJECTED

LOS ANGELES, May 7. (AP)—Orson Welles, actor-writer-director, was rejected Thursday for induction into the army "for physical reasons," an induction center official announced.

Mr. Ching

CHAPTER 9

The Morale Section at Work

WHILE THE MORALE SECTION ORGANIZED within the different ethnic groups, an emotional event occurred that put Ching and Yoshida into the center of public attention. The background dated to the fall of 1940, when Hawai'i's two National Guard regiments were federalized and called to active duty. This left the territorial government without a guard unit to call its own, which in turn led to the creation of the Hawaii Territorial Guard (HTG). On December 7, when the Nisei of the university ROTC were ordered to duty, it was under the command of the HTG. In a famous incident, a squad of students was dispatched to secure a ridgeline above the University of Hawai'i in the face of a rumored parachute invasion. The invaders turned out to be an illusion, but the incident provided anecdotal evidence that Japanese Americans would stand in defense against Japanese troops in the face of an invasion. Thereafter, the HTG guarded power plants, water pumping stations, and government offices. The iconic photograph of this period was of a Japanese American soldier standing guard at the gates of 'Iolani Palace.

Nearly six weeks after December 7, at 3 a.m. on January 19, the Honolulu battalion of the HTG was called out, and the Japanese Americans among them were dismissed. This was about two-thirds of the total unit.

Their dismissal was widely interpreted as a response to pressure from Washington, D.C. This no doubt was a factor, in that Nisei guardsmen had become a subject in the Roberts hearings. As if scoring a point for toughness, General Emmons reported to the War Department that he had inactivated seven hundred "Japanese," an inflated number.[1] What escaped the public, including the Nisei, as well as subsequent recitations of history, was that the HTG was vulnerable to surgery for administrative reasons. Overlooked in the territorial government's archives was a unit record, in which it was apparent that the HTG did not have adequate leadership, financing, equipment, or training. The problem of preparedness was compounded by an outpouring of new volunteers. The unit had swelled from a single outfit of about six hundred men concentrated in Honolulu to three O'ahu battalions and two in Hilo on Hawai'i Island, totaling nearly fourteen hundred.[2] To reduce the payroll, the territory encouraged the non-Japanese members to volunteer for the regular army. A further problem was that HTG competed with the Honolulu Police Department, which regarded the securing of public facilities on O'ahu as part of its job.

Accordingly, the HTG dismissal resulted from a combination of factors, worsened by an uncharacteristic clumsiness and lack of communication on the part of Emmons, for which he would later apologize.[3]

All that said, what mattered most was the apparent discrimination and the intensity of emotions that swept through the ranks. Many had tears in their eyes. Guardsman Ted Tsukiyama would forever recall this as the lowest point in his life, a cry of pain that became the operative response. One of the HTG, Masato Doi, was to write, "Happy have been the days that were, dark is the color of now."[4] The downhearted ROTC students returned to the UH campus, where they debated how to impress the country with their patriotism. What happened next became legend in the story of Hawai'i.

The Varsity Victory Volunteers

A small nucleus of individuals—a total of five, one of whom was Tsukiyama—met with Hung Wai Ching under a shade tree on the University of Hawai'i campus.[5] They were depressed and angry. Ching began: "Tough luck, boys. That was a hard blow." (Silence). "OK, OK. I know exactly how you feel. But what are you going to do about it? Nothing? You going to take it lying down? You going to sit out the war? Do nothing? Just feel sorry for yourselves?"

Having taught countless Sunday school lessons, having led countless youth meetings, and having studied theology at Yale, Ching turned to Christ's admonition in Matthew: "If any one strikes you on the right cheek, turn to him the other also."

"Turn the other cheek," Ching said. "Go the second mile. You think the only way you can serve is with a gun? . . . They're dying for manpower. . . . Why don't you guys volunteer for [a] labor battalion?" The young men were at first appalled. "Labor battalion!" The very thought was demeaning. Ching continued: "Damned right, labor battalion! [Are] you too proud to do common labor? Think of the impact! You guys are at the prime of life. You're willing to give up good defense jobs and education. You're the intellectual cream of the crop, and yet you're telling them you're willing to work with your bare hands to serve your country!"

Hindsight did not lack for claimants of the idea. Ching recounted the story several times. Burns in his oral history said that after Ching's first campus meeting, he met with Ching in the Morale Section office, where he advised organizing a labor battalion.[6] John Young claimed to have held the original meeting. Young recalled they met almost immediately with Emmons, who was said to be receptive from the beginning.

The one person whose role was understated was Yoshida. On behalf of the students, Tsukiyama wrote a first draft of a petition, packed with emotion and excess words. Streamlined by Yoshida, it became, "Hawaii is our home; the United States, our country. We know but one loyalty and that is to the Stars and Stripes. We wish to do our part as loyal Americans in every way possible and we hereby offer ourselves for whatever service you may see fit to use us." The Yoshida of old age was pleased with the wording: "It was to the point, very brief and sincere." Asked if he wrote these often-repeated words, he replied, "Well, now that you ask me, I'll have to say yes."[7]

The resulting Varsity Victory Volunteers (VVV) was the ultimate organizing project of the YMCA. The organizers were from the Atherton House YMCA. They discussed the petition's wording at the Central YMCA. They then held a mass meeting at the Nu'uanu YMCA.

The idea of a labor battalion played well in both Hawai'i and Washington, D.C., for nearly opposite reasons. That is, people in Hawai'i saw it as an entering wedge into the war effort, while in Washington it was a convenient way of shunting eager Japanese Americans into menial labor. For Emmons, approval was an easy call. He told the proponents only that he required a unit of at least 170 men.

Ching worried about both turnout and the tone the unit would strike. He worked relentlessly on shaping the unit, resulting in a group that was well behaved, studious, and not lacking for strongly held opinions. Concerned that it would be exclusively college boys, Ching recruited a renowned boxer, Richard Chinen, who was older and brought street celebrity to the ranks. The early volunteers signed up other volunteers. As the unit developed, it progressively filled space in the minds of observers and the public alike, even though the sign-ups were less than overwhelming. The number of volunteers just made it to Emmons's metric of 170—the unit count actually was 169. It was less than half of the number let go by HTG and a small fraction of the available Japanese American manpower pool. Further, the volunteers were, as Ching observed, substantially of the same demographic. They strongly tended to be the educated sons of pioneer Issei, from whose hard work they had benefited.

Over and over, they were told they were on the spot and that the future—theirs, their families, the Japanese community, and how everyone was to get along in Hawai'i after the war—hung in the balance. The VVV mobilized quickly. Following an emotional rally on the UH campus, they were sworn in at 'Iolani Palace on February 25, a month after the HTG dismissal. Their mobilization stirred a breath of hope in Hawai'i during the same week that President Roosevelt issued Executive Order 9066. Ching stood in his familiar position on the left side of the top steps of the palace. Emmons stood front and center. He was his usual terse self: "Thanks for turning out and the best of luck," he said. "I know you will work hard." He shook hands all around. Both the *Honolulu Star-Bulletin* and the Army Signal Corps photographed the sendoff. The volunteers loaded into army trucks and rode out past Pearl Harbor, up the central plain, and on to Schofield Barracks.

Native Hawaiians played a special role, surrounding the VVV like a protective cover. To house and handle the unit, Ching contacted the most distinguished Native Hawaiian soldier of his time, General Albert Kuali'i Lyman, who was in charge of construction engineering at Schofield Barracks. Lyman gave his wholehearted support, without which the project likely could not have gone forward. Ching arranged an officer's commission for a part-Hawaiian to serve as morale officer—Tommy Kaulukukui, a football hero from the University of Hawai'i. Kaulukukui was placed in charge of an athletic program for the VVV. In addition, two sergeants of Hawaiian ancestry were assigned to the unit as cadre.

General Lyman assigned a Chinese American, Captain Richard Lum, to command the unit. Lum's intermediary to the men was a newly commissioned Japanese American lieutenant, Ralph Yempuku, who came from the University of Hawai'i Athletic Department and agreed to serve as an older-brother figure at the determined urging of Charles Hemenway. From the ranks of the students, Ted Tsukiyama served Yempuku as his number two.

They were mentored constantly. Ching went to Schofield often to check on "the boys" and to manage situations before they became problems. John Young likewise visited Schofield often. Like Ching, he had studied theology. He also had engaged in missionary work in both China and Japan. He spoke Japanese and regularly laced his conversation with value-loaded Japanese words such as *giri* (duty/obligation) and *ganbare* (persistence). Yoshida continued to be involved with the VVV while juggling innumerable concerns and contacts. His personal notes beginning April 21 say, "Had lunch at the Rotary Club. Clocks were presented to the VVV." On Tuesday, April 28, he noted that arrangements for a speaker to the VVV fell through: "Checked with Hung Wai. . . . Must arrange for one next Tuesday"—this suggesting that they tried to send a weekly speaker to Schofield. The following Tuesday Yoshida met with a Congregational pastor from south Kaua'i, who went with Yoshida to Schofield: "Gave a good talk to the VVV boys." A week later Yoshida went to Schofield with Dr. Lind. On April 30, he wrote that "a few of the Triple V boys came in to see me about giving their blood." On Saturday, May 2, he "went to see the boys giving blood at the hospital. Sixteen of them. Got some brandy for them." The hospital staff invited the VVV blood donors to a chop suey lunch. On Sunday, May 3, Yoshida counseled Yoshiaki Fujitani, who was upset because his father, a Buddhist priest, had been interned. "Told the boy to wait a week before he resigns from the Volunteers. Hung Wai and I will do what we can." Fujitani did resign but later volunteered for military intelligence. He later was to marry Yoshida's younger sister and eventually became a distinguished community figure as bishop of the Hongwanji Buddhist Temple.

The college boys proved to be tough and spirited. They quarried and crushed rocks, built roads, moved lumber, and built barracks. Although free to leave at any time, Fujitani was one of only three who did so. A second left to help with his family's coffee harvest in Kona, then returned. The third was the boxer Chinen, who left in a moment of anger but returned and made amends.

Their hard work, the blood donations, and even their sports programs were reported in the government-supervised press. By April 10, 1942, the *Honolulu Star-Bulletin* exclaimed, "The VVV Does It Again!" with an accompanying story on the unit's 100 percent subscription to war bonds. The conscious goal of the members was to work their way into combat service. The theme of creating a more equitable society in the postwar period was also at work. In their spare time, the more intellectual ones took classes, including one entitled "Post-War World."[8]

Tsukiyama took his Brownie camera and photographed everyone over and over. Despite the sweat and grime, all appeared to be having a great time. For some, it was their first chance to get away from home. Tsukiyama had an exceptionally mature understanding of the unit as potentially of historic importance.[9] He was the son of an educated Issei. He was part of the small minority of nonwhites who attended Roosevelt High School, an English Standard school that tested applicants for English proficiency before admission. He regarded himself as "one of Hung Wai's boys" in the YMCA, and he also was acquainted with Yoshida and Burns. He was drafted to give talks in the community on the meaning of the VVV. One such presentation ended with this: "We are not just the VVV. We are yours, the community's, the nation's representatives in a unique war effort. We need your support, your confidence, your good will, and your approval that what we do is right."[10] With many others, Tsukiyama believed the VVV served a great purpose: "It was the finger in the dike to stop the flood of fear, hysteria and prejudice."

Countering Japanese Nationalism

As the responsible individuals in a war zone, Emmons and Green worked with little margin of error. They could hold to their tenuous position of trusting Japanese Americans only under three conditions: first, if they remained confident that sabotage and espionage were absent; second, if people in Hawai'i worked together in a reasonably unified way; and third, if people of Japanese ancestry would actively allay both local and national fears by contributing to the war effort. It was by addressing these conditions that the Morale Section derived its access to the top reaches of the martial law government.

A Morale Section paper conceded that a minority within the Japanese alien population was "nationalistic, strongly loyal to Japan, and dangerous." However, it argued that Japanese nationalism had been greatly diminished by a sense of shame about the surprise nature of the attack and also by gratitude to the American government.[11] The paper mapped ideas for communicating with the pro-Japan element: "1. Stress their obligation to America. . . . 2. Stress the welfare of their American children, the fact that these children are American citizens and owe their education and livelihood to America. 3. Play on their sense of appreciation for the fair treatment they are receiving from American authorities. 4. Interpret the American democratic values in contrast to the totalitarian values now operating in Japan. 5. Urge them to live up to the best in Japanese traits (obedience, respect for constituted authority, sense of appreciation)." Yoshida repeatedly pointed out what well might not have occurred to the ruling American authorities otherwise: namely, that many Issei thought of Hawai'i as their country.

A Work Diary

Yoshida kept his diary-like notes from April 21, 1942, to May 12, 1942, creating a unique close-up view of the Morale Section's work. He can be seen running off to a meeting, checking on his school (which he still served in spare moments as principal), giving a talk, then working into the night. The relationships established in the prewar proved durable in wartime. Yoshida often worked with Shivers, Burns, Bicknell, Lind, Katagiri, and others of Shivers's six Nisei advisers. On the morning of April 21, he spoke to the International Institute of the YMCA on the morale of the Japanese community. He was unhappy that the haole establishment was not more actively supporting the Japanese: "A certain Mrs. George B. Isenberg took exception to my statement concerning the haoles. . . . A call from Miss Towle in the evening assured me that the talk had been well received by everyone else she had talked to."[12] After focusing attention on the VVV in remarks to the Rotary Club, he worked at his school, then returned home to write a progress report on the Emergency Service Committee (ESC).

The next day he, Loomis, and Ching met with an independent-minded attorney named Frank Thomas to discuss ways the haole could help. "[Thomas] advanced the opinion that the Citizens Council and the Big Five were out to save their hides," Yoshida wrote. "[We] need for the little fellows vitally interested in the future of Hawai'i to get together to work for Hawai'i. Get up an inter-racial council."

A little later they met with Lorrin P. Thurston, publisher of the morning newspaper, the *Honolulu Advertiser.* Thurston was the namesake of the missionary descendant who had orchestrated the overthrow of the kingdom and whose newspaper often warned darkly against a yellow tide of Asians. "Presented the need of emphasizing unity and the future of Hawaii," Yoshida wrote. "Got the usual business attitude—everybody has problems, don't press the issue, time will take care of things, etc."

Yoshida, Katagiri, and Dr. Murai next met with Hemenway at his home, where they once had gathered as students to practice their debates. Yoshida then met with Burns's Contact Group in late afternoon. Police Chief Gabrielson participated, as did House Speaker Vitousek. "Both gave encouragement to the boys." Yoshida closed out the day with a meeting among various Japanese on River Street, which had become the heart of Japanese business inside the old boundaries of Chinatown. The next day he followed through with Vitousek, who was known in political circles as "Boss Roy." Vitousek was well regarded for supporting the political participation of elected Japanese Americans—a majority of whom were Republicans at that point. He showed Yoshida a letter he had drafted to the Los Angeles and San Francisco Chambers of Commerce. Yoshida approved.

Yoshida then met with Bicknell of Army Intelligence, reviewing Sam King's attempts to influence the Tolan Committee. He teamed up with a Buddhist priest, Eugene Hunter, to speak to the VVV at Schofield. Evidently Hunter had not been interned because he was Caucasian. "Hunter spoke on post-war plans," Yoshida wrote. "Talk didn't go over too well."

The next day, Friday, after meetings and writing, Yoshida spoke at Waipahu High School. He was disturbed by the tone: "One of the teachers wanted to know if I had any authority to address the students." Yoshida found the students to be languishing from indifference and lack of leadership: "The teachers must make themselves more a part of the community." (In this, he reflected agreement with the estimate of public education in Waipahu written by Lind's student.)

Yoshida worked most of the weekend. Among four events on Saturday, he met with Shivers's group of six Nisei advisers and then with a well-known social worker named Nell Findley, who was moving to the relocation camp in Poston, Arizona, to aid the internees. "I admire her courage and her sense of duty to her ideals," Yoshida wrote. His and Miss Findley's mutual acquaintance, Dr. Miles Cary of the Council for Interracial Unity, also was relocating to the Poston camp to set up a school system for interned children. (When given a choice of the camp administration's housing, Cary would opt to live in the barracks with the imprisoned families.)

On Sunday, Yoshida attended a joint conference of the YMCA and YWCA. He then went to visit Hung Wai Ching, who was suffering from shingles, a stress-related ailment. He thereafter went to a baseball game as the guest of the dentist Katsumi Kometani, who owned the famous Japanese American ball club, the Asahi. It was a poignant moment. Kometani was about to leave for military service. The team had changed its name from the Asahi to the Athletics for the duration. The new general manager was none other than Jack Burns. The coach was Neal S. Blaisdell, a young part-Hawaiian man who would eventually be the longtime mayor of Honolulu. These two would become, respectively, the dominant figures in the Democratic and Republican Parties for much of the next several decades.

The following Monday, Yoshida went to his school and attempted to clear the clutter on his desk. At noon he met with the ESC, encountering a variety of loose ends and budding conflicts. He also met for a second time in the week with Harold T. Kay, a Big Five attorney who was associated with Vitousek and otherwise well connected politically. Kay, just back from Washington, D.C., said they must do something more in Hawai'i "to offset the demand for drastic action," almost certainly referring to a forced relocation of the Japanese population. Yoshida closed out the week with a speech in Aiea and a late-night meeting with a journalist.

In the three-week period covered by his notes, Yoshida reported three conversations with Army Intelligence, one with Green, one with the chief of police, and two with Shivers. Of Shivers he wrote, "Arrived half an hour late and this didn't please him." He met twice with Thurston and three times with Vitousek. He updated his communication with Hemenway. He was in frequent conversation with the superintendent of public education, Oren E. Long. He communicated often with the VVV and took a guest speaker to Schofield Barracks each Tuesday. One night he cooked dinner for Yoshio Hasegawa, the police department's original point of contact with the McKinley High School volunteers, and also for Burns. "Imagine my chagrin at having to feed them in the semi-darkness." He spoke to hundreds of high school students and other community groups, most notably in the YMCA—this in addition to dozens of conversations with people in the ESC or with people otherwise engaged in some level of community organization.

On Sunday, May 3, Yoshida took time out to read materials about the West Coast. He came close to an undiluted bitterness. "My heart goes out to those being evacuated," Yoshida wrote. "If there is justice, and if America is really fighting for democracy, there must be an attempt to correct the injustice that has so far been done." He was upset by a rumor which held that the absence of sabotage was the surest sign that Japanese agents were lying in wait—"The same old story," he wrote.

The Morale Section's West Coast contacts were expanding. Galen Fisher of the Fair Play Committee stayed in close touch. Yoshida was also communicating with Lincoln Kanai, a YMCA secretary in San Francisco. Kanai was originally from Kaua'i and a 1930 graduate in social work from the University of Hawai'i. He was an instantaneous resister to the forced evacuation. When he refused to relocate inland, he was arrested. While awaiting trial, he left California to travel the country looking for colleges that might accept the application of Japanese American students. "Poor Lincoln's doing all he can," Yoshida wrote, "but the odds are too much against him."[13] Kanai went to prison for six months. Long afterward a friend revealed a letter from Kanai in which Kanai wrote, "I have a higher authority than the United States government, and I must follow it."[14]

On May 5, two days after his despairing Sunday, Yoshida finished writing a paper called "UNITED HAWAII, INC." The recurring theme was the search for unity to get through the war and thereafter to build a better society. The outcome would "affect the welfare of not only the Japanese but of everybody else in Hawaii during and after the war." He defined the problems at hand as "(1) the potential disloyalty of a certain percentage of the group and (2) the fear psychosis and the consequent demands for drastic action to meet the problem." Yoshida believed that a substantial portion of the entire community would cooperate with a unity program, if not for the sake of the Japanese then for "the preservation of Hawaii and all that it means to them." He predicted that not only the military in Hawai'i but, in due time, the military in Washington would buy in.

Arguing that all but a small percentage of both aliens and citizens were loyal to the United States, the plan concentrated on finding ways for people to demonstrate their loyalty and to focus public recognition on such demonstrations. Those "on the fence" could be converted by participating in activities "which make them feel that they are with us." To cover the downside, the plan also called for keeping the potentially dangerous "under close surveillance or have them investigated and interned by the authorities." Taken together, he believed, these actions might allay fears sufficiently to prevent a massive removal and incarceration.

Yoshida added, "Place the greater part of the responsibility on the Japanese themselves."

Yoshida asked for a budget of $25,000 to support a public informa-
tion bureau dedicated to countering "fear psychosis"—one of his favorite pairing of words—in both Hawai'i and on the Mainland. In this, he
clearly recognized that fear was running out of control across the continent. Second, he wanted support for expanding ethnic and interethnic
organization across the territory. Funding, Yoshida wrote, should come
not only from the Office of the Military Governor but "as many sources
as possible to avoid the appearance of domination by any one special
interest or group."

Loomis was apparently taken aback by the scope of Yoshida's ideas.
He limited its circulation "to let it incubate." The Morale Section was
left to fend for itself financially, but the plan nonetheless served thereafter as their guide to action.

The Morale Section networked extensively with Burns at HPD. This
collaboration was most important in organizing the plantation communities of rural O'ahu. The prototype was the plantation at Aiea, immediately west of metropolitan Honolulu. Aiea had about five thousand
people, nearly half of Japanese ancestry. In the hope of stabilizing the
downward slide of morale, four meetings were held over two months,
beginning in March 1942. The first meeting was a show of common
purpose by the ESC and the Aiea Plantation.[15] The ESC speakers were
the celebrated attorney Marumoto, the often-present Katagiri, and the
agricultural agent Baron Goto. The Honolulu Plantation Company was
represented by its manager, the Stafford Austin who had vouched for
Hawai'i's Japanese in his affidavit to the Tolan Committee. The chair
was from Burns's Police Contact Group, Yoshito Matsusaka. A cadre of
twenty-five contact people—mostly male—led the way in recruiting a
volunteer labor force. Inspired by the VVV, it was called the Aiea Victory Volunteers. Every Sunday, they cut *kiawe* trees along the beaches to
clear lines of defensive fire in case of an invasion. They also performed
labor for the U.S. Army Corps of Engineers. In the first three months,
the Aiea Victory Volunteers racked up more than sixteen hundred volunteer workdays.

Contact people knocked on doors. They signed up several hundred
blood donors and encouraged everyone to buy war bonds. One aspect
of their appeal was a new ruling that alien bank accounts frozen by
the U.S. government could be unfrozen if invested in U.S. war bonds.
A number of aliens did so. For employees of all races, the plantation

developed a payroll deduction plan for the purchase of bonds. The Aiea
Victory Volunteers mounted community drives to gather wastepaper,
rags, and rubber tires for recycling. The Red Cross appeared in Aiea
in the person of Mrs. Samuel Damon of the missionary Damons. She
recruited forty-five Aiea women, who formed a sewing group.

Burns reported the story of a Filipino plantation hand who was known
for his frequent use of the word "Japs." After a month of watching the
patriotic work at Aiea Plantation, the Filipino man said, "You Japanese
are OK. We take our hats off to you." Burns also quoted an Issei man as
saying he now felt better and that the program had "brought light into
our dark existence and pointed out the way. We did not know what to
do. But now that we know what we can do, we will do our utmost." The
habit of Japanese and Filipino workers talking and eating together over
lunch break was restored.

Burns saw in outwardly humble activities the potential of a new
society. While intolerance is part of the human condition, he wrote,
"If the opportunity is taken and pushed, equal opportunity prevails for
everyone regardless of race." Burns said that whenever newly included
people came to a meeting, committee leaders solicited their thoughts
and opinions: "Everyone contacted has changed his outlook towards
this emergency."

Burns was often to be described as brusque and inclined to watch
events from the back of a meeting room. Be that as it may, he played a
leading role in the community's Educational Committee. He told the
assembled Japanese that, like himself and most other people, they or
their parents had moved from a foreign land. He celebrated America
as the land of the free. He quoted the Declaration of Independence as
the basis of what it meant to be an American: "We hold these truths to
be self-evident: that all men are created equal; that they are endowed by
their Creator with certain unalienable Rights; that among these are life,
liberty and the pursuit of happiness." Burns said it was for this ideal that
Japanese had come to America, and it was the reason for fighting the war.
He plunged on, quoting Lincoln at Gettysburg on government of the
people, for the people, and by the people. In his parting paragraph, he
turned unerringly to the core Japanese themes of loyalty and obligation.
It was not to the Hitlers or the Tojos that the people owed loyalty, he said,
but to the American nation that had given them opportunity. The issue
of loyalty was being sealed in blood: "Those who have died have thrown
the torch to us to carry on," Burns said. "We cannot fail them."[16]

Everyone on the scene seemed to agree that Burns had a special grasp of the situation. The first-generation Japanese had come from a country in which the Meiji leadership and then the military dictatorship had fueled a nationalistic bonfire. Burns posed the essence of America's answer, and never mind the historical accuracy of why most people had immigrated. He understood the power of idealism and loyalty. He understood the ever-nagging presence of discrimination, the devaluing of people of color, and what he was to famously describe as an unwarranted "subtle sense of inferiority." He had one hand on the Nisei and one hand on the Issei. He embraced rather than shrank from a phenomenon of the period, which was the potent influence of a white person who unequivocally cast his lot with nonwhite people.

Burns had gone from writing police reports to writing ideas. He wrote to the retired General Wells commending him for stating there had been no sabotage on December 7. He wrote to the editor of the *Honolulu Star-Bulletin*, Riley Allen, proposing that the newspaper dispense with the hyphenated American-Japanese in favor of Americans of Japanese Ancestry (AJA, on second reference). Allen said he would try it, and thereafter it became widely adopted throughout Hawai'i and elsewhere.[17]

The organizing of Japanese plantation communities spread from neighborhood to neighborhood—to Waipahu, 'Ewa, Kahuku, Hale'iwa, and remote Waialua. These efforts shared in common a cooperative approach including the Police Contact Group, the ESC and Morale Section, plantation managers, the Red Cross, and the Blood Bank. The meeting records reflected thoughtful and courteous discussion, aimed at building consensus. An individual would ask a question or make a proposal. Various members would reflect, followed by a decision attributed to "Group." Work projects helped create a deeper sense of community. The Waipahu Emergency Service Committee sponsored a drive to buy a community ambulance. The Kahuku Patriots trained Boy Scouts in camping and first aid in the event of another attack. At Waialua, the contact teams went door-to-door in fifteen different residential camps, stretching from Hale'iwa to the remote beach at Mokule'ia.

The Island of Kaua'i

On behalf of Kaua'i, the Congregational Church minister Paul Denise appeared at the Morale Section office in early May 1942, asking for help.[18] Yoshida made a note that Kaua'i's situation was not good. "Hope we can go there to get something done." On May 23, a Saturday, Yoshida, Ching, Loomis, and Marumoto traveled to Kaua'i. As a much smaller community, Kaua'i brought the problems of the war into a particularly sharp focus. Nearly half of Kaua'i's thirty-six thousand people were of Japanese ancestry. The island, with abundant water and rich soil, was laced with plantations. More so than elsewhere, the Japanese-ancestry population of Kaua'i still worked in the sugar industry. Many continued to live in the relative isolation of labor camps. This decentralization was reflected in the fact that the island had numerous Japanese-language schools (sixteen), Buddhist churches (twenty-two), and Shinto temples (four). A statue in the county seat town of Līhu'e celebrated the victory of Japan over Russia in the war of 1905, as did a second statue to the north in the town of Kapa'a.

At first glance, Kaua'i was a pastoral backwater. The island's most influential figure was Charles Rice, the grandson of a teacher who had arrived with the New England missionaries. After being elected as a Republican for thirty years, "Charlie" Rice had supported the Democrat Roosevelt for president. In an act of heresy, he gave $5,000 to Roosevelt's first reelection campaign. His brother William was a perennial sheriff of Kaua'i County, and his brother Philip was a prominent lawyer. Together the Rice brothers created a comparatively benign, semiseparate polity at the far end of the archipelago. There was a little something for everyone. The International Longshoremen and Warehousemen's Union (ILWU) had made significant inroads into labor organization prior to the war, and Japanese American political candidates had achieved significant success at the polls.

In contrast to prewar forward movement, the first months of martial law rule had not gone well on Kaua'i. When the army took over the Kaua'i county government on December 7, it was confronted by the threat that Japan might invade a neighboring island that then would serve as a military base for an invasion of O'ahu. Among all the islands, this threat was most imminent for Kaua'i. It is closest to Japan, and it was virtually without military defense. To punctuate Kaua'i's vulnerability, a Japanese submarine lay outside Nāwiliwili Harbor on the night of December 30 and shelled the harbor at will.

Kaua'i's army commander wrote that "through fear or misunderstanding," many people of Japanese ancestry had withdrawn psychologically, believing they were unwanted.[19] Drawing the line connecting internal security and morale, he said that an element of the Japanese community might become dangerously embittered in its isolation. Fearing sabotage, the authorities at first had clamped down. In the several days after December 7, the FBI arrested forty-one leaders of the Japanese communities, including all of the consular representatives and most of the priests and language-school teachers. The first provost marshall court session convicted eight persons of traffic violations in fifteen minutes. A Japanese man was sentenced to five years in jail for reputedly saying, while drinking with American soldiers, "The United States Army is no good and democracy is no good."

Manpower was in short supply, and martial law regulations prevented workers from changing jobs. Absenteeism resulted in thirty days of confinement at hard labor and a fine of $100. The average wage on the plantations was frozen at forty-one cents per hour plus housing and medical care, which was valued at nine cents an hour. The plantations in turn contracted a portion of these workers to the army for sixty-two cents, thereby turning a twelve-cent per hour profit. The captive plantation workers then labored alongside regular civilians who made considerably higher wages, a situation the army attempted to address by ordering everyone to stop talking about how much they were being paid.

When the army organized a home guard on Kaua'i, none were of Japanese ancestry. The majority of its members were Filipino, suggesting that drills were mainly aimed at creating an illusion of participation for Filipinos who otherwise were frozen to their plantation jobs.

Everyone agreed that the morale of the Japanese communities had deteriorated rapidly. Numerous interrogations by the intelligence agencies had preceded the war, so in some instances Japanese community leaders had kept their bags packed awaiting arrest. Gijo Ozawa was a Buddhist priest from Yamanashi Prefecture in Japan. He was raised to the priesthood by his father, also a priest. As a young man he had been conscripted into the Japanese Army. There he made such a positive impression that he was assigned to guard the emperor. After he completed his military service, the Soto Zen sect of Buddhism dispatched him to Kaua'i, where he served a Buddhist congregation in the Wahiawa Camp area above Hanapēpē town. He and his family were supported by contributions of the congregation, much of it coming from the bounty of the land and ocean. When a community member approached the Reverend Ozawa's residence, he or she called out respectfully from the bottom of the staircase and removed his or her shoes. When Reverend Ozawa heard shoes climbing the stairs without anyone calling out, he realized that the FBI had arrived to take him away.

He reached for his small bag, but the agents told him he wouldn't need it. He was jailed for several days without benefit of a toothbrush, until his wife and children caught up with him at the Kaua'i jailhouse.

The arrests were proportionately few—less than 1 percent of the ethnic Japanese population—but their impact on a small community was marked.[20] One young girl on Kaua'i was aware of her uncle, who was a community leader, her Japanese-language schoolteacher, and a Buddhist priest, all disappearing at once.

Officeholders of Japanese ancestry were pressured to step down from public offices that had been dearly won at the ballot box. In 1900, the first territorial election, only 3 percent of the voters were of Japanese ancestry.[21] As the Nisei came of voting age, they not surprisingly led the way in advancing political candidates. In 1930, a spirited man named Noboru Miyake won a seat on the Board of Supervisors representing southwest Kaua'i, the first American of Japanese ancestry elected to public office. As war approached, four Japanese American candidates won in the primary election for Kaua'i's Board of Supervisors and one for the Territorial Legislature.[22] The chairman of the Kaua'i Republican Party, a Chinese American, proposed they withdraw, an opinion taken up by the *New York Times* and *New York Daily News*. The *Garden Island News* then agreed. One by one, all withdrew.

Although the Morale Section leaders from Honolulu were philosophically inclined to build a multiethnic organization across the territory, they yielded to the ethnic pressures of Kaua'i in the short term.[23] Where the FBI arrests had taken away traditional leaders, they sought to develop new ones. They turned to a United Church of Christ pastor, Masao Yamada, who was part of Hung Wai Ching's web of acquaintances. Yamada was born in 1907 in Camp Five of Makaweli Plantation, which made him one of the older Nisei. His father was a skilled carpenter who often worked at the plantation manager's house. Yamada tagged along and was thereby "exposed to Western culture," his wife eventually wrote.[24] In his early youth he converted to Christianity through the Hanapepe Japanese Christian Church. At twelve, he was sent to Honolulu, where he boarded at the Okumura Dormitory, attending McKinley High School and the University of Hawai'i. As an active YMCA member, he campaigned to start YMCA clubs throughout O'ahu. He hoped to work for the YMCA after graduating, but when a job opened it went to a newly arrived haole. Yamada took his grievance to Frank Atherton, the Big Five executive and YMCA president. He announced he was leaving the YMCA. Atherton was adept at juggling white privilege against the rising expectations of the Japanese. He secured a scholarship from the missionary society for Yamada to attend Auburn Theological Seminary in New York. There Yamada met the famous American socialist Norman Thomas, as Ching had before him. He worked in Thomas's 1932 campaign for president of the United States, then returned to Hawai'i and served as pastor in his wife's community in Kona, on Hawai'i Island. He and his wife then were invited to do missionary work in Japan. Shortly thereafter, Japan's army invaded China, and suddenly the military was all powerful. Yamada and his wife were classified as pacifists and hustled out of the country. In 1937 he became pastor of the congregation of his childhood church in Hanapēpē, Kaua'i.

After Pearl Harbor, he was asked to be part of the delegation greeting the new army military commander, who spoke derisively of "the Japanese," unspecified. Yamada cut in and said, "If you hate us so much, why don't you shoot me!" The next day he was invited to army headquarters and given an apology.

From the combined contacts of Yamada, the Rice brothers, and the Morale Section, a steering committee was organized for Kaua'i. The chairman was the head bookkeeper of Rice Ltd., Charles Ishii. The vice chairman was Masaru Shinseki, also a bookkeeper. Yamada was secretary. All were early born Nisei who had risen to leadership positions before the war.

One alien, H. S. Kawakami, served on the original Kaua'i committee. He had been brought to Hawai'i by his older brother, Fukutaro, who worked in the sugar fields to support his education at Mid-Pacific Institute on O'ahu. When H. S. Kawakami returned to work in a plantation store on Kaua'i, he realized that Japanese quickly hit a ceiling of advancement. Bucking plantation pressure, he had gone on his own, taking grocery orders from plantation families in remote camps and delivering them out of the back of a Model T Ford. When the plantation camp police tried to keep him from travelling on plantation roads, he retained Philip Rice at $50 a month to be his lawyer. Rice made a telephone call, and the problem went away. By 1941, Kawakami owned two stores, the beginning of a modest empire called Big Save Markets.[25]

Although he had lived in America twenty-nine years, Kawakami had been prohibited from U.S. citizenship by virtue of his birth in Japan. He had visited the last Japanese naval training ship to call at Port Allen and taken the Japanese naval captain and two other officers on a courtesy call to the County Building. After December 7, he was interrogated repeatedly. Which side of the fence was he on? "All my business and all my savings are right here on Kaua'i," he parried. "My heart is right here. All my children are here."

It helped that he spoke English extensively, that he advocated vigorously for himself, and also that his attorney was Philip Rice. Kawakami was a walking testimonial for acquaintance. "I try to work with all racial groups," he wrote. "This creates understanding. It dissolves suspicions."[26]

The positive effect of the Morale Section was nearly instantaneous. It was as if the Japanese community of the island was suddenly licensed to get moving. With a steering committee in place, Shigeo Yoshida and the others set out to build a mass organization. Their second day on island, a Sunday, he and Marumoto spoke at three stops, including Yamada's church in Hanapēpē. They were accompanied by the head of Army Intelligence on Kaua'i, who told the Japanese they were needed in the war effort. Dr. Murai and Masa Katagiri arrived the following day and recruited district chairmen from around the island, including a bookkeeper in Waimea, an attorney in 'Ele'ele, an engineer in Līhu'e, a bank teller in Kapa'a, and a tax assessor in Hanalei. All were of Japanese ancestry. Each district was divided into sections or camps, which in turn were divided into blocks. Each block had a chairman, who in turn had helpers, called contact men. A contact man was responsible for communicating with a maximum of ten houses. The resulting organization was decentralized in such a way as to reach into virtually every Japanese household while being coordinated from the top down.

Contact men were coached in how to promote giving blood and buying war bonds. A print guide said, "We are untried individuals. We have been indoctrinated for the past thirty to forty years in Japanese thought and culture. The stake for us is precarious. We are American citizens in the making. It is our hour of trial."[27] The contact men conducted a crash survey that asked about household size, ages, occupations, education histories, spoken languages, and citizenship. Based on their observations, workers checked one of several descriptive boxes: Neutral, Frightened, Ignorant, or Cooperative. Of nearly seventeen hundred alien heads of household interviewed, 93 percent were reported to be cooperative. Although numerous observers had described the Japanese as frightened, only 2 percent were identified as such in the survey. Kaua'i was revealed as still a largely stratified society.[28] The survey turned up only one lawyer of Japanese ancestry, five doctors, one banker, 104 teachers, a dozen accountants, and fifty-nine bookkeepers. Otherwise there were smatterings of policemen, social workers, contractors, and photographers. Three were ranchers. Many had risen to the level of skilled tradesman—carpenters, machinists, plumbers—most predictably on the plantations. A small fraction (likely a smaller fraction than in Honolulu) worked as domestics and yard boys.[29]

Fluency in English was the doorway to advanced education. Two hundred forty-six English speakers had attended a university, while only sixteen predominantly Japanese speakers had done so. More than nine thousand people had some level of grade school education. Among aliens, more than twenty-five hundred reported themselves as Buddhists, more than three hundred as Christian, and four as Shinto.[30] Although Shinto observances were woven into their ritual life, usually holidays, people did not regard it as a religion nor themselves as church members.

In the course of the door-to-door interview, contact workers urged people to buy bonds, give blood, give service to the community, and donate to community causes.

The makeup of the island population was changing dramatically. White soldiers were arriving in large numbers, first as an emergency defense force, then for training in jungle warfare. By late summer, the military population outnumbered the resident population. Meanwhile, without fanfare, the Japanese American soldiers of the 299th Army Regiment—many of them native sons of Kaua'i—sailed to O'ahu for military training.

On July 18, two months after their initial foray, Yoshida, Ching, and Loomis returned to Kaua'i. Ching coordinated with the military. Loomis spoke to a conference of social workers. Yoshida again took the lead in a speaking tour. Obviously, he was not only valued as an orator in English but Japanese, because the entire tour was conducted in Japanese.

The crowds swelled. Along the south side of the island, Yoshida spoke at four plantations, numerous camps, and the Waimea Christian Church. Yamada was heartened: "The alien Japanese group freely expressed themselves as follows: 'We are thankful. This clears our hearts.' 'Most of us have lived longer in Hawaii than in Japan. We have been cared for and aided by the American government in our long days here. We have an obligation to this country.'"

"We are *'yoshi'* (adopted sons) of America," Yamada quoted another as saying. "It is our duty to do the will of the American government."

"We must all be one," a man at the hamlet of Lāwaʻi declared. A resolution proposed that all Japanese be 100 percent loyal to America. Everyone voted "aye."

The fact that a number of older Japanese nursed a primary loyalty to Hawaiʻi came out repeatedly. "We believe in Hawaii," an Issei man said. "We are more Hawaiian than otherwise."

H. S. Kawakami told people in Japanese, *"Umi no oya yori sodate no oya,"* which he translated as, "When you have had two mothers, one who brought you into this world and one who brought you up, you owe much more obligation and respect toward the mother who brought you up." Honor America.

The newly empowered Kauaʻi Morale Committee held forty-three meetings in the Japanese language in three months, involving nearly two thousand people. As a means of further involvement, the committee began calling people out in early July to clear a field of defensive weapon fire along the beaches. On the first Sunday, nearly five hundred men turned out. The next week the number tripled, which was more than could be effectively organized and put to work. They were called the Kiawe Corps to celebrate the felling of the tough *kiawe* trees that grew along the vegetation line.

A Japanese women's group transitioned from rolling bandages to performing the hard labor of the Kiawe Corps. The women's chair was a YWCA secretary, Aiko Fujikawa. The vice chair was the wife of Charles Ishi, the Rice brothers' bookkeeper. Chitoko Isonaga, a staff member of the Morale Committee and sister of a VVV founder Herbert Isonaga, was secretary. Others were schoolteachers. Like the Kauaʻi Morale Committee, the women's group had haole advisers, the most prominent of whom was a missionary descendant, Elsie Wilcox, a stalwart of the YWCA who previously had served Kauaʻi as a legislator.[31]

The statistics of Kiawe Corps participation were breathtaking. Between early July and Christmas 1942, work was performed on twenty-five separate days, with a total turnout of 1,431 men and 438 women. Cutting brush, Yamada wrote, "has been the ace-card in making the aliens find themselves in the war effort." In late 1942, rumors spread from Honolulu that all Japanese were to be evacuated. Aliens on Kauaʻi bought blankets and warm clothes. To knock down the rumor, the Morale Committee held thirty-eight meetings in one week, reaching nearly 3,000 people.

Viewed at arm's length, the Kaua'i Morale Committee was in part a substitute for the traditional community leadership that had been swept up by the FBI and jailed. At the point of their arrest, the detainees of Kaua'i did not know where they were going, or what their status would be.[32] Reverend Frederic B. Withington of the Līhu'e Union Church visited the martial law jail on December 9, the day after the first arrests. "The situation was most discouraging," he wrote. Five men were crowded into a cell designed for a maximum of three. One was a fellow Christian minister, likely the Rev. Paul S. Osumi, who had come from Japan and performed humanitarian work in the Japanese community. He was under arrest for writing letters on behalf of dual citizens who sought to shed their Japanese citizenship.[33]

With community support, conditions in the jail improved. Communication was reestablished between detainees and their families, and family visitation was set for two hours a week. Men were allowed to keep money and pocketknives. They performed tasks of their choosing. Some gardened. Others wove mats, carved, played games, or read. Supporters of the detainees were aware of the Geneva Convention and used it as leverage: "We have tried to remember that not only is there an American standard to uphold—but that there is an international agreement which calls for humane and fair treatment, and that the standard that we set may have an effect on the treatment of American nationals detained by other nations at war with us."

Following the initial sweep, another twenty-eight individuals were picked up one by one. Additional family members of the internees were relocated in the name of family reunification under confusing circumstances that involved a combination of enticement and coercion; they became virtual internees themselves. Two families were told they were being repatriated to Japan—that is, they were being forced into prisoner of war exchanges and deported to Japan. No reason was given. One family objected. The army commander initially balked at reversing the order but then agreed to keep the family on Kaua'i if the Morale Committee assumed responsibility for the family's welfare.

Markers of Japanese culture and history were dismantled. The two statues celebrating Japan's victories in the Russo-Japan war were torn down. Half of the Buddhist churches were shut down, as were all the

Japanese-language schools and Shinto temples. In some instances where properties were to be taken over by the U.S. Alien Property custodian, the Kaua'i Morale Committee interceded to take control of the proceeds, putting the money into scholarships that were handed out to students regardless of ethnicity.[34]

In a year-end report for 1942, the committee described itself as alarmed by complacency.[35] Things were going too well for their comfort. Anxiety had abated as a result of sincere friends "who are out of their aloha saying 'you Japanese are doing everything,'" thereby implanting a false security and a short-term satisfaction, making many of the Japanese pseudo-heroes of the island." The Japanese immigrants, the first-year report went on, were regaining self-confidence. The report also complained that the most educated people—meaning haole, although no ethnic group was specified—were not exerting leadership commensurate with their status: "By natural disposition, the highly educated are detached from the common clay." To which the report added, "The Japanese are forcing its own members to relinquish clannishness but the others are just as clannish as the Japanese!"

A follow-through report in the spring of 1943 concluded that the job of orienting the Japanese community to the war effort had been substantially achieved.[36] The larger task was transitioning from "old Japanese thought" to American ways. This introspection went to the Darwinian question of racial inferiority or superiority: "There was from the beginning of time in the Territory, the feeling of the superiority of one race over the other." (Again, the names of the groups in question were politely not mentioned.) "The group on top has by its managerial ability and economic status held the most coveted position socially and politically for a long while. With the importation of alien Japanese and other laboring groups, the laboring group always took the servant's position." However, the Orientals were not completely docile: "They were economic servants but culturally, they felt that they were as good or better than their lords."

The writer, likely Yamada, went on to say what few individuals at the time said aloud: the Japanese community had been on the move in the prewar, and by coping with early wartime problems it was getting in a position to exert high-level leadership. The report asked if the Kaua'i Morale Committee's work should remain under the military. The answer was yes, because the alternative was perceived to be the prewar status quo: "We prefer to have an unbiased authority which

. . . preserves the good will of all groups on the basis of equality. The Military is the only authority that can bring better harmony and peace in our present set-up."

In biting off this slice of the martial law question, the Kaua'i Morale Committee reflected a belief held by many of the less privileged in Hawai'i—that in spite of the injustices of martial law, it was a transitional path toward a social system based on greater equality. The standard of comparison was the previously unfettered influence of the Big Five and the government of the territory of Hawai'i.

Less than a year into the war, the Kaua'i Morale Committee began to use the words "post-war reconstruction" and to propose a multiyear plan to develop what they called the Community Improvement Society.[37] The goal for the second year became organizing across racial boundaries: "The movement for children's playgrounds, better sewer systems, etc. can fuse all groups together into one. What the Japanese Kai did for Japanese only, the Community Improvement Society can do to lift the standard of living for all Americans."

The goal for the third year was to complete "the change from the old world to the new." It was hoped that by 1944 most meetings would be held on an interracial basis and in English: "Rubbing shoulders with one another regardless of race . . . as Americans, can become an experiment of far-reaching benefit." The Kaua'i committee proposed that morale groups on all islands transition into chapters of the Community Improvement Society and then hold a territorial conference on postwar reconstruction. While this was not exactly how events were to unfold, this proposal took varying forms across the Islands.

The army commander on Kaua'i, Major Charles A. Selby, wrote that the central idea all along was to develop an interracial community organization. He invited wide participation "as an initial step in the solution of the inevitable and serious problems of post-war reconstruction." As relationships improved, he sounded less like a military officer and more like a mayor: "Your comments, criticism, and suggestions are invited."[38]

The concepts developed on populous O'ahu had been considerably refined on Kaua'i. What had begun as a desperation response on a small island had become a series of bold steps. While the Morale Section was mapping the way forward, the Kaua'i Community Improvement Program was filling in crucial detail.

Maui

The arc of morale work on Maui was much like Kaua'i. The Pearl Harbor attack caused "a sickening feeling in the hearts of every red-blooded American citizen of Japanese ancestry." The FBI arrests created fear. Older Japanese tended to withdraw. Once more, the arrival of the ESC from Honolulu reversed this downward drift by licensing the involvement of the Japanese community in the war effort. This brought about "a marked change in morale."[39]

Maui County's army commander, Colonel Charles B. Lyman, a product of Hawai'i, had effectively managed the initial wave of fear. He was the brother of General Albert Kuali'i Lyman, whom Ching had sought out to make use of the Varsity Victory Volunteers at Schofield Barracks. The Lyman brothers were descendants of the great chief Kuali'i, the paramount chief of O'ahu in the seventeenth century, at a time when O'ahu was an independent polity. The Lymans also were descended from missionaries, Asian settlers, and a Cherokee Indian. They were said to be the first high-level Asian/Pacific Islander officers of the U.S. Army.[40]

Colonel Lyman understood the importance of culture. As a means of damping down Filipino resentment of Japan, he seized on December 30, Rizal Day, to mount an appeal to the Filipino communities. A flyer addressing Filipinos said, "We know your eyes are filled with unshed tears. . . . We respect you for the self-control you are showing—the fine way you are living up to the spirit of your great statesman, scientist and author, Dr. Jose Rizal." Over the signature of a Miguel Valdez, president of the Maui Filipino Civic Club, the statement continued: "There is no time for ill feeling among the various groups in the islands. There is too much for each one of us to do."[41] It was translated into the predominant Philippine dialects of Tagalog and Ilocano.

The enormous Hawaiian Commercial & Sugar Co. (HC & S) plantation, occupying the north-central plain of Maui, had a population of nearly eight thousand people out of a total island population of forty-six thousand. Its largest element was Japanese, who occupied many of the plantation's thirty camps. In early January 1942, camp leaders converged on the HC & S personnel office.[42] The authority figures were Lawrence "Chu" Baldwin, personnel manager of the plantation; Dr. Homer Izumi, a physician of Japanese ancestry who worked at the Kula tuberculosis sanitorium; and Judge Edna E. Jenkins. The first question was the recurring rumor that concentration camps were being built on Moloka'i to house the entire Japanese alien population. Through a translator, the Japanese camp leaders were told that the rumor was false; further, that the practice of destroying the emperor's picture and pictures of relatives in the Japanese military should cease—that what mattered was not possession of a picture but loyalty to America. The meeting reviewed the martial law prohibitions of firearms, ammunition, explosives, short-wave radios, swords, spears, bows and arrows, cameras, and binoculars. Offshore fishing was prohibited for all, and Japanese were also prohibited from fishing from the shoreline.

A Japanese man who had worked thirty-five years for the plantation spoke up: "My children and grandchildren have been born here. I will live here and I will die here. I am a good citizen. I want to thank you for coming here today and saying these things to us. . . . We will work harder than before. All we want is to know what we shall do."

Probably because of relatively favorable conditions on Maui, the ESC did not come calling until August, seven months into the war.[43] Katagiri and Murai arrived first. Loomis followed, speaking to the plantation managers and haole businessmen. Yoshida and three others from the ESC then arrived for their now familiar barnstorming. In two days, they spoke to 770 people. They recruited district chairmen as they went.[44] Dr. Izumi reported that, after a slow start, the committee quickly gained momentum "and is fairly well up to its neck in work."[45] One of its first acts was to visit the detainees, who were at Ha'ikū on the northern coast of the island. Following the Kaua'i example, layers of contact workers were recruited as outreach to each family. One Sunday the turnout for the Kiawe Corps was seven hundred ("they were getting in each other's way").

By January 1943, the Maui Morale Committee reported that involvement in the war effort had made people feel wanted, lifting much of the fear and uncertainty: "As a result, the Japanese people have regained much of the self-respect which they lost on that fateful seventh of December, 1941."[46] Although Izumi pursued ethnic organization as a short-term imperative, he too sought to create an integrated community: "An inter-racial program for the future is obviously the only solution for all of us in this Territory."[47]

Hawai'i Island

The Island of Hawai'i was not the undivided success of Kaua'i and Maui. It is the island farthest from Japan. It was fortified for defense and troop training without the apparent urgency of Kaua'i. The enormous island traditionally operated on an east-west divide, with Hilo serving as the center of the east side. As elsewhere, Hilo's traditional Japanese leadership was rounded up. The patently unjust arrests of the two leading Japanese political figures, Sanjiro Abe and Thomas Sakakihara, played badly. Nonetheless the Hilo community seemed to reach a kind of equilibrium. Hilo was a sizeable town, heavily Japanese, and the seat of government.

The vast Kona District, which was coffee country, formed the heart of the west side. Prior to the war, Kona was often portrayed as idyllic. Japanese families who picked beans in the coffee fields often sang Japanese songs to one another while they worked. The singing stopped.[48] Stories of conflict abounded, particularly conflict with Filipinos.

Alarmed, the UH sociologists began to inquire about life in Kona.[49] The history of Kona's population derived substantially from the aridness of the land. Houses were dispersed, sometimes down rocky slopes accessible only by footpaths. The Japanese had not lived in close proximity with other ethnic groups, as on the plantations. On the contrary, Kona in the late kingdom days was a place of refuge for Japanese workers who had jumped their labor contracts under the Master's and Servants Act.

Dispersion and more individualistic lifestyles made the military nervous and more inclined to repression. The area military commander was known for restrictive orders. One of his more foolish orders was requiring military permission to go from the traditional district of North Kona to South Kona. He prohibited women of Japanese ancestry from the USO. Farmers could only burn trash on Friday. An elderly Japanese bachelor was fined $700 and given four years in jail for using an uncovered flashlight. A militia group composed mainly of Filipinos, the Hawai'i Rifles, barred Japanese from participation in their group.

A Japanese American sociology student, Helen Ikeda, described a friend of her father's, a Mr. T., who was known before the war as the first to arrive at a gathering and the last to leave. He often dropped by the Ikeda house on his way home from the store. Mother would cook a chicken. Another friend would drop by. The party would be on. With martial law, liquor was rationed and barely available. The customary exchange of gifts at New Year stopped. Once-vibrant people whom Ikeda had known as a child now behaved timidly. They often were disinclined to leave home. Cooped up in blacked-out houses at night, some feared that their neighbors would point the FBI their way. Further,

Ikeda believed that Kona people were less tolerant of interracial dating than city dwellers. If a Japanese girl was seen in a movie house or on the road with a soldier, everyone knew about it.

A second student writer said she often gritted her teeth at the pro-Japan remarks of older community members. The Japanese neighborhood organization, the *kumiai*, was shut down. It then was revived in a thinly disguised form, with Nisei replacing Issei in the leadership. An inquiry into the local Konawaena High School revealed open prejudice and verbal abuse of Japanese Americans. Schoolteachers were reported to have humiliated students by calling them Japs or "Tojo face." When students were prompted to air their dislikes, many did so readily, steaming with ethnically driven resentments.[50] Some of the Japanese students looked down on Filipinos, some of the Filipinos resented the Japanese, and various students resented the haole.

An analysis of Kona dated August 1942 described the first attempt to organize a more far-reaching morale project. The author was Shiku Ogura, a graduate of Konawaena High School who had moved to Honolulu and become active in the YMCA, then returned to examine his home island. "The community is disintegrated," Ogura wrote. He echoed the view that an alarming number of older community members were taking comfort in Japan's military successes. He appealed to the Morale Section to get active in Kona. Seeing positive results elsewhere, he suggested that they delegate responsibility to a Kona Morale Committee.[51]

Professor Lind visited in early 1943 and decided that government price controls had set the price of coffee beans unworkably low. In some instances, demoralized Issei believed their land would be confiscated and they would be arrested. They left their coffee beans in the field. Sons went away to wage jobs or to war, and overflow Filipino labor was restricted by wartime regulation. Many Japanese families turned to *lauhala* weaving, a traditional fiber craft that had been kept alive in the region by Native Hawaiians. In a short time, the hundreds of thousands of soldiers and sailors passing through Hawai'i were buying *lauhala* placemats, fans, and hats as proof of their encounter with paradise. Middlemen dealt the products in Honolulu and around the other islands. As a result, industrious families were reputed to be making more than they ever had made in coffee. Agricultural extension agents from the University of Hawai'i stepped in, headed by Baron Goto of the ESC. Goto cajoled and pressured. He told the people that everyone was watching. GIs needed coffee. He proposed that the farmers and their families devote themselves to coffee beans from sunrise to sunset through the picking season. If they wanted to keep weaving, they could do so inside their blacked-out homes at night. Most agreed.

While Goto's extension service brought about improvements, it apparently never achieved the level of cohesion that the morale groups achieved on the plantations. Various reports indicate the best the extension agents could do was soften the edges of martial law. In a year-end assessment, Ogura wrote that a new military commander had been installed. Farmers were given a modest increase in the ceiling price of the coffee market. The north-south boundary restriction was lifted. Fishing was reestablished. The military was reopening its ranks to Nisei. War bonds were selling. Food markets were flourishing.[52] After two years, Ogura was finally optimistic: "Many feel that happy days are back again, and that old Kona spirit of friendliness and hospitality has returned."[53] If results in Kona were slow in coming, the Neighbor Island campaigns were generally a resounding success for the Morale Section. Most of the Japanese-ancestry populations seemed to be aching for acceptance into the war effort, and the Morale Section pointed the way. Once the energies of Neighbor Island communities were unleashed, their resulting activity took on a life of its own.

CHAPTER 10

War Service or Mass Evacuation?

WHILE COMMUNITY WORK was developing across the territory, federal pressure on the martial law government for a mass removal continued unabated. At President Roosevelt's January 30, 1942, cabinet meeting, Knox again pressed his case. The president told Knox to reach agreement with Stimson on a large-scale evacuation from Hawai'i "and then go ahead and do it as a military project," a wording that gave his approval to indiscriminate removal on the grounds of military necessity, as was soon to occur on the West Coast.

In early February, the War Department ordered Emmons to lay off all Japanese civilians from military jobs. Emmons wrote back saying there were more than four thousand such workers of Japanese ancestry, representing about 95 percent of all skilled workers. Discharging them, he reasoned, would delay the war effort. It would also idle, frustrate, and impoverish people who were otherwise making a vital contribution. Further, a person who went to work every day was much less likely to be dangerous than one who was unemployed and brooding. The effect of such a layoff, Emmons argued, would be to "consolidate pro-Japanese sentiment" and promote disloyalty. Moreover, there would still be thousands of other Japanese and Japanese Americans working on the docks, highways, railroads, utilities, and plantations.

Emmons proposed sticking with the status quo until American troops arrived on a much larger scale. At that point, he wrote, the government could evacuate "a large part" of the Japanese population. This glib and pro forma endorsement of a large-scale evacuation was the sort of ploy that Emmons would use repeatedly. He put up barriers to evacuation and then talked tough, engaging in what Green would eventually describe as a rearguard action.

In response, the War Department backed away from the layoff order but nonetheless pressed the idea of mass evacuation. On February 14,

Washington proposed building a camp on Molokaʻi to hold twenty thousand of the "most dangerous," a novel idea in that no single person ever had been identified as dangerous. How twenty thousand were to be so identified, the War Department did not say. Washington also authorized the evacuation of up to one hundred thousand "Japanese" from Oʻahu to unspecified destinations. To this, Emmons replied that however desirable such an evacuation might be, it was—again—impractical. Between Honolulu and Washington, D.C., this battle of suspicion versus trust, exclusion versus inclusion, continued. While Roosevelt never took active ownership of the exclusion schemes by outright and directly demanding implementation, he repeatedly cleared space for such action. "I do not worry about the constitutional question," he wrote, citing EO 9066 as well as martial law.

In the first several months of the war, the army draftees of the 298th and 299th National Guard Regiments receded into the landscape. Strangely, the presence of a large contingent of uniformed, armed, trained Japanese Americans was all but overlooked. They were assigned to guard the coastlines, which meant they were widely scattered. This was fortuitous, because it would be of utmost importance to future events that they not be pushed out of the army or segregated into a labor battalion.

Two credible strands of story—one navy, one army—describe what happened next. They differ, but they are not mutually exclusive. The navy version has been so widely ignored as to become almost unknown. It is rooted in the role played by the Office of Naval Intelligence through Cecil Coggins, in concert with Kenneth Ringle and Douglas Wada. The historical amnesia about the navy version is particularly odd because Coggins described it in a 1943 article in the nationally distributed *Harper's Magazine*. The prewar Hawaiʻi of Coggins's memory was a melting pot in which children of all races mixed "in an atmosphere of perfect equality." The problem was the loyalty question. When Emmons arrived to govern, he was besieged with advice: "Self-appointed advisers invited him to lunch, buttonholed him in the street, [and] formed lines outside his office door," advancing a multiplicity of views about the Japanese. "But General Emmons refused to be stampeded."[1] Emmons was a rock against the storm.

Coggins continued: a delegation from the Japanese Hawaiian Civic Association petitioned for opening military service to Japanese Americans. "Whereas," they wrote, "to deprive us of the sacred birthright to bear arms in defense of our country is contrary to the principles upon which American democracy is founded, now therefore . . . grant us the opportunity to fight for our country, and to give our lives in its defense."[2] Coggins arranged for the petitioners to meet with Walter Dillingham, who by then was arguably the most influential of the old-school oligarchs of Hawai'i. Dillingham owned or ran a significant part of the Island economy. He kept an office in Washington, D.C. To attack the worker strike of 1919–1920, he had raised the cry of a Japanese conspiracy. Now he seemed to be a new man. He chaired the Territorial Food Committee, which was trying to build up food sufficiency, and he was practically alone as a haole of the corporations who had real entrée with the martial law government. Possibly the military leadership admired him because he was a headstrong autocrat, or possibly because they knew he was a friend of Roosevelt's and occasionally spoke with the president by telephone.

The executive committee of the HJCA—a lawyer, a merchant, a salesman, and an editor ("the leadership of thousands")—made an earnest plea to Dillingham, whom Coggins described as moved to tears. He organized a luncheon at his villa, La Pietra, on the shoulder of Diamond Head, to which he invited the Nisei petitioners and all the top military officers in Hawai'i, chief among them Emmons and the one person who outranked him, the commander in chief of U.S. forces in the Pacific, Admiral Chester W. Nimitz. Both men endorsed the Hawaiian Japanese Civic Association (HJCA) petition and, according to Coggins, Emmons forwarded it to the War Department in Washington.

Coggins said Emmons then reviewed the intelligence records of more than one hundred thousand people. While the number is outlandish, it conveys the pervasive scrutiny to which the Japanese-ancestry population of 160,000 was subjected. In Coggins's account, the War Department began to shift its attitude toward a Japanese American combat unit. This was a streamlined cause-and-effect account that not only Coggins but Douglas Wada believed.

The army story is more complicated. It is also more substantive. It began with the Council of Interracial Unity and its alliance with the FBI and Army Intelligence. At Schofield Barracks, the performance of AJAs in the army contributed to an ever-improving relationship, but whether the Hawaiian Army's inclusive view would ever penetrate Washington, D.C., seemed doubtful.

The variable in the equation of spring 1942 was John J. McCloy, the traveling undersecretary of war, the field man who had served as the cabinet-level architect of the West Coast internment. McCloy was the source of a convoluted twist that makes sense only by carefully reviewing what he had been doing on the West Coast versus what he encountered on the ground in Hawai'i.

McCloy found in Emmons a commander whose calm and focus contrasted with the nervousness and agitation of DeWitt in the Western Defense Command. Emmons spent only a part of his time governing Hawai'i and otherwise had the gravitas of a battle zone commander under enemy threat. Green emerged as Emmons's knowledgeable number-two man who might have been described as McCloy himself had been described—that is, Green had his nose in everything. Green had taken a position against Bendetsen's ideas of a mass internment prior to the war, along with Short, and he had authored the General Order No. 5 promising loyal people of Japanese ancestry "the consideration due all peaceful and law-abiding persons." Fielder of Army Intelligence was charming, while the question of whether a person could be arrested for potential internment was delegated back to the FBI's Shivers, who seemed to command everyone's respect and who insisted after investigation that there had been no sabotage or subversive activity in Hawai'i.

McCloy witnessed firsthand how closely the three-member Morale Section worked with both Army Intelligence and Shivers. They seemed to reach deeply into the Japanese community and bridge the potentially contentious problems of the other ethnic groups. Oddly enough, a scholarly Japanese American named Yoshida was advising the martial law government and writing public addresses for the command. Yoshida had just turned in a report on behalf of the Morale Section reflecting its high level of activity. He wrote reassuringly that there were no signs of significant domestic conflict. In fact, McCloy on his arrival could read on the front page of the *Honolulu Star-Bulletin,* "Racial Groups Form 'Victory Committees.'" The story listed dozens of citizens engaged in the work of the Filipino, Chinese, Korean, Puerto Rican, and Japanese communities under the auspices of the Morale Section.[3]

Further, an impressive representation of Japanese American professionals was organized to exert leadership through the Emergency Service Committee (ESC). The chair was a Harvard Law School graduate, Marumoto, and Yoshida was vice chair. With their encouragement, people of Japanese ancestry, aliens and citizens alike, were donating blood, buying bonds, rolling bandages, digging trenches, and cutting *kiawe* brush from the beaches—in general, contributing real value to the war effort while demonstrating loyalty to the United States. At the Honolulu Police Department, there was Chief Gabrielson, who spoke up for the Japanese community, as well as Captain Burns, who was mysteriously in the know—a white man who had gone local.

And then there was "the Chinaman," Hung Wai Ching. Where McCloy had been surprised to eat noodles in the San Francisco China-town with the Japanese American Citizen's League (JACL), in Hawai'i he found that the most ubiquitous promoter of the Nisei was a char-ismatic person of Chinese ancestry. Ching took McCloy on a guided tour of the Varsity Victory Volunteers at Schofield Barracks. His pur-pose was to explain the volunteer labor brigade with a maximum of fanfare. Ching knew their every detail—their individual personalities as children at the YMCA, the leadership qualities they displayed in Hi-Y groups, their siblings, their parents, what they studied in school, their reactions to their dismissal from the Hawaii Territorial Guard (HTG), their petition to serve the country, and their work habits under the hot sun at Schofield.[4]

The VVV men were divided into twelve work gangs, through which they managed themselves. Ching drove McCloy up the mountain to a stone quarry where one of the gangs was breaking boulders and load-ing them for movement to a wall-building project. Although the VVV had been stripped of their guard uniforms, they now dressed neatly in blue dungarees and blue work shirts, as if their lowly status had become a badge of pride. If these were the lambs sacrificed to Washington's demands for a crackdown on "the Japs," as they were almost always described in McCloy's diary entries, they were resilient. The Hawaiian Army command, the YMCA, community leaders, sociologists, and min-isters—all sang the praises of the VVV.

McCloy also saw firsthand that the majority of the two National Guard units, the 298th and 299th regiments, were made up of Japanese Americans. Self-discipline—as distinct from command discipline—obvi-ously played a major part in their service. For example, an army reserv-ist, Masaichi Goto, brother of Baron Goto, had been drafted in late 1940 and trained at Schofield Barracks. He was shipped to Maui, where he built barracks at an army camp and then ran the kitchen of Headquar-ters Company. After serving out his obligation, he returned to O'ahu in November 1941. On December 7, he wrote in his notebook, "War!

Remember Pearl Harbor."[5] On December 8, he reached an encampment of the 299th on O'ahu but was told to report to the HTG. He found the HTG mess hall operation was in bad shape. "Soldiers almost starving," Goto wrote. He was placed in charge of food supply and promoted to staff sergeant. Of the HTG dismissal, he wrote, "I was really sore for the deal. But I was a soldier." At the point where he could have disappeared into the community, he bought an air ticket to Maui, where he spent four days with his young wife, Fumiko, while he located his prewar unit. Back in the 299th, he lost his sergeant stripes and stood guard duty. "Had to start over." When McCloy arrived, Goto was one of nearly two thousand Japanese Americans still in uniform.

All in all, it was as if McCloy had entered a different country.

Prior to McCloy's trip, Emmons might have seemed confusing, striking contradictory notes, twisting and turning, even risking a charge of insubordination. Whenever Washington had pressed for a large-scale evacuation, Emmons had sent long cables explaining why such a thing was impractical or why he agreed with Washington's goals but suggested doing things a little differently. He was short of shipping; he needed these people in the workforce; maybe later he would ship all of them out, and so on. At close range, the question was what Emmons really thought and whether McCloy and he could see eye to eye on a course of action. The third person in the discussion was Green, who would write that he was fortified in his position by Ching and Yoshida and their cohorts: "I leaned heavily on the intelligence reports given me by members of our Morale Section, which was composed largely of Orientals who were in close touch with large segments of the Oriental population. This group assured me that the local Japanese were trying their level best to cooperate fully with the Office of the Military Governor and that they were cognizant of the difficulties we were having in sustaining our position in treating them fairly." Green said Emmons—in contrast to his cleverly ambiguous cables—clearly spelled out to McCloy that the crux of his approach was to cultivate the loyalty of Japanese Americans and Japanese aliens. Green wrote, "At a conference in our office, General Emmons convinced him of the correctness of our view [opposing] evacuation." The following day, he confirmed to the press in Hawai'i there would be no mass evacuation.[6]

In the discussion, the alternative to evacuation became a Japanese American combat unit, to be drawn from the National Guard. Emmons said they should not be used to fight Japan but, he believed, they would give a good account of themselves against Germany and Italy. It would not only give them a chance to prove their loyalty but also reinforce the loyalty of their families.

Green said McCloy was impressed and promised to take up the idea in Washington. McCloy's light had gone on. In the face of almost complete opposition at the highest levels of his own department and the White House, he now wanted to train, arm, and deploy Japanese Americans. In this, he was at odds with his previous position and also at odds with people he had empowered to ruthlessly pursue the West Coast internment.

On his return, McCloy held a news conference, in which he announced that a mass evacuation of the Japanese-ancestry population from Hawai'i was an impossibility. Too many Japanese Americans were working on defense projects, fortifications, and roads, he said. Better yet, some of the workers were "keen and enthusiastic." A single reporter questioned "why an evacuation on the West Coast was deemed a military necessity when a much larger and more concentrated population of Japanese Americans, living in the midst of a Pacific battlefield, was thought essential to the national defense."[7] Other than that, neither then nor thereafter did the press ask why Japanese Americans were removed from their communities on the Mainland while their much more numerous and potentially more threatening counterparts in Hawai'i were not.

McCloy's about-face was stunning. He was the government's sabotage mind, yet he no longer believed the Pearl Harbor sabotage story. On April 4, 1942, a reporter from the *Detroit Free Press*, Radford E. Mobley, called him about his Hawai'i trip. McCloy told Mobley "there were no authenticated cases of actual sabotage as distinguished from espionage." The sabotage argument in support of the forced evacuation was off McCloy's table. While the debacle of the concentration camps deepened, McCloy became a voice of caution, suddenly concerned about the constitutional issues at stake.

A University of Hawai'i political scientist, Dr. Noel Kent, was to describe McCloy as manifesting "split-mindedness."[8] He held two seemingly opposing views. Charitably, McCloy reflected two long-standing regional attitudes, one being California's, the other being Hawai'i's. In context of California he was an exclusionist, while in Hawai'i he favored inclusion. However influential, McCloy was less the maker of policy than a faithful political conduit and manager, juggling local concerns from hinterlands to the top of the federal decision-making heap. McCloy was not completely unaware of this phenomenon, remarking to his logbook the danger "of yielding to local pressures which demand drastic and unintelligent action."[9]

As one who wrote about the West Coast internment in the moment, the scholarly Morton Grodzins understood the source of McCloy's seemingly contradictory views. Grodzins said the overriding factor in California was "the regional demand for evacuation." The writer Carey McWilliams, also in California at the time, looked into the state's long history of prejudice: "With the aid of the Deep South, [California] had forced the federal government to adopt the Chinese Exclusion Act in 1882." Further, "Since the federal government had capitulated to the South on the Negro question, it found itself powerless to cope with race bigotry on the Pacific Coast."[10] He decried "the alarming extent to which the foreign policy of the government of the United States toward 'colored' races and nations has been determined by the provincial prejudices of a particular region, more precisely of a particular state."[11]

Two days after McCloy's press conference, on April 6, Emmons asked the War Department for approval to organize a Japanese American unit of soldiers from Hawai'i and ship them to a Mainland training camp. Contrary to the fears held by some in Hawai'i, this had nothing to do with removing Japanese from the territory. Rather, straightforwardly, it was aimed at developing a Japanese American combat unit to fight in the European theater of the war.[12]

Opposition in Washington was intense. A brigadier general on Marshall's staff, H. R. Bull, quoted War Department policy to the effect that such a unit should be assigned to noncombat duty in the interior of the United States or in Hawai'i.[13] Four members of Marshall's staff commented in the same vein, including Eisenhower, the future commander of America's European forces and, eventually, president of the United States. Eisenhower held to the view of assigning Japanese Americans to noncombat roles in which, he wrote, "they cannot gain valuable information, or be in a position to execute damage to important installations."[14]

Although McCloy had not presented it as such, the idea of a Japanese American combat regiment was apparently taken as oppositional to a large-scale Hawai'i evacuation. The joint chiefs struck back at Emmons with a proposal for a mass evacuation of the Japanese-ancestry population from Hawai'i. The date was April 15, 1942. Five days later, Secretary of the Navy Knox again weighed in with his argument for removing all Japanese aliens from O'ahu. President Roosevelt again agreed with Knox.

Chaotically, one week later, a joint meeting of War Department and navy war planners seemed to suggest that the Hawai'i viewpoint with regard to evacuation was having an impact. They recommended that Emmons be authorized to send fifteen thousand Japanese males to the Mainland.[15] The key word was "authorized." He was not directed to do so.

In this atmosphere, it was no wonder that Emmons had to haggle and connive. On May 11, he again took up his argument for a Japanese American combat unit. In response to Stimson's belief that Hawai'i's Japanese Americans should be placed in a noncombat service unit, Emmons cabled saying this would have serious repercussions on the Japanese population, "which is now cooperating fully with authorities." Stimson backed off.

Ching and Yoshida became involved in the discussion, as reflected in notes by Yoshida of May 12 describing a meeting with Fielder on the status of the National Guard in Hawai'i. Fielder had been assigned to go to Washington to advocate for a combat unit.[16] He was a strong choice, in that he was a vigorous supporter of the Nisei soldier. He had commanded the 298th National Guard in the field, and now he was the head of Army Intelligence in Hawai'i.

A summary of army views noted tersely that in a May 7 letter, Admiral Nimitz weighed in supporting a combat unit. Apparently, this reflected the groundwork of ONI's Cecil Coggins and the petition of the HJCA. At the time, no one commented on the Pacific navy command recommending formation of a Japanese American Army unit while failing to examine its own racial policies.

On May 18, McCloy warned Emmons that Knox continued to resist and that the president did likewise. He wrote that they continuously "refer to the desirability of moving Japanese from the Island of O'ahu to some other island rather than to bring any numbers of them to the United States."[17] Emmons thanked McCloy for the warning but was undeterred. He wrote back, "I think we can counteract any such suggestions when the time comes."[18] Having previously told the War Department that seven hundred Japanese Americans had been assigned to noncombat units, which was an overstatement, Emmons now understated the number of men that he intended to send for combat training on the Mainland. He gave a figure of one thousand. The actual figure was more than thirteen hundred. In essence, he used a standard number for units of battalion size without explaining that he planned to organize an oversized battalion.

Playing his hand to the limit, Emmons made preliminary moves without securing orders from Chief of Staff George Marshall. On May 26, he notified Washington he had relieved the Japanese Americans from the windward headquarters area of the O'ahu regiment—the 298th—and moved them to Schofield Barracks on the central plain. He said "low morale" made it urgently important to move all the others to Schofield as well. The same day, Marshall wired Emmons to lift Japanese Americans from the National Guard and send them to the Mainland for training. The detailed order that followed included a narrative appendix by staff that squarely put the burden of the decision on Emmons. Throughout, the War Department continued to refer to the Hawai'i troops as "Jap soldiers."[19]

While the stars were finally aligning for the combat training of Japanese Americans from Hawai'i, the idea of a segregated unit was received in the island community with mixed feelings. Ching, Yoshida, and Lind hurriedly gathered feedback. In a never-published document, they reported conversations as follows: "Why only the Japanese boys? Why are not the boys of other nationalities accepted when so many have volunteered to go with us?" And, "We prefer to remain here and fight the Japs," meaning Japan. "By sending us away, they are depriving us of the opportunity of proving that we can and will fight as Americans against enemies of our own race." Also, "If only . . . we could show the rest of the world that men of all races can live and fight and die together as Americans."[20]

The idea of a racially integrated military already had taken root in Hawai'i. At a closed-door meeting among Caucasians on Merchant Street, Hemenway said, "It's bad to keep them segregated—it may have a bad effect when they return after the war. A strong feeling of solidarity may defeat the purposes of maintaining racial harmony in postwar Hawai'i. This is not of their doing; [the U.S. government] is forcing them apart."[21] Ching despised racial segregation but believed a segregated unit was inevitable. Yoshida accepted segregation only grudgingly, realizing it was the best deal possible under the circumstances, being keenly aware that the president and the navy secretary were still pushing for a mass evacuation from Hawai'i. Army major Frank Blake focused the discussion on national realities. He said that when the Hawaiian command had begun pushing for a Japanese American unit, the army in Washington was 95 percent opposed.

Lind wrote a memo to the Morale Section that his most pressing concern was with parents who, "in the absence of any official interpretation of the orders, seem to have made their own interpretation that this is another evidence of discrimination against the Japanese." He said the soldiers' mothers in particular seemed to be "greatly depressed and bewildered." He urged as much communication as possible to put the mobilization in a positive light.

Emmons forced a rapid pace, as if attempting to ensure there would be no turning back. Marshall's order required the troops to turn in their weapons at Schofield Barracks, with the idea that they then would be issued new weapons at their as yet unknown destination. He said the troops should be told enough "to prevent any feeling that soldiers are being disarmed and sent to mainland for internment which is definitely not repeat not the War Department's intention period.'" Sakae Takahashi, an officer as a result of his ROTC training, took all of this at face value, placing a high degree of trust in the army. Others flinched. No less a figure than Spark M. Matsunaga, a future U.S. senator, said, "It was an emotional jerker for me to be forced into turning in my side arms to my commanding officer after having stood ready to defend my country."[22]

Ching and Yoshida addressed the question of mentors for the new combat battalion. They interceded with the army command on behalf of two people who hoped to serve. One was the YMCA executive John Young, who was not accepted. The second was Katsumi Kometani, the well-liked dentist from Kapahulu who had emerged as a leader in the ESC. Kometani was thirty-five years old and had a family. He was commissioned a first lieutenant with the idea of serving as a morale officer.

The army designated the new unit the 100th Battalion (Separate). In Hawaiian pidgin, the 100th became "The One Puka Puka"—one-zero-zero.

Masaichi Goto, who had risen to staff sergeant in the HTG only to be reduced to a private in the 299th, by now had bounced back two pay grades to the rank of corporal. When orders arrived to ship him and his comrades from Maui to O'ahu, Goto's commander gave him two hours to say goodbye to Fumiko. "Perhaps this is the last time I'm going to see Fumi," he wrote in his notes. "Perhaps Goodbye Forever." Fumiko put on a strong face. "Her last words were, 'I have a feeling that you will

come back after.' I hope she is right." The next day, Goto moved into
a tent at Schofield Barracks. His mother had been sick in bed for the
past year and his father was now seventy-three years old. He wondered
about leaving Hawai'i, not knowing where he was going. His brother,
Baron, brought him a watch. On June 5, only eight days after Marshall's
order, he boarded a train from Schofield bound for Pier 27 in Honolulu
Harbor. He glimpsed the title on the marquee of the movie house in the
Schofield theater, "The Man Who Wouldn't Die." Goto asked, "Could
this mean me too?"

Ching was on hand at Schofield to see them off, but there was a
nearly complete absence of public recognition. Once loaded, the troops
sailed immediately. Subsequent propaganda—aimed at offsetting the
stench of the Mainland internment—would cause the 100th Battalion
to be portrayed as a national unit, but in the beginning it was entirely
a Hawai'i unit. Many of its men had never traveled beyond Schofield
Barracks or the Neighbor Islands. If they had, it well could have been
to Japan. Within the 100th, unremarked, was a contingent of *kibei*, a
category of people whom the intelligence agencies purported to view as
a potential security risk. Perhaps nothing so clearly illustrated America's
error in elsewhere marginalizing (and even interning) Americans of
Japanese ancestry who had been educated in Japan.

The decision to ship the 100th Battalion occurred as Admiral Nimitz, General Emmons, and others were focusing on engaging Japan's
advancing navy at Midway Island, at the distant end of the Hawaiian
archipelago. While Emmons was arguing for the 100th Battalion, he
also was planning the U.S. Army Air Corps bombing of Japan's ships.
The actual Battle of Midway began a day before the departure of the
100th Battalion and concluded three days later while the 100th was sail-
ing to San Francisco. The Battle of Midway was America's first major
American victory and—it would be widely agreed—the turning point
in the Pacific War. The overlapping of Midway and the 100th provoked
speculation of a connection, but in fact the timing seems to have been a
coincidence. The salient fact was that the battle had barely started when
the 100th Battalion shipped out.

An army memorandum attempted to shut the door on any further
experimentation, saying that the 100th had dealt with the problem
of Japanese Americans left over from the draft and that the case was
now closed. In reality, the opposite was true. Strengthened by positive
reports from the 100th Battalion training camp, McCloy and Emmons

looked for an opening to create a much larger Japanese American fighting force. This was again a difficult proposition. First, President Roosevelt ascribed to the tokenism by which the 100th was framed as the one and only such unit. Second, the idea of a mass relocation from Hawai'i persisted. Throughout the summer and fall of 1942, these oppositional ideas—of a large-scale fighting force on the one hand and a large-scale forced evacuation on the other—continued to compete. This debate largely went on behind the scenes, involving some of the most influential people in the country.

McCloy advised Emmons to proceed cautiously, given the ongoing animus for anything related to Japan. Meanwhile, he raised four arguments against a mass evacuation: a lack of shipping; the loss of a skilled workforce in Hawai'i; the negative reaction of U.S. Mainland residents to importing more people of Japanese ancestry; and the difficulties of housing such a large number of evacuees. Belatedly, McCloy warned against "legal difficulties in placing American citizens, even of Japanese ancestry, in concentration camps." He suggested that the War Department order to Emmons be modified to allow only for evacuating "potentially dangerous Japanese, whether they be citizens or aliens," subject to the availability of replacement workers, shipping capacity, and housing.

Given that McCloy no longer believed the Japanese of Hawai'i were dangerous, he was essentially proposing an evacuation that approached zero. Meanwhile, Emmons gave continued assurances as to the reliability of the Japanese community in Hawai'i. Where initially he had hedged a bit on the possibility of sabotage, by April 1942 he flatly declared there had been no sabotage in Hawai'i.[23] In late March, Emmons estimated that perhaps fifteen hundred people were actually dangerous and that achieving any greater certainty of security would require an evacuation of one hundred thousand people. This was classic Emmons. He was asking Washington whether he should evacuate fifteen hundred or one hundred thousand. Likely even the fifteen hundred figure was plucked from the air, since he offered no definition of "dangerous." In round numbers, it was the capacity of a good-sized ocean liner.

McCloy advised Emmons that in the interest of placating the president and Knox, Emmons should come up with something more specific. Two weeks after shipping the 100th Battallion, Emmons proposed a voluntary evacuation of families "who were a drain on the war effort and economy of Hawai'i." Meanwhile, the War Department prepared to receive Roosevelt's number, fifteen thousand people, from Hawai'i in an encampment on the West Coast. Bendetsen became involved in planning the logistics, including the use of a relocation center, such as the notorious Tanforan Race Track in San Francisco, where Japanese Americans had been forced to live in horse stalls. On July 1, Emmons announced the conduct of the Japanese-ancestry population in Hawai'i was "highly satisfactory." He urged reducing the fifteen thousand figure to five thousand. Who these might be was not specified, other perhaps than the families of men who had been incarcerated in the initial sweep. These especially vulnerable people were enticed and, in some instances, effectively coerced to join with family fathers who had been shipped to Mainland camps. Most were taken to two camps in Arkansas: Rohwer and Jerome. The resulting problems were numerous, but the running total of evacuations was comparatively small—less than two thousand out of a total Japanese-ancestry population of 160,000 in Hawai'i.[24]

In mid-summer, on July 17, Roosevelt injected a new twist. He issued an order saying that American citizens of Japanese ancestry were not to be evacuated from Hawai'i at all, but up to fifteen thousand aliens could be.[25] This new order called for any citizen considered dangerous to be interned in Hawai'i. This was arguably the genesis of the Honouliuli Detention Camp, which was located in a sun-drenched gully in remote leeward O'ahu. Transparently, the motive for this camp was to keep Japanese Americans under the jurisdiction of martial law, so that in case of incarceration they would be unable to challenge their status by filing writs of mandamus. The camp was built for several thousand people but at most held 350 or so people from Hawai'i. The rest of the camp was turned over to housing prisoners of war.

In October 1942, ten months into the war, Knox again complained to the president about the absence of a mass evacuation from Hawai'i. Emmons responded with yet another proposal, which was to remove three thousand unspecified persons. By this time Roosevelt thought Emmons was playing a game. He said, "General Emmons should be told that the only consideration is that of the safety of the Islands and that the labor situation is not only a secondary matter but should not be given any consideration whatsover."[26] Roosevelt's statement bears emphasis. It reflected a willingness on his part to uproot the entire Japanese work-force in Hawai'i—thereby contradicting the most enduring single-focus explanation for how things would play out in Hawai'i.

That Emmons was not sacked for insubordination—or at least for seriously irritating the president—is a tantalizing aspect of his tenure.

The answer likely lay foremost in the way he had stabilized the situation in Hawai'i. He was a charter member of the Army Air Force and a recognized expert in long-range bombing, which was basic to attacking Japan in the Western Pacific. He was protected by McCloy. Further, by this time more people in key positions were having misgivings about the forced evacuation and resulting mass incarceration. The internment was a public relations disaster. It tarnished America's claim to constitutional democratic government. It caused human suffering for tens of thousands. It was a drag on the war against Japan. Milton Eisenhower, brother of the general, had resigned almost immediately as director of the War Relocation Authority. His successor at the WRA, Dillon Myer, was overwhelmed by logistics even as Bendetsen was trying to figure out how to accommodate Roosevelt's additional fifteen thousand people from Hawai'i.

This went on and on. It was both tragedy and farce.

Finally, on April 1, 1943, the War Department told Emmons to not send any more people to the Mainland. A total of 1,875 persons had been shipped, including those from the original wave of arrests. Another several hundred were kept at Honouliuli. This meant that 98 percent of the Japanese-ancestry population had continued to go about their lives, if under the controls of martial law, in contrast to none on the West Coast.

The push to form a second and much larger Japanese American combat unit continued. As late as September 14, 1942, a War Department board of review reiterated the generals' opposition to further involving Japanese Americans in the military. McCloy held back their recommendation, stalling for time as he searched for allies. On the same day, a proposal labeled "Policy Toward Japan" was published by a young Harvard PhD, Edwin O. Reischauer, the offspring of missionaries to Japan. The internment, he wrote, provided Japan "a powerful argument in their attempt to win the Asiatic peoples to the view that the white race is not prepared to recognize them as equals." The genuine involvement of Japanese Americans in the war effort, Reischauer argued, "would be the best possible proof that this is not a racial war to preserve white supremacy in Asia, but a war to establish a better world order for all, regardless of race." When the war was won, Japanese Americans would become the "opening wedge into the minds and hearts of the Japanese people." Reischauer supported the idea of forming a Japanese American combat team to be deployed in the European theater of war. He also hoped that a sizeable number of Japanese Americans eventually would become part of the occupation of a defeated Japan.[27]

On October 2, 1942, the head of the Office of War Information, Elmer Davis, echoed Reischauer: The internment had reinforced the appearance of a racial war, and the most effective response was to open the U.S. military to Japanese American volunteers.[28] Davis wrote on behalf of both himself and his deputy, none other than Milton Eisenhower. A few days after Davis's statement, Eisenhower wrote a confidential note to McCloy, telling him the president was giving a little ground but not agreeing. Roosevelt had met Davis for lunch and, according to Eisenhower, said he could accept enlistment of Nisei for "restricted duty," which might be followed by "more normal tasks" if all went well.[29]

Advocacy continued. Supporters of a combat unit were identifying one another and in some instances coordinating their tactics with one another. Stimson, who was under the sway of McCloy, wrote a note by hand to Roosevelt saying that the internment had gone to the limit. A War Department paper drafted in Stimson's name said he and General Marshall had agreed that the potential benefits of a large Japanese American force outweighed the risks. Stimson's focus at this point was not on Hawai'i but on the Japanese American men of combat age in the internment camps, whom he estimated at fourteen thousand. Surely, he said, they would be good for at least a regiment. Stimson said it would be a waste to restrict such a unit to the home front, "a faint-hearted compromise which would not fail to rob the plan of most of its value." Stimson cited the potential effect on Japan, India, and elsewhere in Asia: "To the whole world, it would be further evidence of the success of democracy." Echoing a frequently held view, Stimson predicted that Japanese Americans would display "a bravery of a high order," motivated by their desire to prove their loyalty to America. "And when they returned, they would return with pride in their hearts that they had done their bit, instead of being released like lepers to find their places in a world all too eager to reject them."[30]

Unphased, Knox again expressed his opposition to letting Japanese Americans into the navy except, perhaps, as civilian spies—a notion reminiscent of Coggins's ONI operation in Hawai'i in the 1930s. Knox complained to Roosevelt that nothing was being done about "a very large number of Japanese sympathizers, if not actual Japanese agents, still at large in the population of O'ahu, who, in the event of an attack upon these islands, would unquestionably cooperate with our enemies."[31] Roosevelt asked Stimson to comment on Knox's opinion. Stimson replied that all persons known to be hostile to the United States were under restraint, while many others merely suspected of subversive tendencies had also been interned. Citing Roosevelt's benchmark on additional evacuees—by then down to fifteen thousand—Stimson said that another five thousand in the next six months would do. Who these unlucky five thousand were to be, neither Stimson nor Roosevelt nor anyone else knew. When Bendetsen was notified in mid-November to expect more like three thousand or fewer to arrive on the West Coast, it was to be a token evacuation aimed at placating the high-level demand for mass evacuation.

In this way, curiously, the number of people of Japanese ancestry to be swept up in Hawai'i kept shrinking. One hundred thousand became twenty thousand, then fifteen thousand, then five thousand, then three thousand, then fewer still. Emmons cautioned that regardless, none of the imaginary evacuees had in any way behaved suspiciously.

By this circuitous route, at the apex of the American government, the conflicting impulses of exclusion versus inclusion were finally being joined into a single subject. The impulse to exclude had taken the form of massive evacuation and internment, along with barring Japanese Americans from military service. It had come from the president, from the politicians of the West Coast states, and from the U.S. Navy. The impulse to include had come from the community of Hawai'i and from the elements of the U.S. Army on the ground who had become knowledgeable of and sometimes acquainted with Hawai'i's multiethnic peoples.

In his November 11, 1942, wire, Emmons confidently told McCloy that all the concerned parties in Hawai'i strongly supported organization of a large-scale Nisei combat unit. Vastly underestimating, he predicted that four thousand or so men likely would volunteer. He recommended that the ranks be filled by draftees only as a last resort. As an "indication of spirit" he cited a petition by several hundred Nisei on Kaua'i seeking to volunteer.[32]

McCloy directed a particularly qualified staff officer, Colonel Moses W. Pettigrew, to develop a unit plan. Pettigrew was a career soldier who had fought in Europe in World War I. Unusually for his time, he then had studied in Japan from 1931 to 1935. He had served in 1938 and 1939 as the head of Army Intelligence in Hawai'i under General Herron, who had spoken up for the Nisei soldiers in training at Schofield Barracks.

Accordingly, Pettigrew had developed an acute sense of the threat of militarized Japan along with the upside potential of Japanese Americans in Hawai'i. As a high-level white officer fluent in Japanese, Pettigrew also understood that the military's Japanese-language resources were painfully lacking. Prior to the Pearl Harbor bombing, he had played a role in creating the first Japanese-language intelligence school at the Presidio in San Francisco. When the Western Defense Command evacuation orders came down, he was among those who successfully advocated for keeping the school open and the ethnically Japanese in attendance.

Pettigrew enthusiastically endorsed a Nisei unit, above all as a morale project. He predicted it would improve the lives of Japanese Americans in the postwar, change attitudes in America generally, and have a good effect around the globe. He concluded there were enough Nisei to form a fighting division of ten to fifteen thousand men. He volunteered to be its commander.[33]

On the same day that Pettigrew made his recommendations to McCloy, Roosevelt advised Stimson to think small. He said a company would do. He wanted a unit one small fraction the size of what Pettigrew imagined. Roosevelt's goal was not military but, at best, propaganda. Endorsing "Americanization of the Army," he noted the prior existence of the 100th Battalion, as well as a Norwegian battalion and Filipinos who were fighting as guerillas in the Philippines. Roosevelt said a Polish, Czech, or Danish battalion also might be a good idea. He was yielding ground circuitously, advancing modest thoughts that were in no way equivalent to the proposal at hand.

The discussion up to this time mostly had occurred between Honolulu and Washington, but now the scene shifted wholly to Washington. As if the culmination of an opera, the main players appeared in McCloy's office. Emmons and Green arrived on December 7, 1942, a year to the day after the bombing of Pearl Harbor. They had been ordered to Washington to discuss the loosening of martial law but, while there, the discussion of Japanese American combat units rapidly evolved. From Naval Intelligence, Zacharias and Coggins appeared, brimming with opinions. Roosevelt's personal representative, John Franklin Carter, who a year previous had advised the president against the internment, was described in McCloy's logbook as available to work on the Japanese American question, on the authority of the president. In addition, Colonel Pettigrew, Attorney General Francis Biddle, the Interior

Department's Harold Ickes and Abraham Fortas, Dillon Myer of the War Relocation Authority, Secretary Stimson, various generals and admirals from the highest reaches of their services, as well as staff officers who answered directly to McCloy—all became engaged in dozens of overlapping discussions about what to do next.

Although McCloy had warmed to the idea of a large Japanese American force, his logbook entries continued with the racial nomenclature of the day: "Japs," as when he wrote on December 11, "re Japs in Army. (General) White very doubtful about it." That day he had a short meeting with Emmons and Green and a long meeting on the subject of Negro soldiers (a subject for which he was also responsible), followed by a second meeting with the Interior Department.

Emmons came and went, reflecting his lack of tolerance for protracted talking, while Green, a consummate in-fighter, stayed in Washington for weeks. Friction was rife. Attorney General Francis Biddle described Green to FDR as "stuffy, over-zealous [and] unyielding" on the subject of martial law.[34] FDR let it be known that he was sick of Green and thought he should be replaced. McCloy noted meetings with Green on December 12, 16, 17, and then on Christmas Eve, a Thursday. The following Monday, McCloy's day began with Green, followed by Biddle, Ickes, Stimson, Knox, and an admiral who was acting vice chair of Naval Intelligence. A telegram arrived from the president of the Honolulu Chamber of Commerce, Leslie Hicks, a friend of the Nisei, heaping praise on Emmons's handling of martial law.

On Monday, December 28, McCloy met at length with Zacharias and Coggins, whose presence created a sort of full-circle event. They brought the entire sprawling discussion into focus. Following their assignments in Hawai'i, Zacharias had gone to sea, commanding a navy cruiser. Coggins, suffering a fit of boredom, had hitched a ride with him to Micronesia and back to Hawai'i. According to Coggins, they had sunk several Japanese ships at Kwajalein Atoll in the Marshall Islands.[35] Zacharias then had returned to Naval Intelligence, serving as acting director while Coggins served as his idea man. That Zacharias had been so wildly off in his testimony to the Roberts Commission seemed in no way to diminish the weight of his reappearance.

McCloy was excited. After all, Zacharias had studied in Japan, and Coggins had chased Japanese fishing boats off the coast of southern California, then organized the first counterintelligence circle of Nisei in Hawai'i. Possibly they could map the course by which the U.S.

government could proceed toward the propaganda goals that Elmer
Davis had promoted. Each claimed to be an expert on the "Japanese
mind." And who was to say they were not?

McCloy started a packed conference on January 4, 1943, by citing a
nameless paper in the War Department on the use of Japanese combat
troops. He said it was a paper "upon which a decision had already been
reached." More accurately, it was a paper with which he agreed. McCloy
stressed the fighting qualifications of Japanese American soldiers, followed by their propaganda potential in America and Asia. He then
introduced Zacharias, who began his presentation in a brash, boastful
vein. To underscore the fact that ONI was the first agency to have investigated the Japanese community as a security threat, Zacharias said that
the navy's knowledge of the subject was much better than the army's.
He said he had tried to interest Army Intelligence in the prewar on the
West Coast, when he, Coggins, and Kenneth Ringle were all engaged in
surveillance. The army, he said, had only one man available for the job
but he was overwhelmed and threw up his hands. In essence, Zacharias
was turning back the clock to what then must have seemed like light
years in the past—the squabble of 1940 and 1941 over intelligence jurisdiction. Although his observation was dated, conceited, and even insult-
ing, he seems to have gotten by with it. He then turned the meeting over
to Coggins.

Coggins described the old days under cover in Hawai'i. He reiterated his claim to having formed a large counterintelligence circle of
loyal Nisei. He said he based his litmus test on a forty-point checklist,
as if he had reduced screening to a science. He harked to the content
of what would become his anonymous *Harper's Magazine* article. Allud-
ing to his claimed understanding of the Japanese mind, he estimated
that 80 percent of the Nisei were actively loyal (thereby shaving five
points off Ringle's number). This went on, covering opinions on Japanese American officers, training grounds, volunteers versus draftees,
and more.

A colonel from Military Intelligence, W. E. Crist, agreed that the
navy comment on the army's lack of information was regrettably true.
During a break, he approached Zacharias and Coggins informally and
asked them to help the army with screening. McCloy entered the conversation, wanting to know what the head of Army Intelligence, General
George V. Strong, thought. Crist said Strong likewise worried that the
army didn't know enough. Crist speculated that Strong "had vividly in

mind the Japanese fifth-column activities which preceded their occupation of other countries." Zacharias reassured both Crist and McCloy that about 85 percent of the Nisei would be loyal, retrieving the 5 percent of Ringle's number that had gone missing from Coggins's presentation.

From this convergence of navy smugness and army insecurity, an ill-fated screening process was to soon be devised that was to limit the recruitment of Nisei from the Mainland concentration camps. Broadly, this reflected the fact that prior to the war the United States did not have a coherent, integrated intelligence system and that the services freelanced with limited information and little expertise. The influence that Coggins was to exert brought to mind the line originally rendered in Latin: *In regione caecorum rex est luscus* (In the valley of the blind, the one-eyed man is king).

In the discussions, a Japanese American combat team was usually referred to as a propaganda counterweight to the mass internment. While occasionally there was testimony for the patriotism of the Nisei, or even the rectitude of the Issei, war propaganda tipped the scales of decision making. It was agreed that maximum effect was to be derived by bringing a fighting force out of the internment camps. The plan was for at least 60 percent to come from the camps of the continental United States. What could be a more stirring testimony to the motivational power and righteousness of the American nation? The rest were to come from Hawai'i.

CHAPTER 11

The Mobilization

IN ANNOUNCING FORMATION OF THE UNIT, President Roosevelt wrote grandly, "The principles on which this country was founded and by which it has always been governed, is that Americanism is a matter of the mind and heart; Americanism is not, and never was, a matter of race or ancestry." According to the War Department's call to arms, the unit was designated a regimental combat team. It was not to be the larger combat division that Pettigrew had recommended, but it was still to be a formidable fighting force, a unit of forty-five hundred men, which was to make it three and one-half times the size of the 100th Battalion. It was literally to be a combination of fighting forces resulting in a team. It was to have three infantry battalions, its own artillery battalion, an antitank company, a marching band, and a medical detachment. It was to be called the 442nd Regimental Combat Team (RCT), which in conversation would become the "Four Four-Two" or the "Four forty-second." For an outfit that Roosevelt only recently had wanted to perform labor in the Midwest and not to carry rifles, the 442nd was a turnabout. Not only were its troops to be trained for combat, but its cannon were to be armed with a capacity for attacking enemy positions at a range of seven miles. Further, it was to have an on-the-move engineering capacity for such contingencies as the rapid assembly of bridges in pursuit of enemy forces.

Officers at the regimental, battalion, and company levels were to be what the table of organization called "white American citizens." In contrast to the 100th Battalion, which organizationally hung suspended as "(Separate)," the 442nd RCT was attached to the Third U.S. Army. This was to change as its battlefield experience played out, but the Third Army designation reflected the fact that the army had a clearer idea of what it intended for the 442nd than it first had for the 100th.

The recruiters were to open volunteering throughout the camps and across Hawai'i in early January and to activate the unit at Camp Shelby,

Mississippi, on February 1. This would prove to be an overly ambitious timetable, but it succeeded in creating a pressure to move quickly.

The noncommissioned officers who were to serve as training cadre were all to be citizens who had resided in the United States since birth. This was interpreted to mean individuals who resided in the U.S. Mainland, which became a sore point with the soldiers from Hawai'i.

The question of how many would come from the internment camps and how many would come from Hawai'i took on a life of its own. Army Intelligence estimated that there were more eligible Japanese Americans in Hawai'i than on the continent (30,400 versus 26,600). Nonetheless, the initial idea was that up to two-thirds of the force would come from the continent, and only one-third would come from Hawai'i.

That meant that three thousand were to be recruited from the Mainland. Within Hawai'i, each of the major islands was to be represented proportionately. To secure fifteen hundred Hawai'i recruits, twenty-five hundred were to be marked as acceptable. The extra one thousand were to serve as a buffer against rejections based on physical issues or loyalty issues.

News of Washington's approval was received in Hawai'i with a mixture of elation and anxiety. Yoshida remarked that he knew the directive was coming three weeks in advance. During that time, he spoke to leaders in the Japanese community who feared the recruitment would fall short. As with the previous shipment of the 100th Battalion to training camp, the Morale Section wanted a racially integrated unit representing the spectrum of people in Hawai'i. At one of its meetings, Yoshida said, "I still feel that a Hawaiian Rainbow Division would be a good thing. I was originally completely opposed to segregation. For the sake of expediency, I have given up my opposition, and I can see some positive good." The Emergency Service Committee stalwart Masa Katagiri wrote a letter to Selective Service advocating integration for the good of postwar Hawai'i: "We are all Americans and we shall have to live together after the war as Americans and the less differentiation there is among us, the better it will be for all." After talking with UH faculty, Lind reported a measure of ambivalence. Some faculty objected to the racial segregation on principle. Others feared that it would cause ill will by unduly bringing attention to Japanese Americans, to the exclusion of others serving in the war.

Despite its misgivings, the Morale Section was determined to make things work. Publicly, Yoshida struck a militant note. He told the press,

"The treacherous sneak attack on Pearl Harbor was the work of a band of military martinets who have a strangle clutch on the Japanese nation. We Americans of Japanese descent may have a similar ancestry with Tojo and his brigands, but you can bet our values, hopes, and desires are vastly different. We welcome this chance to strike a blow against the Axis."[1]

This was, after all, the long-sought moment of full-scale participation in the war effort. The recruitment drive that followed was a compressed retracing of the preceding several years. Relationships that had developed slowly were now tapped. Well-crafted phrases were thrown into the campaign. Pressure on the Nisei ratcheted up. In late January, the Morale Section pulled the ESC and various allied representatives in from rural Oʻahu and the Neighbor Islands. They met for two days, mapping a territory-wide campaign to ensure that the quota would be met. ESC speakers then fanned out across the islands, holding hundreds of meetings, reaching groups large and small. Grassroots leaders such as Yoshida, Ching, Loomis, Burns, and a wide range of ESC members took turns speaking at these meetings. They stressed the historic nature of the situation and the imperative of settling the loyalty question. The FBI's Shivers and Fielder of Army Intelligence joined in. "You're on the spot," Nisei were told over and over. Speakers combined a call to service with a threat of shame and guilt. If the Nisei failed, the ill effects would fall not only on them but their parents, their children, and on their future position in Hawaiʻi and the United States.

In Honolulu, the tide of enlistees strained the capacity of the Selective Service boards. Work tables were populated by rows of clerks, each facing a queue of eager young men. Demand to complete the paperwork was so great that the city experienced a shortage of typewriters. Predictably, the Varsity Victory Volunteers signed up en masse.

While thousands volunteered without nudging, in some instances individuals were "recruited." The plantations seemingly supported recruitment without reservation. In leeward Oʻahu, the Ewa Morale Committee, representing Ewa Plantation, announced in a flyer, "A golden opportunity has arrived—to show your loyalty to the United States!" The company provided transportation to anyone who wanted to go to Waipahu to enlist.

Community pressure was possibly even more explicit on the Neighbor Islands. In one week, from January 30 to February 5, recruiting teams addressed nearly seventeen hundred people on Kauaʻi. In the remote west-end community of Waimea, the ESC held no fewer than sixty-six meetings with an average of four to five people per meeting.[2] The recruitment teams reached 300 people in the nearby 'Ele'ele district in south Kaua'i; 277 in Kōloa; 545 in the island's central district, Līhu'e; and 100 apiece in each of the two less densely populated northern districts. When the volume of enlistments swamped the capacity of Selective Service, the Kaua'i ESC provided thirty-two typewriters and clerk typists to go with them.

A young Japanese American wrote to his fiancée on O'ahu, "The Morale Committee members claim they are not using pressure but they're certainly doing it. First, they pass out mimeographed forms of intentions of volunteering and ask people to sign it if they wish. . . . This isn't all in my case. Reverend Yamada stopped me on the road and asked me if I signed up. I said no—then he hands me the official form and tells me to sign it and bring it to his house."[3] In addition to Yamada's central role in the Kaua'i Morale Section, he volunteered to serve as a chaplain, even though he was easily old enough to avoid service.

After rejects, Kaua'i produced 787 enlistees in this first round, which meant that one small island alone had filled more than half of the army's quota for Hawai'i. Ching nonetheless worried about numbers. He told his companions he would have liked to see more volunteers from Kaua'i. Maui's Morale Committee reported that the spontaneous approval of businessmen and army officials was apparent from the first meeting. Returning from the two-day orientation in Honolulu, Dr. Izumi launched a bilingual tour around his island, closing with a rally at Baldwin High School.

The process on the Big Island was, predictably, not as efficient. To complement the East Hawai'i effort, VVV members were handpicked from O'ahu to speak at a bandstand rally above Hilo Bay. One of the speakers was Ted Tsukiyama, whose sister would eventually write that a great deal of beer was consumed on the trip—whether by her brother she did not say. Dr. Lind, continuing to monitor morale in Kona, elicited a handwritten report from a Nisei social worker who, himself, had not volunteered. The social worker described pressure from the viewpoint of a person he referred to as "X," an employee of the Kona Coffee Company in the small town of Kealakekua. Outwardly healthy, X suffered from a sinus condition. Everywhere he went, people asked him if he had volunteered. He said no. Why had he not? He entered into a pact with a friend against volunteering. Among another set of friends, he presented himself as divided. This group was older and some were married with several children. They were agreeable to volunteering but hoped they would be among the last actually mobilized, so they could watch out for their families. The enlistment crusade arrived in X's town in the person of Tomekichi Okino, a deputy county attorney. Okino said the army was giving the Japanese a chance and they must take it. Although the call was for fifteen hundred recruits, Okino hoped for ten thousand. Included in this meeting were a Native Hawaiian sheriff, a police captain of Japanese ancestry, a second sheriff who was also of Japanese ancestry, three agents of Baron Goto's UH Extension Service (which hosted the meeting), a dentist, a doctor, several schoolteachers, and the head bookkeeper of the Kona Coffee Company. The next day, the head bookkeeper called X to a company meeting. Hoping to escape the pressure, X first objected to the meeting even being held, saying "the enlistment was a voluntary one and the decision should be left to the individual." His protest was in vain. A fellow employee said the enlistment was voluntary in name only. Ultimately, all the employees volunteered, X included.

Among those who went around giving talks was an officer named Aoki. If young men wanted to sign up, he drove them to a draft board. A young office boy said everywhere he went, the talk was of volunteering, but he could not do so because of his mother's advanced age and his obligation to care for her. He couldn't sleep and couldn't keep his mind on his work. He feared people would call him a slacker. At the district high school, all the Japanese teachers volunteered except one. High school boys said the one teacher had a yellow streak. Upper classmen were also volunteering, but not all. One boy was "made to feel 'small' because he had not yet volunteered. This boy cried all the way home."

Enlistment in Hawai'i rapidly reached the original recruitment goal, then surpassed it more than six times over. Simultaneously, the enlistment drive in the concentration camps of the U.S. continent was faltering. The tale of two divergent populations, two different attitudes, two communities—the stark contrast between exclusion and a growing trend toward inclusion—long in the making, was becoming more vividly clear.

Mistake by mistake, first in Washington, D.C., and then in the camps, faulty thinking and nagging fears undermined the possibility of a successful recruitment drive on the U.S. continent. The source of trouble was a loyalty questionnaire that, in the crass language of the war planners, promised to separate the sheep from the goats, the loyal from the disloyal.

At the conferences in McCloy's office, Coggins had proposed such a questionnaire, and the army's Colonel Crist had latched onto it. From this odd collaboration came the infamous Form 304a. Although the recruiters were to be army soldiers, the navy—with its supposedly superior knowledge—was put in charge of developing the screen questions and also put in charge of training recruiters. Further, the navy was to form a joint board with the army, with two officers from each of the services who were to evaluate the questionnaires, from which to determine whether a person was accepted for service.

General Strong of Army Intelligence, advised by Crist, directed that the questionnaire be filled out in quadruplicate. One copy was to be analyzed by Selective Service, one sent to Army Intelligence, one to the Hawaiian Army Department, and one to the individual soldier's personnel file.[4]

The army brought teams of four soldiers together for recruiting in each of the ten War Relocation Authority (WRA) camps of the Western states. Each team had an officer and three enlisted men, one of whom was of Japanese ancestry and bilingual.

President Roosevelt was aware of the process, writing in an announcement letter that he was pleased by the collaboration of the War Department with the navy.[5] McCloy was integrally involved. On January 26 at the Munitions Building in Washington, D.C., he gave a ten-minute pep talk on the first day of the five-day training of the recruitment teams.

Coggins was the main attraction in the training of screeners. He was on the one hand well meaning, even profound and empathetic; on the other, he was egocentric, glib, and illogical. "It is a fundamental mistake in the United States that because a man is a descendant of Japanese that he thinks as Japanese do," he began. "That is entirely wrong." Following Pearl Harbor, no Nisei aided the enemy, he said, rumors notwithstanding. No one had blocked the roads. No one from McKinley High School had come crashing down in a Japanese airplane. "They did a lot of work," Coggins said. "They turned around and manned the guns." He recounted the Japanese Civic Association petition for participation in the war effort, the Kiawe Corps, formation of the 100th Battalion, and the VVV petition. He congratulated his army listeners for giving the Nisei a chance. He took a swipe at the navy for not doing so. He turned to the trust doctrine: "If you deal with them honestly you get loyalty back, no tricks, no subterfuges, no indirection, no deception. You have to play it square, put your cards right on the table."[6]

There had been conflicts in the camps, yes, but conflicts largely of the government's making. Although General DeWitt originally had done the right thing in forcing the evacuation from the West Coast, Coggins said, the camps were all wrong and the sooner they were closed, the better: "Any effort to solve this problem such as it is without dissolving those camps is like sitting on a pile of manure with a fly swatter trying to dispose of the flies"—a vivid image. In Hawai'i, he said, he had been personally reassured by acquaintance with his Nisei circle. He would not only vouch for their loyalty but "go to hell and back" on their behalf. "The method we use to determine the loyalty of any person is to make their entire lives speak for themselves and actions speak louder than words."[7]

From Coggins's basis in whole-life analysis, he spiraled into the ether of Japanese psychology. He attempted to open an expert space for himself, per his self-image, by asserting that hardly anyone understood the Japanese mind. In any case, he continued, no such analysis applied to second-generation Japanese Americans, because the Nisei were 100 percent Americans. He asked his audience to imagine a friend of ten or twenty years. They would have no doubt about where that friend stood. The catch, which he did not acknowledge, was that the recruiters would be administering a loyalty questionnaire without benefit of personal acquaintance or other knowledge. Nonetheless the questionnaire would be, Coggins said, "a very satisfactory system for evaluating loyalty."

The transcript of Coggins's instruction ran to eleven pages, single-spaced. Word by word, it must have been entertaining. Unmistakably, he was taken as an authentic voice. His testimonial for the Nisei of Hawai'i was no doubt heartfelt. And his belief in the questionnaire went unexamined.

The work proceeded with what were taken to be high-minded goals. However, what appeared to be army-navy cooperation was actually reminiscent of the army, navy, and FBI fumbling around in 1940 and 1941 over who was doing what in the field of intelligence gathering.

The teams were sent out from Washington, D.C., to the deserts and remote wilderness and forests—to places called Heart Mountain, Manzanar, Minidoka, Poston, Amache, Gila River, Topaz, Tule Lake, Jerome, and Rohwer.

In Hawai'i, the forms were simply shipped to Selective Service. Only potential inductees were expected to fill them out, which translated to a pool of young men who actively wanted to serve in the military. Hawai'i recruits remembered a blur of paperwork but did not specifically recall the loyalty questionnaire. "We would have signed any paper they put in front of us, so eager were we to volunteer," a Hawai'i Nisei wrote. The difference "can only be explained by the simple fact that in the [camps] the loyalty screening was involuntarily imposed behind barbed wire enclosures in a liberty-deprived environment, whereas in Hawai'i it was not."[8] Per War Department orders, the forms were reviewed by the assistant chief of staff for intelligence in the Hawaiian Army Department, the Nisei-friendly Fielder. If an applicant cleared a records check, he was not investigated further.

In the ten WRA camps of the U.S. Mainland, use of the questionnaire was expanded to screening all adults for the purpose of granting or denying leaves from the camps. To answer one way was potentially to be let out, while to answer another way was to be put into the conflict-ridden Tule Lake Segregation Center. The controversies centered on Questions 27 and 28, which affected the Nisei and Issei generations both separately and in combination. Question 28 asked, "Will you swear unqualified allegiance to the United States of America and faithfully defend the United States from any or all attack by foreign or domestic forces, and forswear any form of allegiance or obedience to the Japanese emperor, or any other foreign government, power or organization?" Many Issei reacted by recalling that they had been denied U.S. citizenship and now, if they answered yes, they might become stateless people. Question 27 was, "Are you willing to serve in the armed forces of the United States on combat duty, wherever ordered?" Many Nisei either said no, not until their civil rights were restored, or until their families were set free.

These were the broad strokes of reaction, with many variations arising from the explosive issue of loyalty. The gravity of the questions became even greater in context of the Japanese cultural standard of loyal military service, which was to never surrender but, rather, to die honorably on the field of battle. Was Question 27 a de facto death warrant, made out by the country that had jailed you?

Per Coggins's instruction, recruitment teams sometimes told "No/No" respondents that the internment was a mistake, and that a Japanese American combat team was the instrument for making things right.

Volunteering for the army was the chance to turn over a new leaf. If the respondent wished, he had a second chance to give the "right" answers, usually to no avail.

In Hawai'i, around four thousand men signed up in the first two weeks. This was about ten times the number who signed up on the continent in this time frame. By the end of January, activation of the 442nd was pushed back a month. By mid-February, the ratio of ten Hawai'i volunteers for every Mainland volunteer remained unchanged. Camp by camp, the numbers took on a heightened drama. In the desert camp of Topaz, Utah, only fifty-eight Japanese Americans volunteered in the first two months out of a population of more than eight thousand people. The four-person army team packed up, leaving recruitment to the WRA. By March 8, with two months gone, Army Intelligence reported that only 829 applications had been received from the Mainland, while 9,500 had arrived from Hawai'i.[9]

The separation of sheep from goats had landed in a heap. Long afterwards, witnesses before the Commission on Wartime Relocation and Internment of Civilians talked about the effects of the loyalty test. Chizuko Omori, a writer and filmmaker, was keenly aware that her parents were embittered by internment and particularly by the loyalty screening. They decided to repatriate to Japan, which young Chizuko opposed. "The alienation was so complete I did not speak to my parents for what seemed like months," she testified. "It ripped families apart, set neighbor against neighbor, and was the cause of much anguish."[10] Lawson Fusao Inada, a poet and English professor, himself interned, said the loyalty test was "a bad idea in a bad situation, made worse by government mishandling."[11]

The future of the combat unit was in jeopardy. In response to two months of resistance from the camps, General Strong threw up his hands. He recommended that the deficit be made up by increasing Hawai'i's quota "to the necessary number."[12] In a word, the answer to the recruitment dilemma was Hawai'i: "The Japanese American community of Hawaii had become the recruitment pool of last resort. It had become America's way of saving face."[13] The Hawai'i quota rose, then rose again. Soon the quotas were more than reversed. Ultimately the continent was to produce about one thousand trainees and Hawai'i was to produce nearly three thousand, or double its original quota. Given that ten thousand had volunteered in Hawai'i, the figure of three thousand actual recruits was no problem. Thousands of disappointed young men were turned away.

Many months were to separate the recruits from the field of battle, but the mere existence of the 442nd Regimental Combat Team emboldened supporters to address the closing of the Mainland camps and the reopening of the Western states to Japanese Americans. On February 11, 1943, McCloy wrote to General DeWitt—he of the line "Once a Jap, always a Jap"—saying that in light of the 442nd, War Department policy was undergoing revision. Plans to release "loyal Japanese" from the camps were being accelerated. Employment in war industries was to be opened. Further, McCloy wrote, DeWitt should now consider reversing one of his most cruel policies—by which he had forced the relocation of spouses of mixed marriages out of the West Coast. McCloy concluded by asserting that War Department policy now recognized "the loyalty of individuals" rather than assuming the disloyalty of the entire group. It was a significant statement, but it was many thousands of interned victims away from being true.[14]

DeWitt reacted angrily. He questioned McCloy as to whether he actually had written and signed the letter, or whether it was a forgery in McCloy's name.[15] Thereafter Karl Bendetsen shuttled to Washington to present, in strident terms, his and DeWitt's objections to McCloy's new line of thought.[16] In return, McCloy complained bitterly to Bendetsen that the rapport they once had enjoyed was no longer forthcoming. They were no longer a team.

Coincident with formation of the 442nd, in March 1943 a colonel in army planning, William P. Scobey, wrote to Dillon Myer at the WRA noting Hawai'i's ten thousand volunteers. He asked Myer to secure an agreement with Secretary of the Navy Knox to withdraw Knox's longtime advocacy of a mass evacuation of Hawai'i.[17] In April, the army opened the Women's Army Auxiliary Corps to Japanese American women.

Yoshida, Ching, and Loomis held an after-action discussion on the 442nd drive with the UH sociologists, Lind and Bernard Hormann. Verbatim notes were taken. Having set out in a climate of skepticism on the task of recruiting fifteen hundred, they had hurtled to a level of success many times over. Loomis credited the impact of the 100th Battalion's outstanding training record. Yoshida thought it had to do with something beyond organization. "It is hard to explain why the thing succeeded," Yoshida said. "Something seemed to develop from within the group." Ching was wary of overthinking the question in the presence of a transcriber. "In a changing situation, we all change our points of view from hour to hour," he said. "To put our oral statements into writing gives them a stability which they do not intrinsically possess."

The sendoff of the 442nd from 'Iolani Palace drew a crowd of seventeen thousand people. The sea of faces and piles of lei were a reminder that the hopes of Hawai'i were loaded onto the shoulders of the 442nd RCT. Famously, Ching was at the dock to see the 442nd off. The struggle for inclusion in the war effort was complete. The struggle to avoid a mass removal and internment was substantially won. The strands of the Hawai'i strategy—minimize internment, maximize involvement in the war effort—were weaving ever more tightly together.

Green, having made powerful enemies in Washington, was reassigned shortly after, in April. Emmons was reassigned in June. They left behind a great legacy. Green said Emmons had succeeded by a combination of courage, brazenness, and a sleight of hand that bordered on deception: "We were on the defensive all the way, but in the face of tremendous odds we succeeded in a major degree in preventing the plan of ruthlessly tearing all the Japanese of whatever station or origin from their homes and placing them in detention camps."[18]

The question of how the Japanese American troops might perform in battle loomed. The question of Hawai'i's future loomed.

CHAPTER 12

Missionaries to America

Hung Wai Ching was on the dock in Honolulu to see the soldiers off to the West Coast. He then overflew them, thanks to Army Intelligence, which secured a seat for him on a flight otherwise loaded with high-ranking military officers. "Plenty brass hats," Ching wrote to Loomis and Yoshida. Ching checked into a low-cost San Francisco hotel on Grant Avenue near the entry to Chinatown. For advice he turned to a friend, Carl Palmer, political editor of the *Los Angeles Times*. Palmer had traveled to Hawai'i in the fall of 1941 gathering material for a story on the supposed Fifth Column threat. Ching and Yoshida, along with Katagiri, had gone to talk with Palmer. "Meet the potential enemies," Ching had said, motioning to Katagiri and Yoshida. The story died.

Now, a year and a half later, Palmer checked into a first-class hotel at San Francisco's Union Square, and Ching camped out with him for two days. They drank the hotel's scotch and talked about the future of the 442nd. Through Palmer, Ching strengthened acquaintances with the California Fair Play Committee, the elite group that had tried, however feebly, to stand up for the now-incarcerated Japanese community.

At the Presidio of San Francisco, headquarters of the Western Defense Command, Ching produced a letter from Fielder saying that he, Ching, was a confidential adviser who "is probably more familiar with the racial problem in Hawai'i than any other individual."[1] Ching had a high-level security clearance and was a commissioned officer in the army reserves. He was accustomed to dealing with disagreeable views. He was even familiar with the geography of the Presidio as an ROTC student visitor.

He met with General DeWitt, who was shortly to tell Congress, "A Jap's a Jap. It makes no difference whether he is a citizen or not."[2] From the first moment, DeWitt had objected to the idea of a Japanese American regiment. As early as January 18, he had written to McCloy arguing that the government's search for loyal people in the camps meant admitting to a mistake. "Otherwise," DeWitt wrote, "we wouldn't have evacuated these people at all if we could determine their loyalty." Ching found DeWitt to be predictably hostile. He quoted DeWitt as saying, in an accusatory tone, "You know about troop movements. That's a court-martial item." Ching recalled replying, "If you're going to court-martial me, let me know when. In the meantime, the boys are arriving and I want to see them treated well."

Ching thought the worst that could happen was to be thrown out. Instead, he was briefed by two colonels on their plans for managing the troop movement. On the second day he had a long talk with none other than Karl Bendetsen. Bendetsen gave him a jeep and a driver, who took him to San Francisco's Pier 10. Ching was there as the ship docked. As a result, he was both the last person the 442nd soldiers saw in Hawai'i and their first recognizable figure in the continental United States. He boarded, greeting the young people he had known for much of their lives.

The troops were unloaded, then ferried across San Francisco Bay to the port of Oakland, where they were loaded onto a train. Ching reported to Hawai'i that the troops were well treated, which seems to have been a bit of public relations aimed at keeping things on a positive track. What Ching eventually remembered was how appalled he was that the 442nd was escorted by troops with side arms, then put on a train with the blinds drawn. He complained to the Western Command, to no apparent avail, that this looked like imprisonment. Most ominously, the troop's destination was Camp Shelby, Mississippi, deep in the violently segregationist South.

The 442nd recruits arrived at Hattiesburg, Mississippi, on April 13, 1943. In contrast to the welcoming environment surrounding the 100th Battalion in Wisconsin, Mississippi was ominous. In his Yale days, Ching had gone only as far south as Virginia, and he was extremely apprehensive about the deep South. John Rankin—the Mississippi congressman who had cast aspersions on Hawai'i and the Japanese in the 1937 statehood hearing—had taken the War Department to task for organizing the 442nd. He predicted its troops would sabotage the Tennessee River Valley Authority. The local paper, the *Hattiesburg American,* greeted the troops with a headline, "Japs Invade Mississippi." Signs in Hattiesburg said, "Japs Go Home."

The first YMCA executive from Hawai'i to visit Camp Shelby was apparently Lloyd Killam. He reported that racial problems had materialized quickly. On April 24, Killam reported that when Hawai'i troops went to a USO (United Service Organization) dance, white women several times had refused to dance with them. Killam quoted an army colonel as saying, "If you don't keep those Japs out of here, you will have a riot." The USO closed its doors to Japanese Americans. Killam said the USO governing committee was swayed by local lawyers who argued that Mississippi law prohibited encouraging ideas of equality between "the white race and the colored races." The Camp Shelby commander pushed back, demanding that the USO rescind its ban. In response, the USO shut down its dances on the excuse of hot weather.[3]

Meanwhile, Ching had ridden by train to Washington, D.C., where he enlisted the help of Hawai'i's new delegate to Congress, Joseph R. Farrington, successor to Sam King, who had moved from the reserves to full-time service in the U.S. Navy. Farrington called McCloy and told him that Ching was the most important person in the mass mobilization in Hawai'i, an opinion that McCloy's office eventually echoed.[4] Reconnected to McCloy, Ching complained vigorously about the prejudice the 442nd was encountering. He argued that the troops be relocated to a more benign environment, suggesting either Wisconsin or Colorado. McCloy commiserated without agreeing that the unit move. He instead wrote a letter of introduction for Ching, and he assigned a colonel from his staff to support Ching, who then took the train back to Shelby to tackle the situation head-on.

Ching met with the Camp Shelby commander, the company commander, the Hattiesburg police chief, and the local newspaper editor. The nasty editorials stopped. The anti-Japanese signs came down. Ching also met with a chaplain assigned by the army to the 442nd. The minister was a Baptist who told him, "I'm gonna make good Americans out of your kids, Hung Wai." Ching recoiled. He lobbied for the man to be dismissed in favor of two Congregational ministers from Hawai'i: Masao Yamada of the Kaua'i Morale Committee and the Reverend Hiro Higuchi of Honolulu. As Ching's recommendations were being approved, he was asked if he also would like a Buddhist chaplain in light of the religious background of many of the men. In an act of uncharacteristic narrow-mindedness, Ching declined, a decision for which he later castigated himself.

Ching returned to Washington, where he reported to Farrington and McCloy. Farrington then got Ching an appointment to meet with First Lady Eleanor Roosevelt. From the beginning of the war, Mrs. Roosevelt was on record as advocating for loyal Japanese Americans. She had been taken by surprise by the president's EO 9066. Thereafter she was torn between her dislike for the internment and her political loyalty to her husband. In addition, her views were muted by her original acceptance of the conventional wisdom that Japanese had engaged in sabotage at Pearl Harbor. However, in early 1943 she began to question the widely held sabotage story, ironically turning to the Democratic congressman from California, John Tolan, whose own opinions as an inquiring lawmaker had been all over the map. Changing his story for at least the third time, Tolan told Mrs. Roosevelt there had been no sabotage.[5]

In late April 1943, Mrs. Roosevelt visited the Gila River internment camp in Arizona, which was located in the desert on an Indian reservation. Afterward she said the camps should be closed as soon as possible. She wrote about her visit in her then-famous newspaper column, "My Day," describing the ingenuity and determination displayed by the people in the camps. On April 26 she spoke in Los Angeles. She none too subtly challenged General DeWitt by saying that the idea that a Jap is a Jap "leads nowhere and solves nothing." At the Gila River camp, she met with Dillon Myer, the War Relocation Authority director, who was looking for ways to furlough people out of the camps.

Fresh from her outing, on a Thursday, the sixth day of May, she received Farrington and Ching at the White House.[6] That night, Ching sat in his room at the nearby Mayflower Hotel and wrote, in hand, a detailed account: "Two Negro butlers came to [the] door and took our hats," then showed him and Farrington into the Red Room, where they waited for about fifteen minutes. Mrs. Roosevelt shook Farrington's hand, then his. "Because of her gracious informal spirit," Ching wrote, "I was immediately put at ease." He thought her better looking than her pictures. "I find her very pleasant, forthright, honest and above all very human. No condescension on her part, not stiff despite her position in the country and in this world at present moment." He saw her as exuding enthusiasm, thereby detecting in her one of his own most obvious traits. "It can easily be seen why she is such a great woman of this age."

Ching described his own background to her. Mrs. Roosevelt said she was surprised to hear there were races other than Japanese in Hawai'i. "I was amazed at her lack of knowledge of Hawaii." Ching sketched what he had begun calling "the Hawai'i story," or what made Hawai'i different. "She inquired whether the story had been circulated." She told him about her visit to Gila River and her ensuing "My Day" column. She said

Eleanor Roosevelt. President Roosevelt Library.

the president thought her article ill timed. She drew a parallel between the internment camps in America and the Nazi's rounding up of Jews in Europe.

Ching drew her back to the subject of Hawai'i. He reminded her of the sabotage myth by describing the possible damage that could have been done on December 7 by the Japanese community, had it actually been disloyal. He talked about Hawai'i having better race relations than most places. He talked about the "Democracy experiment in Hawai'i. That surprised her." "[I] noticed her very keen and sympathetic interest in Hawai'i." He described the unit at Shelby and discussed the racial situation there. Mrs. Roosevelt asked to whom he was talking about the 442nd being located in Mississippi. McCloy, he said. She asked how long Ching would be in Washington. "She wanted me to tell the same story to [the] President." Rather abruptly, she stood. Farrington asked her to visit Hawai'i. She said she wanted to, but the president didn't want her to because various congressmen were pushing to travel to Hawai'i, and if she, a woman, went, then they would feel entitled to go as well.

She soon sent word that Ching should return on Sunday morning to speak to her husband. The date was May 9, 1943. In the two-day interlude, she had traveled to New York but was back in Washington by late morning. Roosevelt himself had been up late, until 1:15 a.m., according to the White House usher's log, and a man named Hung Wei (sic) Ching was his first appointment.

Ching walked from his hotel to the White House. On his arrival, Mrs. Roosevelt cautioned him that, uninterrupted, her husband might frustrate the purpose of the meeting by taking over the entire conversation. The message was clear. Mrs. Roosevelt led him through the Red Room to the elevator, which took them to an upstairs library, which in turn connected to the president's private study. He found Roosevelt in his shirtsleeves, his desk littered with papers and "all kinds of junk." Roosevelt apologized for not wearing a necktie. As with Mrs. Roosevelt, Ching quickly felt at ease: "I felt rather like I am speaking to someone whom I have known for many years—like speaking to Mr. Hemenway. Very attentive—says yes all the time when he agrees with parts of an opinion."

Roosevelt asked about Hawai'i's appointed territorial civilian governor, now Ingram Stainback, a figurehead under martial law. He also asked about the Japanese-language schools, food production, and Stainback's predecessor, Poindexter. Roosevelt welcomed the closing of the language schools, which elements of the Japanese community were systematically pursuing. Without endorsing the relocation of the Japanese to Moloka'i, Roosevelt talked about the pressure *on him* to do so—possibly a reference to navy secretary Knox. He asked Ching's opinion on resettling people out of the Mainland camps and was of the opinion that internees should be spread around the country. He also digressed into his own ancestry, saying that his maternal grandfather, Warren Delano, was involved in the China trade. Roosevelt said that as a result he had felt predisposed from childhood to a rapport with China but not Japan.[7]

"Excuse me, Mr. President," Ching interjected, "but I must tell you what I have come five thousand miles to tell you."[8] He talked about the planning of the Council for Interracial Unity, about army policy in Hawai'i, the Varsity Victory Volunteers, and finally about the 442nd and the choice of training at Camp Shelby. He believed that despite the president's proclivity for filling the air space, Roosevelt had listened carefully. Roosevelt's famous Scottie dog Fala came into the study and gave Ching a sniff. Roosevelt said that in victory he wanted to disarm Japan for fifty years. He talked about his correspondence with Chiang Kai-shek regarding the development of democratic self-government in the Far East. He talked optimistically about the future of the Philippines.

Mrs. Roosevelt entered. Roosevelt continued his discussion of Asia. On his completion, she made sure they actually had discussed the racial situation at Shelby. She asked the president to call Ching's concerns to the attention of the army chief of staff, General Marshall. Ching distinctly heard Roosevelt say he favored moving the 442nd out of the South.

While her apparent intention was to let Ching know that his appointment time was up, the conversation had momentum. The president offered Ching a cigarette, a Camel. While Mrs. Roosevelt talked, FDR lighted it for him. With a conspiratorial touch, Ching announced that on behalf of the president of the University of Hawai'i he was inviting Mrs. Roosevelt to come to Honolulu to deliver the commencement address. She seemed to him "very flattered" but explained that, as President Roosevelt had said, too many congressmen wanted to come to Hawai'i. Although demurring to Franklin, she nonetheless said she was contemplating a trip to Australia and might drop in on her way by.

Ching said that perhaps congressmen who had been critical of Hawai'i's Japanese should come with her and get the real story. "In my invitation," Ching wrote, "I spoke of the possibility of focusing attention on Hawai'i as a great demonstration of democracy working." The president predicted "great changes in Hawai'i to come," which in context was tantalizingly close to a prediction of statehood.

According to the White House usher's log, the meeting lasted twenty-five minutes. As Ching was leaving, Mrs. Roosevelt stopped him in the library: "She specifically told me that she wants me to keep [her] informed re Shelby." In passing he saw that the president's next meeting was with Dillon Myer, administrator of the camps. Mrs. Roosevelt had met with Myer on her recent trip and wanted the president to hear his views on how to release large numbers of people from internment.[9] Thereafter the president met in succession not only with the camp administrators but his top military advisers, who were preparing for the imminent arrival of British premier Winston Churchill for a discussion

President Roosevelt. President Roosevelt Library.

of the invasion via North Africa of Italy, in which the 100th Battalion and 442nd RCT were to become intimately involved.

In memory, Ching framed his message in terms of the pivotal importance of Robert Shivers. ("I told the President we had this FBI agent, and everything was under control. 'Just leave things alone.'") Otherwise Ching liked to recall a repartee with Roosevelt in which Ching played the Yale man and Roosevelt acknowledged being a Harvard man—with a complicated allusion to Harvard's ceremonial "pee pot." Ching said he saved the cigarette butt in his jacket pocket as a souvenir, only to realize it was still smoldering.[10]

As history, Ching fretted that his story might not strike people as believable. In fact, validating press coverage resulted from his meetings with both Eleanor and Franklin Roosevelt. Following May 1, the *Honolulu Star-Bulletin* carried a story headlined, "Hung Wai Ching Tells Mrs. Roosevelt About Hawaii's Role in War." It included an aside to the effect that, in connection with the meeting, the WRA had announced "that Americans of Japanese Ancestry held in relocation camps for more than a year are being returned to normal life on farms and in cities." (More accurately, they were being furloughed into student or employment situations away from the West Coast.) On Tuesday, May 11, 1943, the story of the White House meetings went national. Mrs. Roosevelt held a press conference in which she said Hawai'i had demonstrated "how to get along." Hawai'i had presented an alternative approach to Japanese Americans. As an extension of this observation, she advocated closing the camps, a plea aimed not only at American public opinion but, above all, at her husband, who was, as she had told Ching, already irritated by her previous statements.

Although Ching had gone away thinking FDR had said yes to relocating the 442nd, McCloy said no. In Ching's reconstruction: "Well, Mr. Ching, don't you think it [Mississippi] is part of America too? The boys are gonna learn a hell of a lot." Given the logistical issues of moving thirty-five hundred troops and their training cadre, the outcome was all but inevitable. However, in his advocacy Ching had succeeded in curing some of the more glaring problems of Shelby. More generally, he had heightened awareness of the Japanese American units in both Washington, D.C., and within the army. He also had helped make the connection between the Japanese American soldier and phasing out the internment camps.

Both McCloy and Mrs. Roosevelt continued to check on the well-being of the 442nd. At the end of May, McCloy sent a second officer to report on training conditions. By letter McCloy told Mrs. Roosevelt there had been no serious clashes with the people of Hattiesburg, although he acknowledged there had been some "problems" (street fights) with white troops who called them Japs: "Since they are very sensitive about their loyalty, this is resented by them." He said he would stay on top of the situation and that he would move the unit to a new base if necessary.[11]

When eventually the 100th Battalion deployed to the European theater of war, Mrs. Roosevelt wrote a letter to General Eisenhower, by then theater commander and a longtime skeptic of the project, asking that Eisenhower watch over them.[12]

Meanwhile, Ching met with members of Congress, talking about Hawai'i's approach to Japanese Americans. He also was drawn into discussion with Congress members about the grievous Chinese Exclusion Act of 1882, which soon would be repealed as a means of improving the country's reputation in China. "As a whole," Ching later wrote, "I felt that all of them were keenly interested in Hawaii and very much pleased with the way Hawaii handled her own internal problems." One month into his journey, he decided to keep moving. "Somebody," he wrote home, "should be here going all over the country telling the story of Hawaii." Beginning on May 18, he made a series of appearances at Oberlin College in Ohio, a religiously inspired progressive institution with student ties to Hawai'i.[13] He spoke to a faculty group, as well as a Rotary Club. He was also invited to preach at church, which he regarded as an honor, "but since Shigeo isn't here to write my talk, I turned down the invitation."

Ching reported spending an average of $10 a day for food and travel, which was financed in Hawai'i by passing the hat. Yoshida in particular went around Honolulu touching members of the Emergency Service Committee for donations, raising a few to several hundred dollars at a time.

In the course of his travels, Ching met with various figures in California who advocated for Japanese Americans through the Fair Play Committee. Among other things, he arranged a meeting between them and Army Intelligence. The committee had some of the most influential citizens of California, but Ching left feeling they lacked fight. "They had a guilt complex," he was to say, describing them as members of a majority-white culture that struggled to imagine the majority-nonwhite culture of Hawai'i.

As he interacted with people around the country, he developed a compelling notion about externalizing what had gone on inside Hawai'i. His freewheeling approach to travel, his ability to make acquaintances quickly, and his dedication to working with and on behalf of young people all came into play. To this should be added his infectious enthusiasm and his considerable self-confidence. He spent eighty-six days in the continental United States. He had become a missionary of a sort—a missionary in reverse, a proselytizer for a more genuine democracy.

After his return to Hawai'i, Ching spoke repeatedly and at length to community groups about the content of his travels. He spoke in a moral voice, with a combination of intelligence, improvisation, and gumption. While the crisis of the AJA was ever present, he brought the same concern for equal treatment to other groups as well. He organized a dinner at the locally famous Wo Fat's restaurant in Chinatown in what was described as a joint meeting of the haole and Chinese race relations steering committees.[14] In his warm-up talk, he went straight at the hypocrisy of haole discrimination in the economy against young Chinese, "as it contradicted the high ideals they had as a result of their school and church contacts." This was a sharp cut; it told haole leaders that the noble concepts of the public sphere were not to be found in the business sphere. He cited racially restrictive covenants in elite white neighborhoods as a major irritant, along with exclusion from the Pacific Club and restrictions on certain golf courses. Further, he said younger Chinese Americans felt they were "on the spot," the phrase usually reserved for the Japanese, because they were being portrayed as profiting from the war when many were serving in uniform.

He also spoke up for the Filipino workforce: "There is unrest in their hearts. They want to fight [but] feel that they are held back by their plantation managers. They hate the [job] freeze order. . . . They are mad because the Army took volunteers on the mainland but did not offer a similar opportunity to Filipinos in Hawai'i."[15]

Ching was not alone in his sociopolitical missionary work. As war-wounded AJA veterans returned from Europe, the army made use of their speaking abilities and their stories. The first was Captain Jack Mizuha, who from his hospital bed wrote impassioned letters advocating for postwar veteran programs. Among his correspondents was Mrs. Roosevelt, who invited him to the White House for tea. Mizuha urged her to support naturalized citizenship for the first-generation Asian immigrant, a position Mrs. Roosevelt at first thought premature but eventually adopted (and which was to become law in 1952). Thereafter Mizuha gave talks around the Mainland and in Hawai'i about the 100th Battalion. A second such traveler was Spark M. Matsunaga, also of the 100th Battalion. After being wounded in Italy, Matsunaga worked on morale issues with the War Relocation Authority. He gave hundreds of testimonial talks across the United States aimed at persuading employers to hire Japanese Americans who were being released from the camps.

One-time *kibei* Thomas Taro Higa became one of the most traveled in this far-flung version of barnstorming. Higa was twice wounded in battle. After recuperating, he was having a drink in the Nihon Machi

of Denver, Colorado, where he met a man named Joe Masaoka, who
turned out to be the brother of the JACL staffer Mike Masaoka. Joe
Masaoka talked Higa into speaking at a rally that night about the 100th
Battalion. Afterward a fellow speaker took Higa to a prison, where he
met with Japanese American draft resisters who became known as the
"no-no" boys for their negative answers to Questions 27 and 28. Saburo
Kido, the Hawai'i-born president of the JACL, prevailed on the army to
put Higa on a much longer tour, accompanied by Joe Masaoka. The two
men jumped around the American West, visiting little Japanese communities in Pocatello, Idaho, and Ogden, Utah, where Higa talked to
Japanese Buddhists, Japanese Protestants, and Japanese Mormons. At
the Amache camp, Higa addressed rumors that Japanese troops, followed by Negro troops, were being deployed as human shields before
white soldiers were committed to battle. He spoke to a Blue Star Mother's Group, then addressed the entire camp: "I took the opportunity to
stress the important relationship between the war front and the home
front."[16]

At Fort Lupton, Colorado, he estimated that a prewar population
of sixty-five Japanese families had tripled as a result of people moving
inland. He found about two hundred Japanese in Milwaukee. With no
real economic base, most were working as office help or domestics. In
Minneapolis, he stayed at Hostel House, where he made the acquaintance of an Adelicia Allen, who had served as a Christian missionary
in Japan for thirty years. Hostel House gave furloughed individuals up
to three weeks of free room and board as a base for developing self-
sufficiency. Higa spoke in Cleveland and Detroit before moving on to
Chicago, where he was surprised to find that the Japanese population
had swollen from 1,000 to an estimated 6,000. He spoke in Cincinnati,
St. Louis (which he estimated to have 350 Japanese), and Kansas City
(an estimated 300). From New York, he reported that a prewar population of 2,500 had collapsed to fewer than 1,000, then grown back to
more than 3,000. In New Jersey, he spoke at Seabrook Farms, a packing
house that at the time employed about 600 Japanese and would soon
employ hundreds more. In Washington, D.C., the syndicated columnist
Drew Pearson drove him around the city, picking his brain on Japanese
American issues and the war. Higa and Farrington went to Arlington
National Cemetery together in remembrance of the dead.

At Camp McCoy, Wisconsin, Higa went to the barracks where he had
lived in basic combat training. It was now the home of Japanese POWs.

He asked in Japanese, "How are you?" They replied, "Fine, thank you." At one of his talks, a Korean woman came to listen because she was homesick for Hawai'i.

He attended the JACL national convention, then spoke at the Manzanar camp in the desert east of Los Angeles. Twenty-eight hundred people listened, many standing outside the meeting hall in the cold. Mitsugo Sakihara, later a professor of history at UH, then an internee, wrote, "He had done in one night what the Caucasian staff had been trying to do for a long time—make the Issei understand the Nisei viewpoint in the latter's volunteering and going into the Army."

Higa toured for six months, travelling twenty-three hundred miles over forty states.

Such work fulfilled Hung Wai Ching's belief that telling Hawai'i's story across the Mainland should be a full-time job. It set Hawai'i apart. It inevitably underscored the U.S. government's urgent need to minimize the divisions set in motion by the forced evacuation and internment.

PART V

Home Front and Battlefront

LOOKING AHEAD

By Shigeo Yoshida

nce today has placed before us a great number

ve been created or at least intensified by th

rstand these problems more clearly and to s

helped us to evaluate more effectively th

e past and to give us a renewed courage

r the difficulties and disappointments

clearer understanding of our many obl

ation to see that these obligations

se whom we represent.

ly the beginnin

CHAPTER 13

The Home Front Doldrums

MEMBERS OF THE MORALE SECTION and their allied groups periodically complained that, with individual exceptions, the white power structure was not doing what it could and should do to help the community through the war. Not far beneath the surface of this complaint seethed the question of what Hawai'i was to become when the war at last would be over.

What was to happen between the dominant haoles and the most populous if momentarily beleaguered group, the Japanese, as well as the other nonwhite groups? If the economic and power relationships between whites and nonwhites changed, what were they to become? Conversely, who in the boardrooms and on the plantations harbored the idea that as soon as martial law was out of the way, the system of white dominance would resume? Would it be status quo ante?

As between Ching and Yoshida, it was Ching who relished the challenge of influencing the haole establishment. He was a passionate combatant against racial inequality and discrimination, and he enjoyed demonstrating that he could assert himself in any situation. Yoshida was likewise determined to challenge the dominant role of haoles. He was at times frustrated by the obtuseness and arrogance of key individuals. He occasionally lost his temper, but he felt constrained by the demands of the situation not to show it.

Less than two months into the war, Yoshida wrote two pages of talking points on how to proceed in Morale Section meetings with haole groups. He recommended asking haole leaders whether they were going to help the Japanese of Hawai'i get a fair deal "and maintain their loyalty, or are we going to let [them] become disgruntled and bitter and carry their emotional scars to the postwar period?"[1]

Documentation of tension came to be stored in vast quantity in the files of the Morale Section, the most interesting of which was labelled

"HAOLE" in Yoshida's handwritten block letters.[2] The picture that emerges is of early attempts initiated by Charles Loomis at a collaborative relationship between haole leaders and the Morale Section. The idea was to form a haole coordinating group equivalent to the ESC, and then to integrate it into a multiethnic leadership system. This proposal was rebuffed on the ground that such organizations already existed.

In the early months of the war, the business elite had promoted its agenda through a Citizen's Council, which had a hundred or so members.[3] Its composition reflected the interlocking grip of Caucasians on the political and economic life of the territory. Territorial House Speaker Roy Vitousek was chairman. The board of directors was made up of Leslie A. Hicks, manager of the Hawaiian Electric Company and president of the Honolulu Chamber of Commerce; Frederick D. Lowrey, president of the Lewers and Cooke building supply house; Louis W. Jongeneel, manager of California Packing Company; Walter Dillingham; business executive Walter J. Macfarlane; Lorrin P. Thurston, publisher of the *Honolulu Advertiser;* Edward E. Bodge, a corporate executive; Hemenway, who was still president of the wealth-managing Hawaiian Trust Company; John E. Russell, president of Theo H. Davies Company and acting president of the Hawaiian Sugar Planters Association (HSPA); L. H. Riley, manager of the McInerny Company, a retailing chain, and president of the Honolulu Retail Board of Trade; and C. B. Wightman, the secretary of the HSPA. Among the additional members were Frank C. Atherton of Castle & Cooke, Ltd., president of the *Honolulu Star-Bulletin* and a director of numerous other interests—he was, along with Dillingham, likely the most powerful figure in the territory; A. G. Budge, president of Castle & Cooke; E. W. Carden, president of the Bank of Hawaii; Harold K. L. Castle, president of Kaneohe Ranch Company, which owned a large part of windward Oʻahu; Riley Allen, editor of the *Honolulu Star-Bulletin;* Frank E. Midkiff, manager of the J. B. Atherton Estate; Lester Petrie, mayor of the City and County of Honolulu; John Waterhouse, president of Alexander & Baldwin, Ltd.; and H. A. White, president of the Hawaiian Pineapple Company, Ltd. (later renamed for its founder James Drummond Dole), to name a few. All were white except the attorney William H. Heen, a territorial senator of mixed Chinese-Hawaiian ancestry who had access to the white establishment as a result of his political prominence.

Vitousek chaired the group. While individual members (such as Hemenway, Hicks, and Riley Allen) had responded with deep concern for the war crisis, the Citizen's Council pursued narrow self-interest. Initially, it lobbied for businesses needing cargo space on the ships running to and from the Mainland. Thereafter, their only archival record was a letter to the territorial governor appealing for passage home for wives who had fled the islands after December 7. The wives were now "willing and anxious to return." They were needed to boost the morale of their husbands, the letter said, and also to do Red Cross work.[4]

Irritated by his fellow whites, Hemenway convened a freewheeling discussion at his Mānoa home on a Sunday afternoon in July 1942, a month after the battle of Midway, bringing together haole, Japanese, Hawaiian, Filipino, and Chinese. "The biggest problem here is the haole group," he said. "They don't practice what they preach." He was slightly encouraged by what he detected as more haoles remarking favorably on Hawai'i's Japanese, but he was newly alarmed by the negative attitudes of the white in-migrant defense workers. "This is bad," Hemenway said. "We should continually strive to break all the race lines."[5]

He pressed for reframing the war in terms of expanding democracy. "We need to state our war aims in terms of the ideals we are fighting for," Hemenway said. "Washington leaders have failed to do this." He argued that Congress should immediately repeal the Japanese Exclusion Act of 1924. Further, the University of Hawai'i, which he had served for thirty-five years, should be regarded as a sacrosanct model, "the one place where no race distinction is made."

Attorney Katsuro Miho, a member of the ESC, was fired up by Hemenway's remarks. "This is a different war," Miho said, "a war for all humanity, and it cannot be won by hatred alone. We need to kindle a real fire of idealism. Hawai'i should show the world the real way to win the war." Miho said the Pilgrim fathers and those who fought in the Civil War had stood for ideals on which America was built. "When I was on the mainland as a student, I always had the thought, 'You haoles don't appreciate America. The world is crying for the brotherhood of mankind.'" Dr. Harold Loper, who had served the martial law government as a volunteer, agreed. "We know what we are fighting against but very few know what we are fighting for," Loper said. The sociologist Lind said that profound social changes were under way but questioned what percent of the kama'āina haole sincerely believed in practicing interracial relationships based on equality.

N. C. Villanueva said, "Frankly, morale work is needed among the haoles." He complained that as a Filipino leader he was "always between the devil and the deep blue sea." The army was urging him to promote enlistments while the Sugar Planters Association was pressuring him in the opposite direction because the plantations needed laborers. "The Filipinos feel that they are the underdogs and it's high time they are recognized," Villanueva said. "Sometimes it's to the advantage of the United States to treat them as aliens and other times as citizens."

Thereafter Yoshida's HAOLE file went silent for three months, until October 2, 1942. The occasion was a revealing debate weighing the traditional oligarchic dominance of territorial government against the merits of the martial law government. The executive vice president of the Chamber of Commerce, John Hamilton, complained that civilians seemed "all too ready to relinquish their normal civilian controls to the military." To this the Chinese American businessman Richard Tongg, a close friend of Ching's, replied, "The Orientals in the community feel that this is the first time that they have had a fair break, not realizing of course they might at the same time relinquish forever certain civilian rights. . . . In the eyes of the military everybody is equal. There is no tendency to kowtow to the Big Five." Not one to sit in silence, Ching added, "Everybody gets their ten gallons of gas regardless of race, and the Orientals are getting a kick out of seeing the way in which some of the high-hat *haoles* have to stand in line along with all the rest." Straddling these viewpoints, one participant said the military showed "a genuine interest in maintaining democratic principles, although their whole mode of action is one which is essentially nondemocratic."[6]

In a subsequent discussion, tensions over martial law clearly seemed to be increasing. Attorney Cades spoke "emphatically on the abuse of civilian rights under the military setup and urged that a civil liberties committee be formed." Cades said the army's handling of individual court cases was atrocious. He proposed forming a citizen's organization "to put the heat on the military." Ching asked Cades why he now professed such interest in civil liberties when there had been no such interest among the haole elite prior to the war. He said if there was to be a civilian examination of martial law, it should not be under the influence of the Chamber of Commerce and the Big Five. Organized labor, he said, should be integrally involved. Cades stood his ground. "Is it going to get worse here?" he asked. "And do we have to generate more and more hate to prosecute the war? What is Hawaii doing to prevent this? What can we do to . . . keep the war based on ideals?"[7]

Yoshida sympathized with the idea of organizing a group to address civilian rights but cautioned against it behaving as a pressure group. While he was obviously concerned about the army government's violation of due process in the martial law provost courts, he clearly was not about to confront the military, in which he had placed his trust.

Much of the same group convened again a month later and began to more systematically focus on the problems of the Japanese community. The Morale Section members were alarmed by the recurrence of rumors that a mass evacuation was coming. Japanese families were again buying coats, suits, and heavy blankets. Loomis had talked to the essentially powerless civilian governor, Stainback, with no apparent result. He told Bicknell of Army Intelligence that something had to be done to calm people down. "[Bicknell] replied that nothing could be done—that a public announcement would simply serve to stimulate the people who are rather anti-Japanese and would encourage witch-hunting," Loomis agreed: "Everybody would be reporting their neighbors and saying that they ought to be evacuated." Retired general Briant Wells said he had taken up evacuation rumors with Emmons at the Pacific Club, but that Emmons was unmoved. Wells asked that Emmons at least talk with his old friend, who turned out to be the Rev. Takie Okumura, organizer of the New American Conference. "Of course, the funny part of it was that old man Okumura had to bring his son along to interpret for him," Loomis said, "this after all these years he had been working on Americanization." Emmons again said nothing could be done, but at a press conference the next day he abruptly stated—again—there was to be no mass evacuation.

Baron Goto had just run across an army notice that twenty-four Japanese farm families in Leeward O'ahu would be evacuated because of the proximity of their farms to military installations. The farmers had assumed they could stay elsewhere on the island but were told they were to be resettled to the Mainland. Goto said if that happened, "all the other farmers would ask, 'What's the use?'" Goto was working on food production with Walter Dillingham, who did not stand on ceremony. When he and Goto were confronted by an army sentry outside an ammunition depot in Waianae, Dillingham yelled at him, "I am Walter Dillingham," and barreled his way through to talk with the Japanese farmers. Dillingham, Goto said, was the only prominent haole still functioning within the martial law government. This he attributed to Dillingham's thick skin.

* * *

In early 1943, almost coterminously with mobilization of the 442nd
RCT, a booklet appeared titled "Shall the Japanese Be Allowed to Dominate Hawaii?" A tract of thirty-eight pages, it was the work of a John A.
Balch. Far from being a fringe figure, Balch was an influential businessman. His booklet seized on President Roosevelt's original evacuation
goal, one hundred thousand. Balch said sixty thousand of the hundred
thousand should be children, and that all should be moved directly to
the U.S. continental interior. If the Japanese continued on their course,
Balch wrote, they would take over Hawai'i and "we shall be forced out
of our jobs and our homes." He took inspiration from Nazi Germany's
holocaust: "If the Germans can move three million men from occupied
Europe within a short period, surely our great Government can move
one hundred thousand from Hawaii without grave difficulty."[8]

Balch held to a fervent settler belief that America was a white man's
country. He was descended from a John Balch who had arrived at
Salem, Massachusetts, in 1623 at a time when English colonists either
starved to death in winter or stole food to survive.[9] As his clan multi-
plied, they migrated west. A Daniel Webster Balch helped build a railroad from Nevada to California. He was shot by an irate stockholder
but survived to later be described as a pioneer Californian. The John
Balch of wartime Hawai'i first was employed in the American West
as an engineer in the mining business. He boasted of working along
the Arizona and Mexico border and of having "learned the necessity
of outthinking the numerous marauding bands of outlaws and rene-
gade Apaches." At age twenty-eight he migrated to the new territory of
Hawai'i, where he devoted himself to developing interisland communication.[10] During an economic bust that followed the 1898 annexation boom, Balch bought the Wireless Telegraph Company, through
which he eventually leveraged a large piece of the Mutual Telephone
Company of O'ahu.

Nothing in his experience had disabused him of the idea that white
men were supposed to run everything. Following World War I, he had
served for two years as the radio superintendent of the 14th Naval
District, an all-white domain. The board of Mutual Telephone was all
white, as was the Pacific Club to which he retreated after a day of work.
In 1936, Balch published an advertisement in the *Honolulu Advertiser*
conjuring an apocalyptic vision of an attack by Japan. It was entitled,
"An Entire Civilization Perished at One Blow." He proceeded after the

Pearl Harbor bombing as if he possessed prophetic powers. He evoked images of Japanese Americans with machine guns mowing down American soldiers at the YMCA and of bus drivers of Japanese descent suddenly swerving their buses athwart the streets, crippling transit.

Two of his sons were in military service in the Pacific. "I am at a loss," Balch wrote, "to understand just why they should be out fighting Japan if it is only to turn Hawai'i into a super-Japanese colony after the war has been won." He complained of "mollycoddling of the Japanese" and of maintaining the University of Hawai'i primarily for their benefit.

Reaching for respectability, he based his booklet on correspondence with the army, navy, and the U.S. Department of the Interior. In retrospect, it is shocking to read that he received brief pro forma responses from Admiral Nimitz, General Emmons, and B. W. Thoron, director of the Office of Territories and Island Possessions of the U.S. government. His one enthusiastic response was from a Californian, H. J. McClatchy, executive secretary of the California Joint Immigration Committee, which was at the heart of the anti-Japanese movement that had propelled the evacuation and internment. McClatchy took credit for congressional passage of the 1924 Exclusion Act. He pointed proudly to passage of the alien land laws of the Western states. He also put in a word of opposition to statehood for Hawai'i, "holding that such grant would make the Islands a Japanese outpost through gradual voting control." McClatchy was pleased with the forced evacuation. "There are none loose," McClatchy wrote to Balch, "and their former strongholds in cities like Los Angeles, San Francisco and Sacramento look like blighted areas. They are definitely out of here for the duration. We hope to make it permanent."

Balch claimed that white executives shared his fears of the Japanese, but Morale Section members gave no indication that Balch was gaining traction in Hawai'i. They were irritated, but their main concern was for Balch's effect on the Mainland. Loomis said Balch had given forty speeches across the continent, stoking the cause of limiting American citizenship to people of European ancestry. Loomis worked with Galen Fisher of the Fair Play Committee to discredit Balch on the West Coast. Hemenway led a Chamber of Commerce group in adopting a denunciation of Balch addressed to its Mainland chamber counterparts. Lind developed a statement with a national network called the Interfaith Federation, and the Hawai'i branch of the American Friends Service Committee similarly worked on the Balch problem with Mainland churches.

* * *

A group of thirteen Caucasian leaders convened on October 19, 1943.[11]
All at one time or another had expressed concern for the status of
Japanese aliens and Japanese Americans.[12] In addition to Hemenway,
Loomis, editor Riley Allen, and attorney Garner Anthony, the group
included several Big Five executives, two plantation managers, and a
Chamber of Commerce executive. The minutes no longer described
them as a discussion group but, more purposefully, as a "Group on Race
Relations." Possibly this was the point at which those present acknowl-
edged they too were part of an ethnic group, with a stake in the well-
being of other ethnic groups.

The discussion occurred around the boardroom table on the fourth
floor of the Merchant Street headquarters of the Alexander & Baldwin
Corporation. Ted Trent, a financial trust executive, opened the meeting
awkwardly. Rising tension around "the Japanese problem" potentially
threatened everyone, he said. "This [Japanese] group is a part of the
community and is here to stay, whether we like it or not." Trent was
equipped to have phrased this better—he had served as president of the
Honolulu YMCA and also was an original participant in the Council for
Interracial Unity.

Hemenway announced he was not sure he could join the white group
because he regarded himself as a "fifth-wheel member" of the Japanese
American ESC, which he credited with promoting harmony, "correct-
ing evils and carrying on a program of Americanization in the Japanese
community." Hemenway ranged over a variety of current issues—such
as labor conflicts and the maid and yard boy situation—before arriving at his most remarkable statement: "We haoles have to get over the
notion that we are heaven-born to rule the earth. I don't believe it any
more. It's character and ability that count, not the color of the skin.
They want equality, not favors. I know [the Nisei]. You don't. I have
them in my home as groups and individually and follow them through
the university and into business," to which he added, "Get on a friendly
basis with them."

Garner Anthony condemned the federal Selective Service for not
following the Selective Service Act of 1940, which provided for drafting
eligible young men without regard to race, creed, or color. "We say to
citizens of Japanese ancestry, 'You will not be drafted like other Americans but you can volunteer as a separate racial group.'" Anthony was
correct. Like no other place in the country, the draft in Hawai'i was

being manipulated by federal war aims—first to exclude the Japanese, then to include the Japanese on a large scale as segregated troops, and also to protect the interests of the plantations to the detriment of the Filipinos. Anthony was raising an issue that finally would be discussed publicly by resentful draft boards throughout Hawai'i in 1945.

Riley Allen, editor of the *Star-Bulletin,* was surprisingly explicit about the propaganda goals behind the 100th and 442nd. "The Army wanted the publicity and initiated it," Allen said. "They want publicity about our AJA soldiers to keep the home folks informed and to sell the idea to the Far East. They want to prove to Asia that the United States system accepted the AJAs as loyal citizens." He said this had resulted in a backlash in Hawai'i that had led the *Star-Bulletin* to "ease off on AJA publicity so as not to excite the Japanophobia." On a positive note, Allen ventured that arriving American troops quickly distinguished between enemy "Japs" and the Japanese-ancestry community in Hawai'i. "Many soldiers say the only friendly contacts they have had since coming to Hawaii have been with Japanese families," Allen said.

A plantation manager, H. P. Faye, joined in castigating the segregation represented by the formation of Japanese American combat units. Other ethnic groups saw their sons drafted or mobilized by the guard without fanfare and, he said, they resented all the attention paid to the AJA. Faye said Japanese workers were also being unfairly criticized for participating in unions. "It's unfortunate that at this time the majority of the workers are Japanese and consequently many union members are of Japanese ancestry," Faye said, "especially when their *haole* leadership leads them at a critical time to slow-downs and strikes."

The participants proceeded haltingly to become a group. Loomis and Trent said the conversation was informal and they might or might not agree to meet again. They then agreed to meet the following week, when the discussion again revolved around rising tension.

"It's getting extremely difficult to talk sanely with people about the Japanese problem," Leslie Deacon said, "as their feelings seem so charged now."[13] The plantation manager Stafford Austin said, "I have people who tell me that [the Japanese] are all sons of bitches and should be put back in the trees where they came from." Fred Lowrey said an element of the public believed a psychology of hate was necessary to win the war. He had heard people say that after the war all people of Japanese ancestry should move back to Japan. Lowrey blamed the upwelling of prejudice on recent arrivals to Hawai'i, which he defined as those arriving anytime within the preceding ten years. Individual *malihini* had kept quiet but on exposure to military prejudice were speaking up. Faye said army officers had called him a "Jap lover" for saying Hawai'i's approach to the Japanese issue was better than California's. Faye said the answer was for everyone to refer to everyone else as Hawaiians.

The business executive Edward Bodge brought up the ESC view that haole leadership had not done enough to help manage the situation. Bodge said haole executives could start by telling their wives to stop complaining about losing Japanese maids and yard boys: "Tell them to stop talking and realize that they'll have to learn how to use brooms."[14]

Cades said, "My wife told me it was a shame that only once a year the *haoles* work with Japanese women on the Welfare Campaign and go through the entire year without hearing or seeing them again. I think we should put it on a more personal basis." He added, "Scapegoatism is rising."

Riley Allen said the *Star-Bulletin* had decided to ease off on covering labor strife, which at that point had occurred in the city's bus system, a major dairy, and the Theo H. Davies Corporation, one of the Big Five. As soon would be proven, he warned the businessmen that despite the war, the unions were gaining ground. "[The unions] appealed to the Japanese because they feel at sea and are bewildered. The union calls them brothers and treats them as equals. It makes an impression on them because they are wondering what their place will be after the war. The unions are getting closer to the boys as individuals than their employers are."

Contrasting the performance of the afternoon *Star-Bulletin* with the morning *Advertiser*, Galen Fisher said, "The Star-Bulletin has done a swell job. The Advertiser should be run out of town. It has done a stinking job."

An occasional speaker seemed to genuinely empathize with the experience of Japanese Americans. Leslie Deacon, who worked consistently to make the most of veteran benefits, had just attended the first islandwide conference of the Japanese community since the onset of war. He reported, "[I] made the observation that when the ESC boys asked for help from the other races they always got a scolding." He said such support as existed was often freighted with condescension. As if to illustrate that point, Austin said, "These people need a continual kick in their pants to make them keep up their fight, and I occasionally do so. . . . I told them to meet with *haoles,* Hawaiians and other leaders.

I told them they needed the help of all their friends to lick the problem and criticized them for being too much to themselves and for not being free with other races."

Finally, a shift in tone occurred in a series of meetings held in late 1943.[15] During this period, news of the first AJA battlefield casualties filtered home. John Hamilton, the Chamber of Commerce representative, struck a strongly inclusive note. He called for the schools to actively teach that America had no place for racial intolerance; for churches to organize social gatherings with a view to incorporating Japanese women; and for the service clubs such as Rotary and Lions to include a percentage of all ethnic groups in their memberships. In the business sector, he advocated for wage scales based not on race (a widespread practice) but on the quality of work performed. For the press, he proposed referring to Japanese Americans as simply Americans.

The (White) Group on Race Relations formed committees devoted to counteracting rumors, labor relations, and the future of Hawai'i. Each was assigned to merge its efforts with a counterpart group from the ESC.[16] A steering committee was formed to coordinate their combined efforts. Ted Trent appointed three vocal proponents of improving relations—Bodge, Leslie Deacon, and Galen Fisher—while the ESC assigned Yoshida, Ernest Murai, and Masa Katagiri.[17]

The scale of the problem of achieving proportionate representation on territorial boards and commissions gained a certain specificity in a report by the *Honolulu Star-Bulletin*. It said that of 254 appointments surveyed, 200 were Caucasians and 41 were Hawaiian. Only 7 were Japanese and 6 were Chinese. As in many other settings, the sizeable Filipino population was unrepresented, as if they did not exist.[18]

CHAPTER 14

Imagining a New Hawai'i

VISIONS OF A more GENUINELY MULTIRACIAL and inclusive Hawai'i arose incrementally from the war crisis. The Morale Section repeatedly advanced strategies for achieving it. Everyone was to be respected. Everyone was to have a place at the table. Inclusivity was at the heart of the Morale Section campaign to organize every ethnic group on every major island and then to weave them together into an interracial leadership system. Inclusivity was the heartbeat of Yoshida's paper, "United Hawaii." Here and there, the theme of inclusivity had risen to the top of people's aspirations spontaneously, as within the Kauai Morale Committee. Inclusivity was likewise the main theme of Hemenway, Ching, and Yoshida as they pounded on the doors of the white power system.

The more strategically minded Nisei carried the goal of an open, inclusive society into their military experience. While on a long, grueling maneuver in mid-1943 in Louisiana, men of the 100th met around a campfire on weekends, far into the night, discussing the situation in Hawai'i. This group included all the junior Nisei officers, a few Caucasian officers, and the Korean American Young Ok Kim, who was developing what became a lifelong friendship with Lt. Sakae Takahashi. Their goal was to create a society based on equality through participation in politics and business. "The discussions became endless and very passionate," Kim was to recall. "Sakae and I fought for only two points. The 100th must excel in combat and we as individuals must set the example or none of the solutions proposed would work." With success on the battlefield, the "quick solution was to change the political equation in Hawaii. Throw out the Republicans."[1]

A correspondence on postwar society developed between Nisei soldiers and community leaders in Hawai'i. The urgency of the soldiers' message spurred the home front to remain vigilant in the present while creating a map into the future. The most essential work of the home front effort continued in the Morale Section and its progeny, the Emergency Service Committee. Over the course of two years, they held four conferences dedicated to postwar planning.[2]

The first conference was on Sunday, September 12, 1943. Predictably, it was at the Nu'uanu YMCA. Katagiri served as chairman. The conference secretary was Mitsuyuki Kido, a teacher at the inner-city Farrington High School. Thirty-one people participated, all of Japanese ancestry except for Ching and Loomis.

Ching and Yoshida warned of the dangers of a letdown following the mobilization of the 442nd RCT. Ching opened the conference by saying its purpose was "not to look back but to look ahead." He suggested that the hardest days in Hawai'i might yet be to come, partly because Pacific combat was intensifying, and partly because of friction points within the Islands, such as labor unrest, complaints about yardmen and maids, and the irritation resulting from the continued speaking of Japanese in public places. Ching said the Japanese community had to be no less disciplined than its soldiers: "You have jobs that you must do. You have obligations. The home front is just as important as the front lines."

"Our friends have stood by us," Yoshida said. "It is up to us to show that their confidence in our Americanism has not been misplaced." He exhorted the group to an ever-greater effort. The conferees, he said, had an obligation to promote cooperation in race relations not only in Hawai'i but "the invaluable contribution it can make in the future in other parts of the world, including the mainland U.S."

Yoshida described the AJA not as victims of history but as authors: "The old world is irrevocably gone. What the future shall be is partly for us to decide. We are helping to set certain precedents in the handling of racial minorities in a democratic society. What we do now is not only going to determine our place in the larger American community for generations to come; it will also determine to some extent the policies . . . of other governments in the handling of racial problems."

Yoshida said the moment had arrived to become a real part of the American community: "But we've got to work for it. Some of us are going to die for it. . . . Either we make use of the present opportunity or we let it slip out of our hands and we remain forever a kind of second-rate, pseudo American so far as the rest of our fellow Americans are concerned."

This first conference was limited to O'ahu, with the intent of organizing a follow-through gathering of delegates from all the islands. The second conference was held ten months later on Maui in the county seat town of Wailuku. It was on a more ambitious two-day schedule and better organized. By this time, AJA had gone from their long period of training to the battlefield, so the conference heard reports of casualties. War-wounded veterans of the 100th Battalion participated, telling the delegates that the challenge of mid-1944 July was to focus on what the veterans would return to.

The host and chair of the territory-wide conference was the Dr. Izumi, who led Maui's Morale Committee. Twelve Maui ESC members, eight area chairs, another ten Maui contact men, and thirty Maui delegates attended. Eleven delegates arrived from Oʻahu and four each from Kauaʻi and Hawaiʻi Island. An additional two dozen people were guests, including representatives of the army, navy, and FBI, public schools, the plantations, the Red Cross, and the four county governments.

The leadership was much the same. Hung Wai Ching gave the opening speech. "Can we say at this moment that we are safely out of the woods?" Ching asked. As usual he tried to keep the pressure on, announcing the time had come to "realign sights, revamp your objectives and redefine your goals." At Camp Shelby, Ching had interviewed many of the 442nd RCT soldiers: "They feel they are doing more than their share and expect the people back home to come through with their share." Ching produced a letter he always carried with him, quoting a Nisei soldier as writing, "My hero will be whoever steers the war to winning the peace after the guns are silenced."

Ching previously had criticized Japanese habits of mind, thereby underscoring his intimate relationship as a non-Japanese with the Japanese community. Japanese, Ching contended, tended to withdraw when faced with critical and potentially embarrassing situations. "[Such behavior] seems to stifle progressive action and negates constructive thoughts," Ching said. "Typical is an expression: 'Why are we picked on? Aren't we Americans and aren't we doing as much as other groups?' This attitude of mind fails utterly to see the special position imposed on the group."

"Rightly or wrongly," Ching said, Japanese Americans had to do more than other people. "You simply cannot lay down. You have to make good."

Dr. Izumi entitled his remarks "Developing Better Personal Relationships with People of Other Races." Izumi said the absence of a massive internment in Hawaiʻi could be attributed "in no small measure to the unshakable faith of some of our Territory's leading citizens and officials of other races." More than anything, he said, Pearl Harbor had taught Japanese that interracial friendships were not merely a nice idea but a necessity. He noted that one of three people in Hawai'i was Japanese, compared to one of eighty on the West Coast. He cited the "common occurrence" of interracial marriage in Hawai'i as dramatic evidence of tolerance and bonding.

Echoing Ching, Izumi took Japanese to task for "a lack of frankness." Withdrawal, he said, led to a self-defeating self-pity. "Any psychological attitude of defeatism because of ancestry is bound to hinder that individual's initiative and ambition. So this feeling of being sorry for oneself must be one of the first hurdles to be overcome." He called for a "liberal intermingling" and intentional association with other racial groups through the public schools, the YMCA and YWCA, civic associations, and business.

Self-criticism by Japanese continued. Various speakers depicted the Japanese population as clannish and prone to support the class barriers of traditional Japanese society. Japanese "can improve their attitude toward certain other races which they have a tendency to look down upon," the conference minutes reported. For example, Japanese from the four main Japanese islands tended to look down on the Okinawans, and all looked down on Japan's caste of untouchables, the Eta. Delegates repeated, as a social gospel, that better relationships were their own responsibility as well as that of other racial groups, and also that all groups must evolve through genuine personal fellowship of free, equal people dedicated to working together on common concerns.

Army captain Jack Mizuha traced the deployment of the 100th Battalion in Europe and Nisei linguists in the Pacific. The cost in dead and wounded was mounting. Untold numbers of Nisei veterans were scattered in hospitals across Europe and the United States. The question of "rehabilitation," or more broadly what the veterans would come home to, took over a major part of the discussion.

Leslie Deacon, a staunch white ally of the Japanese community, corresponded with several soldiers overseas. He had investigated making use of organizations ranging from employment agencies to mental health providers, welfare, chambers of commerce, and the Red Cross. The ensuing discussion reflected a keen interest in using the education subsidies of the GI Bill of Rights, formally known as the Servicemen's Readjustment Act, which Congress had passed and President Roosevelt had signed into law one month previously.

The problems of people with mixed or conflicting national loyalties crept into the conversation in a modest way. Katagiri talked about a class in Americanization for young men paroled from the internment camp at Honouliuli. Most were *kibei*. Katagiri said the class had twelve lessons and was being conducted by Dr. Miles Cary, the McKinley High School principal who recently had returned from setting up the education system at the Poston internment camp.

Mitsuyuki Kido was described as the conference discussion leader. Yoshida served the conference as coordinator and was assigned the familiar task of summarizing. Together they stated what was going to happen, what was happening as talk progressed, and what had just happened.

A third AJA conference was held six months later on January 28, 1945, at the Nu'uanu YMCA. Again, the atmosphere had changed as the result of an ever-growing impact of AJA participation in the military. The letter that Ching carried in his pocket, widely circulated, was from Sgt. Joe Itagaki, written from "Somewhere in France": "The families of the deceased, the maimed and their dependents, and the fortunate few who will return sound in mind and body, all will need help in the difficult days ahead," Itagaki wrote. The letter was to become widely read throughout the community and would be cited by Jack Burns as a spur to political action.

The third conference was, again, an O'ahu conference. Two teenagers were included: George R. Ariyoshi, representing McKinley High School, who would eventually be the first Japanese American governor; and Nelson K. Doi, of Hawai'i Island, who was to become Ariyoshi's lieutenant governor, a power in the Hawai'i Senate, and a distinguished judge.

Yoshida opened the conference by saying the Japanese community had experienced a major change for the better in race relations since the onset of the crisis on December 7, 1941. The challenge now was to accelerate Japanese American participation despite an accumulating complacency. Dr. Murai led a discussion of home front assistance to servicemen and their families covering life insurance, pay and pensions, hospitalization, loans, jobs, unemployment compensation, dependent benefits in the event of death, burial allowance, nursing care, and prominently, again, the educational benefits of the GI Bill.

An ESC delegate reported that 124 Japanese-language schools had been dissolved, but 42 were intact. After discussions about the various types of Japanese-language schools—for example, schools under community control versus schools run by the Buddhist sects—the conferees supported a resolution favoring the complete dissolution of the schools. The resolution was joined to a call for the public schools to take responsibility for teaching Japanese, as well as Korean and Chinese. The conference favored what some Japanese schools already had done—either selling their assets or donating their assets outright to a foundation dedicated to the benefit of veterans. The foundation officers included Hemenway as president; Shivers, vice president; Robert K. Murakami, secretary; and Kido, Colonel Farrant Turner, and Garner Anthony as trustees.

In contrast to the narrow Americanism at work in the language issue, the conference struck a more self-assured tone on the long-standing question of dual citizenship. The researcher on the subject, Ethel Mori, stressed the fact that many of the 100th Battalion were dual citizens. Accordingly, she said, the war had proven that dual citizenship "had no bearing on one's Americanism." Shimeji Ryusaki, on the staff of the Swedish consulate, described a work-around for expatriation, in which a dual citizen could file a declaration of intent to expatriate his or her Japanese citizenship. She then would issue a statement acknowledging receipt of the declaration in lieu of meeting Japan's expatriation requirements in wartime. Ryusaki reported more than a thousand such declarations were on file. Yoshida, who had labored over expatriation between 1939 and 1941, said that the veterans' war records had proven that dual citizenship "does not mean anything."

Thirty-nine people were listed as guests, prominently including Hemenway, Cary, and Lind. The conference began on a Saturday, March 24, 1945, and continued for three days. A new professor of sociology at the University of Hawai'i, Dr. John A. Rademaker, served as recorder, producing a blow-by-blow, single-spaced, sixty-one-page narrative of the proceedings.[3]

The fourth and final conference was held at McKinley High School and attracted sixty delegates. Twenty-seven were from O'ahu, fourteen from Hawai'i, ten from Kaua'i, seven from Maui, and two from Lāna'i. Yoshida was the discussion leader on day one, and Hung Wai Ching led the second day. Although the conversation was couched in the evolving history of the war, its past-present-future structure was as Yoshida, Ching, and a few others had mapped the goals of the Council for Interracial Unity four years previously. Having once anticipated the war, they continued to analyze how it was evolving, and what people must do to make the most of the postwar.

Yoshida was ever wary of ethnic insularity. He proposed that the participants transform their immediate group concerns into overall community concerns. This, he said, would require a realignment not only of influence and relationships but of how Japanese thought of themselves. He critiqued ethnic groups as self-absorbed. Interracial cooperation, he said, was the key to community progress. Therefore, the conferees should "evaluate all things in terms of their effect on the larger community." Yoshida asked in what ways Japanese could contribute to integrating themselves. In what ways could other groups contribute to an inclusive process? AJA had proven themselves to be loyal Americans, "but Americanism means more than willingness to sacrifice one's life for America. . . . It also means feeling at ease among other Americans, speaking out, acting, and using freely the customs of America."[4]

By now, the ever-present Mitsuyuki Kido praised the Kauaʻi Morale Committee for its pioneering efforts to form interracial systems of community leadership. From the discussion, it appeared Kauaʻi's goal of an effective interracial council had been only partially realized. However, support of Philippine relief work was cited favorably, as well as broad inclusion in the observance of Memorial Day and in Boy and Girl Scouts, the American Legion, Lions Clubs, and the Chamber of Commerce. In a self-critical vein, delegate Charles Ishii of Kauaʻi said people still sat back while criticizing haoles "for not coming half way."[5]

Katagiri, vice chair of the conference, said that AJAs who participated in community-wide efforts tended to be perceived not as leaders but as AJA representatives. "We have to educate ourselves so well that we'll be appointed to groups as individual members on the basis of our own talents," Katagiri said, "not as representatives of AJAs."

Noburo Miyake of Kauaʻi spoke as a pioneering officeholder who had stepped down under the pressures of the war. He said before Pearl Harbor there were fourteen Japanese associations on Kauaʻi. Eleven were religious or educational, two represented business, and one was a *hui* of fishermen. He said most had been open regardless of ethnicity but were predominantly Japanese. Now all were shut down. This, he said, had created an opportunity in disguise by forcing Japanese to seek wider participation in multiethnic associations, which he urgently favored.

In response, one delegate advanced a critical view of the underlying history of institutional segregation throughout plantation Hawai'i, namely that both the planters and the planter-dominated territorial government "encouraged persons of Japanese ancestry to group together." By his count, twelve of Kaua'i's Japanese-language schools were located on plantations and five on land paid for by the territorial government. Further, "out of nineteen churches, eleven were on plantations, [and] six were on property purchased from the Territory."

Izumi Kansako of Hawai'i Island pointed to the existence of Swedish, German, and Italian enclaves on the Mainland, saying it was natural for immigrant groups to form settlements and then engage more extensively with others. He said the Japanese were being criticized, and were criticizing themselves, for perpetuating ethnic ties and customs that would have been acceptable except for the war with Japan.

Murai struck a note for the more affluent, suggesting weekly poker and golf and entertaining in one's home. Kido held up Hemenway and Deacon as role models: "They are constantly out doing something for the community."[6] For a haole perspective, Yoshida called on Deacon, who said haoles did not think in terms of participation with other groups because haoles did not regard themselves as a group. To this he added, with considerable candor, "The haoles are not to be expected to push the matter of racial integration anyhow, for they are the haves while the others are the have-nots."

A delegate from Hawai'i Island, Thomas Takamune, sharpened an emerging theme. Were they dedicated merely to getting ahead or to creating a better society? He cited a Japanese man who spoke ill of Filipinos. He said if AJA were obsessed with gaining acceptance "from the top, and are not interested in building acceptance of everyone by everyone else, we are merely trying to elevate ourselves as a racial group." He said the Japanese were approaching a choice: "Either we will have to fight for acceptance as a general principle or admit that we're just trying to advance ourselves for strictly selfish reasons." Self-seeking would result in "reciprocal discrimination and unrestricted competition with no holds barred," he said. He warned that if, in the main, Japanese leaders engaged in self-seeking after the war, it would spell the end to hopes for acceptance, tolerance, and real democracy. Echoing the pioneering themes of Kaua'i's Community Improvement Society, his solution was building better public schools and recreation facilities, developing better health care, and creating a stronger economy in which everyone could benefit.[7]

How Japanese Americans went about exerting their full potential for influence was a delicate issue. Kaua'i, which had led in the prewar in electing AJAs, was ripe for returning AJAs to office. The biggest problem, according to a guest from Kaua'i, was allaying non-Japanese fears of an AJA political bloc: "These critics will say, 'See what we told you? They are just using you to get their chestnuts out of the fire and to secure political control of the Territory.'"

Labor organizing figured in the conversation, if minimally, given the impact that labor soon was to have. Takamune said increases in the minimum wage showed what could happen when people worked together. The attorney Miho said the organization of labor must be a central concern of postwar planning. In his view, this was well along and could be activated with the cessation of war, resulting among other things in displacing "strong-armed plantation managers."

A prominent school principal from O'ahu, Stanley Miyamoto, quoted studies documenting the disparity between public schools and private schools. He cited Punahou School and Kamehameha School in particular. The gap, he said, could only be narrowed by "supporting and voting for candidates who favor adequate teachers and progressive education."[8]

At this point, in Yoshida's view, neither the Emergency Service Committee nor AJA in general were yet adequately prepared to do the hard work of a multiracial political landscape. He complained of approaching fellow educators to testify with him at the legislature for expanding the budget, but they were always too busy. Both Ching and Yoshida acknowledged that the ESC was weakened by the fact it had been chosen from above, not elected.

Rademaker recommended the groupwork techniques of the YMCA for developing discussion skills on an individual by individual basis.

Day two was a puzzle. How far into the future should the Morale Section and ESC continue to operate? As circumstances changed, what should their relationship be with the military? To what extent should they publicize the heroics of AJA? What story was arising from the battlefield?

The ESC groups had tried to work quietly, but now—seeming to lack the discipline of the three-member Morale Section to work in anonymity—they were bothered by the fact that only a fraction of the public understood who they were. One delegate said 90 percent of the public had never heard of them, as if that was not good.

Speakers occasionally referred to soldiers who resented the ESC as home-town elitists who had sent the young off to battle. To this point, the war-wounded Jack Mizuha advised, "Don't be too concerned about the criticism of the veterans. . . . Work with them, guide and help them . . . we must lead. . . . There is no one to take our places now. We've got to stay with it."[9]

Kido criticized the ESC for its preponderance of businessmen and professionals: "People who work with their hands and veterans are not represented."[10] Murai jumped in to advocate for the inclusion of "less high-brow" people, such as stevedores, farmers, contractors, and sports figures. Kido advocated generating more publicity for the AJA war effort. Loomis agreed, saying the anti-Japanese movement had advanced its views across the country, backed by large sums of money. "We have not," he said. "Hawaii is taking a beating in Washington D.C. We need a number of paid steamer fares right after the war with the motto stamped on the ticket, 'Hawaii is an integral part of the United States.'"

Ching welcomed the Hawai'i delegate to Congress, Joseph Farrington, to the conference as one who had always helped him in Washington, D.C. Farrington reassured the audience that national opinion of the AJA had improved. Further, the War Department was unwavering in its commitment to the 100th and the 442nd RCT. Such well-known figures as Mrs. Roosevelt, McCloy, Secretary of the Interior Harold Ickes, and Dillon Myer were all staunchly in support. Farrington had just returned from visiting the combat units in Europe, acquiring immediacy for his words. He had met with General Mark Clark, commander of the American forces in the Italian theater of war, whom he found "warm and sincere" and deeply appreciative of the Nisei's soldiering qualities. Farrington described the rows of white crosses marking the European graves of AJA who had died so "democracy and freedom might live."[11] There followed another exhaustive session on veteran affairs.

Spiritual and religious practices were also discussed in depth, revealing a continuing vein of superstition and fear at work in the community. Dating to the December 7 roundup, traditional religious life had been suppressed. The result was a vacant space into which folk practices, cults, and what some viewed as grifting had entered. Stanley Miyamoto abstracted the subject by saying, "We live in a world of dual culture, that of the Orient and the Occident. Our parents live more in the culture of the Orient. They were put in a precarious position with the coming of the war." Katagiri cut in, insisting that Shinto not be discussed, because

Shinto was the state religion of Japan and the U.S. government rightly had seized its assets. Attention focused on the small fraction of Buddhist priests who had been allowed to return to Hawai'i from internment camps. A Kaua'i delegate told the story of a female priest who was offering prayers for the safety of servicemen. "Parents flock to her and enormous amounts are turned in to her in the collection." Once or twice a week, as many as three hundred mothers from the north end of Kaua'i traveled around to Waimea on the southwest end for prayers, each giving the priest a dollar or two. The walls of her temple had pictures of Nisei GIs. The delegate's conclusion was ambiguous. Although he felt the woman was "racketeering," he nonetheless reported, "Not one of these boys has been killed." One by one, delegates acknowledged similar prayers of intercession were ongoing on their islands. Collectively, the response was to advocate for more Buddhist priests and Christian ministers to be released into the community to draw people back to aboveground religious practices. The discussion also favored activating the Young Men's Buddhist Association (YMBA), which had been shut down in the war.

Several participants talked about the loss of parental control in the turbulence of war, most painfully a loss of control over teenaged daughters. Lind reassured them they were not alone. The ESC being a virtually all-male society, the status of females was often only to be inferred. This particular conference listed thirteen female guests, five of whom were Caucasian. The conference noted with approval that the first small contingent of Women's Army Corps had been recruited in Hawai'i, and that Japanese American females were disproportionately represented.

The prospects for internees on their return provoked a long discussion. Several delegates knew about internment in depth.[12] Yoshida had worked on developing Americanization classes for returnees. Dr. Murai, along with the acting Swedish consul Shimeji Ryusaki, had traveled with the wives of internees who had gone with their children to the Rohwer and Jerome camps in Arkansas to join their husbands. Reverend Miho had visited internment camps on the Mainland. Loomis reported his correspondence with the Fair Play Committee, which was attempting to line up jobs and housing for people in the camps. Two representatives of the American Friends' Service Committee (AFSC) were introduced as having been "of inestimable value" to the support of internees. Both were of the pacifist Quaker sect. William Morris Maier, an attorney, was executive secretary of the Hawai'i branch of the AFSC throughout the war. He was a friend of Ching's, who credited him with helping to facilitate access to Eleanor Roosevelt. The second was Dr. Gilbert Bowles, originally a Quaker missionary to Japan who worked full time in Honolulu with Maier.[13]

Maier estimated that fourteen hundred internees and family members would be returning to Hawai'i. Before the war, many of the internees were prominent community members. "If they come back embittered and feel that their place is no longer here," Maier said, "unfortunate repercussions may result." Bowles said the question was whether they would be welcomed back as rightful members of the community. Various speakers stressed the importance of renewing personal friendships with internees on their return.

Yoshida and Ching periodically intervened to keep the conversation from bogging down. The majority of the participants were the older Nisei leaders who had seized the moment on December 7. Now, with the crisis past and a level of definable success coming into sight, the obvious imperatives of crisis management were giving way to subjects of greater complexity. Ching asked how their wartime work would be integrated into the wider community. The challenge of the Council for Interracial Unity remained: How were they to create an inclusive society? As delegate Takamune had insisted on discussing, was their work for the advancement of everyone, or was it for the advancement of an emerging privileged class of Japanese? Was this about self-interest or democracy?

The philosophy of the actors was clearly evident. Yoshida, Ching, and Loomis represented an assertive democratic idealism. They were taken seriously not only because of their skills but because they advocated an ideology and an organizing plan that Hawai'i needed—and that the country needed. The white people in the equation, the "guests" of the conferences, were a combination of religious leaders, educators, and businessmen blessed either by high ideals or enlightened self-interest. Some approached the task with a democratic and missionary spirit, while others were wary of a postwar restructuring.

Perhaps the most enduring feature of the ESC organizing process was the interaction of the Japanese with the dominant haole group. Acquaintance had expanded considerably. Although the Morale Section had sought the inclusion of all ethnic groups into their paradigm, the Japanese were the one group with the numbers, education level, and determination to lead a movement for inclusivity. A certain level of change had occurred in the shadow of the U.S. military and more generally in the colonial administration of the U.S. government. Whether Hawai'i would evolve further toward a genuine democracy after the war, or whether it would revert to race-based colonialism, was impossible to predict.

While speakers at the conferences repeatedly identified ways in which the ESC might be useful in the future, advancement via ethnically based organization was judged to be ultimately self-defeating. At the end of the last day of the conference, a committee headed by the attorney Robert Murakami proposed the ESC's answer. He presented a resolution saying more and more citizens recognized that ESC's concerns were "no longer peculiar only to persons of Japanese ancestry but are of vital concern to all."

Therefore, the resolution read, "We do not approve of the creation or perpetuation of any purely racial organization." Accordingly, as soon as peace was at hand, the Morale and Emergency Service Committees of Hawai'i "shall be dissolved and disbanded." Shigeo Yoshida moved that the resolution be passed, and it was seconded and carried.[14]

CHAPTER 15

Sealed with Sacrifice

IN CONTRAST TO THE HURRIED DEPARTURE from Hawai'i of the 100th Battalion, the 442nd Regimental Combat Team was given a grand send-off on the grounds of 'Iolani Palace. The Varsity Victory Volunteers members stood in the front ranks. The others filled the grounds, facing the palace steps, which overflowed with generals and dignitaries. The crowd was estimated at seventeen thousand, weighing the soldiers down with leis that represented the hopes and prayers of Hawai'i. The Army Signal Corps photographed their every move, as did the hometown press.

What the Council for Interracial Unity had envisioned in the prewar, and what the 100th Battalion had discussed in training camp, could only be realized if the Nisei units made a good showing on the battlefield. From Japanese culture, "Do not bring shame," was repeated countless times. "Do your best," was an almost hypnotic phrase. Mentors talked with the Nisei volunteers repeatedly, to the effect that they carried on their shoulders the honor of their families, the reputation of Japanese Americans, and the future of Hawai'i.

At full strength, the outfit totaled more than four thousand men. When assembled, they struck one soldier as looking like a wheat field that stretched on and on. In truth they were a tiny part of an American army that by 1943 had swelled to 8 million. Karl Bendetsen predicted they would not amount to, in his words, "a hill of beans."[1]

The most common prediction was that Japanese American combat soldiers would do well—how well, no one seemed to imagine—as a way of proving their loyalty. This was a truism that failed to convey the complexity and range of the troops. Mobilizing in the shadow of Pearl Harbor, they were front-row students of the world drama. They were tricultural: American, Japanese, and local/Hawaiian. Many were bilingual or, counting pidgin, trilingual. The more far seeing were determined

Swearing in of the 442nd filled the grounds of 'Iolani Palace.

to enter politics, business, and the professions, and even to redefining how minorities were treated in America. They were a choice group mentally and intellectually, which translated to a high battlefield IQ.[2] They had been introduced to military culture in high school ROTC, and many had continued this training in college. As potential fighters, they were products of the hard-working, athletically competitive culture of Hawai'i. They were swimmers and often farm boys or laborers of some type. They had played all the sports, boxed, and studied martial arts—judo, karate, and kendo—and thereby conditioned from a young age to engage in face-to-face, hand-to-hand struggle.

They were further advantaged by sharing the relationship skills of Hawai'i's all-for-one grassroots lifestyle. They were well mannered and respectful, while also on the ready for a fight. Their outgoing demeanor upended the stereotype of the unknowable Oriental. In print, "aloha" was a nice-sounding word. In practice, it was an elemental influence. A soldier of the 100th, Conrad Tsukayama, had grown up in a community of first-generation Japanese farmers. He regarded the neighboring Issei as ethnocentric to a fault. He believed the "Japanese" had been rescued by a fellowship that was Native Hawaiian in origin. "We were all Hawaiian at heart," he wrote of the 100th. "The basic ohana [family] spirit came from the Native Hawaiian people, an ethnic group filled with genuine aloha, the magic ingredient that brought together the hearts of all the oppressed immigrants' sons. We carried this spirit of aloha wherever we went."[3]

Tsukayama credited the multiethnic National Guard units, from which the 100th was drawn, for enhancing the development of a Hawaiian attitude. Regimentation was more like that of a sports team than a military outfit: "Officers and NCOs [noncommissioned officers] led us rather than ordering us around, and orders were more of a request than a command," Tsukayama wrote. "Being assigned to a local unit was definitely a break and a blessing, and every ethnic group contributed to the unit's cohesiveness . . . 'all for one and one for all' . . . your fellow soldiers will take care of you and fight for you, whatever the risk." Soldiers from the Mainland, he said, were amazed by the solidarity of the islanders.[4]

Isaac Akinaka of the 100th kept a diary. In it, he described the circuitous train ride from the port of San Francisco to Camp McCoy, Wisconsin. The train stopped in a small town, Liberal, Kansas, where the troops were allowed to get off and stretch. The townspeople were all eyes. Most, he said, knew nothing about Hawai'i except for Japan's attack on Pearl Harbor. He and his friends gave out matchbook covers with images of the islands. One of the men also handed out fifty scenic postcards that he had brought for just such an occasion. "These acts on the part of our men will surely create goodwill for Hawaii's soldiers in the U.S. Army," Akinaka wrote. "Most of the people here think of Hawaii as a foreign land. I informed them of the true status of our islands." Akinaka saved an article from a Wisconsin newspaper describing the soldiers from Hawai'i as "friendly and eager talkers." Night spots near the training camp began playing Hawaiian music. "There the Hawaiians are happy to buy any stranger a drink in exchange for conversation," the newspaper reported.[5]

To affirm community-to-community friendship, people in Hawai'i put on a luau for the townspeople of Camp McCoy, Wisconsin, with great success.

When the 100th eventually moved to racially troubled Mississippi, Akinaka went for a Sunday stroll. "Every person we passed said a 'Good morning' first before we did," Akinaka wrote. "This is really a good sign and we will be making many new friends before we know it."

A Nisei soldier from an internment camp described the Japanese Hawaiians as "happy-go-lucky, extroverted, loaded [with gambling money], and very outspoken, while we came out of camp introverted, broke, and carrying a chip on our shoulders."[6]

Self-confidence flowed from their high degree of cohesion. Although they were usually treated as whites on the black-white color line, Nisei were appalled by the segregation of African Americans. Veteran Mike Tokunaga told of riding a bus to New Orleans on pass. The bus stopped to pick up a black soldier. The driver snarled his order: "Back of the bus." The Japanese Americans challenged the driver, but he persisted, at which point they threw him off the bus and drove themselves to New Orleans, where they ditched the vehicle, with impunity.

A young white lieutenant in the 442nd, William Davenport, wrote to his mother in Lincoln Park, Michigan, that he was never to use the word "Jap": "They resent it very much." He reported that they were prepared for brawling and occasionally engaged in it as necessary.[7]

The introspective Thomas Higa set out to visit his Japanese-language teacher at Camp Livingston, Louisiana. A news vender nearby shouted, "He is the one! No mistake!" Two police jumped Higa and put him in handcuffs, loudly announcing that he was a Japanese spy. Higa was surrounded by soldiers with rifles and machine guns, as well as newsmen with cameras. He was put into the back room of a jail for interrogation. "All of a sudden I was seized with fear," Higa wrote. "I knew lynchings took place often in the South and I had heard that people had been hung from tree branches and burned alive." After convincing his captors that he was indeed an American soldier, he was told to get out. He refused, demanding to speak to everyone. "I am a Japanese American," he announced. "If you have anything to say to me, let me hear it." The captain in charge bent over to Higa's height and said, "I apologize."[8]

Contrary to the image of a segregated unit, not all were of Japanese ancestry. Both the 100th and the 442nd contained bridging figures from other ethnic groups: Native Hawaiians, Chinese, mixed Japanese-Caucasians, Korean Americans, and Caucasians. On War Department orders, a majority of the officers were haole.

The highest-ranking Asian American of the 100th was Young Ok Kim, a Korean American. Kim was from the old downtown of Los Angeles. He had been drafted into the army and then attended Officer's Candidate School. Whoever assigned him to the 100th did not understand that Japan had brutally taken over Korea. When told he could transfer out because he might harbor a distaste for Japanese, Kim replied, "I am an American, and they are Americans, and we will fight together as Americans." Young Ok Kim became a legend of personal courage and military strategy, eventually rising to the rank of colonel.[9]

Caucasians were typically welcomed. "There may have been a few misunderstandings when we started training," Chester Tanaka recalled, "but there were very few even then. When we hit combat, there were none. We were one fighting team. To us, our Caucasian officers were Nisei, like us."[10] Major John "Jack" Johnson was a graduate of the then nearly all-white Punahou School. He had played several sports for UH and excelled in football, most famously in an improbable and famous victory over the University of California. As a sugar industry executive, he was eligible for an exemption from service, but he insisted on going to war with the 100th. Through battlefield attrition, he was to rise to second in command.

A young white lieutenant, Kurt E. Schemel, struck a nerve with certain individuals for entirely different reasons. His parents were immigrants from Germany. He talked with Thomas Higa about the forced evacuation and internment. Schemel had entered the war knowing he might be fighting his cousins from Germany. "Germany is my motherland," he told Higa. "I learned German customs at home, and I love Germany as well as America." He believed that Japanese Americans could understand his dilemma: "I joined the one hundredth battalion . . . to be with you."[11]

Among soldiers of Japanese ancestry, their diversity was as the sociologist Lind had said—they were "a congery" of groups. Akinaka was a devout Mormon. He knew of only one other soldier who was a member of the Japanese mission of Latter-day Saints. They discussed their hope of creating a good record for other Japanese LDS members who might follow. Higa was one of the twenty or so *kibei* who attended a special English-language class. Others spoke so little English that "Doc" Kometani would translate for them. If they went drinking in a bar, he would follow them, apprehensive of their tendency to sing Japanese martial songs after a few drinks.

Kaoru Suzuki was a *kibei* of a sort, the son of a struggling rice farmer from Fukushima Prefecture. His father had immigrated in the early 1900s to work on a plantation on Oʻahu. Thereafter he brought a picture bride from the old country, and their marriage produced four boys. When Kaoru was six, the family returned to the rice fields of Japan. There they lived in a bamboo house chinked with mud and grass. The living room was covered by tatami. A fire pit burned in the middle of the living space. They drank water from a well they had dug by hand. They doctored themselves from a stash of pills and herbs that a medicine man left to them on his twice-yearly visits to their village. At age twelve, Kaoru followed his father back to Waipahu Plantation in Leeward Oʻahu. He commuted to Honolulu, where he made false teeth for a dentist for $30 a month. He studied English in a class at St. Andrew's Episcopal Church, which was seemingly the closest he ever came to an Americanization activity until he was drafted into the U.S. Army in 1941.[12]

Stanley Izumigawa of Maui was less than enamored with army life. "You don't know how many jackasses there are in this world," he wrote, "until you get into an organization like the Army."[13]

With elements so diverse, it was not uniformity of family or ethnic background that empowered the Nisei soldiers so much as their unique comradery. Compared to a usual training of somewhere between three and six months, the 100th Battalion trained for thirteen months, first in Wisconsin and then in Mississippi. This reflected their unattached "Separate" status and, more fundamentally, the army's indecision about what to do with them. Finally, they shipped in August 1943 to North

Africa, where hard-won Allied successes had created a staging area for the invasion of Italy. Over several weeks the 100th commander, Colonel Farrant Turner, was forced to haggle for deployment into the war zone.

On September 22, 1943, the first of the Japanese American fighting forces landed in southern Italy. Despite the skepticism of America's military planners, the Italian front was opened at the insistence of British prime minister Winston Churchill, who contended that it would tear at Germany's "soft underbelly." This was to prove more evocative than descriptive. The Allied goal was not about Italy as an enemy state, in that Italy had changed governments and surrendered as the invasion began. Rather, the attack on Italy was an elaborate and costly diversion, aimed at tying down large elements of the German army from what was to be the Allied invasion of France across the English Channel.

In its first campaign, the 100th Battalion was a subset of the 34th Infantry Division, which was part of the VI Corps, which in turn was part of the Fifth U.S. Army, which was part of the 15th Army Group or, simply, the Allies. It consisted of not only Americans, British, and Free French but Algerians, Belgians, Cypriots, Moroccans, Canadians, Indians, Ghurka from Nepal, Lebanese, New Zealanders, Greeks, Poles, Carpathians, Brazilians, Jews from Palestine, Berber tribesmen, Seychelle islanders, Italian partisans, and others. Among the Americans were outfits of African Americans, Mexican Americans, and, finally, Japanese Americans. In terms of diversity, the Allied invasion force foreshadowed the postwar United Nations. Under these circumstances, the soldiers from Hawai'i might have all but disappeared. But they did just the opposite.

From the Salerno beachhead, the 100th Battalion struck out on a winding course through the mountains. On September 29, it ran into German machine-gun fire. Sergeant Joe Takata rushed the German gunners, shooting as he ran. He was killed by an enemy shell. News of his death spread quickly, not only as the first casualty but because he had been a star player on Kometani's Asahi baseball team. Takata was posthumously awarded the Distinguished Service Cross.[14] The diarist Masaichi Goto—by then a medic—ran to the rescue of four wounded soldiers. Enemy shells fell all around him. This was the Goto whose bride had promised him he would survive. He rendered aid to one of the wounded, then the next and the next, for which he was awarded a Silver Star for bravery. Conrad Tsukayama set a tone for unit solidarity.

Wounded, he left the hospital without being discharged, returning to the front to be with his comrades. This was to be repeated many times by others.[15]

The Italian theater commander, General Mark Clark, reported to Eisenhower, with what must have been a certain self-satisfaction, "In initial baptism of fire, leading company had twelve casualties but pushed coolly on." In twenty-four hours, they advanced twenty-five kilometers. "Efficiency of the Battalion very good. Quick reaction to hostile opposition." Clark's personal history intersected positively with the Nisei for reasons that ran deeper than battlefield experiences alone. In the early days of 1942, when DeWitt was panicking over imagined sabotage on the West Coast, Clark had visited him at General Marshall's direction. When Clark returned to Washington, he told Marshall that DeWitt was overreacting. He said there was no chance of a Japanese invasion and no real Fifth Column threat. When Roosevelt signed Executive Order 9066, Clark was opposed to a mass evacuation and the inevitable jail-like detention camps that would follow. He said it would be an injustice to Japanese Americans and also tie up army personnel who were needed to fight.[16] When the generals in the War Department had refused to support Emmons's plan for a Japanese American fighting force, McCloy found an ally in Mark Clark.[17] When the 100th Battalion was finally deployed, Marshall asked General Dwight D. Eisenhower, as overall commander in Europe, if he wanted the Japanese Americans for the invasion of northern France. Eisenhower previously had opposed formation of the 442nd, and now he declined to take the 100th into his command.[18] Mark Clark took them eagerly, assigning them to a fighting general, Charles Ryder, who previously had been to Hawai'i and who shared his open-mindedness regarding the possibilities of the unit.

Clark had a strong background in troop training. "Without question," he wrote critically, "our training has not yet produced disciplined officers and disciplined men." In the 100th he found discipline. Their battle cry was "Remember Pearl Harbor," and now they were part of Ryder's "Red Bull" 34th Division, the motto of which was "Attack, Attack, Attack." Clark needed soldiers who would, without hesitation, attack.

For months at a time, the Italian front resembled a war of attrition as much as a war of decisive invasion. When John J. McCloy eventually toured Italy, he observed, "It was more like the last war than anything I had seen."[19] If it was not quite a Somme or Verdun of World War I, it was nonetheless a slow-moving, desperate struggle with uncertain results.

It is an axiom of warfare that an invading force, to succeed, needs to outnumber a defending force. The first Italian theater commander, a British general, had hoped for a three-to-one advantage in manpower, but the ratio hovered around one-to-one.

Under these conditions, the hostile terrain did not allow for sweeping moves by field armies but rather demanded close-range combat, which created opportunities for a comparatively small outfit that was intent on proving itself. The military historian Milton Blumenson would write, "The true war in Italy took place on the level of platoons, companies and battalions that battled from one hill to the next."[20] Gaining ground required extraordinary losses. And it was in this militarily tenuous situation that the Japanese American soldier began to rise to the top of the Allied initiative. As the Italian front pierced the German underbelly, in Churchill's phrase, the Japanese American soldier became the tip of the spear.

Carrying belongings and weaponry, the infantrymen pushed forward through downpours and rivers of mud, followed by freezing cold. They crawled through barbed wire and minefields while the German cannons screamed at them. Many died or were wounded as they struggled to get within combat range. If successful, they came face-to-face with German machine guns with overlapping fields of fire. There was nothing to do but press themselves against the earth or charge forward. When assigned to take a town or village, they fought house to house. This meant crawling or running up to what might be a heavily fortified dwelling, hoping not to be killed as they went. A soldier might then throw grenades through an opening and follow the blast by tumbling in, hoping for the best.

From Thanksgiving 1943 into mid-January 1944, the 100th tore relentlessly at the German defenses. They climbed, slid, and fought their way through the snow and ice of high mountains. At one point it took twenty-four hours to evacuate a casualty. "We reached new limits of physical endurance," Higa wrote. "Though our feet moved mechanically, our conscious minds were asleep due to extreme exhaustion and drowsiness. It is difficult to conceive that one can sleep while walking, but after an hour or so, it is possible to regain one's strength." Higa's friend, the German American Kurt Schemel, was killed in the black of night while leading a bayonet charge against the Germans. On New Year's Eve, 1944, Higa's platoon took refuge from a blizzard in a mountain cave. They had been reduced by about one-fourth, with thirty men remaining. They pooled the wax from the wax paper of their rations and made a candle, which they lit. One of the soldiers produced a bottle of homemade wine that an Italian had given him that day. They brought out crackers and talked about the New Year traditions of home: fresh fish, *ozoni* soup, and soba noodles. Higa said they mostly spoke in Japanese through the night.[21]

McCloy's enthusiasm for them was heightened by the early news from the Italian front. He wrote to the head of Selective Service, saying their performance was proof that the experiment was working; that, with screening, Japanese Americans were not a security risk; and further, "the propaganda value is tremendous." McCloy recommended that the drafting of Japanese Americans be reinstated.[22] On the New Year day that Higa burned a candle in a mountain cave, the U.S. government reclassified Japanese Americans 1-A.

After contributing substantially to breaking the German's first line of defense, the 100th ran into a second and more daunting barrier, called the Gustav Line. Its most imposing feature was the Rapido River and a cliff that towered above, Monte Cassino, which was defended by a murderous array of German firepower. The Rapido River was a natural trap. German engineers had flooded its surrounding plain and planted mines every few feet. The terrain problems were compounded by the existence of an ancient abbey on top of the mountain, which for a long while was designated off limits to shelling or bombing for historic, cultural, and religious reasons. After other units had failed, the 100th Battalion was ordered to cross the river and attack the mountaintop. What happened next became a tangled if often-told story.

By the battle of Cassino, the 100th Battalion had shrunk to three understrength rifle companies. Companies A and C were ordered to cross the river at night. Although covered by darkness, they encountered a horrendous combination of artillery, mines, sniper fire, and mud. Only a fraction of the men made it across the river to the base of the cliff. B Company was in reserve. With daylight, it was ordered to cross, causing a bitter debate among various officers. The haole field commander assigned to lead the Battalion refused to relay the order from headquarters and, as an insubordinate, he was relieved. His replacement then agreed with him. The executive officer, Young Ok Kim, argued that the order was a death sentence. Kim's close friend, Captain Sakae Takahashi, was by this time in charge of Company B. Takahashi shared Kim's view but resolved that he and his men had not come this far to have their soldiering questioned. With the Germans firing down from the mountain, he led a daylight charge onto the river, across an open field of fire. Only 14 of 187 men actually made it to the base of the cliffs, including Takahashi. The substitute battalion commander insisted that if he was to be in charge, he would cross with the men. Wounded, he was replaced by his insubordinate predecessor. Soon thereafter Jim Lovell of Hawai'i took command, only to be wounded and evacuated.[23] The popular Jack Johnson, the football player turned sugar industry executive, second in command, was mortally wounded.

Takahashi's remnant was called back. After a brief rest, it was made part of a second assault, which also ended in failure. By then, the original force of 1,300 numbered 521. Captain Mitsuyuki Fukuda's Company A had been reduced from 173 to 23. It was here that the unit first was referred to as the Purple Heart Battalion. The 100th had fought with great courage and aggressiveness. Eventually thousands more Allied soldiers would be required to drive the Germans off the mountaintop.

Lyn Crost, a correspondent of the *Honolulu Star-Bulletin,* wrote a bitter epitaph to the battle of Cassino: "It exemplified the neglectful treatment of the Italian campaign by U.S. War Department officials in Washington and by General Eisenhower as they gathered and hoarded men and matériel for the cross-Channel invasion of Normandy in France. Supplies for Italy were always short; fresh troops were never enough; adequate air support was not forthcoming—even in the most important and devastating situations. Italy was the stepchild of the war."[24]

With the future of Cassino left hanging, the 100th was moved up the Italian coast to a second beachhead, Anzio, as part of a move to liberate Rome. The Anzio landing went well enough, but the Allied forces were almost immediately isolated. Mounting an offensive against such an entrenched defense was proving to be much harder than imagined. Assigned to pierce Germany's soft underbelly, General Clark was to say he ran into a "tough old gut." German counterattacks threatened to drive the Allies into the sea.

After four months at Anzio, the Allies broke out with 150,000 troops, the 100th Battalion among them. The drive north was stalled by the German defense at a town outside of Rome. After two battalions failed to break through, the 100th battalion was ordered to attack. In thirty-six hours of fighting, it cleared out an array of machine-gun nests and minefields. It then cleared out a German-held intersection on the road north.[25] Because of their decisive role, the 100th battalion was actually leading the Allies toward Rome, only to be sidetracked and to watch motorized units go roaring past them. Two explanations were given, neither satisfying: one that they were awaiting truck transport, and one that the command was working out the arrival of the 442nd RCT.

The 100th had been in the field for nearly nine months. With the 442's own extended training finally ending, Hung Wai Ching had returned to Mississippi to give them a final word of encouragement. He told them social and economic conditions in Hawai'i were improving. "He still is the same fighting Chinaman," Chaplain Yamada wrote to his wife. "We do love him and can't forget his faith, optimism and courage. . . . He really is the idol of our men."[26]

Individuals from the 442nd previously had joined the 100th as replacements. When the 442nd arrived in force on June 11, it far outnumbered the 100th—thereby raising the delicate question of how to combine the two forces while acknowledging the accomplishments of the original battalion. The answer was to make the 100th Battalion the first of three infantry battalions of the 442nd RCT. The One Puka Puka thereby retained its distinctive, hard-won designation even as it became part of the otherwise untested combat team.

Thereafter the new unit was officially, as well as popularly, known as 442nd Regimental Combat Team.

In history, the image of the Purple Heart was to stick to the Japanese American soldiers. It was an image of sacrifice and, to a certain extent, an image of victimhood. They would repeatedly be thrown into murderous circumstances, raising the question of whether they were being treated as cannon fodder. Inarguably, they were a much-needed strategic variable. Where others fell short, the Japanese Americans would break through. Beyond Rome, the Allies again were stalled by a German defense at a town called Belvedere. The 442nd attacked, then its 100th Battalion interceded to defeat the Germans in one of its most brilliant battles. An entire SS battalion was wiped out. The wording of the Presidential Unit Citation was vivid: "Doggedly the members of the 100th Infantry Battalion fought their way into the strongly defended positions. The stubborn desire of the men to close with a numerically superior enemy and the rapidity with which they fought enabled the 100th Infantry Battalion to destroy completely the right flank positions of a German Army."[27]

On the Fourth of July 1944, Secretary of War Henry Stimson conducted a review of the troops in Italy. Clark requested that the 100th

Battalion be represented by Company B, under the command of Captain Takahashi, who had planned the battle at Belvedere. When General Ryder and Stimson came to Takahashi, Ryder put his hand on Takahashi's shoulder and announced, "Mr. Secretary, this is my best outfit."[28] This observation recurred. On a particular day when General Ryder walked Secretary of the Navy James Forrestal in review of the 34th Division, he likewise stopped in front of the 100th and said this was his best unit. In light of what was at stake—America's need to offset Japan's propaganda campaign, as well as America's need to soften domestic animosity aimed at the internees—battlefield heroism provided a perfect stage on which American leaders could dramatize the army's wisdom in making a controversial decision. Other high-level reviewers were to include Robert Patterson, assistant secretary of war; most poignantly, John J. McCloy; and, down the road, the president of the United States.

McCloy first had reviewed the 442nd in training camp. When he reviewed the 442nd in Europe, the one-time Wall Street lawyer was reaping the dividend on what others had regarded as a risky investment. The return for America was amazing. In the month following Rome, the 442nd was the subject of positive stories in both *Time Magazine* and the *New York Times*. Chaplain Yamada wrote home describing how reporters and columnists were being embedded in each of the battalions. "The army now wants a lot of publicity," he wrote. "All the haole soldiers are now spreading the stories for us."[29]

Breakthroughs continued. The unit looped inland, securing the approach to the German-held port of Livorno. This was followed by yet another strike inland, in which the 442nd crossed the Arno River, connecting the great Italian city of Florence to Pisa. Clark praised the Nisei lavishly: "I can depend on the 100th to successfully carry out any mission. I have absolute faith in every soldier in the 100th."[30]

To Clark's chagrin, the unit then was pulled out of the invasion of Italy by the Allied command. Their departure was a great blow to Clark.[31] In late September 1944, they were shipped to Marseilles, France, where they became part of a fast-moving push northward into the Vosges Mountains, beyond which lay the German homeland. This campaign turned out to be a nightmare of another sort. Once more, the widely propagated story line of France was to be about the number of killed and wounded, when it was, on the ground in real time, about making strategic breakthroughs in battle.

Within a little more than two weeks of its landing in France, the 442nd was thrown against the defensive line protecting Germany. Their objective was the railroad town of Bruyeres, which was crawling with German troops, as were the four hills surrounding it. In three days of fighting, the unit captured one hill outright, took part of a second hill, and fought their way house-to-house into the town. On the fourth day, Bruyeres was fully liberated, setting off an outpouring of affection from the French townspeople. The unit then cleared a ridge over a second town, Belmont, and was ordered immediately to take a third town, Biffontaine.

While commanding officers changed repeatedly, field officers such as "Mits" Fukuda and Sakae Takahashi ably led their troop through great dangers. They were coordinated by the talented Young Ok Kim, who ascended to the gritty role of plans and operations officer. Kim and Takahashi fought together almost constantly for months, plotting their moves by radio or in person, often in the dark of night. "Throughout northern Italy and France," Kim recalled, "Sakae and I took great risks to win battles quickly to reduce casualties. Once we both had bullet holes in our uniforms, but were not physically wounded."[32]

The unit had been detached from the 34th Division, with its Midwestern roots, and attached to the 36th Division, of Texas origins. Here loomed an inexperienced but willful division commander, Major General John E. Dahlquist. Dahlquist must have harbored delusions of becoming a storied fighter, but he became a story of another sort, pushing his troops too far too fast. In the hills over Biffontaine, overextended, the 442nd was surrounded on all sides and cut off from supplies and reinforcements. Nearing exhaustion, with ammunition running low, the unit was in danger of being overrun. Dahlquist nonetheless ordered them to descend and take the town of Biffontaine, which they did, only to again be surrounded. Dahlquist next ordered the unit to press on through the mountains to rescue a battalion of Texans who would become known in military lore as the Lost Battalion. With less of a propaganda twist, the Texans were a stranded battalion—or yet another overextended unit.

Two regiments already had tried and failed to free the Lost Battalion. The tension heightened when German prisoners disclosed that Hitler was watching, and that he had ordered the Texans to be annihilated at all cost. A circuitous nine-mile route separated the 442nd from the Lost Battalion. Facing interlocking fields of machine-gun fire, grenades, mortars, and artillery, the 442nd pushed forward. Dahlquist hovered over their shoulders, occasionally yelling at them moment by moment. Fog and the density of the forest turned day to night. Trees shattered from the impact of artillery. Tree trunks, limbs, and splinters crashed out of nowhere. These were known as tree bursts. "Trees with human parts. Humans with tree parts," soldier John Tsukano wrote.[33] As they advanced, they passed foxholes shared by dead Germans and dead Americans.

Shuji Takamoto would remember that although they suffered from the icy rain, most did not wear their ponchos. The pop of raindrops on a solid surface attracted the enemy.[34] Chester Tanaka had been promoted to acting first sergeant of "K" Company and then to acting company commander. Out of 188 riflemen, he had 17 left. He met with a sergeant from "I" Company, who likewise had become a company commander. "I" had eight men left. They sat down to confer. Tanaka sat on his helmet. The sergeant from "K" sat down on what he thought was a log, but on examination he discovered it was a frozen German corpse.

After five days, the 442nd broke through to the Texans. Hitler's project of annihilation had been thwarted. A newsreel of the rescue was shown in movie houses as a short subject throughout the United States. It depicted the soldiers from Texas gulping the sweet air of survival and, only secondarily, did the newsreel show their liberators.[35] Two hundred and eleven Texans were still alive. Counting their losses at Bruyeres and Biffontaine, the 442nd had suffered an estimated eight hundred casualties.

Improbably, Dahlquist ordered the combat team to continue on the battle line, and they were given no rest until the second week in November, twenty-five days after their ascent into the Vosges Mountains. Dahlquist ordered the unit to stand in review as a means of tribute. Surveying about one-eighth of what previously had been four thousand men, Dahlquist grumpily demanded to know where the others were. One hundred forty were dead, some were missing, and eighteen hundred were hospitalized from wounds, sickness, and trench foot. An officer replied, "Sir, these are all that are left." The usually resilient Chaplain Yamada wrote, "I am spiritually low for once. My heart weeps."[36]

Accounts of the first Italian campaign and the subsequent campaign in France run on as whole lifetimes of experience, yet there remained a third part to the epic, adding further weight to the record. On the Italian front, Clark was planning what the Allies hoped would be a final blow. Simultaneously, the American press was realizing (or finally reporting) that the Allies were fighting in Italy with inadequate resources. Chief of Staff Marshall flew to Italy to signal an increased commitment to the Italian front and in the process to review the 442nd under Clark's command.

For the first time the unit was split up, an act that added evidence of competition among the generals for their service. The artillery battalion, the 522nd, had pounded the German Army with great effectiveness. Now it was detached from the unit and assigned to serve as an advance element of the invasion of German soil. Its fighting capacity on the road to Berlin was part of the assurance of overwhelming American force. The best-known event resulting from this was its encounter with victims of the German death camp, Dachau. As the 522nd Artillery pushed eastward, emaciated figures in prison garb began to appear, wandering along the highway. This led to a subcamp of Dachau, where men of the 522nd stopped and shot the locks off the gates, setting the survivors free. The idea of the victims of America's internment camps liberating a German death camp created an irresistible story line. It was a true story, but it was more of symbolic value than real consequence. It was yet again the type of narrative wherein the military value of the artillery battalion was obscured, much as the overall military importance of the 100th battalion and the 442nd RCT would be obscured by the drama of their fighting and dying for a country that had incarcerated people of Japanese ancestry wholesale.

In late March 1945, the infantrymen of the 442nd sailed back to Italy, landing at Naples. Their presence was kept under wraps, because Clark was convinced the Germans automatically strengthened their line wherever the 442nd appeared. When the spring offensive began, he directed the unit to make a feint, designed to throw off the Germans. Sure enough, German reinforcements followed.[37] Axis Sally, a German broadcast propagandist, told the Nisei they were fighting on the wrong side, that they should be part of the alliance of Germany and Japan. A Nisei prisoner of war, taken to Berlin for interrogation, was asked why, as a person of Japanese ancestry, he was fighting in the American army. Because I am an American, he said. Around this time the army's newspaper, *Stars and Stripes*, reported that the Nisei had the highest average IQ of any infantry unit in the U.S. Army—something of a blow to the theory of white supremacy.

The Allied goal was to break the last German line of defense in the mountains of Italy, the Gustav Line, then descend into the favorable fighting terrain of the Po River Valley, and finally strike at the German homeland. The 442nd was the left flank of a pincer movement, assigned to the difficult mission of driving the Germans out of the mountain range that stands over the western coast. With on-the-job training, the men became mountain fighters, untethered from the wheeled warfare of trucks and tanks. They took off by foot and backpack, leading mules on inclines that sometimes seemed nearly straight up. Lyn Crost said the slopes were as steep as 60 degrees. The men crawled upward, clinging to grass, stones, crevices, and each other. They climbed silently through the night. Their orders were to make no sound, even if they fell, and some did fall. Whether anyone fell to their deaths is a matter of argument, but their disciplined silence is not. The aim was to surprise the German Army at first daylight, which they did, with great result. In brutal close-range fighting, they drove the Germans from their gun nests, artillery posts, and command centers.

Where the original idea was to push the Germans down into the river valley, the breakthrough became even more decisive. The Germans ran. Exceeding Clark's own ambitious plans, the 442nd chased the enemy across the plain.

With veterans such as Takahashi and Kim hospitalized, new leadership emerged. A field-commissioned second lieutenant, Daniel K. Inouye, of the Mo'ili'ili district of Honolulu, attacked three enemy machine-gun posts, running in front of his platoon. He was knocked down by a bullet to the stomach but rose and ran to within several yards of the enemy, where he uncorked a grenade and wiped out a submachine-gun nest. He staggered forward and threw two more grenades into a second machine-gun post. Aiming for yet a third, he pulled the pin out of another grenade, which he was holding in his right hand. An enemy grenade hit his right arm, nearly tearing it off. Inouye responded by plucking the grenade from his dangling right hand with his good left hand, throwing it, and taking down most of the German crew. He then shot the last gunners, after which he took a second bullet—this one to the leg. He survived.

The date of Inouye's charge was April 21, 1945. On April 28, the Fascist dictator of Italy, Benito Mussolini, and his mistress were executed by Italian partisans. Lyn Crost saw their corpses hanging upside down in Milan. Mussolini's face was covered with blood. Italians threw stones

at the person who had led them into this mess. His mistress was likewise
in an undignified position but "some solicitous soul had tied the woman's dress to her legs so that the skirt would not fall away and bare her
body."[38] The same day, Allied elements entered the northern industrial
city of Turin.

The soldiers of the Third Reich, so often depicted as unwaver-
ingly disciplined, were throwing down their arms. On April 30, 1945,
Adolph Hitler took his own life. On May 2, 1945, the German command in Italy surrendered. On May 8, the German nation surrendered
unconditionally.

The unit held a formation to honor the fallen. The last commander,
Col. Virgil R. Miller, was prophetic: "By your fighting you have made for
yourselves stronger friends than ever—friends who will go to bat for you
to the last ditch."

Eisenhower awarded the combat team with yet another Presidential Unit Citation. He credited them with breaking the left flank of the
German's last line of defense: "In 4 days, the attack destroyed positions
which had withstood the efforts of friendly troops for 5 months." What
had been planned as a flanking diversion became a "victorious offensive, which played an important part in the final destruction of the
German armies in Italy." At the port of Leghorn, Italy, three thousand
members of the 442nd were placed in the front rank of a victory parade.
Another twelve thousand U.S. troops followed. A Mississippi editor, who
had risked his life fighting the Ku Klux Klan, Hodding Carter, wrote,
"The Nisei slogan of 'Go for Broke' could be adopted by all Americans
of good will in the days ahead. We've got to shoot the works in a fight
for tolerance."[39]

Praise flowed from the highest levels of the army. "Superb!" General
Marshall exclaimed. "That word exactly describes it: superb! They took
terrific casualties. They showed rare courage and tremendous fighting
spirit."[40] One of McCloy's last acts before returning to Wall Street was to
receive Major Fukuda, the 100th Battalion's last wartime commander.
Fukuda asked that the unit be perpetuated as an army reserve unit in
Honolulu and that it no longer be segregated on racial lines. McCloy
supported both these requests, to which the War Department agreed.[41]

The losses of Hawai'i's Japanese Americans, quietly absorbed, were
grim indeed. Where people of Japanese ancestry comprised one-third of
the population, they suffered two-thirds of the deaths. By one account,
they made up nearly nine-tenths of the wounded.[42]

* * *

The war in the Pacific continued for another three months. In secret, Genro Iwai had served in Army Intelligence since 1931, and Douglas Wada had served in Naval Intelligence since 1937. In the aftermath of the Pearl Harbor bombing, they jointly had interrogated the first Japanese prisoner of the war, the pilot of a miniature submarine that had beached on Windward Oʻahu. Throughout the war and deep into the occupation of Japan, these two pioneering figures of the Pacific war had continued to play sensitive roles in their respective branches of service. Two other Nisei of Hawaiʻi, Arthur S. Komori and Richard Sakakida, were recruited into Army Intelligence in the year prior to the war and assigned to General Douglas MacArthur in the Philippines. They had gone underground and gathered intelligence on Japan's expatriate community in Manila.

Through such figures, the army had glimpsed the potential contribution of the Nisei in the Pacific theater. Six months into the training of the 100th Battalion, recruiters from the Military Intelligence Service (MIS) scooped up fifty-nine Nisei and moved them to language school. These *senpai gumi* (roughly, "pioneer team") became the language school's first sizeable class, badly needed. A second scoop was made from the 442nd training camp. MIS also made a fruitful recruiting drive throughout the Hawaiian Islands. Individuals who for one or another reason had not volunteered for the 442nd now volunteered for the MIS—for example, Yoshiaki Fujitani, who had left the VVV camp at Schofield Barracks in upset over his father being interned.

As the scope of the American counterattack against Japan expanded, the need for linguists grew. Here and there, such as with the famous Merill's Marauders in Burma, Nisei worked in teams to monitor and translate the radio transmissions of unsuspecting Japanese military. Many Nisei were widely dispersed to invading combat units. As specialists, they were everywhere and nowhere. They read and decoded Japanese battle plans, listened to battlefield communications, translated, and interrogated prisoners. Most poignantly, often at great risk to themselves, they made face-to-face appeals to Japanese soldiers and civilians to surrender, rather than commit suicide, such as at the Battle of Okinawa and the invasion of Saipan.

In all, the Japanese American ranks of the MIS swelled to somewhere between four and five thousand participants, counting the far-flung zones of combat and the Occupation.[43] By Victory over Japan Day, there were more Nisei in the Pacific than in Europe. Col. Charles Willoughby, MacArthur's chief of intelligence, praised the MIS extravagantly. He said they had saved a million lives and cut the duration of the Pacific war by a year.

While the Nisei played a ubiquitous role throughout Asia and the Pacific Islands, their comparative anonymity was in contrast to the spotlight that shined on the 100th and then the 442nd. The linguists were told their work was confidential, and that they should never talk about it, a nonsensical taboo that held into the 1970s. Valiant and effective as they were, they were never adequately recognized (and certainly that is the case here). They were agents of war but not agents of far-reaching sociopolitical change. They had not been joined to liberating the powers of Europe. They were not the subject of a major propaganda project of the U.S. government. Neither did they suffer injury or the loss of life in great numbers in such a way as to forge a primitive blood pact with their nation. Here and there, MIS servicemen devalued their own work, regretting that they were not on the ground with their brothers in Europe. They trickled home. There were no parades.

CHAPTER 16

All the People, All the Time

WHAT WAS LEFT OF THE 100TH BATTALION shipped out of Europe
first, followed in late June 1946 by the remaining bulk of the 442nd
Regimental Combat Team. The now-famous Four Four Two arrived in
New York Harbor on the auspicious date of July 4, 1946. "Small crafts,
decked with streamers, went offshore to welcome them," Crost wrote.
"On shore, crowds shouted and whistled and waved American flags."[1]
The veteran war correspondent from Honolulu wept. "I have learned
that we are dependent on each other," she wrote, "and the future will be
based on the ability of our diverse races, religions and cultures to weave
an understanding that will rise above inevitable conflicts."[2] The unit laid
over until a parade could be organized in Washington, D.C., in which
President Truman would be available to review the troops.

Crowds again lined the streets, cheering and waving American flags.
Truman's purpose was clear. In his reedy voice, he recalled the mobilizing letter of his predecessor—he did not utter Roosevelt's name—saying that to be American was not a matter of race or creed but of the
heart. He went on: "You fought not only the enemy, but you fought
prejudice—and you have won. Keep up that fight, and we will continue
to win—to make this great Republic stand for just what the Constitution
says it stands for: the welfare of all the people all the time."[3]

Truman had bluntly acknowledged the chasm that lay between the
wartime propaganda and the American condition. The first battle was
over. The second battle was about to begin. It was a call for the 100th
Bn/442nd RCT to leverage its record on behalf of racial equality. Truman subsequently was to do his part. In 1948, he issued an executive
order directing desegregation of the United States armed forces. The
same year, he urged Congress to grant statehood to Hawai'i. He ran for
reelection in 1948 on a civil rights platform that alienated the South
and nearly cost him the presidency.

The Four-Four-Two sailed into Honolulu Harbor on August 9, 1946. Hula dancers boarded their ship and danced with the men. A passing boat unfurled a huge banner, "Aloha, 442nd." The men marched from the pier past adoring crowds to 'Iolani Palace, where they originally had been sworn to duty. Impending social and political change seemed self-evident. Skirmishes lay ahead, but it was as if the transformation of Hawai'i to a more egalitarian and genuinely multiracial society already had occurred. When the unit was dismissed, the throng exploded with lei, tears, embrace, and kisses. The surviving film suggests an atmosphere of ecstasy, of people floating on air.

The most recurring description became that the 442nd was the most decorated unit of its size for its time in American history. It was a narrative of deaths, wounds, and Purple Hearts that in some odd way obscured the unit's strategic battlefield successes and also failed to convey the impact of the Nisei on Hawai'i and the country.

The second-most quoted observation was about the soldiers who had volunteered from the Mainland detention camps. Again something crucial got lost—the central importance of Hawai'i to the entire venture. The legacy value of the aloha spirit, and of the resulting cohesion, tended to be forgotten—the postcards distributed at the train station in Kansas; the crossing of the color line at Camp Shelby; the friendship in Italy with the Midwestern 34th Division and in France with the Texas 36th Division; and eventually even the bonding with Jewish Americans who tracked such events as the liberation of Dachau.

Among individuals of the home front who had imagined the transformational possibilities of the war, Hemenway was the most immediately acknowledged. The University of Hawai'i library was named for him, and a scholarship was established in his name. Many decades later, the scholarship continues to help young people make their way through UH. Charles Hemenway died in 1947.[4]

Shigeo Yoshida went back to the public schools. As the intellectual navigator of the Japanese community of Hawai'i in wartime, it could be argued that Yoshida was the single most important person of the entire saga. Working behind the scenes, he never became widely known. In his crucial five years in the public sphere, he derived his influence from the authoring of ideas, cultivating personal relationships, and—paradoxically—his acceptance of relative anonymity. The question of credit seems to have not crossed his mind. Most of his acquaintances in public school and church circles had little to no idea what he had done during the war. Neither did his two sons, whose middle names respectively were Charles and Reed, in memory of Mr. Hemenway. When the 442nd returned, Yoshida was thirty-nine years old. He was offered high-level posts in the centralized school system but backed away in favor of a more hands-on role as a school principal. He thought about law school but decided he was too old and his family responsibilities too great. He served in the background of Jack Burns's campaigns for governor as a speechwriter. He offered himself as a delegate to the 1968 Constitutional Convention for the state of Hawai'i, but lost. Most voters did not know who he was. In retirement, he was injured in an automobile accident and spent his final years in pain. He gave an interview to Dr. Franklin Odo in which he handwrote his answers. He did not exult. He said the war had caused "many injustices" but that it had sped up the process of social and political change in Hawai'i. He died in 1986 at the age of seventy-eight. His ashes are in a crypt in the sanctuary of Church of the Crossroads.

Hung Wai Ching did not leave the public scene quietly. In the postwar he became the central figure in seeing to the higher education of the Nisei soldier. He goaded the well heeled to contribute to veterans' scholarship funds, which he distributed on an as-needed basis to supplement the GI Bill. An untold number of prominent veterans owed completion of their college work—typically professional degrees and advanced studies—to the brokering of Hung Wai Ching. Despite his repeated tributes to his "brain," Yoshida, Ching received the main share of credit for the Varsity Victory Volunteers and, in many circles, the 442nd.

Passed over for the job of director at the Nu'uanu Y in favor of a haole from the Mainland—still then a common practice—he quit his YMCA job as youth director. Nonetheless, lifelong he spoke highly of the YMCA, which eventually lifted him up to heroic proportions.

Having put his family in economic jeopardy during the war, Ching made money in the early postwar. He founded the predecessor to Aloha Airlines, co-owned the once-famous Lau Yee Chai Restaurant in Waikīkī, and developed housing for an emerging middle class. His head and heart were in the clouds, and after making money he lost most of it. He was appointed a member of the University of Hawai'i's Board of Regents. He was a force in the university's periodic East-West Philosophers Conference, and he received two honorary doctorates, one from

UH and one from Pacific College. Despite his smoldering liberalism, he was a lifelong Republican—in the mold of Delegate Joe Farrington and his classmate and friend, U.S. senator Hiram L. Fong. He died in 2002 at the age of ninety-six. His ashes were placed in a crypt in Community Church.

Robert Shivers had a heart problem, which lay behind the FBI director J. Edgar Hoover reassigning him in midwar from the strains of Hawai'i to light duty on the U.S. Mainland. His impact had been enormous. He left behind many people who believed that if he had been of an oppressive bent, events would have gone badly for Hawai'i. Wishing to return, Shivers passed the word to Hung Wai Ching that he would like to be collector of customs when the position opened. Ching's ESC/Morale network took up a collection and sent Ching back to Washington, D.C., to advocate for Shivers's appointment. He again met with Mrs. Roosevelt, who said she must speak to Henry, meaning Treasury Secretary Henry Morgenthau. Shivers returned as customs chief. When the position of appointed territorial governor opened in 1949, John Burns lobbied for months in Washington on behalf of the Democratic Party of Hawai'i for Shivers to be appointed by President Truman. Whether this might have happened cannot be known. Shivers was tempted but backed away for reasons of health.

Asked about the relative absence of internment in Hawai'i, Shivers said he could never have imagined his *hanai* daughter, Sue (Shizue), or people like her, being put in a camp behind barbed wire. It was perhaps the most existential expression by an authority figure on the entire vast subject. Dressed in a white suit, he walked Sue down the aisle at her marriage to a handsome young fellow from the VVV and 442nd, Herb Isonaga, a protégé of Ching, who had introduced the couple. Shivers died in 1950. He was buried in Diamond Head Memorial Cemetery in a grave secured by Ching. Lifelong, Sue Isonaga took flowers to his gravesite. She maintained a relationship with his Tennessee family and otherwise honored his memory. She passed away in 2018 at the age of ninety-two.

"Doc" Kometani, the morale officer, undertook a speaking campaign on his return from the war. In the vein of Truman, he said, "We have helped win the war on the battlefront, but we have not yet won the war on the home front. We shall have won when we attain those things for which our country is dedicated, namely, equality of opportunity and the dignity of man."

John A. Burns resigned from the Police Department in late summer 1945, several weeks before the end of the war. Among those who read the messages from the war front, it was Burns who responded with the greatest clarity of purpose. Lifelong he would cite Sergeant Joe Itagaki's letter as a motivating force for his actions. The veterans had changed as a result of their complicated and challenging experiences. It followed that Hawai'i must change. Burns single-mindedly devoted himself to politics. He developed a circle of coffee drinkers at the Nu'uanu YMCA who were determined to take over the traditionally unsuccessful Hawai'i Democratic Party and give it new life and direction. His inner circle consisted of two individuals from the Emergency Service Committee, Dr. Ernest Murai and the educator Mitsuyuki Kido; also Jack Kawano of the ILWU; and a Chinese American member of the City and County Board of Supervisors, attorney Chuck Mau, who was best known for proposing and then maintaining rent control in the war-fueled housing market.

Burns read political philosophy under the guidance of a progressive UH professor, Dr. Allan Saunders. He was particularly impressed by Jefferson and, devout Catholic that he was, St. Thomas Aquinas. In the party-building effort, Burns volunteered to recruit war veterans. Unable to draft a party candidate for delegate to Congress in the 1948 election, he personally filled the ticket at the last moment. He won only a quarter of the vote but nonetheless enlisted key war veterans into his campaign.

The ensuing cascade of social and political change was inseparable from the community work that had begun in 1939—the work of the Council for Interracial Unity; the discussions of soldiers; the Kaua'i plan for postwar reconstruction; the constant exchange of letters; and, perhaps most importantly, the Japanese American conferences of 1943, 1944, and 1945. More broadly, this movement toward creating an inclusive democratic society owed its vitality to the Hawai'i public schools, the University of Hawai'i, the YMCA, the internationalist movement, the progressive churches, and the Hawaiian Army's commitment to the idea, "Trust breeds trust."

Between 1939 and 1941, the ILWU had made significant gains in workforce organization, particularly on the island of Kaua'i. The militant union then was sidetracked by martial law during the war. Immediately following, the union's membership exploded, rising from less than a thousand to nearly thirty thousand. Led by Kawano and Jack Hall, the ILWU mounted and won a long strike against the Big Five and the sugar plantations.

The struggle for the future of Hawai'i accelerated. It pitted a coalition of war veterans and labor organizers against the prewar Republicans. In 1946, half of the Territorial House turned Democrat, one of whom was the ESC's Mitsuyuki Kido.

Reflecting the wartime reluctance of the white elite to embrace far-reaching change, the Republicans pushed back, attempting to retrench into something resembling their prewar position. The pervasive phobia of Communism temporarily worked in their favor, as well as a shrinking economy and the fact that many of the veterans were away in college.

In 1949, the ILWU mounted a second long strike to bring the waterfront and shipping industries under their control.

In the 1954 election, Burns, in his capacity as Democratic Party chairman, led a drive to recruit veterans as candidates and campaign workers, resulting in a historic Democratic sweep of the Territorial Legislature. The long era of top-to-bottom oligarchic dominance had ended. The Democratic victory immediately became known as the "Revolution of 1954" and is still referred to as such these many decades later.[5] The Democrats pushed for expanding support for public education, for more equitable taxation, collective bargaining between labor and business, and an end to the interlocking boards of directors of the big corporations.

In 1956, Burns was elected territorial delegate to Congress. In the pursuit of statehood, he called on the friendships and alliances that the 100th and 442nd had made. The most effective was the Texas delegation, which remembered the rescue of the Lost Battalion. The support of a large Southern state was the wedge that broke through the hold of the Southern segregationists who previously had opposed the admission of a majority nonwhite state. Texans Lyndon Baines Johnson, the Senate majority leader, and Sam Rayburn, House speaker, became Hawai'i's most influential supporters.

In an agreement worked out by Burns, Rayburn, and Johnson, Alaska was granted statehood in 1958 and Hawai'i was granted statehood in 1959. While the surface narrative was about which would go first (and which state likely would be Republican and which would be Democratic), the underlying reality was about bringing in Alaska as cover for the admission of Hawai'i. In the geopolitics of the postwar Pax Americana, Hawai'i was of great strategic importance, while Alaska was a distant second. In the interrelated realm of racial definitions and civil rights, Johnson—in the spirit of Truman—found in Hawai'i a means of undermining Jim Crow segregation. By his own account, merely to be in Hawai'i lightened his burdened and gloomy side. He counted statehood for Hawai'i as one of his highest achievements.

The Statehood Bill was signed into law by President Dwight D. Eisenhower, who as a general had dragged his feet on formation of the 442nd.

After a stumble in the first statehood election, Burns was elected governor in 1962 for the first of three four-year terms. He died in 1975 at the age of sixty-six. He is buried in Punchbowl National Cemetery.

Two individuals involved in the wartime transformation were the first to be elected to the U.S. Senate. Democrat Oren E. Long, superintendent of territorial schools, had facilitated Yoshida's wartime absence from his school job and was generally a force for progressive education. The second was the Republican Fong, Ching's friend and classmate. He had served on the Chinese American committee of the Morale Section before going to war as a commissioned officer.

Daniel K. Inouye, who had attacked the three German machine-gun nests, was elected to the U.S. House of Representatives. In 1962 he was elected to Long's seat in the U.S. Senate. He was reelected without significant opposition, following Burns as the most influential political figure in Hawai'i and also, according to various surveys, the most influential and best-known Asian American.[6] He drew high marks for his participation on the Senate Watergate Committee. He subsequently cochaired the Iran-Contra investigative hearings and played a major role in the Senate Intelligence Committee. At the time of his death at eighty-eight in 2012, he was third in the constitutional line of succession for the presidency by virtue of being the Senate's longest-serving member.

Spark M. Matsunaga, he of the eight hundred meetings on veteran accomplishments, ran successfully for the Territorial House in 1954 and the U.S. House in 1962. In 1976, he moved up to the Senate, where he served until his death in 1990 at age seventy-three. He championed such diverse subjects as civil rights, peace studies, and space travel.

True to his campfire plan, Sakae Takahashi became a pathfinder in both business and politics. In 1952, he served as territorial treasurer, then was elected to the Honolulu Board of Supervisors. In 1954 he founded Central Pacific Bank and was elected to the Hawai'i Senate, in which he served for sixteen years. He remained active in the U.S. Army Reserve, eventually commanding what in the postwar became the racially integrated 442nd Infantry Regiment.

Vestiges of white exclusivity, such as the Pacific Club and the racial covenants that attempted to cover certain neighborhoods, became verboten.

A timeline comparison of the social and political development of Hawai'i to the forty-eight continental states is noteworthy. The 1954 Democratic Revolution of Hawai'i occurred in the year of the U.S. Supreme Court's ruling against "separate but equal" education in the case of Linda Brown vs. the Board of Education of Topeka, Kansas. In 1955, while the new Hawai'i Legislature was passing a raft of progressive legislation, Rosa Parks refused to sit in the back of the bus in Montgomery, Alabama.

A combination of statehood for Hawai'i, the introduction of much larger and faster jet airliners, and a rapid expansion of the national economy occurred coterminously. Hawai'i as a distant paradise, and then a war zone, overnight became a middle-class travel destination. Everyone wanted to come to Hawai'i. In the process, the idea that Hawai'i was a model for a genuinely inclusive multiracial society circulated widely. It fortified those who believed that such a thing was possible. It gave the country—and the entire Pacific—a mental picture of what a successful, racially integrated society looked and felt like. A month after the president's signature on the Hawai'i Statehood Bill, Dr. Martin Luther King Jr. visited Hawai'i. He addressed the first session of the Hawai'i Legislature as follows: "You can never know what it means to those of us caught for the moment in the tragic and often dark midnight of man's inhumanity to man, to come to a place where we see the glowing daybreak of freedom and dignity and racial justice."[7]

If democracy was to live, King said, racial segregation must die.

"We are seeking to free the soul of America. . . . We are [determined] to free all men, all races and all groups. This is our responsibility and this is our challenge, and we look to this great new state in our Union as the example and the inspiration."[8] If there was a single photographic image to represent King's speech, it was of a multiracial delegation from Hawai'i carrying a banner into the civil rights march at Selma, Alabama, in 1965. It said, "Hawaii Knows Integration Works." In the front row, Dr. King and the top leaders of the civil rights marchers locked arms, wearing crosses and flower lei.

In a 1963 address to the U.S. Conference of Mayors in Honolulu, President John F. Kennedy said Hawai'i "is what the rest of the world is striving to become." By 1964, Lyndon Johnson was president. He

Ties between Hawai'i and the Rev. Martin Luther King Jr. culminated in the Selma voting rights march, in which a Hawai'i delegation marched under a banner reinforcing the concept of a multiethnic society. Courtesy of U.S. Rep. Mark Takai collection.

used the fifth anniversary of statehood to issue a statement proclaiming Hawai'i as "a symbol to people everywhere of what it is possible to achieve within the American system of Government."[9] Johnson's Republican successor, Richard M. Nixon, weighed in similarly. Visiting Hawai'i in 1970 in conjunction with the landing of U.S. astronauts, he attended Reverend Abraham Akaka's service at Kawaiahao Church. Akaka gave his *aloha* sermon. Strumming his four-stringed ukulele, he described the harmony that resulted from black, brown, yellow, and white people working together. "I have never heard a sermon that was more eloquent, more appropriate, and timely for not only this event, this day, but for this period in the history of this world," Nixon wrote. "I wish it could be heard all over the world."[10]

Hawai'i's impact on the country was not only atmospheric but literal. Its congressional delegation became a force for change. In 1964, the country aflame, Johnson—pressured by Dr. King—was determined to pass a comprehensive civil rights act. The ultimate key to passage was breaking the Southern Democratic filibuster in the Senate, to which the four votes of Hawai'i and Alaska made a crucial contribution.

Together the 1964, 1965, and 1966 sessions of Congress poured out the Great Society legislation that continues to shape American life, prominently including the Voting Rights Act, the Immigration and Nationality Act, Medicare, Medicaid, and the Food Stamp Act, among others.

Hawai'i's contribution to the cause of racial equality stands out. In 1964, a young one-term congressman from Hawai'i, Thomas P. Gill, authored labor aspects of the Civil Rights Act and served as a floor manager in the House at President Johnson's request. In 1965, Senator Hiram Fong played a role in repealing the race-based, discriminatory immigration laws that had governed the country since 1924. The effect was to put an end to the system favoring northern Europeans while expanding immigration from Asia and Africa. In 1972, Congresswoman Patsy Takemoto Mink coauthored the Title IX amendment to the Elementary and Secondary Education Act. This became known as the Mink amendment, prohibiting discrimination on the basis of gender in any education program receiving federal money. In a brief time, Title IX contributed substantially to revolutionizing female participation in competitive athletics. How women were thought of, and how they thought of themselves, took a leap forward.

Senator Matsunaga kept a record in his pocket of his personal discussion with every one of his ninety-nine Senate colleagues about the injustice of the wartime forced evacuation and incarceration. After each conversation, he made a checkmark beside the senator's name. Mike Masaoka, the central figure of the Japanese American Citizen's League, credited Matsunaga with rounding up the votes and credited Senator Inouye with the crucial step of forming the Commission on Wartime Relocation and Internment of Civilians, which laid groundwork with the public. The result was the nation's apology for internment and a reparation of $20,000 for each of its victims. After years of shocking revelation and agonizing dialogue, Congress passed and President Ronald Reagan signed the bill into law as the Civil Rights Act of 1988.

At Hawai'i's new capitol building, Burns was succeeded by his lieutenant governor, George R. Ariyoshi, the first American governor of Asian ancestry and the first nonwhite governor since Reconstruction. Like Burns, Ariyoshi was elected to three four-year terms. He was followed by his lieutenant governor, John D. Waihe'e III, the first governor of Native Hawaiian ancestry, who was in turn succeeded by his lieutenant governor, Benjamin J. Cayetano, the first governor of Filipino ancestry. Together they spanned a Democratic political genealogy of four different ethnicities over ten elections and forty years of service.

Hawai'i came to be widely viewed as the most liberal or progressive state of the union. This reputation rested in part on a first-in-the-nation prepaid health insurance program (1973), which resulted in near-universal insurance coverage. Hawai'i's labor laws were comprehensive, including a state-level temporary disability insurance program.

A woman's reproductive right to abortion was legalized in 1970 for the first time in the country. The Hawai'i Legislature was the first to support the proposed Equal Rights Amendment, ratifying it on the same day as its congressional passage.

During the first decade of statehood, university education was nearly tuition-free, including out-of-state students, who were regarded (by Burns, prominently) as potential conduits of aloha. Traditional trade schools were transformed into a far-reaching network of community colleges that promoted liberal education and a ladder to four-year degrees. Despite inefficiencies of scale, the University of Hawai'i established law and medical schools, with programs aimed at levelling the playing field for access to these professions.

The Hawai'i Constitution, revised in 1978, incorporated a doctrine of public trust. This meant that the state exercised domain over all waters, surface and subsurface, as well as the zoning and appropriate use of all lands. Each individual was explicitly granted a right to a clean environment and also to standing in court as an individual in pursuit thereof. The Hawaiian language was designated along with English as the official language of the state. Access for traditional practices of religion and culture were protected, as well as traditional gathering rights, from the mountaintops into the sea. Native land awards under five acres were protected against adverse possession.

A powerful sense of Hawai'i's identity was embedded in the new Constitution's preamble: "We reserve the right to control our destiny, to nurture the integrity of our people and culture, and to preserve the quality of life that we desire."

Finally, Hawai'i became the cradle into which a child of mixed African and Caucasian ancestry, Barack Obama, was born, and the spirit of inclusivity from which he evolved into the first nonwhite president of the United States (2008–2016). The influences on him were many and varied, but in the description of his spouse, Michelle Obama, "You can't really understand Barack until you understand Hawai'i."

Conclusion

I DID NOT SET OUT TO WRITE ABOUT INCLUSION as a concept but rather was compelled by the question of how Hawaiʻi navigated World War II and, by extension, how contemporary Hawaiʻi came to be. The title arose in the final edit, in which I more fully realized that the practice of inclusion had so deeply influenced people and events. Inclusivity held Hawaiʻi together under the stress of war and helped lay the foundation for its evolution thereafter.

As protection of Japanese Americans in their time of crisis, inclusion was by no means perfect. Over two thousand people were interned as a result of federal policy. More so than others, people of Japanese ancestry were lectured, pressured, hectored, and harassed.

Inclusion was imperfection in motion. In retrospect it is not to be confused with higher standards of measure such as integration, equality, and the attainment of civil rights, nor with the critical examination of wrongdoing and injustice. The conversation of the times did not so much as acknowledge the root fact that the United States had taken the Native Hawaiian's country. Neither did it address the manipulative grip of the plantation economy on the Filipino population. These and other battles were left to future years and future generations.

But with an acknowledgment of such limitations, the record nonetheless demonstrates that inclusion was a powerful idea and practice. The message was that each person mattered. People—often badly frightened people—were encouraged to get together, mobilize themselves, and generate energy and purpose. Inclusion was health giving. It counteracted alienation.

"Live and let live" and an ease of relationships, as originally practiced by Native Hawaiian society, came to the fore. In the brief years of the war crisis, the strides toward inclusion undermined the oligarchic structure that had been consolidated in the forced annexation of 1898.

Inclusion undermined attitudes of white supremacy. It began the undo-
ing of Hawai'i's forms of segregation. The genie was loose in the land.
The oligarchy's postwar attempt to resurrect the status quo fizzled, and
the era of unfettered privilege was taken down in the 1950s and early
1960s with relative ease.

The work of the Council for Interracial Relations, the intentional
organization of interethnic networks, the battlefield accomplishments,
the legislative breakthroughs, the origins of an Obama—all have a root in
the work of inclusion. The Morale Section's farsighted plan for minimizing oppression and maximizing involvement in the war effort mattered
greatly. The practice of friendliness and the making of acquaintance
mattered greatly. People who consciously or unconsciously worked
across ethnic lines became society's navigators. The incessant recita-
tion of democratic principles aided this process even in the absence of
democracy. The concept of aloha was an animating force. The cultural
legacy of not only Hawaiians but the Kingdom of Hawai'i was causal.
Healthy institutions shaped events. The networks of people who led the
process overlapped one another at many institutional points: the public schools, the University of Hawai'i, the YMCA, progressive churches,
and, yes, an inclusive U.S. Army. The resulting cohesion was at the heart
of Hawai'i's success in working its way through the cataclysm. Shigeo
Yoshida was right when he wrote, "How we get along during the war will
determine how we get along when the war is over."

As to why federal policy in Hawai'i and on the West Coast differed,
the most fundamental reason was simply the differing nature of the
two surrounding societies. Each harbored values that ultimately swayed
events. Hawai'i's pattern of inclusivity diverged from the regional prejudices of the West Coast states in ways that reached to Washington, D.C.
In the end—all the wrestling aside—the great figures of history and
their functionaries took their cues from the ground up, even President
Roosevelt. For the final piece of individual evidence, there is John J.
McCloy. Although widely vilified by contemporary historians for his pivotal role in the West Coast internment, his portrait hangs in the club-
house of the 100th Battalion in Honolulu as one of its first honorary
members.

The intentionality of the wartime envisioning of postwar Hawai'i is
stunning. Hawai'i's status as the "most liberal" state was an irrepressible
manifestation of aloha and egalitarian democracy at work. The results
are a tribute to people such as Hemenway, Yoshida, Ching, Burns, and

more generally, to the steadfastness and restraint of the Japanese community and to their friends.

Because of Hawai'i's extraordinary history and circumstances, I do not attempt to contend that Hawai'i is a model for the future. My sense is that history does not repeat itself but loops and tumbles forward. Hawai'i is suggestive. What America needs is to develop its own authentic version of inclusion, leading to genuine mutual regard, and then we will become a more whole and cohesive nation.

Notes

Prologue

1. This and subsequent unattributed quotes from Mr. Ching are from my documentary film interviews and repeated conversations with him. The film work resulted in *Ganbaré*, 1996, ten minutes, which has shown continuously in the theater of the Japanese Cultural Center of Hawai`i; and the one-hour *The First Battle*, 2005, distributed widely on PBS and continuously for educational purposes by the Center for Asian American Media.

2. Yoshida wrote massively during the wartime crisis and saved this material in a cramped fashion in his makeshift file boxes. Where possible, the reader is directed to a source by Box Number (1, 2, 3) and file name. Unattributed quotes from Yoshida are descended from these file references.

Chapter 1: On the Ground

1. University of Hawai`i, Hamilton Library, Archives and Manuscript Collections (hereafter UHAM), Romanzo Adams Social Research Laboratory (RASRL), Morale Section, Box 2.

2. Author interview with Dr. Michael Yoshida, a nephew and confidante of Shigeo Yoshida, ca. 2005.

3. Issei (first generation); Nisei (second generation); Sansei (third generation). These words now occur in the *New Oxford American Dictionary* and are not italicized.

4. The painting was left in China until many years later, when Hung Wai Ching's youngest brother, Hung Wo, a financier, retrieved it. The image is similar to many such stylized paintings of the period.

5. The story of Ching Yei being washed overboard was recorded in separate oral interviews of the YMCA worker John Young, one by Ted

T. Tsukiyama and a second by Diane Mark. Daughter Bessie Ching Young, at a lucid 102 years old, told her grand-nephew K. L. Ching that Ching Yei consistently sent his paycheck to his family.

6. Hung Wai Ching, oral history interview, Dr. Franklin Odo and Chris Conybeare, University of Hawai'i Hamilton Library Archives, 6.

7. The author gratefully acknowledges Leigh Wai Doo and the Doo, Ching, and Young families of Honolulu for inclusion in an educational tour of these villages and other sites associated with the life of Sun Yat-sen. For a village-level written account, see Luke Chan and Betty Tebbetts Taylor, *Sun Yat-sen, as I Knew Him: Memoirs of Luke Chan, Boyhood Friend of Sun Yat-sen* (n.p., 2008), 135–149.

8. Yusheng M. Lum and Raymond M. K. Lum, *Sun Yat-sen in Hawaii: Activities and Supporters* (Honolulu: Chinese History Center and Dr. Sun Yat-sen Foundation), 7.

9. Eileen Tamura, *"Americanization, Acculturation, and Ethnic Identity: The Nisei Generation in Hawai'i"* (Honolulu: University of Hawai'i Press, 1993), 199. Tamura described the Hawai'i public schools of the 1920s as "adequate but far from outstanding." She cited a 1920 study that ranked the territory of Hawai'i twenty-third among fifty-three states and territories.

10. *Black and Gold,* McKinley High School annual (Honolulu, 1921), 14.

11. Conversations with Dr. Richard H. Kosaki, a political scientist and chancellor of the Mānoa campus of the University of Hawai'i, who played a key role in keeping alive the memory of democratic practice at McKinley High School. He was student body president in 1941. His wife, Mildred Doi Kosaki, was a research assistant to Dr. Miles Cary at the University of Minnesota.

12. Dan Ainoa preceded Hung Wai Ching as president of the University of Hawai'i senior class. He eventually headed the Hawaiian Government Employees Association, which became the largest public worker union in Hawai'i.

13. Hung Wai Ching, interview by Dr. Franklin Odo and Chris Conybeare, Honolulu, ca. 1983.

14. The 'Round the World debate accounts are from clippings in Yoshida's scrapbooks, courtesy of Gerald and Bonnie Yoshida.

15. Dr. George Akita eventually became a distinguished professor of history at the University of Hawai'i and a writer and speaker in academic circles in both the United States and Japan.

16. Tamura, *Americanization*, 93.

17. Kazuo Miyamoto, *Hawaii, End of the Rainbow* (Tokyo: Charles E. Tuttle, 1964), 65. Miyamoto was later to be interned.

18. Shigeo Yoshida, "Evaluation in Reading," *Hawaii Educational Review* (September 1940): 10–11.

19. Editorial, *Hawaii Education Review* (September 1940): 47.

20. Diane Mei Lin Mark, *Seasons of Light: A History of Chinese Christian Churches in Hawaiʻi* (Honolulu: Chinese Christian Association of Hawaiʻi, 1989), 3.

21. Mark, *Seasons of Light,* 281.

22. Gwenfread E. Allen, *The YMCA in Hawaii, 1869–1969* (Honolulu: YMCA, 1969), 22.

23. Ching, interview by Ted T. Tsukiyama, ca. 1995. Similar figures—an original budget of $60,000, a final budget of $120,000—are reported in Allen, *The YMCA in Hawaii,* 67–68. The "challenge" aspect of the fundraising is from Ching.

24. Allen, *The YMCA in Hawaii,* 67.

25. From notes in Ching's memorabilia, the Toronto conference was held July 27 to August 2, 1930. The Canadian incident is based on conversation with Ching and on the news clipping files of Tsukiyama, inclusive of the responses of the Canadian commissioner of immigration and Henry L. Stimson. Additional details are in the U.S. State Department archives at College Park, Maryland.

26. *Honolulu Advertiser,* "Chinese-American Complains," August 26, 1931.

27. Ching, conversation with author. Communicating with "high muck-a-muck Christians" was part of Ching's explanation. Clearly, he was uninterested in becoming a minister.

28. Mark, *Seasons of Light,* 279.

29. D. Neal MacPherson, *Church at a Crossroads* (Eugene, OR: Wipf & Stock, 2008), 33–40.

30. Andrew H. Lind, "Ethnic Sources in Hawaiʻi," *Social Process in Hawaiʻi* 29 (special issue, 1982): 112. An equality of relationship was evident in the relationship between Kamehemeha I and the explorer George Vancouver, for example. However, inequality of firepower was quickly at work in the encounter between the Cook expedition and the great Makahiki gathering of Hawaiians (including Kamehameha) at Kealakekua Bay on Hawaiʻi Island. It ended in the deaths of several British, including Cook, and dozens of Hawaiians.

31. W. R. Castle, *Hawaiʻi Past and Present* (New York: Dodd, Mead, 1917).

32. Miyamoto, *Hawaii: End of the Rainbow,* 66.

Chapter 2: Next to the Ocean

1. Carey McWilliams, *Prejudice: Japanese-Americans, Symbol of Racial Intolerance* (Boston: Little, Brown, 1944), 6.

2. Allen, *Bridge Builders*, 60.

3. Allen, *Bridge Builders*, 132, quoting Theodore Richards, "The Future of the Japanese in Hawai'i: Things Problematic, Things Probable, Things Potential," *Journal of Race Development* 2, no. 4 (April 1912): 399–423.

4. Ralph S. Kuykendall, *Hawaii in the World War* (Honolulu: Hawaiian Historical Commission, Territory of Hawaii, 1928), 437.

5. Ibid., 444.

6. Several times, the two thousand interned during World War I were picked up and released.

7. American Factors ("Amfac") and its Liberty House subsidiary became household names in Hawai'i for more than half a century, until acquired by a U.S. Mainland corporation in the 1980s and dismembered once again, this time for financial reasons.

8. Kuykendall, *Hawaii in the World War*, 435.

9. Ibid., 91–93.

10. Yukiko Kimura, *Issei: Japanese Immigrants in Hawaii* (Honolulu: University of Hawai'i Press, 1988), 197.

11. The labor history of Hawai'i was eventually documented comprehensively by Dr. Edward Beechert, *Working in Hawai'i: A Labor History* (Honolulu: University of Hawai'i Press, 1985).

12. United Japanese Society of Hawaii (UJSH), *A History of Japanese in Hawaii* (Honolulu: UJSH, 1971); statement of the Japanese Labor Federation in Hawai'i, December 1, 1919, 187.

13. UJSH, *History of Japanese in Hawaii*, 189.

14. Ibid., 192.

15. See Masayo U. Duus, *The Japanese Conspiracy* (Berkeley: University of California Press, 1999) in its entirety. With painstaking research, Duus opened new veins of local, national, and international history.

16. UJSH, *History of Japanese in Hawaii*, 196. A representative of the planters told a subsequent congressional hearing that approximately three-fourths returned to their jobs.

17. This "systemic" concept is most often attributed to Harvard's Talcott Parsons, a trained economist who played a major role in developing the field of sociology.

18. For example, Earl Nishimura, 1994 interview with author; Sakae Takahashi, 1994 interview with author.

19. The impact of the Exclusion Act is virtually unknown to the U.S. public but widely accepted by historians, the most prominent and persuasive being Dr. Akira Iriye in several books on the origins of World War II. He spoke emphatically to this in an interview with the author in 1995 for the documentary film *The First Battle: The Battle for Equality in Wartime Hawai'i*.

20. The (U.S.) Senate's Declaration of War, *Japan Times and Mail*, April 19, 1924.

21. William L. Holland, *Remembering the Institute for Pacific Relations* (Tokyo: Ryukei Shyosha, 1995), 2: "The Institute had been organized in 1925, largely by YMCA people in Hawai'i who were acutely conscious of the racial tensions building between Japan and the United States over American immigration policy." The historian Paul F. Hooper, who studied the IPR from inception to demise, made a virtually identical statement in the introduction.

22. *Pan-Pacific Union Bulletin* #1, University of Hawai'i Archives and Manuscripts (UHAM).

23. *Pan-Pacific Union Bulletin* #3.

24. This was likely Nicolas Dizon, a Methodist minister and later a labor organizer and head of the Filipino National Association.

25. Yoshida's residence with Ford was recorded in the 1930 Federal Census. His housemates, distinguished either by names or pastimes, included Sivaa Fahani, Andrew Juitelelewaga, Jokoichi Ichiyama, and Ellen Shofse; also Edwin Grey, a photographer; Z. S. Zschokke, the offspring of Theodore C. Zschokke, an early day ecologist; and Thelma Rothwell, sister of the iconoclast Guy M. Rothwell, the second member of Ford's Outrigger Canoe Club. Rothwell supported Queen Lili'uokalani in the overthrow. He designed Honolulu Hale (City Hall), the Atherton House next to the university, and many other distinctive buildings.

26. Writing about statehood tends to be anecdotal. In contrast, Dr. Roger Bell, *Last Among Equals* (Honolulu: University of Hawai'i Press, 1984), systematically analyzes the long arc of the statehood movement in the context of U.S. political history, with a focus on civil rights.

27. Joint Committee on Hawaii, *Statehood for Hawaii: Hearings before the Joint Committee on Hawaii, Congress of the United States, Seventy-Fifth Congress, . . . October 6–22, 1937* (Washington, D.C.: U.S. Government Printing Office, 1938), 313–323. The most readily available volume is a 1946 compilation of Hawai'i hearings by the Subcommittee of the Committee on the Territories, 79th Congress, 2nd Session.

28. Joint Committee, *Statehood for Hawaii.*

29. Ibid.

30. Ibid.

31. The word "expatriate" is commonly used as a noun, referring to one who lives abroad, or away from one's country—an "expat," in slang. Here it is a verb and refers to ending one's citizenship in a given country.

32. Shigeo Yoshida, "Why and How to Expatriate," *Hawaii Educational Review* (January 1938): 137.

33. A rediscovery of the records of the Hawaiian Japanese Civic Association would expand understanding of Nisei development. As I have retrieved names from the HJCA, I have found only Nisei as members. Most recently, the dozens of brief biographies in L. C. Newton, *Who's Who: Americans of Japanese Ancestry, Territory of Hawaii* (Wailuku: Maui Publishing, 1941), point to the HJCA being a Nisei organization. According to notice of a memorial service for early day attorney Arthur K. Ozawa, HJCA was preceded by the Society of American Citizens (see *Honolulu Star-Bulletin,* June 26, 1939, 7).

34. The nature and extent of Yoshida's involvement in the HJCA is unclear. Eventually, Yoshida became critical of the HJCA's ethnic boundaries.

35. Edwin G. Burrows, *Chinese and Japanese in Hawaii during the Sino-Japanese Conflict* (Honolulu: Hawai'i Group, American Council, Institute of Pacific Relations, 1939), 33–35.

36. Ibid. The study method was obviously crude. Such rough assessments of ethnic voting, or "plunking" for one's own ethnic group, continued into the statehood period, with similar results. Generally, it appears that voters have tended to vote in disproportionate numbers to facilitate a member of their own ethnic group making a breakthrough in officeholding, then return to a more individual-by-individual approach to voting once such a breakthrough becomes part of the status quo. In multimember legislative districts, voting across ethnic lines indisputably was a common practice.

37. Burrows, *Chinese and Japanese in Hawaii,* 65.

38. Ibid., 49. Ching was not mentioned by name. The presumption is based on Ching's prominent role in the YMCA and in the study.

39. Ibid., 46, quoting the Rev. Galen Weaver, founding pastor of the Church of the Crossroads.

40. Ibid., 70.

41. Dr. Gregory Robinson, *By Order of the President: FDR and the Internment of Japanese Americans* (Cambridge, MA: Harvard University Press, 2003), 16, 30, 38. The latter quotes FDR as describing Japanese as "non-assimilable immigrants."

42. Frederick Samuels, *The Japanese and the Haoles of Honolulu: Durable Group Interaction* (New Haven, CT: College & University Press, 1970), 94.

43. Miyamoto, *Hawaii: End of the Rainbow,* 66.

44. Possibly their benefactor was a celebrated African American flyer, Hubert Julian, known as "Black Eagle," who was in and out of Europe around this time. Hung Wai Ching told the story to his son King Lit Ching. The reference to the World Congress of Christian Youth is from the Reverend Abraham Akaka website. A world peace conference in Zurich coincided with the start of the European land war.

Chapter 3: External and Internal Security

1. Tom Coffman, *Nation Within: The Story of America's Annexation of the Nation of Hawai'i* (Kenmore, WA: EpiCenter, 1998), 17.

2. Coffman, *Nation Within,* 213–222, establishes this history, otherwise unrecognized in written American history: Francis Hatch, ambassador of the Republic of Hawai'i to Washington, came up with the idea of provoking an incident with Japan, and Henry Cooper, another Cabinet member, executed it. This information is fundamental to understanding America's entry into the Pacific.

3. Ibid., 247.

4. Brian McAllister Linn, *Guardians of Empire: The U.S. Army and the Pacific* (Chapel Hill: University of North Carolina Press, 1997), 84–88.

5. Ibid., 85. As Linn points out, American writers have obsessed over the several days before Japan's attack, leaving an impression that the U.S. Army was sleeping. Linn placed the army's weak position in context of Pacific history resulting from the 1898 annexation of Hawai'i, the Spanish-American War, and the ensuing Philippine American War.

6. Ibid., 153.

7. Ibid., xiii.

8. Edward J. Moralda, ed., *FDR and the Navy* (New York: St. Martin's Press, 1998), from a presentation by Dr. Jonathan G. Utley, 56. Also see Thomas Hone and Trent Hone, *Battle Line: The United States Navy, 1919–1939* (Annapolis, MD: Naval Institute Press, 2006), 99.

9. Linn, *Guardians of Empire,* 154.

10. *MISLS Album,* "Gero Iwai" (Minneapolis: Military Intelligence Service Language School, 1946), 31. The author is indebted to the writer Mark Matsunaga for calling his attention to Iwai.

11. Linn, *Guardians of Empire,* 161.

12. Michael Slackman, "The Orange Race: George S. Patton, Jr.'s Japanese-American Hostage Plan," *Biography* 1, no. 7 (Winter 1984): 1–22.

13. Slackman's "Orange Race" article was not literally inaccurate, but its implications have been removed from context, resulting in a wide and sensationalized impact that has fed simplistic accounts of the victimization of Issei. Linn's *Guardians of Empire* is a more whole and illuminating account of the U.S. military's thinking and role.

14. "Herron Orders Increase for ROTC at McKinley," *Honolulu Advertiser*, n.d., 16.

15. Linn, *Guardians of Empire*, 156.

16. Archives of Hawai'i, Hawai'i National Guard file, Colonel Perry Smoot to Major General Charles D. Herron, Commanding General, Hawaiian Department, Fort Shafter, Territory of Hawai'i, October 6, 1939.

17. *Collier's Weekly Magazine*, October 19, 1940.

18. *Pittsburgh Courier*, February 7, 1942. The *Courier* was one of the largest African American newspapers of its time and is given major credit by historians for driving the Double V campaign.

19. Archives of Hawai'i, 1939 Report of Territorial Adjutant General, Hawai'i National Guard.

20. About 1,400 Nisei troops were in the federalized guard units, and several hundred more were in training at Schofield Barracks. Of the 600 members of HTG, about three-fourths were of Japanese ancestry. The adjutant general estimated that about 400 were sufficiently trained to stand guard duty, 300 of whom were likely of Japanese ancestry.

21. Author interview with Cecil H. Coggins, 1985, 24–25. Subsequent quotes from Coggins are from this interview.

22. Stephenson was a familiar figure to attorney and later federal judge Samuel P. King (not to be confused with his father, Samuel Wilder King). The younger King served with Stephenson in Naval Intelligence during World War II.

23. Federal Bureau of Investigation, *Memorandum on Pearl Harbor Attack and Bureau's Activities Before and After*, vol. 1 of 2, December 6, 1945, 107.

24. Author interview with Douglas Wada, ca. 1995. Col. Wada was supported in this effort by a mutual friend, Dr. Bertram Kobayashi.

25. Ibid.

26. Ibid. The attorney Masaji Marumoto became aware of his role but said nothing. The Language School Archival Project article said, "He found himself isolated socially from the Japanese community in Hawaii." University of Colorado Libraries, *US Navy Japanese/Oriental Language School Archival Project* no. 69 (November 1, 2003).

27. Wada worked with a customs agent, George Roberts, later collector of customs.

28. University of Colorado Libraries, *Language School Archival Project.*

29. Blake Clark, *Hawaii: The 49th State* (Garden City, NJ: Doubleday, 1947), 115.

30. J. Edgar Hoover, *Persons in Hiding* (Boston: Little, Brown, 1938), 280.

31. Shivers personal file, courtesy of Sue Isonaga, Hoover to Shivers, May 20, 1938.

32. "FBI to Handle All Subversive Activities Here," *Honolulu Star-Bulletin,* September 15, 1939.

33. Author interview with Sue Isonaga, ca. 2004; also, conversation with Wendall Marumoto, son of Masaji Marumoto.

34. Shivers, personal file, Shivers to Hoover, May 14, 1943. Although the letter was considerably after the fact, it is consistent with what Shivers said about his early months in Hawai'i.

35. FBI, *Memorandum on Pearl Harbor Attack,* vol. 1, 2. This is a massive after-action report on all states and territories. Its transmittal letter is from D. M. Ladd, head of the Domestic Intelligence Division, to J. Edgar Hoover, FBI director. Given Hoover's eventual reputation for self-aggrandizing distortions, the memorandum should be read with care. The accounts of Hawai'i in the crucial period 1939 to 1943 were derived from the files of Shivers's. These reports were obtained through the Freedom of Information Act and were minimally redacted.

36. FBI, *Memorandum on Pearl Harbor Attack,* vol. 1, 400.

37. Pearl Harbor Archive, Roberts Commission, Pearl Harbor Attack, Part 25, Shivers's testimony, 1405. The numerous investigations into the Pearl Harbor attack are online in the Boston Public Library site (bpl.com).

38. Clark, *Hawaii: The 49th State,* 118.

39. No records and only a few widely scattered references regarding the Hawaiian Japanese Civic Association appear to have survived. Information appears in brief press references during the 1930s in the Yoshida files with reference to the Honolulu Police Contact Group and in the papers of Cecil Coggins.

40. Newton, *Who's Who.*

41. Clark, *Hawaii: The 49th State,* 120.

42. Roberts Commission, Pearl Harbor Attack, 1406.

43. Shivers personal file, Shivers to Hemenway, October 8, 1943.

44. A copy of this memorandum in Andrew H. Lind's files at Hamilton Library archives bore the note, "Written about Dec. 14."

45. This memorandum was issued on December 22, 1941, in an expanded form, by the martial law government to explain the working principles of the Morale Section.

46. FBI, *Memorandum on Pearl Harbor Attack*, vol. 1, 103.

47. Ibid., 107. For a broader context, see 100–109. To correct the impressions of the Roberts Commission investigating the lead-up to the Pearl Harbor attack, the report is obviously preoccupied with convincing readers that the FBI only briefly had exclusive jurisdiction over civilian investigations and otherwise shared this responsibility with the better-staffed ONI.

48. Ibid., vol. 1, 107.

Chapter 4: A Swing toward Americanization

1. Archives of Hawai'i, "Burns Oral History Project," Tape #2 (transcript), 7.

2. Pearl Harbor Attack, Pearl Harbor Board, Part 25, 1406–1407.

3. Pearl Harbor Attack, FBI Report, vol. 1, 411.

4. Ibid., 412. A footnote acknowledges this important point: "There were no Consular agents in Honolulu, their work being done by the Japanese Consulate."

5. Miyamoto, *Hawaii: End of the Rainbow*, 70.

6. Pearl Harbor Attack, FBI Report, vol. 1, 407–408: Shivers to FBI headquarters, Washington, D.C., September 3, 1940.

7. Shivers personal files, Shivers to Hoover, September 3, 1940; also Pearl Harbor Attack, Part 24, 1409.

8. Pearl Harbor Attack, Part 24, 35. To my knowledge, this is the single reference to the consul's alleged use of consular representatives for intelligence. The allegation was not repeated by Shivers or in other documents. The statement was made by William B. Stephenson, Fourteenth District Intelligence Office, to the Hart Commission.

9. Linn, *Guardians of Empire*, 155.

10. Pearl Harbor Attack, Part 24, 1414: Stimson to Biddle, July 22, 1941.

11. Pearl Harbor Attack, Part 25, 1413.

12. George Bicknell, unpublished MSS in possession of author.

13. "Walker, Shivers at Maui Rally," *Honolulu Star-Bulletin*, August 22, 1941.

14. Bicknell, unpublished memoir, 18.

15. The phrasing foreshadowed Yoshida's rewrite eight months later of the Varsity Victory Volunteers's petition to serve the country.

16. Bicknell, unpublished memoir, 18.

17. *Honolulu Star-Bulletin*, editorial, June 14, 1941.

18. Archives of Hawai'i, M471, Box 23, King Papers, Riley Allen to King, June 18, 1941.

19. University of Hawai'i Archives and Manuscripts (hereafter UHAM), Romanzo Adams Social Research Laboratory (hereafter RASRL), Box 1 of 3, Ching Correspondence file, Hung Wai Ching speech notes, September 12, 1943. Ching was looking back over a two-year period.

20. With the Hawai'i National Guard federalized and relocated to Scho-field Barracks, six hundred people were being trained on Maui as police reserves, and a police reserve also was being organized on Kaua'i.

21. Archives of Hawai'i, National Guard: Territorial Adjutant General P. M. Smoot proposed a large-scale police reserve in the absence of the National Guard, which had been federalized and relocated to Schofield Barracks on January 24, 1941. Smoot said that, in addition to the six hundred people being trained on Maui as police reserves, a police reserve was being organized on Kaua'i.

22. UHAM, RASRL Box 1, HPD Contact Group. The Honolulu Police Contact Group was cursorily described in various books. It was first described to the author by Burns when he was governor of Hawai'i. The more detailed description is derived from a memo in the files of Yoshida, noted here.

23. Ibid.

24. Ibid. Shivers, Gabrielson, Burns, Hasegawa, Sakamaki, and Jack Wakayama reviewed the draft plan on August 25, 1941. Sakamaki, Wakayama, Hasegawa, W. Amioka, G. Eguchi (presumably territorial leg-islator George Eguchi), Masatoshi Katagiri, M. Maneki, S. Higashino, Paul Morihara, Clifton Yamamoto, and Yoshida attended a follow-up meeting. They were described as representing the O'ahu Citizens Committee for Home Defense.

25. Ibid. In addition to Shivers's advisers at the HPD meeting, Yoshida listed W. Amioka, G. Eguchi, M. Maneki, S. Higashino, and Paul Morihara.

26. Archives of Hawai'i, "Burns Oral History Project," 9.

27. Ibid., 2, 1.

28. Ibid., 1, 6.

29. Ibid., 1, 11.

30. Ibid., 2, 5.

31. Author interview with Burns, 1971. He expanded on the subject in "Burns Oral History Project," Tape 2, 6, 1975. The investigator Kanazawa,

by then a prominent dentist, described his work in a 2003 interview at the home of a mutual friend, Helen Doi.

32. UHAM, RASRL Box 2, Miller report, Morale Section.

33. Burns once said that his brother Edward's IQ score on the HPD entrance examination was 154, and that his own was higher, which he ascribed to his wide travels as a youth.

34. UHAM, RASRL Box 1, from a draft manuscript, Remington Stone, submitted to Major Frank Blake out of concern for security, intended for publication in *Collier's,* located in file marked "Japanese." The Stone manuscript is undated.

35. UHAM, RASRL Box 1. Burns and Riley Allen exchanged views on the AJA idea in early 1942.

Chapter 5: A Climate of Fear

1. FBI, *Memorandum on Pearl Harbor Attack,* vol. 1, 212, gives the date of Roosevelt's directive as September 6, 1939. The directive included other U.S. territories: Alaska, Puerto Rico, Virgin Islands, and the Panama Canal Zone.

2. Ibid. Tetsuden Kashima, *Judgment Without Trial* (Seattle: University of Washington Press, 2003) describes this system at length. Kashima fits the Hawai'i experience inside the national story of what is usually described as "internment." The Special Defense Unit is described at length by Kashima.

3. FBI, *Memorandum on Pearl Harbor Attack,* vol. 1, 213.

4. Kashima, *Judgment Without Trial,* 30.

5. FBI, *Memorandum on Pearl Harbor Attack,* vol. 1, 300.

6. Plan III called for arresting fifty-seven male Germans and forty-six German females, as well nineteen male Italians and ten female Italians.

7. FBI, *Memorandum on Pearl Harbor Attack,* vol. 1, 212.

8. Ibid., Letter of agreement, July 18, 1941.

9. Kashima, *Judgment Without Trial,* 50–51. This approximate number is inferred from the first-week arrests described by Kashima.

10. FBI, *Memorandum on Pearl Harbor Attack,* vol. 1, 213.

11. Ibid., 801.

12. Kashima, *Judgment Without Trial,* 47.

13. My 1996 documentary film, *The First Battle,* portrayed the scene between Shivers and Burns without describing Hoover's cable to Shivers, about which I did not know at the time of production. The effect was to create a suggestion erroneously that Shivers not only had been warned of an impending attack, which he had, but that it likely would be on Hawai'i, which was not the case.

14. UHAM, RASRL, Miller report, Morale Section, Box 2.

15. Ibid.

16. FBI, *Memorandum on Pearl Harbor Attack,* vol. 1, 301.

17. UHAM, RASRL, Box 2, Yoshida account of council history, 4–5.

18. Ibid.

19. General Thomas H. Green, *Martial Law in Hawaii, December 7, 1941–April 4, 1943,* Library of Congress, Military Legal Resources, OCLC # 461333055, an unpublished typescript of Green's crucial role in Hawai'i, chapter 4. The pages of his voluminous manuscript are unnumbered and are referred to herein by chapter. Available online at https://www.loc.gov /rr/frd/Military_Law/pdf/Martial-Law_Green.pdf.

20. George F. Nellist, *The Story of Hawaii and Its Builders* (Honolulu: Honolulu Star-Bulletin, 1925).

21. Green, *Martial Law in Hawaii,* chapter 4.

22. Kashima, *Judgment Without Trial,* 49.

23. Green, *Martial Law in Hawaii,* chapter 4.

24. Ibid.

25. *Honolulu Star-Bulletin,* editorial page, November 18, 1941. Burns was walking a fine line as a police officer and investigator assigned to the FBI. The article was initialed "JB" but not signed.

26. Green, *Martial Law in Hawaii,* chapter 4.

27. Kai Bird, *The Chairman, John J. McCloy and the Making of the American Establishment* (New York: Simon & Schuster, 1992), 93–94. The portrayal of McCloy draws heavily on Bird's work.

28. John J. McCloy Papers, Amherst College Archives (ACA), McCloy diary (more accurately, a day log), online digital collection, available at http://asteria.fivecolleges.edu/findaids/amherst/ma35.html.

29. Ibid.

30. Nancy Clark de Nevers, *The Colonel and the Pacifist* (Salt Lake City: University of Utah Press, 2004), 313.

31. Bird, *The Chairman,* 148.

32. Ibid., 150.

33. Bendetsen Papers, Hoover Institution, Personal Correspondence Box 683, Bendetsen to Col. Harry A. Auer (retired), June 3, 1942.

34. Green, *Martial Law in Hawaii,* chapter 13; also chapter 17, a nearly identical statement.

35. Bendetsen Papers, Bendetsen to Finance Officer, U.S. Army, Sept. 22, 1941 (re: travel performed), Box 683.

36. Bendetsen Papers, Box 683.

37. Ibid. Bendetsen's second trip to Hawai'i is explicitly described in trip notes in his personal papers at Hoover Institution, Stanford University. Bendetsen was also to claim that he continued on to Manila to meet with General Douglas MacArthur. In *The Colonel and the Pacifist,* de Nevers wrote that such a trip did not appear in Bendetsen's records, which the eminent Roger Daniels, in his introduction to the book, cited to support her contention that Bendetsen was a chronic liar; de Nevers gives other instances in which she concluded Bendetsen was untruthful.

38. Green, *Martial Law in Hawaii.*

39. Stetson Conn, Rose C. Engelman, and Byron Fairchild, *Guarding the United States and Its Outposts* (Washington, D.C.: Center for Military History, U.S. Army, 2000). This is an example of the "wartime hysteria" interpretation: "During the first few days after the Pearl Harbor attack the west coast was alarmed by a number of reports—all false—of enemy ships offshore. It was in the midst of this atmosphere that the first proposal for a mass evacuation of the Japanese developed." In much the same terms, the U.S. Commission on Wartime Relocation and Internment also blamed wartime hysteria.

Chapter 6: Resetting the Clock

1. "Knox's Warning," *Honolulu Star-Bulletin,* September 16, 1940.

2. Archives of Hawai'i, King papers.

3. UHAM, Hawaii War Records Division, 27.01, Letters to John Reinecke.

4. Thomas Taro Higa, *Memoirs of a Certain Nisei, Aru Nisei no Wadachi* (Kāne'ohe: Higa Publications, 1988), 27.

5. Conn, Engelman, and Fairchild, *Guarding the United States,* 173.

6. Pearl Harbor Attack, Joint Hearings, Roberts Commission, Part 23, 1081. This is the report of the Joint Congressional Committees, 79th Congress, a combination of postwar hearings and the previous seven inquiries, including the Roberts Commission. In addition to being online in the Boston Public Library archive, it can be found at www.ibiblio.org/pha /congress.

7. Pearl Harbor Attack, Part 22, 36.

8. Conn, Engelman, and Fairchild, *Guarding the United States,* 187.

9. Author interview with Sue Isonaga, 2005.

10. Author interview with Mary Beth Sheenagh Burns, 2005.

11. Archives of Hawai'i, King papers, M-472, File 957, Vitousek to Samuel W. King, July 28, 1942.

12. FBI, *Memorandum on Pearl Harbor Attack,* vol. 1, 905.

13. Sumitomo Bank was to make a comeback in the postwar market through the Central Pacific Bank of Hawai'i.

14. Green, "Martial Law in Hawaii," chapter 8.

15. Ibid., chapter 10 (Poindexter's quotes in the following paragraphs are from this source). The most widely quoted account of this meeting was by Charles Hite, Poindexter's assistant.

16. The title of "military governor" was apt and is used in this text. The succeeding appointed civilian governor, Ingram Stainback, eventually disputed it, as did the U.S. Interior Department.

17. Blake Clark, *Remember Pearl Harbor!* (New York: Modern Age, 1942), 14.

18. Yoshida, written in response to interview questions by Odo and Tsukiyama, ca. 1980.

19. Yasutaro Soga, *Life behind Barbed Wire: The World War II Internment Memoirs of a Hawai'i Issei* (Honolulu: University of Hawai'i Press, 2008), 37. First published in 1946 in Japanese in Soga's *Nippu Jiji* newspaper, his memoirs were translated by Kihei Hirai with an introduction by Dr. Tetsuden Kashima and republished.

20. As I was introduced to the wartime story, I heard repeated references to vouching. My research contradicts the statement made by John A. Burns in our 1971 interview as reflected in my notes, which clearly record his saying that as many as half of those on the arrest list were released. This was, and to some extent still is, politically charged information about a moment in time wracked by emotion and confusion.

21. Conn, Engelman, and Fairchild, *Guarding the United States,* 207.

22. University of Hawai'i Archives and Manuscripts, RASRL, Box 2, Morale Division.

23. Government officials in the advisory group were J. B. Poindexter, civilian governor of the territory; Charles M. Hite, secretary of the territory; Mayor Lester Petrie; Frank H. Locey, chair of the Board of Agriculture and Forestry; and Acting Attorney General Ernest K. Kai.

24. University of Hawai'i Archives and Manuscripts, RASRL, Box 2, Hamilton Research Library, University of Hawai'i, beginning "This office would conceive of its function . . ."; it is unsigned but written in the style and repeated themes of Yoshida.

25. The idea of preconceived plans prevailing in crisis was the central thesis of Naomi Klein's *Shock Doctrine.*

26. *Honolulu Star-Bulletin,* December 18, 1941, 1.

27. Transfer was effected by General Order 56. The description was from OMG to Poindexter, dated April 14, 1942, located in Archives of Hawai'i, Gov. 8-20.

28. See Fielder address to the thirty-fifth anniversary dinner, www.100thbattalion.org.

29. King Lit Ching, conversation with author, ca. 2017; Hung Wai Ching's oldest son, King Lit, remembered their family repeatedly visiting Loomis's beach cottage.

30. Green, "Martial Law in Hawaii," chapter 3.

31. Mike Markrich, quoting Dr. Michael Okihiro, www.100thbattalion .org.

32. University of Hawai'i Archives and Manuscripts, RASRL, Box 2, Morale Section, Progress Report I, December 28, 1941, 2.

33. Green, "Martial Law in Hawaii," chapter 17. In addition, Green credited an unnamed Filipino American as a fourth associate. This was probably N. C. Villanueva, a broadcaster. He described Loomis as the "inspirational head of the entire movement," one of the few references to Loomis playing a dominant role.

34. Green, "Martial Law in Hawaii," chapter 21.

35. Ibid.

Chapter 7: The Cry of Sabotage

1. Francis MacDonnell, *Insidious Foes: The Axis Fifth Column & the American Home Front* (New York and Oxford: Oxford University Press, 1995), 12–17.

2. Ibid., 23.

3. Archives of Hawai'i, Gov. 8–20, the basis of the writer Anita Manning reconstructing Roosevelt's 1934 trip to Hawai'i, part of an Elks Club history project.

4. National Archives and Records Administration (NARA), Roosevelt Memorandum to the Chief of Operations, August 10, 1936.

5. Robert Dallek, *Franklin Roosevelt and American Foreign Policy, 1932–1948* (London: Oxford University Press, 1979), 225. For a more deailed exploration of the Fifth Column phenomenon, see MacDonnell, *Insidious Foes.*

6. Dallek, *Franklin Roosevelt,* 225.

7. Robinson, *By Order of the President,* 77.

8. "Secretary Knox to be Honored at Luncheon," *Honolulu Star-Bulletin,* September, 4, 1940.

9. Pearl Harbor Attack, Part 25, 1630, Joint Congressional Committee.

10. UHAM, RASRL Box 2, Mrs. Robert Shivers to husband, December 16, 1941, reporting an account by Leon P. Lovett, commander of the USS *Cassin,* a ship attacked at Pearl Harbor.

11. Pearl Harbor Attack, Part 25, Kimmel to Admiral Stark.

12. *Honolulu Star-Bulletin,* December 15, 1941, 1. Knox's added words, "except in Norway," referred to collaboration with invading Nazi Germany, the most notorious collaborator being Viskund Quisling, whose name in the lower case became a noun equating to collaboration.

13. Pearl Harbor Attack, Part 25, 1756.

14. Pearl Harbor Attack, Part 24, extensively summarizes press comments, reflecting the power of editorial writers of an earlier time. See *Christian Science Monitor* reference, 1293. Numerous others follow.

15. *New York Times,* January 8, 1942.

16. Densho Encyclopedia, https://encyclopedia.densho.org, originally from National Archives and Records Administration, John Franklin Carter to Roosevelt, Memorandum on Summary of West Coast and Honolulu Report by Munson, December 16, 1941.

17. Conn, Engelman, and Fairchild, *Guarding the United States,* 207.

18. Amherst College Archives, McCloy diary/logbook, December 16, 1941.

19. MacDonnell, *Insidious Foes,* 17. I am concerned that the Fifth Column narrative around Roosevelt, Stimson, McCloy, Knox, Donovan, and, here, Justice Owen Roberts, begins to sound like a conspiracy theory. To further consider the information base, I recommend MacDonnell's *Insidious Foes.*

20. See Robinson, *By Order of the President,* Roberts Commission.

21. Pearl Harbor Attack, Part 23, 1311–1329.

22. See Robinson, *By Order of the President,* 95–97, for a detailing of the impact of Roberts and his commission's report.

23. Ibid., 96.

24. Pearl Harbor Attack, National Defense Migration, Tolan Committee, 77th Congress, 2nd session, Part 29, "Problems of Evacuation of Enemy Aliens and Others from Prohibited Military Zones," testimony of California Attorney General Earl Warren, 10973, www.bpl.org/online/govdocs/interstate_migration.html.

25. National Defense Migration Committee (hereinafter NDMC), United States Congress, House Select Committee (Tolan Committee), Parts 29, 30, 31, 77th Congress, 2nd session.

26. McWilliams, *Prejudice*, 121.

27. Morton Grodzins, *Americans Betrayed: Politics and the Japanese Evacuation* (Chicago: University of Chicago Press, 1949), 254.

28. NDMC, 11153.

29. NDMC, 10974–10975.

30. Ibid.

31. NDMC, 11139–11141.

32. NDMC, 11130.

33. NDMC, 11178.

34. NDMC, 11157.

35. Ruth Kingman, oral history (Earl Warren Oral History Project, Bancroft Libary, UC Berkeley) put organization of the committee in August 1942. Masaoka said it was well after Pearl Harbor.

36. Mike Masaoka, with Bill Hosokawa, *They Call Me Moses Masaoka: An American Saga* (New York: William Morrow, 1987), 78.

37. Ibid., 86–87.

38. Archives of Hawai'i, King papers, M 472, Boxes 39–40, Kido to King, February 23, 1942.

39. Archives of Hawai'i, Telegram, King to Tolan, Boxes 39–40, February 25, 1942.

40. Archives of Hawai'i, King papers, Box 38, File 1454.

41. Archives of Hawai'i, Box 38, File 1459. Phleger wrote a concise letter to King on March 5, addressing "Dear Sam," and a longer and more detailed March 6 letter to Vitousek.

42. Amherst College Archives, McCloy logbook/diary, April 10, 1942.

43. "Fifth Column in U.S.—Fighting the Foe Within," *United States News,* February 27, 1942, 75.

44. Archives of Hawai'i, King papers; the graphic heading of the excerpt reads, "The National Week."

45. Archives of Hawai'i, King papers, John O'Donnell, Capitol Stuff, *Washington Times-Herald,* March 16, 1942.

46. NDMC, Fourth Interim Report, Vitousek letter, 49–50, located online at www.hathitrust.org. Vitousek wrote he had not realized until early April that he was expected to gather and file statements in affadavit form for the committee.

47. Burns and all other testimony to the Tolan Committee can be found in NDMC, "Fourth Interim Report," 48–57.

48. Floyd Healey, "The Tolan Committee," *San Francisco Chronicle,* March 20, 1942, 1.

49. Bird, *The Chairman,* 160. Milton Eisenhower planned to rapidly resettle people out of the assembly centers into camps throughout the Western states of the sort developed by the Civilian Conservation Corps during the Great Depression. In Eisenhower's original idea, people would be free to come and go and to find work at market rates. All governors except the governor of Colorado opposed this. They demanded that people be kept under armed guard in prisonlike conditions. Eisenhower, in despair, soon resigned.

50. Ibid., 680n36, quoting Jules Witcover, *Sabotage at Black Tom* (Chapel Hill, NC: Algonquin, 1989), 311.

51. Ibid., 152.

52. Ibid., quoting Report of the Commission on Wartime Relocation and Internment of Civilians, *Personal Justice Denied,* 79.

53. Ibid., 157.

54. Ibid., quoting Bill Hosokawa, *JACL: In Quest of Justice* (Japanese American Citizens League, 1982), 166.

55. Hoover Institution, Bendetsen speech to the Commonwealth Club of San Francisco, May 20, 1942.

Chapter 8: The Threat of Demoralization

1. The reports were not addressed to persons or agencies. However, Ching talked repeatedly of reporting to Fielder at Army Intelligence. Green, "Martial Law in Hawaii," describes the two-way communication process and also specific reports.

2. RASRL, Morale Section, Box 2, Progress Report 3, 3.

3. As indicated previously, Yoshida/Morale Section files were given by Yoshida's widow, Thelma, to the Archives and Manuscripts Room of Hamilton Research Library, University of Hawai'i and are available under the heading of RASRL (the Romanzo Adams Social Research Laboratory). Additional references in this section are to the files of the sociologist Dr. Andrew Lind, also at UH Archives and Manuscripts. Copies of Honolulu Police Department files are (I think uniquely) in Yoshida's files.

4. The progressive educator John Dewey consulted on the development of the kindergarten movement in Hawai'i. Chicago's George H. Mead, a philosopher who played a role in defining the field of sociology, was influenced by his missionary-descended wife and his intellectual brother-in-law, Henry Castle. Warwick Anderson, "Racial Hybridity, Physical Anthropology, and Human Biology in the Colonial Laboratories of the United States,"

Current Anthropology 53, no. S5 (April 1, 2012), focuses on the progression of physical anthropology to sociology. Park and Mead are widely discussed in academic literature in connection with shaping the Chicago School, including its relationship to Hawai'i. I am indebted to Dr. Lori Pierce of DePaul University, "a *kama'āina* by proxy," for guiding me to these connections.

5. RASRL (unaccessed Lind files), Lind Box 17, Lind to Fielder (Morale, December 19, 1941).

6. RASRL, Lind Papers, File 17, Racial Discrimination, AJA Reactions 1940, which is also the source of succeeding vignettes.

7. RASRL, Lind Papers, File 17, Morale Committee minutes, October 22, 1942. At a meeting of a Morale Advisory Group, Lind reported that one of his information sources was from "an anonymous group of students," likely Student House.

8. RASRL, Honolulu Police Department file. Following HPD quotes are from this source.

9. Even though seventy years have passed, stigma and hurt remain; also, the people singled out for this process were both helpless and blameless of criminality—hence the reduction of names to initials.

10. Yukiko Kimura, "Some Effects of the War Situation Upon the Alien Japanese in Hawaii," *Social Process in Hawaii* 8 (1943): 18.

11. Ibid., 19.

12. Ibid., 21.

13. Ibid., 23.

14. RASRL, Yoshida file, Box 1, "Waipahu Japanese Community," 3.

15. Green, "Martial Law in Hawaii," chapter 12.

16. Pearl Harbor Attack, 14135–14136.

17. RASRL, Lind, "Confidential Files" (his marking), Box 20, Teachers/Schools, TS 80–1, Misc. Circular 669.

18. RASRL, Yoshida Box 1, "Japanese" file.

19. RASRL, Yoshida Box 1, Emergency Service Committee. Membership changed and expanded. The listing of the seven original members relies on Yoshida's handwritten account dated May 10, 1972.

20. RASRL, Box 2, Morale Section, United Hawaii, Inc., May 5, 1942.

21. RASRL, Box 1, Japanese file.

22. RASRL, Box 1, Oi to Loomis, February 24, 1942, with accompanying two-page report of activities.

23. RASRL, Box 2, Yoshida, United Hawaii, Inc., 4.

24. Tom Coffman, *Tadaima! I Am Home* (Honolulu: University of Hawai'i Press, 2018), 81.

25. Author interview with Shimeji Ryusaki Kanazawa, 1995. At the time I had no understanding of the "protecting power" aspect of her story. The writer Dorothea "Dee" Buckingham wrote a valuable interview-based account, available at http://www.hawaiireporter.com/shimeji-ryusaki -kanazawa-deemed-"florence-nightingale-of-hawaii"-for-wwii-actions.

26. RASRL, Box 2. Two documents from the Yoshida-Ching collection particularly focus on the Korean community: "Report on Attitudes and Needs Expressed by Various Sections of the Civilian Population," January 20, 1942; and "Third Progress Report (Morale Section to Army Intelligence) Supplementary Report on Koreans," March 5, 1942.

27. RASRL, Morale Section, Progress Report II, January 19, 1942.

28. RASRL, Morale Section, Third Progress Report, "Supplementary Report on Chinese," March 5, 1942.

Chapter 9: The Morale Section at Work

1. Hoover Institution, Emmons Papers. In retirement, Emmons wrote, somewhat disingenuously, that he regretted not communicating his real reason to the HTG, which he said was to protect the Japanese members of the unit. This statement is contained in his fifteen-page autobiographical notes.

2. Archives of Hawai'i, Gov. 8–20, P. M. Smoot, Adjutant General TH, to Joseph B. Poindexter, Governor, December 9, 1941.

3. Hoover Institution, Emmons Papers, autobiographical notes.

4. Dr. Franklin Odo, *No Sword to Bury* (Philadelphia: Temple University Press, 2004), 205–206.

5. As with any legend, there were variations in the accounts. One is that the original group first contacted the Nu'uanu YMCA worker John Young, who had relocated to Hawai'i from his missionary work in Asia. Young said he in turn directed them to Yoshida.

6. Burns Oral History Project, Tape 4, 15.

7. RASRL, Yoshida, written notes in response to Odo interview, 6.

8. Odo, *No Sword to Bury,* 202.

9. Ibid., 159: "Tsukiyama was uniquely aware of the potentially momentous nature of the VVV. His private experience became the public model of VVV emotion, motivation, dedication, and success."

10. Odo, *No Sword to Bury,* 217.

11. RASRL, Box 2, "Propaganda Among the Japanese Aliens," January 15, 1942, 2–3.

12. Hung Wai Ching Papers (HWCP), Yoshida diary. Yoshida quotes in following paragraphs are from the Yoshida diary.

13. Ibid., May 3, 1942, 7. Succeeding quotes on the West Coast situation are from this source.

14. Dr. Greg Robinson, *Nichi Bei Weekly,* January 1, 2012, from his column "The GREAT UNKNOWN and the UNKNOWN GREAT."

15. RASRL, Box 2, Police Contact Group, includes all Aiea and subsequent Oʻahu plantation material.

16. Ibid.

17. Whether the acronym AJA was a wholly new idea, or whether Burns only thought of it as such, is not indisputably clear.

18. RASRL Box 1, Kauaʻi Morale Committee, Report I.

19. RASRL Box 1, Kauaʻi Morale, Headquarters Kauaʻi Service Command, Office for Military Intelligence, Port Allen Kauaʻi T.H., October 10, 1942, Charles A. Selby, Major. To my knowledge, this large file is the single best source of information on Kauaʻi, containing the views of both the army and the ESC. The letters of the Rev. Masao Yamada (UHAM) and the publication "World War II on Kauaʻi" by Timothy Klass also are useful.

20. Researchers at the Japanese Cultural Center of Hawaiʻi estimate that about two hundred persons on Kauaʻi were incarcerated.

21. Electoral and other demographic data are from Reports of the (U.S.) Department of Interior, 1902 and 1918, Volume II, Indian Affairs, Territories, Report of Governor of Hawaii.

22. Report of Governor of Hawaii, 1936, said that 18,698 of 75,000 registered voters were of Japanese ancestry, 13. Of 3,891 newly registered voters, 3,291 were of Japanese ancestry.

23. RASRL, Box 1, Kauaʻi, Selby.

24. UHAM. See book format, Ai Yamada, introduction to the wartime letters of the Rev. Masao Yamada.

25. H. S. Kawakami, with Tom Coffman, *From Japan to Hawaii.* In the introduction to his autobiography I wrote, "Today [the Issei] are often portrayed as scrimping and saving to educate their children, preparing for the day of change. . . . Overlooked in this description are the substantial number of Japanese and other Oriental-Americans like H.S. who had created businesses or professional lives for themselves."

26. Kawakami, *From Japan to Hawaii.*

27. RASRL, Box 1, Kauaʻi. Instructions were eventually reduced to a Worker's Handbook, which is quoted here.

28. RASRL Box 1, Kauaʻi file: Table I Occupation Skills derived from Family Survey covering 7,713 persons of Japanese ancestry: 5 doctors, 1 lawyer, 104 teachers, 1 banker, 3 bank tellers, 12 accountants and 1 appraiser, 59 bookkeepers, 6 cashiers, 10 chemists, 247 clerks, 7 contractors, 5 dental hygienists, 4 dentists, 20 ditch men, 11 engineers, 58 electricians, 217 farmers, 18 fishermen, 3 gardeners, 2 hospital orderlies, 10 insurance underwriters, 25 managers, 22 nurses, 9 nurses' aides, 2 opticians, 80 overseers, 7 photographers, 1 pharmacist, 3 pineapple growers, 6 policemen, 1 priestess, 2 printers, 3 ranchers, 11 restaurateurs, 17 salesmen, 12 secretaries, 1 social worker, 23 surveyors, 74 storekeepers, 1,506 students, 35 tailors.

29. Ibid.: 428 carpenters; 104 machinists; 54 plumbers; 63 maids; 72 yard boys.

30. RASRL Box 1, Kauaʻi file. Possibly the respondents were cued to distance themselves from Shinto. Recall there were twenty-two Buddhist temples and only four Shinto temples. Also both Buddhist and Shinto priests had been arrested, so the relationship to either might have seemed threatening.

31. Ibid. The teachers were Helene Sugihara of Kekaha; Mrs. Edward Watase from ʻEleʻele; Mrs. Tsukasa Miyake from Kōloa; and Mrs. Koichi Kanna from Waimea. The two other Caucasian advisers were Mrs. Eleanor Hobby, principal at ʻEleʻele Grammar School; and Alice Bakeman, who was engaged in humanitarian work with the jailed detainees.

32. Ibid. Rev. Frederic B. Withington (Morale Officer Kauaʻi Detainees) to Lt. Col. Eugene J. FitzGerald—Commanding the District of Kauaʻi.

33. Finding aid for Osumi Papers, which are on file at the Japanese Cultural Center of Hawaiʻi. Osumi would eventually write for many years an inspirational front-page paragraph for the *Honolulu Advertiser* entitled "Daily Thoughts."

34. Disorganized and unprincipled appropriation of alien property is, in my view, one of the little-examined aspects of the war.

35. RASRL Box 1, Kauaʻi Morale Committee.

36. Ibid.

37. RASRL Box 1, Kauaʻi Morale Committee, October 12, 1942, Division of Research Bulletin Number One: Three-Year Plan for Morale Work among Residents of Japanese Ancestry.

38. RASRL Box 1, Major Charles A. Selby, Kauaʻi Service Command, October 10, 1942, SUBJECT: INTERNAL SECURITY, Memo to CITIZENS OF KAUAʻI.

39. RASRL Box 1, Maui Emergency Service Committee file, first report dated October 16, 1942, covering two and a half months of operation.

40. Japanese American Veterans Association, vol. 2, no. 51. After providing crucial support to the VVV, Albert Lyman was promoted to brigadier general. Charles was cited for bravery for leading troops in battle in the retaking of New Guinea.

41. RASRL Box 1, Maui ESC, Army Bulletin #6, translated into Ilocano by P. O. Gamponia and into Tagalog by Rev. Makapagal.

42. RASRL, Box 1. By name and camp, the leaders were Noboru Kobayashi, Kihei Camp 3; Masaichi Yamada, Yung Hee Camp; Yeizo Oda, McGerrow Camp; Keizo Abe, Camp 2; Shichinosuke Kawano, Camp 1; Ichijiro Kunitake, Alabama Camp; Keichiro Kimura, Lower Camp 3; Toyokuma Yoshizawa, Lower Camp 3; Nisaku Miyagawa, Hawaiian Camp; Yutake Matsui, McGerrow Camp; Sadao Kon, Alabama Camp; Tanishi Sorayama, Camp 6; Masaru Mukai, Spanish B.

43. RASRL, Box 1. The ESC met with Maui Morale members including Dr. Edward S. Kushi, Masao Aizawa, Harry Inouye, Dean Shigeta, Toshi Kuwada, Masaru Omori, and George Hasegawa.

44. Ibid. The district chairs were reported to be Shuji Seki, James Tagawa, Shizuichi Mizuha, Sadao Hirata, Shuichi Yamamoto, George Ito, Eddie Sakamoto, James Shigeta, Minoru Tanaka, and Oliver Kamita.

45. Ibid. Izumi to Loomis, November 1942.

46. RASRL, Box 1, Maui ESC—2nd Report, October 16, 1942 to January 31, 1943.

47. RASRL, Box 1. Others were Dr. Edward S. Kushi, Masao Aizawa, Harry Inouye, Dean Shigeta, Toshi Kuwada, Masaru Omori, and George Hasegawa.

48. RASRL, Box 3, Morale Section, Lind, notes on informational conference at Kealakekua, January 14, 1943.

49. Ibid.

50. RASRL, Box 3, "Kona in Wartime," recorded on single sheets of paper, dated 1945 but quoted here on the assumption that it reveals hard feelings that were likely even more intense in 1942.

51. RASRL, Box 3, Shiku Ogura to Emergency Service Committee, report of August 21, 1942.

52. RASRL, Box 3, Ogura, "Morale of the Japanese in Kona," ca. August 1943, Morale Office files.

53. RASRL, Box 3, Ogura, "Life in Kona," November 30, 1944.

Chapter 10: War Service or Mass Evacuation?

1. Coggins, "Japanese-Americans in Hawaii," 78.

2. Ibid.

3. Members as reported by the *Honolulu Star-Bulletin* were as follows: (Filipino) Gregorio A. Labrador, chair, A. J. Avecilla, Dr. N. B. Borja, K. I. Fernandez, Jose O. Galura, C. O. Gorospe, Cayetano Ligo, Clemente V. Reyes, Mrs. Juan A. Valentin, N. C. Villanueva, and Dr. Jose M.Gonzales; (Korean) Jacob K. Dunn, chair, Nodie Sohn, secretary, Won Soon Lee, Y. K. Kim, Rev. D. W. Lim, Rev. C. H. Ahn, David C. Youth, Father Noah Cho, C. D. Choy, and Hasoo Whang; (Chinese) Hiram Leong Fong, chair, T. F. Farm, Richard Tongg, Sam Young, Lau Tang, Doo Wai Sing, C. K. Amona, Theodore Char, Dr. Dai Yen Chang, Kam Tai Lee, Dr. Min Hin, Lt. T. Y. Char, Willis Leong, Dr. Fred K. Lam, Leonard Fong, and Y. Chinn Wa; (Puerto Rican) Antonio R. Rivera, chair, Margaret Santiago, Fred C. Belmont, Rev. John Feliciano, Candelario Martinez, Erminia Morales, Carmen Pacheco, Tomas Peres, and Father Carabalo; (Japanese) Marumoto, Yoshida, Dr. Katsumi Kometani, Dr. Ernest Murai, Baron Yasuo Goto, and Jack Wakayama.

4. Odo, *No Sword to Bury,* 188.

5. RASLR Box 1, Masaichi Goto notebook. Subsequent Goto quotations are from this source.

6. Green, "Martial Law in Hawaii," chapter 17.

7. Amherst College Archives, McCloy diary entry, April 4, 1942.

8. Kent paper, coauthored by Brian Niiya, titled "Dual Discourses, Bureaucratic 'Splits,' and Hawaii's Japanese Americans in 1942," for presentation at the Asian American Studies Association 1998 meeting in Honolulu.

9. Amherst College Archives, McCloy diary entry February 17, 1942, which was prior to his Hawai'i trip.

10. Ibid., 12.

11. McWilliams, *Prejudice,* 32.

12. National Archives and Records Administration, RG 407-360, Box 147, Folder 1, Item 16, p. 1, Emmons to the Adjutant General, April 6, 1942.

13. National Archives and Records Administration, H. R. Bull, April 21, 1942, p. 2.

14. Ibid.

15. Conn, Engelman, and Fairchild, *Guarding the United States,* 211–212.

16. To whom Fielder spoke in Washington, D.C., and to what effect, are undeveloped aspects of the story.

17. Archives of Hawai'i, Box 8, File 15, McCloy to Emmons, May 18, 1942.

18. Archives of Hawai'i, Box 8, File 21, Emmons to McCloy, June 18, 1942.

19. The staff narrative describes Emmons moving the Kāne'ohe troops, and his repeated reference to "low morale," presents a clear picture that Emmons's preemptive maneuvers preceded Marshall's approval.

20. Duus, *Unlikely Liberators: Men of the 100th and 442nd* (Honolulu: University of Hawai'i Press, 1987), 151.

21. RASRL, Box 1, Haole file, Fourth Meeting of the Group on Race Relations, November 9, 1943.

22. Originally published by the *Hawaii Herald* and subsequently quoted in the Matsunaga biography by Richard Halloran, *Sparky* (Honolulu: Watermark, 2002), 38.

23. Archives of Hawai'i, Emmons to McCloy, April 29, 1942.

24. Starting with FBI arrests and including family members sent for reunification, the total by one count of the "internment" of Hawai'i's people came to 1,875. Slowly a picture of this experience emerged, thanks to the work of the Japanese Cultural Center of Hawai'i. See, for example, Yasutaro Soga's *Life behind Barbed Wire* and Otokichi Muin Ozaki's *Family Torn Apart*.

25. Archives of Hawai'i, War Department, Chief of Staff to McCloy, July 17, 1942.

26. National Archives and Records Administration, RFG 107, President Roosevelt to Stimson and Marshall, November 2, 1942.

27. National Archives and Records Administration, RG 407-360, Box 147, Folder 5, Item 15, Edwin O. Reischauer, Memorandum on Policy Toward Japan, dated September 14, 1942, forwarded to the War Department by the Steering Committee of the American Defense Harvard Group, October 2, 1942.

28. Roosevelt Library, File 4849 (WRA), Elmer Davis to President Roosevelt, 2 Oct 1942.

29. National Archives and Records Administration, RG 407-360, Box 147, Folder 5, Item 17, Milton Eisenhower to McCloy, October 13, 1942.

30. Drafted as Stimson to Roosevelt, this memorandum referenced Elmer Davis's October 2 letter. Whether or in what form it was transmitted is unknown. However, it clearly reflects the development of arguments in the October 1942 push to form a Japanese American fighting regiment.

31. National Archives and Records Administration, RG 107-47-8, Knox to Roosevelt, October 17, 1942.

32. Emmons to McCloy, November 11, 1942.

33. National Archives and Records Administration, RG 407-36, Box 147, Folder 5, Item 20, Pettigrew to McCloy, November 17, 1942.

34. Biddle to President Roosevelt, December 7, 1942, Franklin D. Roosevelt Library, courtesy of Dr. Greg Robinson. Biddle said McCloy agreed that Green should be replaced.

35. Coggins oral history, 1985, Dr. Katherine Herbig interviewer.

Chapter 11: The Mobilization

1. *Honolulu Advertiser,* "Volunteers Ready to Serve Country," January 30, 1943, 2.

2. RASRL, Kaua'i Morale Committee quarterly report, January to March, 1943.

3. Melody Miyamoto Walters, *In Love and War: The World War II Courtship Letters of a Nisei Couple* (Norman: University of Oklahoma Press, 2015), Yoshiharu Ogata to Naoko Tsukiyama.

4. National Archives and Records Administration, draft for Strong apparently to the Hawaiian War Department, MID/G-2 MID 291.2, January 8, 1943.

5. Roosevelt to Stimson, February 1, 1943.

6. National Archives and Records Administration, Box 1738, Folder 5, Item 2, 35–46, War Department record of recruiter training, session one, January 26, 1942.

7. Ibid.

8. Personal journals of Ted T. Tsukiyama, edited by author.

9. National Archives and Records Administration, David G. Erskine to Strong, May 8, 1943.

10. Densho Digital Repository, Chizuko Omori, testimony to the Commission on Wartime Relocation and Internment, 1981.

11. Densho Digital Repository, Lawson F. Inada, testimony to the Commission on Wartime Relocation and Internment, 1981.

12. Military Intelligence Division, 291.2, Japanese, Major General George V. Strong to the Assistant Chief of Staff, March 6, 1943.

13. Coffman, *Island Edge of America,* 89–92.

14. RG 107-47-8, McCloy to DeWitt, February 11, 1943.

15. National Archives and Records Administration, RG 107-47-8, DeWitt to McCloy, February 15, 1943.

16. Hoover Institution, Bendetsen (report) to DeWitt, May 3, 1943.

17. Scobey to Myer, March 11, 1943.

18. Green, "Martial Law in Hawaii," chapter 17.

Chapter 12: Missionaries to America

1. Archives of Hawai'i, Fielder to Col. John Weckerling, A.C. of S., G-2.

2. RASRL, Box 1, File 15, Ching Correspondence, Ching to Yoshida and Loomis.

3. RASRL, Box 2, Ching file, Killam to file, April 23–24, 1943.

4. National Archives and Records Administration, Scobey (McCloy staff) to Pence (442nd RCT commander), Box 41, Folder 7, Item 65, April 26, 1943: Ching "is instrumental to a large degree in the success for the volunteering of the Japanese Americans in Hawaii."

5. Densho Digital Repository; Dr. Gregory Robinson. The account of Mrs. Roosevelt's understanding of sabotage and the internment is drawn from the Densho Repository and also from personal conversation with Dr. Robinson, for which the author is grateful.

6. RASRL, Box 1, File 15, Public Morale Committee/Hung Wai Ching Correspondence. The quotes following are from his extensive handwritten notes.

7. President Roosevelt more than once cited his family tie to the China trade, which has been interpreted by various historians as a reason for his support of the "China Open Door" and antipathy for Japan.

8. Ching's interruption of the president is from his long, videotaped interview and ensuing conversations with the author, not his notes.

9. Densho Digital Repository; Robinson.

10. Ching, interview with author, 1995.

11. National Archives and Records Administration, Box 47, Folder 7, Item 65, McCloy letter to Mrs. Roosevelt, May 31, 1943.

12. Ching's recollection of conversation with Mrs. Roosevelt, interview with author.

13. RASRL, Box 1, File 15, Ching letter to Loomis, Yoshida, and Baron Goto; May 18, 1943, twelve days after meeting with Mrs. Roosevelt.

14. RASRL, Box 1, Joint Meeting of Haole and Chinese Race Relations Steering Committees, June 14, 1944. Those present in addition to Hung Wai Ching were Dai Yen Chang, Raymond Kong, Henry Chun Hoon, and Wong Buck Hung, along with Trent, Fisher, Bodge, Deacon, and Lomis.

15. RASRL, Box 1, Ching, Activities of the Morale Section, June 1942.

16. Higa, *Memoirs of a Certain Nisei*, 97.

Chapter 13: The Home Front Doldrums

1. RASRL papers, Loomis file. I think these talking points were directed at Loomis by Yoshida.

2. ' RASRL, Box 3, Japanese file.

3. Archives of Hawai'i, Gov. 9-32, Citizens Council file. The group name conjures the violent segregationist White Citizen's Council, which was active in the American South and particularly in Mississippi in the 1960s. There was no institutional relationship.

4. Archives of Hawai'i, letter dated November 12, 1942.

5. Yoshida, HAOLE file. The quotes in the following paragraphs are from this file.

6. University of Hawai'i Archives and Manuscripts, Lind, "Unprocessed" Box 17, file marked "Morale/Lind," document headed "Meeting of Discussion Group," dated October 2, 1942.

7. Ibid., "Meeting of Discussion Group," October 22, 1942.

8. John H. Balch, *Shall the Japanese Be Allowed to Dominate Hawaii?* (Honolulu: privately printed, 1943).

9. Galusha B. Balch, *Genealogy of the Balch Families in America,* balchipedia .wikidot.com.

10. Balch testimony in Washington, D.C., January 26, 1917, to the U.S. House Committee on Merchant Marine and Fisheries, www .earlyradiohistory.

11. RASRL, Box 3, Haole file, Group on Race Relations, First Meeting, Alexander & Baldwin Directors' Room, October 19, 1943.

12. University of Hawai'i Archives and Manuscripts, Lind Box 17, file marked "Morale/Lind File—CONFIDENTIAL," discussion of Loomis, Yoshida, and Ching to Hormann and (apparently) Lind, dated February 23, 1943; also RASRL, Box 1, Haole file, Meeting October 1943, 3 p.m.

13. RASRL, Box 3, Haole file, Group on Race Relations, Second Meeting.

14. Ibid.

15. RASRL, Box 1, Haole file. This and following material on increased Caucasian engagement is drawn from minutes of what appear to be the fourth, fifth, and sixth meetings of the haoles as a group, occurring between early November 1943 and early January 1944. The latter are not numbered but are clearly dated.

16. RASRL, Box 1.

17. Ibid.

18. *Honolulu Star-Bulletin,* April 28, 1945, courtesy of Mark Matsunaga's research. The 256 appointments presumably were part of Stainback's effort to revive civilian government in Hawai'i.

Chapter 14: Imagining a New Hawai'i

1. Young Ok Kim remarks at the funeral service of Sakae Takahashi, handwritten notes given to author, dated April 23, 2001.

2. Each of the four conferences produced a published report. These are available in the Hawai'i War Records Division, Manuscripts and Archives Room of the University of Hawai'i, in the Pacific Room of the Hawai'i State Library, various regional branches of the Hawai'i Library System, and the ESC files in RASRL, Box 3. Each report is described in sequence in the text, and all quotations are from the respective reports, which are readily accessible through tables of content.

3. Previous to his arrival in Hawai'i, Dr. John A. Rademaker studied the internment camp at Amache, Colorado, most interestingly documenting the camp conflicts over loyalty oaths, Questions 27 and 28, and Nisei participation in the U.S. military.

4. John A. Rademaker, "Summary of Proceedings, Fourth Territorial Conference of Morale and Emergency Service Committees," 4.

5. Ibid., 9.

6. Ibid., 10–12.

7. Ibid., 16–17.

8. Ibid., 18.

9. Ibid., 33.

10. Ibid., 28.

11. Ibid., 40–41.

12. Ibid., 54–56.

13. Quaker and Special Collections, Haverford College, Pennsylvania; Bowles and Maier papers. The steadfast AFSC involvement in wartime Hawai'i is an untold story.

14. Rademaker, "Summary of Proceedings."

Chapter 15: Sealed with Sacrifice

1. Hoover Institution, Bendetsen Papers.

2. Duus, *Unlikely Liberators,* 228.

3. Conrad Tsukayama, *Japanese Eyes, American Heart: Personal Reflections of Hawaii's World War II Nisei Soldiers* (Honolulu: Tendai Educational Foundation, 1998), 20.

4. Ibid., 19.

5. Akinaka Diary, June 15, 1942, 100th Infantry Battalion Veterans, Education Center, https://www.100thbattalion.org/archives/memoirs-and-journals/issac-akinaka-diaries/.

6. Eddie Yamasaki, *And Then There Were Eight,* Victor Izui entry (Honolulu: I Chapter/442nd Veterans Club, 2007), 165.

7. Ibid., 371.

8. Higa, *Memoirs of a Certain Nisei,* 49–51.

9. Young Ok Kim, interview with author, 2002. This was one of the more famous stories of the outfit, thanks to Kim's prominence and passion. Because of his combination of skill and commitment, he surely would have been promoted to general across his long career, if only he had been white.

10. *Fort Point Salvo,* newsletter of the Fort Point and Army Museum Association, 5:3 (June 1981).

11. Higa, *Memoirs of a Certain Nisei,* 49–51.

12. Kaoru Suzuki, 100th Infantry Battalion Veterans, Education Center, https://www.100thbattalion.org/archives/memoirs-and-journals/kaoru-suzuki/.

13. Stanley Izumigawa, 100th Infantry Battalion Veterans, Education Center, https://www.100thbattalion.org/archives/memoirs-and-journals/stan-izumigawa/.

14. Lyn Crost, *Honor by Fire: Japanese Americans at War in Europe and the Pacific* (Novato, CA: Presidio Press, 1994), 79; Clark to Eisenhower #2710, Mark Clark Archive, Hamilton Library, The Citadel, Charleston, SC, Box 65, Clark diary, vol. 9, 76.

15. Crost, *Honor by Fire,* 78.

16. Martin Blumenson, *Mark Clark* (New York: Congdon & Weed, 1984), 55.

17. Bird, *The Chairman,* 195.

18. Duus, *Japanese Conspiracy,* 159.

19. Bird, *The Chairman,* 195.

20. Blumenson, *Mark Clark,* 288.

21. Higa, *Memoirs of a Certain Nisei,* 80–82.

22. Duus, *Japanese Conspiracy,* 152, quoting McCloy to Maj. Gen. White, October 12, 1943.

23. Crost, *Honor by Fire,* 97.

24. Ibid.

25. Ibid., 145.

26. Masao Yamada to spouse Ai Yamada, April 4, 1944. University of Hawai'i Archives and Manuscripts.

27. Crost, *Honor by Fire,* 149, quoting First Presidential Unit Citation, 100th Battalion.

28. Ibid.

29. Masao Yamada letter to Ai Yamada.

30. Crost, *Honor by Fire,* 156.

31. Blumenson, *Mark Clark,* 228.

32. Young Ok Kim, speaking at Sakae Takahashi's funeral service.

33. John Tsukano, *Bridge of Love* (Honolulu: Hawaii Hosts, 1985), 247.

34. Yamasaki, *Then There Were Eight,* Shuji Takamoto entry, 317.

35. War newsreels are in the motion picture room of the National Archives/Maryland.

36. Yamada to Ai Yamada.

37. Blumenson, *Mark Clark,* 243.

38. Crost, *Honor by Fire,* 261.

39. Hodding Carter, "Go for Broke," *Delta Democrat-Times,* August 27, 1945.

40. Blumenson, *Mark Clark,* 56.

41. Lyn Crost, "War Department Will Be Asked to Perpetuate 100th Battalion," *Honolulu Star-Bulletin,* November 15, 1945, 21.

42. The generalization is derived from the writer Mark Matsunaga, who consulted numerous sources, none exactly agreeing. The quote on percentage of the wounded is from Professor Lind.

43. The estimate of over four thousand is from research reported by the *Japanese American Veterans Association* in its winter 2016–2017 issue.

Chapter 16: All the People, All the Time

1. Crost, *Honor by Fire,* 305.

2. Ibid., 310.

3. Duus, *Japanese Conspiracy,* 234, quoting Truman in biography by Merle Miller, *Plain Speaking: An Oral Biography of Harry S Truman.*

4. This and ensuing epilogue material on key individuals are from numerous conversations and interviews with Hung Wai Ching, his son King Lit Ching, Yoshida's son Gerald and daughter-in-law Bonnie, members of

Church of the Crossroads, John A. Burns, Sue Isonaga, Daniel K. Inouye, Sakae Takahashi, George R. Ariyoshi, and others.

5. This brief summary of social and political change in Hawaii between 1945 and 1954 is developed in a longer, more nuanced way in my earlier political history, *The Island Edge of America*. See chapters 6–7, 103–160; also in *Catch A Wave*, in its entirety.

6. www.goldsea.com put Inouye's name on the top of a list of 130 most inspiring Asian Americans, this in 2018, six years after his death. Previous surveys (unscientific) similarly described him as the most influential Asian American.

7. Dr. Martin Luther King Jr., September 17, 1959, First Special Session, Hawaii State Legislature.

8. Ibid.

9. Lyndon Baines Johnson, "Statement by the President on the Fifth Anniversary of Statehood for Hawaii," August 21, 1964, The American Presidency Project, by Gerhard Peters and John T. Woolley, http://www.presidency.ucsb.edu/ws.

10. The record of Dr. King and Presidents Kennedy, Johnson, and Nixon in Hawai'i relative to civil rights, racial tolerance, and the aloha spirit have been diligently researched by Pualani Akaka, daughter of the Rev. Abraham Akaka and niece of former U.S. senator Daniel Akaka. See, for example, *Daily Kos*, September 2, 2011.

BIBLIOGRAPHY

Allen, Gwenfread E. *Bridge Builders: The Story of Theodore and Mary Atherton Richards.* Honolulu: Hawaii Conference Foundation, 1970.

———. *The YMCA in Hawaii, 1869–1969.* Honolulu: YMCA, 1969.

Beechert, Edward. *Working in Hawai'i: A Labor History.* Honolulu: University of Hawai'i Press, 1985.

Bell, Dr. Roger. *Last Among Equals.* Honolulu: University of Hawai'i Press, 1984.

Bicknell, George. Unpublished memoir in author's collection.

Bird, Kai. *The Chairman, John J. McCloy and the Making of the American Establishment.* New York: Simon & Schuster, 1992.

Black and Gold. McKinley High School annual. Honolulu, 1921.

Blumenson, Martin. *Mark Clark.* New York: Congdon & Weed, 1984.

Burrows, Edwin G. *Chinese and Japanese in Hawaii during the Sino-Japanese Conflict.* Honolulu: Hawai'i Group, American Council, Institute of Pacific Relations, 1939.

Castle, W. R. *Hawai'i Past and Present.* New York: Dodd, Mead, 1917.

Chan, Luke, and Betty Tebbetts Taylor. *Sun Yat-sen, as I Knew Him: Memoirs of Luke Chan, Boyhood Friend of Sun Yat-sen.* N.p., 2008.

Clark, Blake. *Hawaii: The 49th State.* Garden City, NJ: Doubleday, 1947.

———. *Remember Pearl Harbor!* New York: Modern Age, 1942.

Coffman, Tom. *The Island Edge of America: A Political History of Hawai'i.* Honolulu: University of Hawai'i Press, 2003.

———. *Nation Within: The Story of America's Annexation of the Nation of Hawai'i.* Honolulu: EpiCenter, 1998; currently republished by Duke University Press.

Conn, Stetson, Rose C. Engelman, and Byron Fairchild. *Guarding the United States and Its Outposts.* Washington, D.C.: Center for Military History, U.S. Army, 2000.

Crost, Lyn. *Honor by Fire: Japanese Americans at War in Europe and the Pacific.* Novato, CA: Presidio Press, 1994.

Dallek, Robert. *Franklin Roosevelt and American Foreign Policy, 1932–1948.* London: Oxford University Press, 1979.

de Nevers, Nancy Clark. *The Colonel and the Pacifist.* Salt Lake City: University of Utah Press, 2004.

Duus, Masayo U. *The Japanese Conspiracy.* Berkeley: University of California Press, 1999.

———. *Unlikely Liberators: Men of the 100th and 442nd.* Honolulu: University of Hawai'i Press, 1987.

Green, Maj. Gen. Thomas H. "Martial Law in Hawaii, December 7, 1941–April 4, 1943." Unpublished typescript, Library of Congress, Military Legal Resources, OCLC #461333055. Available at https://www.loc.gov/rr/frd/Military_Law/pdf/Martial-Law_Green.pdf.

Grodzins, Morton. *Americans Betrayed: Politics and the Japanese Evacuation.* Chicago, University of Chicago Press, 1949.

Halloran, Richard. *Sparky.* Honolulu: Watermark, 2002.

Higa, Thomas Taro. *Memoirs of a Certain Nisei, Aru Nisei no Wadachi.* Kāne'ohe: Higa Publications, 1988.

Holland, William L. *Remembering the Institute for Pacific Relations.* Tokyo: Ryukei Shyosha, 1995.

Hoover, J. Edgar. *Persons in Hiding.* Boston: Little, Brown, 1938.

Kashima, Tetsuden. *Judgment Without Trial.* Seattle: University of Washington Press, 2003.

Kawakami, H. S. with Tom Coffman. *From Japan to Hawaii: My Journey.* Self-published by Kawakami, Honolulu, 1976.

Kimura, Yukiko. *Issei: Japanese Immigrants in Hawaii.* Honolulu: University of Hawai'i Press, 1988.

Kuykendall, Ralph S. *Hawaii in the World War.* Honolulu: Hawaiian Historical Commission, Territory of Hawaii, 1928.

Linn, Brian McAllister. *Guardians of Empire: The U.S. Army and the Pacific.* Chapel Hill: University of North Carolina Press, 1997,

Lum, Yusheng M., and Raymond M. K. Lum. *Sun Yat-sen in Hawaii: Activities and Supporters.* Honolulu: Chinese History Center and Dr. Sun Yat-sen Foundation, 1999.

MacDonnell, Francis. *Insidious Foes: The Axis Fifth Column & the American Home Front.* New York and Oxford: Oxford University Press, 1995.

MacPherson, D. Neal. *Church at a Crossroads: Being the Church after Christendom.* Eugene, OR: Wipf & Stock, 2008.

Mark, Diane Mei Lin. *Seasons of Light: A History of Chinese Christian Churches in Hawai'i.* Honolulu: Chinese Christian Association of Hawai'i, 1989.

Masaoka, Mike, with Bill Hosokawa. *They Call Me Moses Masaoka: An American Saga.* New York: William Morrow, 1987.

McWilliams, Carey. *Prejudice: Japanese-Americans: Symbols of Racial Intolerance.* Boston: Little, Brown, 1944.

Miyamoto, Kazuo. *Hawaii: End of the Rainbow.* Tokyo: Charles E. Tuttle, 1964.

Newton, L. C., ed. *Who's Who: Americans of Japanese Ancestry.* Wailuku: Maui Publishing, 1941.

Odo, Dr. Franklin. *No Sword to Bury.* Philadelphia: Temple University Press, 2004.

Robinson, Dr. Gregory. *By Order of the President: FDR and the Internment of Japanese Americans.* Cambridge, MA: Harvard University Press, 2003.

Samuels, Frederick. *The Japanese and the Haoles of Honolulu: Durable Group Interaction.* New Haven, CT: College & University Press, 1970.

Slackman, Michael. "The Orange Race: George S. Patton, Jr.'s Japanese-American Hostage Plan." *Biography* 1, no. 7 (Winter 1984): 1–22.

Soga, Yasutaro. *Life behind Barbed Wire: The World War II Internment Memoirs of a Hawai'i Issei.* Honolulu: University of Hawai'i Press, 2008.

Tamura, Eileen. *Americanization, Acculturation, and Ethnic Identity: The Nisei Generation in Hawai'i.* Honolulu: University of Hawai'i Press, 1993.

Tsukano, John. *Bridge of Love.* Honolulu: Hawaii Hosts, 1985.

United Japanese Society of Hawaii (UJSH). *A History of Japanese in Hawaii.* Honolulu: UJSH, 1971.

Yamasaki, Eddie. *And Then There Were Eight.* Honolulu: I Chapter/442nd Veterans Club, 2007.

Other Publications

Coggins, Cecil H. "The Japanese-Americans in Hawaii." *Harper's Magazine* (June 1943): 75–83.

Collier's Magazine, October 19, 1940.

Federal Bureau of Investigation. *Memorandum on Pearl Harbor Attack and Bureau's Activities Before and After,* vol. 1 of 2, December 6, 1945.

Japan Times and Mail, April 19, 1924.

Joint Committee on Hawaii. *Statehood for Hawaii: Hearings before the Joint Committee on Hawaii, Congress of the United States, Seventy-Fifth Congress, ... October 6–12, 1937.* Washington, D.C.: U.S. Government Printing Office, 1938.

Kimura, Yukiko. "Some Effects of the War Situation Upon the Alien Japanese in Hawaii." *Social Process in Hawaii* 8 (1943): 18–28.

Lind, Andrew H. "Ethnic Sources in Hawai'i." *Social Process in Hawai'i* 29 (special issue, 1982).

National Defense Migration Committee (NDMC). *Problems of Evacuation of Enemy Aliens and Others from Prohibited Military Zones.* Tolan Committee, 77th Congress, 2nd Session, Part 29.

Nellist, George F. *The Story of Hawaii and Its Builders.* Honolulu: Honolulu Star-Bulletin, 1925.

Pan-Pacific Union Bulletin #1, #3. University of Hawai'i Archives and Manuscripts.

Pittsburgh Courier, February 7, 1942.
Yoshida, Shigeo. "Evaluation in Reading." *Hawaii Educational Review* (September 1940): 10–11.

Archives

ACA, Amherst College Archives
AH, Archives of Hawai'i
BOHP, Burns Oral History Project
DDR, Densho Digital Repository
HA, *Honolulu Advertiser*
HI, Hoover Institution
HSB, *Honolulu Star-Bulletin*
HWCP, Hung Wai Ching Papers
NARA, National Archives and Records Administration
NDMC, National Defense Migration Committee, 77th Congress, Tolan Committee
PHA, Pearl Harbor Attack, Joint Congressional Committees, 79th Congress
RASRL, Romanzo Adams Social Research Laboratory
UHAM, University of Hawai'i Archives and Manuscript Collections

Index

Page numbers in **boldface** refer to illustrations.

About the Author

Tom Coffman's first window into Hawai'i was as chief political reporter of the *Honolulu Star-Bulletin* (1968–1973). A major character of *Inclusion*, John A. Burns, was governor, and Japanese American war veterans prominently populated the State Legislature and congressional delegation. Since 1973 the author has worked as an independent writer and producer. He is the recipient of the State of Hawai'i Award for Literature, three Hawai'i Book Publishers Association awards for Best Nonfiction, and numerous documentary film awards.

The connecting thread of his work is the social and political development of Hawai'i in context of the American nation and the Pacific Rim.

He has often been involved in community projects. He helped write the OHA Culture Plan/Draft One. He served on the storyline work group of the historical gallery of the Japanese Cultural Center of Hawai'i, as well as director/producer of its theme film, *Ganbare*. He wrote and directed the Judiciary History Center's film on martial law. He has spoken at institutions, to community groups, and to classes of young people across Hawai'i and around the United States.

His books include *Catch A Wave; Nation Within: The History of America's Occupation of Hawai'i; The Island Edge of America; I Respectfully Dissent: A Biography of Edward H. Nakamura;* and *Tadaima! I Am Home.*

His PBS films include *O Hawai'i, From First Settlement to Kingdom; Nation Within; Arirang—The Korean American Journey; Ninoy Aquino and the Rise of People Power;* and *First Battle: The Battle for Equality in Wartime Hawai'i.*